Large paper.

Dawson Turner Esq.
from his friend, the author

Inserted

an Original note from the author.

& etching of Sir T. Gresham's portrait & proofs, before the letters, of most of the plates, in addition to the finished impressions.

VI ET ARTE.
Robert Cutlar Fergusson
of Craigdarroch.

THE

LIFE AND TIMES

OF

SIR THOMAS GRESHAM.

VOL. I.

R. Woodman, Sculpsit.

R. Woodman, sc.

THE

LIFE AND TIMES

OF

SIR THOMAS GRESHAM;

COMPILED CHIEFLY FROM HIS CORRESPONDENCE PRESERVED IN
HER MAJESTY'S STATE-PAPER OFFICE:

INCLUDING

NOTICES OF MANY OF HIS CONTEMPORARIES.

WITH ILLUSTRATIONS.

By JOHN WILLIAM BURGON.

IN TWO VOLUMES.

VOL. I.

LONDON:
ROBERT JENNINGS, 62, CHEAPSIDE.

MDCCCXXXIX.

LONDON:
PRINTED BY MAURICE, CLARK, & CO.
FENCHURCH-STREET.

PARENTIBVS·

DILECTISSIMIS·

SACRVM.

PREFACE.

TWO volumes on a subject apparently so little fertile in materials as the present, seem to require a few preliminary remarks; and I should be sorry to forego the opportunity of stating in this place, that which could not with equal propriety be stated elsewhere, principally in explanation of the length to which the following pages have most unexpectedly extended.

This memoir was commenced some years ago, in consequence of an announcement that a premium would be given by William Taylor Copeland, Esq. M.P., then Lord Mayor, to the author of the best Essay "on the Life and Character of Sir Thomas Gresham;" which was to be comprised within such limits, that the public recitation of it should not exceed half an hour. Altogether unacquainted with the subject, it was presumed by the writer that a few pages would indeed have comprised all that was discoverable concerning one who lived at so distant a period, and of whom but little had been recorded in printed books; but a diligent search led to a vast accumulation of materials, and the Essay, instead of forming a slight pamphlet as was anticipated, soon assumed the size of a small volume. The object with which it was written having been attained, in compliance with the conditions under which the prize was bestowed, such portions of the Essay as seemed best adapted for the purpose, were publicly read at the Mansion-house, May 14th, 1836; the office of reader having been undertaken with singular kindness by the Rev. George Cecil Renouard, B.D., Rector of

Swanscombe, Kent; of the value of whose long-standing friendship the writer is deeply sensible; and whose good offices on this, and many other occasions, he gladly avails himself of the present opportunity to acknowledge.—It was further intended that, as the successful composition, the Gresham Essay should have been published; but the narrow limits within which it had been comprised were judged so unfavourable to its probable success, that the MS. was soon laid aside; and, after a few months, the expectation of seeing it printed was completely abandoned.

Two years had elapsed, when the destruction of the Royal Exchange by fire in the beginning of 1838, seems to have suggested the idea that a more auspicious moment had arrived for the appearance of the life of its founder; and inquiries were made for the neglected MS. But, before it left his hands, the writer determined to apply for permission to inspect the correspondence of Sir Thomas Gresham, which he was told existed in the State-Paper Office; and the necessary facilities having been promptly, as well as very obligingly granted him by the Right Hon. Lord John Russell,—a favour which the writer begs leave respectfully and gratefully to acknowledge,—to the State-Paper Office he repaired. Great indeed was his surprise and satisfaction at discovering such a mass of historic evidence as was then first disclosed to him. Hundreds of letters now appeared in place of the scanty documents which he had hitherto known of; and—these volumes are the result.

There can be no presumption in hoping that the present will be found to be a more satisfactory Life of Sir Thomas Gresham than any which has hitherto appeared; for that eminent man has had the singular fate of leaving behind him a name with which every one is familiar, without ever having found a biographer who would take the pains to collect the scattered rays of information concerning him, which time has failed to dissipate. Dr. John Ward, who one hundred years ago filled the chair of rhetoric at Gresham College, may be considered to be the first and only person who ever fairly undertook to write a sketch of his history; for the worthless publication which had previously appeared in 1707, entitled, "An Account of the Rise, Foundation, Progress, and Present State of Gresham College in London, with the Life of the Founder," contains *no* Life, and does not correspond with its title-page: and the seemingly laborious (and certainly heavy) article on the subject in the Biographia Britannica is little else than a transcript from Ward's work,—encumbered with an apparatus of notes.

The Professor's performance has been so often quoted and referred to in print, that it is scarcely necessary to state that it precedes a valuable collection of Lives, published in 1740, with the following title: "The Lives of the Professors of Gresham College, to which is prefixed the Life of the Founder," &c. An interleaved copy of this work, which belonged to Dr. Ward, and has been enriched by him with many valuable MS. additions, is preserved in the British Museum.

Ward's Life of Gresham is a very creditable performance; and it must be remembered that it was an *original* compilation, executed at a time when the facilities which are at present within the reach of every student, were but very imperfectly accessible. Notwithstanding, however, that he has inserted at length, with all its legal verbosity, Gresham's will, his Life barely extends to the length of thirty-two pages: a degree of conciseness scarcely compatible with that minuteness of information which biography professedly requires. All subsequent Lives, — possessing more or less literary merit, according to the talents of their respective authors,—may be said to have added nothing to our stock of knowledge concerning Sir Thomas Gresham.

It may be as well to state something in this place of the method which has been adopted in editing the numerous letters, or parts of letters, which the ensuing pages will be found to contain. —In the opinion of some antiquaries, ancient letters should be printed with a strict adherence to the ancient spelling. Others advocate a contrary system, and are for altogether remodelling the orthography; so that (say they) 'he that runs may read.' Now, either method is liable to some grave objections. I certainly think that when old letters are printed for their own sake, as *a collection of old letters*, or *for purposes of reference*, they cannot be too accurately printed: the importance and interest of the preservation of the ancient spelling is, in many instances, susceptible of direct proof; while it cannot be doubted that the history of language and literature derives illustration from such sources. But when it is only intended to give authenticity to a biographical or historical relation, it is perhaps a matter of doubt whether a more judicious course might not be pursued. The evil of strictly adhering to the ancient orthography is principally this:—that it prevents one's narrative from being read with fluency, and may even have a tendency to disgust and repel ordinary readers; which surely is to purchase a reputation for accuracy at too dear a rate. Altogether to modernise the spelling, on the other hand, in the writer's opinion, besides being sometimes a very hazardous operation, is to destroy an integral part of an old epistle: a certain degree of quaintness in this particular being as much its characteristic, as the obsolete and often difficult phraseology,—which no one presumes to correct.

After much deliberation, I have, in consequence, pursued a middle course; removing occasionally a few letters where they seemed particularly uncouth or redundant; and sometimes spelling a word correctly, where the sense of a passage depended upon it, or seemed likely to suffer by its retaining the antiquated form. Far oftener have I observed the practice of merely spelling a word according to the most intelligible method adopted by the same writer. Thus, since Gresham sometimes spells the word *possibly*,—"possibelly," and sometimes according to the modern method, I have thought it allowable occasionally to reject the word containing four syllables in favour of the word with only three. *Possibelly*, in attempting to steer this middle course, instead of reconciling two classes of antiquaries, I shall find that I have incurred the disapprobation of both: in which case, I shall beg leave to inform the advocates for literal accuracy of my firm belief, that, even by themselves, (the initiated,) the orthography of these letters would never have been suspected without this explanation; and to state that I have only made it, lest I should be hereafter charged with more inaccuracies than I have really been guilty of. I have also a word to whisper in the ear of the lovers of modern orthography, but it must not be overheard by the other party: namely, that I dismiss these volumes not without a suspicion that I should have acted more wisely, had I remodelled the spelling throughout; and that, considering what is due to the prejudices of the great bulk of readers, I verily believe their method to be the right method after all.

It should also be stated, that I have purposely abstained from transferring to my pages any of the contractions with which old letters and papers abound: and lastly, that when a writer's mode of expression seemed too elliptical, and the meaning of a whole passage was rendered obscure by the want of a single word, as a pronoun or a conjunction,—I have ventured to supply such deficiency *between brackets*. The genuineness of the original has consequently been in no single instance impaired; and it is therefore hoped, that no reader will feel offended by a practice which has been pursued solely for *his* convenience.

The principal source whence the materials for these volumes have been derived, has been already mentioned. The writer had access also to the registers preserved in the Council-Office, from which some useful information was obtained. It is impossible to visit that valuable repository of archives without a feeling of gratitude to C. C. F. Greville, Esq., for having supplied the (before almost useless) volumes with that indispensable appendage,—an Index: and most earnestly is it to be desired that Government, when it sees their importance, will encourage him to crown his noble task by supplying them in addition with a general *Index Nominum*. This, to the historian and biographer, would be of paramount interest; for many great and shining characters are necessarily mixed up with events, trifling in themselves, but highly important to personal history: and these unavoidably escape notice in the analytical indexes with which alone the Council-books are as yet furnished.

The assistance which I have derived from the valuable communications of many kind friends has been so carefully recorded, in almost every instance, in my notes, that the subject might be excluded with propriety from my preface: but I am desirous of recording in this place my obligations to a few persons to whom I feel myself more especially indebted; and to no one more distinctly than to my kind friend Dawson Turner, Esq., of Yarmouth, not only in affording me opportunities of access to his valuable MS. library, but for the zealous manner in which, from the beginning, he has uniformly done every thing in his power to facilitate my researches. My learned friend Dr. J. M. Lappenberg, of Hamburg, will allow me publicly to acknowledge the zeal and ability with which, at my request, he examined the archives of that city, in his custody, in search of documents illustrative of this memoir: and less cannot be said in connexion with the name of M. Fréderic Verachter, the *archiviste* of Antwerp; to whom I feel equally indebted, and equally grateful.

Let me not forget to add to the preceding names, with many thanks for the valuable information they have occasionally imparted, those of Robert Lemon, Esq. of the State Paper-Office, Sir Francis Palgrave, and the Rev. Joseph Hunter. To William Jacob, Esq. I am also much obliged; and to John Gough Nichols, Esq. I am indebted for his numerous communications. My kind friend P. Fraser Tytler, Esq., in particular, has my hearty thanks for his frequent good counsel and kind assistance: and it may be that there are others, nearer and dearer still, but who must be nameless, to whom still heartier thanks are due, and on the very same grounds.

To Joseph Neeld, Esq., M. P., I am much obliged for leave to engrave Gresham's portrait from a beautiful picture in his possession: and the Rev. J. Forshall, of the British Museum, has my best thanks for obtaining permission for the fac-similes of autographs to be executed, which precede the second volume.

The lady to whose indefatigable and munificent exertions Englishmen are indebted for the preservation of Crosby Hall, will I trust allow me the gratification of thanking her in this place for a long succession of kind offices, most cheerfully rendered throughout this undertaking: and if I have reserved for the last the mention of my kind friend, the Rev. Alfred Butler Clough, B. D., Rector of Braunston, late Fellow of Jesus College, Oxford, he may be assured that it is not because his frequent and very valuable communications on the subject of his ancestor have been least prized; but for a contrary reason.

Here I shall dismiss these volumes, which have been compiled not without considerable care and anxiety; and if it should be objected to them that the author has not sufficiently adhered to his principal subject, but has in many instances noticed persons and events only indirectly connected with Sir Thomas Gresham, let it be remembered that his object was to carry the reader back to the *times* in which Sir Thomas Gresham flourished, as well as to narrate the incidents of his *life*. It will, moreover, be generally found that some new light has been thrown on the subjects treated of incidentally in the ensuing pages. It is too much to require of a traveller whose journey lies across a picturesque country, that he should look neither to this side nor to that, but "hold his course right on:" and, to vary the illustration, it seems as unreasonable to dwell on one solitary character, and call one's narrative a *life*, as it would be to cut a single portrait out of a family group, and call the irregular piece of canvas so obtained, a *picture*. History presents us with groups of men rather than with individuals: and what is antiquarian biography, but the magnifying-glass applied to a particular portion of history?

Brunswick Square,
July 12, 1839.

CONTENTS

OF VOLUME THE FIRST.

CHAPTER I.

[1519 TO 1550.]

CHAPTER II.

[1551 TO 1553.]

CHAPTER III.

[1553 TO 1558.]

CHAPTER IV.

[1558 TO 1562.]

ILLUSTRATIONS IN VOL. I.

Preceding the Preface, are engraved the seals habitually used by Sir Thomas Gresham and his servants, faithfully copied from the originals, or from fragments of the originals, attached to their letters. The Vignette to Chapter I., representing Gresham-Church, is from a sketch made on the spot, in April 1838:—that preceding Chapter II., representing the Burse at Antwerp, is from an old print, communicated by M. Verachter:—that preceding Chapter III., shows the costume of an English, Flemish, and Venetian merchant, in the sixteenth century, and is noticed at p. 209.—Mainan-Abbey, a view of which precedes Chapter IV., (reduced to perspective from a curious original painting,) is mentioned in vol. ii. p. 367.—Gresham's wedding-ring, represented in the initial letter to Chapter I. is noticed at p. 51.—The initial letters of Chapter II., III., and IV., respectively exhibit pennies of Edward VI., Queen Mary, and Queen Elizabeth: communicated by my kind friend, Edward Hawkins, Esq., of the British Museum.

GRESHAM CHURCH, NORFOLK.

CHAPTER I.

[1519 TO 1550.]

INTRODUCTION—SOME ACCOUNT OF THE GRESHAM FAMILY—MEMOIRS OF SIR JOHN AND SIR RICHARD GRESHAM—SIR THOMAS GRESHAM—HIS EDUCATION, EARLY LIFE, AND MARRIAGE.

HE name of Sir Thomas Gresham is conspicuous among the number of those who have been an ornament to the land which gave them birth, and a blessing to the age in which they lived. His life was at once so actively and so usefully spent, that had he left no other memorial of himself than the space he occupies in the page of the historian, his career would have been far from an uninteresting subject of literary inquiry: but when we consider besides, how greatly he adorned and enriched the metropolis of this country, he appears to possess a peculiar claim on our attention; and it seems but natural that we should desire to become better acquainted with his personal history and character.

Living during the reigns of Henry the Eighth, Edward the Sixth, Mary, and Elizabeth, it may be said of the period at which Sir Thomas Gresham flourished, that it is precisely the period of English History to which the student is accustomed to refer with most interest, and which he is able to contemplate with most satisfaction. Sufficiently remote to be invested with that air of romance which is inseparable from antiquity, and which the multitudinous evidence of a later age fails not to dissipate, it is nevertheless not so far removed from the period at which we live, as to partake of the doubt and obscurity in which our earlier annals are involved. We seem also to be connected with the epoch at which he flourished by an intimate, and as it were a domestic tie; for while all our older families trace their line with certainty to about that period, few can adduce any better evidence of a more ancient origin than such as the partiality of the herald has supplied.[a] The descendants of many of the families which became ennobled during the sixteenth century in particular, are still to be found among us: and this circumstance, while it renders the names which were famous then, familiar to ourselves as household words, seems to keep up a living interest, to give us a personal concern, as it were, in all that relates to the history of their illustrious predecessors, and to their times.

The reign of the eighth Henry, during which Sir Thomas Gresham's family first acquired distinction, seems to be the grand transition period in our history;—the epoch during which our ancestors first emerged from darkness, ecclesiastical and civil, to enduring light in every department of the commonwealth. Then, in the dying words of the venerable martyr Latimer, was "lighted such a candle in England, as shall never be extinguished." It was then that the influence of the art of printing first began to be felt: letters from this period dated their revival,

[a] Hear the evidence of a contemporary on this subject,—Paulet, Marquis of Winchester; a man of ancient family, and certainly a very competent judge of such matters: "Heralds make their books at adventure, and not by the records." The letter which contains this passage, was addressed to Cecil on the subject of the preservation of the Tower Records. It bears date April 11, 1567, and is preserved in the Domestic Correspondence, State-Paper Office.

and superstition and ignorance the termination of their long reign: commerce, the source of our national wealth, then made a gigantic stride; and all the arts of war and peace being sedulously promoted, England was raised to that proud eminence in the scale of nations which she has ever since maintained.

Remarkable periods ever produce remarkable men; and the influence which the Reformation, perhaps more than any other event, exerted over the spirit of society, is apparent in every page of the history of that time. The turbulent nobles, and the ignorant priesthood of a preceding age, made way for a race of Worthies in church and state,—widely differing indeed in their opinions and characters, but all, in a greater or less degree, stamped with the impress of the more enlightened age in which they lived. These men it has been occasionally the object of envy to blacken, or of ignorance to depreciate. It requires, in truth, very little acumen or discrimination to perceive that, as men, they all partook of the foibles to which humanity is subject; and as public characters, that most of them exhibited in their actions the influences of the system of society, and state of manners, in which they lived. But taken collectively, they exhibit a mass of virtue, of talent, of wisdom, and of valour, such as a succeeding age would find it difficult to parallel.

Throughout the period to which reference has been made, Sir Thomas Gresham is to be distinctly traced: not indeed as a brilliant star amid the constellation of great names alluded to, but as one readily discernible, and capable of being identified with certainty. It is a vulgar error to suppose that his ancient celebrity depended on a few munificent acts; or that his pretension to the notice of a succeeding age is founded on no other grounds. Gresham was a statesman as well as a merchant: he resided for a short time at a foreign court in the capacity of an ambassador; and both at home and abroad was the companion and correspondent of princes and nobles. After the lapse of nearly three centuries, our means of developing his life and actions are necessarily much impaired; but enough evidence remains to prove that he was neither an inactive spectator of his country's prosperity, nor altogether uninfluential in promoting its rising greatness. It shall be our endeavour to follow him through the successive stages of his busy life; in order to do which effectually, it will be desirable, in the first place, to state somewhat concerning his origin and lineage.

The family from which Sir Thomas Gresham was descended, like most other old Norfolk families, derived its name from a little village where it had been settled for many generations.[b] Tradition points out the ruins of an ancient fortified mansion near Gresham church as their former residence; but historical evidence is altogether wanting in support of this statement. Neither does the curious little round-towered village-church itself, (which is represented in the engraving at the head of the present chapter,) record the existence of the Gresham family at any time in the neighbourhood. The heralds alone (and they all tell the same story) speak of one John Gresham,[c] who resided at Gresham during the latter part of the fourteenth century. His son James appears to have been clerk to Sir William Paston, the judge: he was lord of the manor of East Beckham, and is said to have settled at Holt, which is only a few miles from the village where his father resided. In quitting Gresham, he certainly exchanged a picturesque

[b] "Gresham, nomen faciens ditissimæ exinde prosapiæ," &c. Sir H. Spelman's English Works, 1723, fol. p. 152. See also Camden's Britannia, ed. 1722, c. 467. There are villages in Norfolk which bear the names of Coke, Paston, Repps, Walsingham, Walpole, Wodehouse, Wyndham, &c.

[c] The reader is referred to a pedigree of the family, (Appendix, No. I.) for a few genealogical particulars which it was thought requisite to supply, but with which it was not deemed necessary to encumber the text. In the Appendix to Dr. Ward's Lives, &c., a fuller pedigree may be found.

neighbourhood for one singularly bleak and unproductive; for Holt stands, or rather stood, in the midst of a wild heathy moor, in the most northern part of Norfolk, being only four miles distant from the sea. Here he probably erected the old manor-house, which occupied the centre of the town; and having since been reconstructed and converted into a free-school, now constitutes the chief ornament of Holt. It is represented in plate II. Eleven of the letters of James Gresham, written between the years 1443 and 1464, have been published among those of the Paston family.[d] They are dated from London, and sealed with a grasshopper;—a sufficient refutation, by the way, of an idle tradition accounting for the adoption of that heraldic symbol by Sir Thomas Gresham, which Mr. Lodge, in his "Portraits of Illustrious Personages," has not thought undeserving of notice.

James Gresham was succeeded by his son John, who married Alice, daughter of Alexander Blyth, of Stratton, Esquire: this lady brought her husband an ample fortune, and by her he had four sons,—William, Thomas, Richard, and John: the two younger of whom had the honour of knighthood conferred upon them by King Henry VIII.;

[d] Original Letters, &c., edited by Sir John Fenn, 4to. See vol. ii. plate xiv. fig. 2.

but Richard more especially claims our notice, as being the father of the distinguished individual whose history forms the peculiar subject of these pages. Before we enter on the life of Sir Thomas Gresham, it may not be improper to give some account of his uncles, who were also 'memorable men in their generation.'

Of William and Thomas, we know little more than is set forth in the family pedigree. The eldest, a mercer and merchant-adventurer of London, and the last of the family who resided at Holt, married a lady of the Bodley family; and in 1537 was registered one of the principal freemen householders of the Mercers' Company.[e] Hakluyt says, "it appears out of certain auncient Ligier Bookes of Master John Gresham," that between the years 1511 and 1534, many English ships traded to the Levant; among which he mentions "the Mary George, wherein was factor William Gresham."[f] This was, perhaps, the individual of whom we have so little else to recount; but it is certain, that in the year 1545 he was ranked among the most considerable merchants connected with the Low-Countries. He died at an early age, and was interred in Our-Lady-Chapel,

[e] Herbert's History of the Twelve Companies, &c., vol. i. p. 227.

[f] Principal Navigations, &c., vol. ii. p. 96.

in the church of St. Pancras, Soper-lane, (now Bow-lane,) on the 20th of March, 1548.[g]

The commercial importance which Norfolk acquired at a very early period, and for which it was indebted to its geographical position, is well known. So far back as the beginning of the twelfth century, many Flemish weavers came over and settled at Worsted in that county,—then a large and populous town, but at present only remarkable for having bestowed its name on a particular description of woollen manufacture: and in the year 1336, a large company of artisans of the same nation, invited over by Edward III., established themselves permanently at Norwich.[h] Their fleets found anchorage in Kirkley-road, near Lowestoft; a haven which has been disused ever since the reign of Richard II. Besides their manufactures, the Flemings brought with them the arts of their country; of which traces are visible to this day in the painted screens wherewith they

[g] In 1544, among the most liberal citizens who advanced money to King Henry VIII. on a mortgage of common lands, we find the names of Sir Richard, Sir John, and William Gresham; who, between them, furnished the king with 1073*l*. 6*s*. 8*d*.; viz. 500*l*., 800 marks, (or 533*l*. 6*s*. 8*d*.) and 40*l*. respectively.—Stowe's Survey, ed. 1720, book i. p. 282.

[h] Blomefield's Norfolk, vol. iii. p. 83. In 1332, Yarmouth yielded in importance to scarcely any English maritime town. It sent 43 ships, and 1905 mariners, to assist Edward III. in the siege of Calais.

decorated the churches of Norfolk, and the style of domestic architecture which they introduced. Of the former, the church of Worsted itself supplies us with a capital specimen: and a comparison of the views of Holt grammar-school, the old manorial residence of the Greshams, in plate II., and of Intwood Hall, in plate IV., with the Hôtel van Lyere, or house allotted to the English merchants at Antwerp, in plate III., will show how clearly imitative of the Flemish style of architecture were the residences of the Norfolk gentry in old times. The art of building with brick, which had been lost since the departure of the Romans, was introduced by the same people early in the fourteenth century.

About the year 1500, the trade with Flanders had attained its highest degree of prosperity; and this may explain why, of the four sons of John Gresham, three devoted themselves to a commercial career, in which two of them, John and Richard, (of whom more hereafter,) made such distinguished figures. It serves in particular to explain the origin of their connexion with Flanders, which in the end was productive of such important results to the family.

Thomas entered the church, and was presented to the rectorship of the adjoining parishes of South Repps and North Repps, in 1515 and 1519 respectively.[i] These villages are only a few miles distant from that whence the Gresham family derived its name. Thomas became a prebendary of Winchester, and in 1535 was collated to the chancellorship of the cathedral of Lichfield. In his will, which was proved in 1558,[j] we have a picture of him in his last moments. "He, the sayde Maister Thomas Gresham, parsone aforesaid, being asked, if God dyd call hym, who sholde be his Executor and Dower for hymn,—laye styll awhyle, and pawsed. Then, he being asked ones again,—'For youe have always borne your good will to Maister Edmund Gresham, your nephew, howe saye ye? Shall he be Dower for you, if God do calle you to his mercy?' He answered and said, 'Yee.'"

John, the youngest son, was a merchant of considerable importance. He was born at Holt; but apprenticed in London to a mercer, by name Mr. John Middleton, and admitted a member of the Mercers' Company in 1517. At that early period, and even earlier, the English traded to the Levant, and John Gresham was one of the principal adventurers. On one occasion, having hired

[i] Tanner's MS. in the registry of the Bishop of Norwich.

[j] September 17th, Prerogative-Office. Noodes. quire xlvi. In the Bishop's registry at Norwich, I found another will of this person, of a similar tenour, but quite differently worded. Jerves, ccxlvj. It was proved September 16th. See Appendix, No. II.

a Portuguese vessel, and loaded it at Scio with merchandise for the English market, the Portuguese, to whom the vessel belonged, dishonestly detained it in Portugal, and made himself master of the cargo, which was valued at 12,000 ducats. Henry VIII. deemed this injury done to a British subject not unworthy of his notice, and wrote to John, King of Portugal, desiring that the property might be restored: the letter is dated the 15th of October, 1531, and has been preserved by Hakluyt.[k] Another illustration of the early traffic of this family with the Levant, is supplied by the will of Lady Isabella Gresham, (Sir John's sister-in-law,) where particular mention is made of her 'Turkey carpets,'—a great luxury for a private individual, in an age when rushes formed part of the furniture of the court.[l] John Gresham became sheriff of London in 1537, (the year of his brother Richard's mayoralty,) and was knighted while in that office.

After the lapse of three centuries, we catch but imperfect glimpses of such a character as Sir John Gresham: but we may infer, that he was held in

[k] Principal Navigations, &c., vol. ii. p. 96. A marvellous story told by George Sandys, the traveller, in which a merchant named Gresham is a principal performer, probably refers to Sir John.—Sandys' Travels, book iv. p. 194.

[l] In 1602, a Turkey carpet, sixteen feet long, cost 27*l.*, equivalent to nearly 200*l.* at the present day.

high consideration, and lived, as our ancestors would have said, in great worship, from the following entry in an old MS. account of payments made "by John Gostwyk, treasurer unto the King's Majestie of the first-fruits and tenths, to these personnes ensuyng for diverse and sundry his Majestie's affaires;" from which we learn that when Anne of Cleves came to England in 1539, for the purpose of being united to the ill-mannered Henry, the task of entertaining certain of her train fell to the share of our knight:

"To certain Inholders of Grenewiche and London, for their dietts, and lodging of certain gentilmen that came over with the Quene's said grace, 387*l.* 6*s.* 7*d.*

"To Sir John Gressham for the charge of the ambassadors lodged in his house, 56*l.* 4*s.* 4*d.*"

In the same document mention is made of Sir Richard, father of Sir Thomas Gresham, and brother of the preceding, viz.

"To Sir Richerde Gressham for a cheyne of fyne golde whiche was geven to a gent. that came from the Duke of Bavyer, 100*l.* 13*s.* 9*d.*"[m]

Liberality and benevolence appear to have been qualities inherent in this family; for in 1546, hav-

[m] Cott. MS. Append. xxviii. l. 128. The Gostwicks were an ancient family of Willington, in Bedfordshire. As gentry they are extinct.

ing purchased of his eldest brother, William, the mansion-house at Holt,[n] where their father had lived, and where himself and his brothers were born, Sir John Gresham converted it into a free grammar-school, which he endowed with the manors of Pereers and Holt Hales, in Norfolk, with all their appurtenances; besides upwards of ten freehold estates in the same county, and three more in London. Had the trustees of this school been formerly distinguished for the same vigilance which characterizes their representatives at the present day, it would not have been our painful duty to state, that of the extensive demesnes with which Holt grammar-school was endowed by its founder,—sufficient, had they been properly managed, to have set it on a level with the first establishments of a similar nature in England,—there remains at present but 162 acres of land. Its total revenue amounts to not quite 350*l.*, about two-thirds of which arise from the rents of its estates in London. Most of the above-named property seems to have lapsed previous to the year 1592; for the Fishmongers' Company (to whom the management of the school was confided by its founder) have no evidence that the greater part

[n] Blomefield's Norfolk, vol. ix. p. 396. The deed of sale is dated October 14, 39 [38?] Henry VIII.; and the purchase-money was 170*l.* Holt school was incorporated April 27, 1 and 2 Philip and Mary, (1555.)

Plate II.

HOLT SCHOOL, NORFOLK: FORMERLY THE RESIDENCE OF THE GRESHAM FAMILY.

From a sketch made on the spot in 1838.

of it was in their possession in that year,—the earliest period to which they are able to refer. In the manor of Holt Hales they have no interest beyond the receipt of a fee-farm rent of 7*l.* per annum, paid to them by the present lord of the manor. Notwithstanding every disadvantage, this school, liberally conducted, and regulated by salutary statutes, is in a flourishing condition at the present day, and educates fifty free-scholars; to any one of whom removing to either of the universities, an annual exhibition of 20*l.* is allowed.[o] A representation of Holt school may be seen in the annexed plate. It is an ornament and a blessing to the county, and reflects much credit on the trustees and its worthy principal—the Rev. B. Pulleyne.

Nor is it altogether destitute of historical interest; for in the year 1650, a few loyal inhabitants of Norfolk having agreed to adventure their lives and fortunes in the service of their royal master, we are told that one Mr. Cooper, a minister and schoolmaster, was apprehended, and sentenced by the minions of Cromwell to be tried on Christmas-day, "partly to show their dislike of the observacion of that day, and partly to add to his affliction, whom they knew to honour that festival-day.

[o] Twelfth Report of the Parliamentary Commissioners on Charities in England and Wales. 1825, vol. x. p. 103.

And though they had no evidence against him but presumption that he was privy to the plot, yet they condemned him, and . . . . . he was executed at Holt, before his schoole-house doore."[p]

Sir John Gresham succeeded in obtaining from Henry VIII. the Hospital of St. Mary Bethlem, which has continued ever since in the hands of the Corporation of London, as an asylum for lunatics. In 1547, being lord mayor, he revived the splendid pageant of the Marching Watch;[q] a ceremony which had been practised from time immemorial by the citizens of London at Midsummer; but having been prohibited by royal command in 1528,[r] and again in 1539, was discontinued till the year of Sir John Gresham's mayoralty. The period fixed for its celebration was the eves of St. John and St. Peter; and what rendered it particularly attractive on the present occasion was, an accession of "more than 300 demi-launces and light-horsemen, that were prepared by the citizens to be sent into Scotland."[s]

[p] Archæologia, vol. xxv. p. 593.

[q] Stowe's Survey, ed. 1720, book i. p. 256.

[r] On account of the Sweating Sickness.—Hall's Chronicle, fol. 177, ed. 1548. A brief account of that malady may be found in Sir H. Ellis's interesting selection of "Letters," &c. first Series, vol. i. p. 269.

[s] Stowe's Chronicle, ed. 1631, p. 595. For a description of the Marching Watch, see Strutt's Sports and Pastimes, 4to. p. 269, or Stowe, ed. 1603, p. 159. But the curious reader should

In the Lady Long's household-book, preserved at Hengrave in Suffolk, the following entry occurs, relating to this ceremony: "Paid to xxx men, for weying of your La: harneys on Midsommer eve and St. Peter's eve; that is to say, x*s.* to my L. Mayor, and xx to Sir Roland Hill;"[t]—"my Lord Mayor" being Sir John Gresham. In proof of the interest this pageant excited, Stowe relates that Henry VIII. and his queen, Jane Seymour, "stood in Mercers' Hall, and saw the watch of the city most bravely set out," during the mayoralty of his privy-counsellor, Sir John Aleyn.

Stowe somewhat graphically mentions Sir John Gresham, when he describes how Protector Somerset, on the afternoon of October 14, 1549, "was brought from Windsor, riding betwixt the Earls of Southampton and Huntingdon, through Oldbourne, in at Newgate, to the Tower of London, accompanied with divers lords and gentlemen, and 300 horse." The Lord Mayor, Sir Ralph Warren, Sir John Gresham, Mr. Recorder, and other city dignitaries, he says, "sat on their

consult the Harl. MS., No. 3741; "A booke conteyning the manner and order of a watche," &c. [1585]: which has been reprinted in the Harleian Miscellany by Park, 4to. 1812, vol. ix. p. 389.

[t] Gage's History of Hengrave, p. 198, Note.

horses against Soper-lane," [Bow-lane,] the officers standing with bills and halberds while the Duke passed.

It was to this person that the subject of these pages was apprenticed; and from a passage in one of the letters he addressed to Queen Mary in 1558, it is evident that Sir John was repeatedly employed as agent in Flanders to Henry VIII. Nor did his commission cease with that monarch's reign, as appears from the council-book of his successor, where he obtains frequent notice as a financial agent.[u]

After having amassed a considerable fortune in trade, by which he was enabled to purchase many

[u] Three extracts may suffice. "12 April, 1547. Warrant to Sr John Gresham and Andrew Judde, aldermen of London, for delivery owte of the money rysing by sale of the King's Maties allom and fustians, the summe of cccc *li.* to thands of Leonard Shorer and his brother, for so much by them delivered at Antwerp to William Damesell for his Maties affaires there."

"13 February, 1547-8. Sr John Gresham had warrant to pay to Mr. Damosell, repayring to Antwerp in his Maties affaires, ccc crownes."

"28 April, 1548. Sir John Gresham, now lord mayor of London, had warrant for xviii c *li.* [1800*l.*], to be sent to Sr Richard Cotton, Thresaurer of Bulloin, for payment of things under his charge; which money to be parcell of that same receyved of the same Sr John sold for fustyanes of the King's Matie deceassed, delyvered to him whyle his Highnes lived." For access to a very beautiful transcript of the council-book of Edward VI., I am indebted to the kindness of my friend, P. Fraser Tytler, Esq.

estates in Norfolk, besides the manor of Titsey in Surrey,[v] he died of a malignant fever, on the 23rd of October, 1556,—seven days after he had made final dispositions for the government of Holt-school,—and was interred in the beautiful church of St. Michael Bassishaw, in which parish he resided at the time of his death. "He dwelt," says Stowe, "where Sir Leonard Halliday, who was mayor *anno* 1605, afterwards dwelt."[w]

Strype has given us a list of several worthies, who, in a short space, fell victims to the same pestilential malady; and he does not omit to mention Sir John Gresham among the number. The day of his interment happening to be a fast-day, he says an extraordinary fish-dinner was provided on the occasion, at which were admitted

[v] In Henry VIII.'s Privy-council book, it is stated that, in 1541, "a frame of tymbre belonging to Sir John Gressam of London, knyght," was destroyed by incendiaries in Surrey: whereupon a letter was addressed to Justice Willoughby, and other justice gentlemen dwelling in the said county, ordering them to examine all suspected persons at the Sessions at Godstone.—Proceedings and Ordinances of the Privy-council of England, 8vo. 1837, vol. vii. p. 174.

[w] It appears, from his will, that he had first lived in Milk-street, and subsequently in the parish of St. Mary, Aldermanbury. "He gave the coat of the Greshams with a chief, or; a trefoil, azure, between two asses' heads, erased, sable, collared."—Stowe's Survey, ed. 1720, book v. p. 176. Among the armorial bearings painted in the old hall of the Mercers' Company, were those of Sir John and Sir Richard Gresham.

all that came; and the funeral sermon was preached by the celebrated Dr. Harpsfeld.[x] To judge from the ceremonial of his interment, he must have been a personage of great consideration. "He was buried," says Stowe, "with a standard and penon of arms, and a coat armour of damask, [Damascus steel,] and four penons of arms; besides a helmet, a target and a sword, mantles and the crest, a goodly hearse of wax, ten dozen of pensils, and twelve dozen of escutcheons. He had four dozen of great staff torches, and a dozen of great long torches........ The church and the streets were all hung with black, and arms in great store; and on the morrow three goodly masses were sung; one of the Trinity, another of Our Lady, and the third of Requiem."[y] Many were his charitable bequests. Besides 100*l.* to poor maids' marriages, and considerable sums to the different prisons and hospitals of London, he left to sixty poor men, and forty poor women, as many black gowns, of the value of 26*s.* 8*d.* and 20*s.* each, respectively. Sir Rowland Hill, and Sir Andrew Judd, Knts., conjointly with his 'well-beloved nephew, Thomas Gresham,'

[x] Lowndes mentions "A notable and learned Sermon or Homilie vpon St. Andrewes Day last past, 1556, &c., by Mayster John Harpesfield. D.D.," &c.

[y] Stowe's Survey, ed. 1720, book i. p. 258-9.

were appointed overseers of his will. To the Mercers' Company he left 13*l.* 6*s.* 8*d.* for a feast,—"desiring theim, aftre dynner, to have my soul in remembrance with their prayers." He was twice married,[z] and by his first wife had eleven children, from the eldest of which was descended Sir John Gresham, the representative and last baronet of the family, who died at Titsey, on the 20th of October, 1801.[a]

Sir Richard, brother of the preceding, and father of Sir Thomas Gresham, was born at Holt,[b] but brought up in London, where he was apprenticed to Mr. John Middleton, an eminent mercer, and merchant of the staple at Calais.[c] In 1507 he was admitted to the freedom of the Mercers' Company. Though occasionally engaged in Flanders, he pursued his business at home, and there appears to be no evidence whatever that he was appointed to the office of Royal Agent in the Low Countries,[d] as many have as-

[z] See the family pedigree in the Appendix, No. I.

[a] Gent. Mag. vol. lxxi. pp. 962, 1049.

[b] Blomefield's Norfolk, vol. ix. p. 396.

[c] Middleton seems to have been a Hertfordshire man. He died in London in October or November 1509, and was buried before the image of St. Katharine Coleman. Prerogative-Office, Bennett. quire 22.

[d] In the Privy-purse expenses of King Henry VIII., from Nov. 1529 to Dec. 1532, he is merely styled "of London, mercer."—See pp. 7, 116, and 261, of that interesting publication.

serted. In confirmation of this statement, it is worth remarking that he attained, in succession, to the several honours of citizenship; from all of which his son was excluded, by his periodical residence in the capacity of Royal Agent at Antwerp. That he was frequently employed in the service of the state,[e] and was its accredited financial agent, is however certain; and he appears to have been one of those individuals, of whose number were Sir John Hackett, John Hutton, and others, on whom Wolsey and Crumwell, as prime-ministers, were accustomed to depend for foreign intelligence, and co-operation in the working out of their plans at home. Thus, in 1526, Richard Gresham wrote to the cardinal from Flanders, apprizing him of an arrest of the English, and a general seizure of merchandise at Nieuport;[f] and about the same time we find him among his fellow-citizens, supporting the demands of the crown with a degree of warmth which called forth the unqualified expression of their displeasure. Supplies were required to enable Henry

[e] See a letter, reprinted in Cavendish's Life of Wolsey, by Singer, 1827, p. 461. It is from the Cott. MS. Otho. C. x. fol. 223.

[f] Cott. MS. Galba. b. ix. fol. 12. This was in revenge of the arrest of the imperial ambassadors in England. The writer recommends to the Cardinal's notice Jochēm Howsteter, a German merchant, who was the bearer of the letter.

VIII. to carry on the war with France; and Wolsey, after attempting some arbitrary impositions, which drove the Londoners very nearly into a state of rebellion, solicited a voluntary contribution of the mayor and aldermen. This they also refused to comply with, until they had communicated his request to the common-council; who so indignantly rejected it, that the court moved for expelling Richard Gresham, John Hewster, and Richard Gibson, three of their members, who ventured to speak in favour of the measure.[g] On his death-bed, Wolsey spoke of Gresham as his 'friend.' Sir William Kingston, constable of the Tower, desired the cardinal to state what had become of a sum of money lately in his possession. "This money that ye demand of me," replied the dying cardinal, "I assure you it is none of mine; for I borrowed it of divers of my friends to bury me, and to bestow among my servants, who have taken great pains about me, like true and faithful men."[h] He then explained how he was indebted for 200*l.* to Richard Gresham. This happened in the year 1530.

In 1531 Richard became sheriff of the city of London; and in October 1537 was elected lord

[g] Hall's Chronicle, by Ellis, 4to. 1809, p. 699.

[h] Cavendish's Life of Wolsey, by Singer, 1827, p. 384.

mayor.[i] The dignity of the chief civic officer was at that time commonly augmented by the honour of knighthood; and during his mayoralty, Gresham received that distinction at the hands of his royal master.[j] It is rather remarkable, that of the four letters of Sir Richard known to exist, three were written during his mayoralty; each being in its way highly interesting, important, and characteristic.

The first in order is probably the following, dated only a few days after the writer's election to the civic chair. It was addressed to Crumwell on the occasion of the death of Queen Jane Seymour, an event which occurred a few days after she had given birth to Edward VI.

"Myne humble dieuty rememberyd to your good lordeshipe, &c. Yet shale please you to untherstand, that by the commaundement of the Ducke of Northefolk, I have cawssyd xii c. [1200] massys to be seyde, within the Cite of London,

[i] In which year (30th November) Christopher Barker, Garter King of Arms, granted to him and his posterity the following augmentation to his arms;—on a chief, gules, a pelican between two lions' gambs erased, or, armed, azure. The grant may be found in "Miscellanies Historical and Philological," &c. 8vo. 1703, p. 175.

[j] His knighthood is referred to 1537, because he is styled *Gentleman* in the grant just cited, and *Sir* Richard Gresham in documents dated in the succeeding year: but Ward, and others, state that he was knighted in 1531.

for the sowle of our moste gracious Quene. And whereas the Mayer and Aldyrmen, with the Commenors, was lattely at Powlles, [St. Paul's,] and ther gave thanckes unto God for the byrthe of our Prynce,—my Lorde, I doo thyncke yt wher convenyent that ther shulld bee allsoo at Powlles a sollem derige and masse; and that the Mayer, Alldyrmen, with the Commeners, to be there, for to praye and offer for Hyr Grace's sowle. My Lorde, yt shall please you to move the Kynges Highnes, and hys pleasser knowen in thys behelfve, I ame and shale be redy to accomplyche his moste gracious pleasser. As knowethe God, who gyve unto you goode helthe with long lyve. From London, thys Thurssdaye, the viiith daye of November.

"My Lord, yf ther be eny allmes to be gyvyn, ther ys many power pepyll within the Cite.

Your owne, at your Lordeshepes
Commaundementes,
RYC. GRESHAM."[k]

This letter merits preservation, were it only for the humanity which dictated the concluding

[k] Cott. MS. Nero. C. x. f. 2 b. Thus, on the occasion of Queen Katherine's pregnancy, (5th July, 1518,) Henry VIII. commanded *Te Deum laudamus* "to be solempnely sunge in Powlys."—See Pace's Letter to Wolsey. State Papers, vol. i. K. Henry VIII. 4to. 1830, p. 2,—a publication replete with interest of the highest order.

sentence. But the charitable spirit of Sir Thomas Gresham's father will best appear from the following very remarkable petition; wherein he prefers no selfish suit, but avails himself of his influence with the king to plead the cause of the afflicted and the friendless. One scarcely knows which to admire most; the benevolence of the writer, the earnestness with which he presses his request, or the dexterity with which he avails himself of the arguments likely to have most weight with the king, and best calculated to secure a favourable result to his application. The letter is as follows:—

"Most redowted, puysant, and noble prynce; my most dradd, beloved, and naturall sovraigne Lorde; I, your pore, humble, and most obedient servaunt, dailly consideryng, and ever more and more perceyvyng by your vertuus begynnyngs, and charitable procedyngs in all your cawses, your persone and majestie Royall to be the elected and chosen vessell of God; by whome not alonly the very and true worde of God is, and shal be sett forthe, and accordyng to the trewghth and verytie of the same,—but also to be he, whom God hath constituted and ordeyned bothe to redresse and reforme all crymes, offences, and enormyties, beyng repugnant to his doctryne, or to the detryment of the comon welthe and hurt of the pore people, beyng your naturall subjects; and forder, to forsee and vigilantly to provyde for the charitable reformacion of the same,—whyche thynge hath, and yet dothe encorrage me, and also my bounden dewtie obligethe me, (in especiall beyng most unworthy your Levetenaunt and Mayer of your Cytie Royall of London,) to enforme and advertise your most gracious highnes of one thyng in especiall, for the ayde and comforte of the pore, sykk, blynde, aged, and impotent persons beyng not able to helpe theymselffes, nor havyng no place certen where they may be refresshed or lodged at, tyll they be holpen and cured of theyr diseases and syknes. So it is, most gracious Lorde, that nere, and withyn the Cytie of London, be iij Hospytalls, or Spytells, commonly called seynt Maryes spytell,[l] seynt Barthilmewes spytell, and seynt Thomas spytell; and the new abbey of Tower-Hyll,[m] founded of good devocion by auncient Faders, and endowed with great possessions and rents, onely for the releffe, comforte, and helpyng of the pore and impotent people, not beyng able to helpe theymselffes; and not to the mayntenaunce of Chanons, Preests, and Monks,

[l] Now called Bethlehem Hospital.—Stowe's Survey, ed. 1720, b. i. p. 192.

[m] This was the Abbey of St. Clare, called the Minories.—Ibid. b. ii. p. 14.

to lyve in pleasure, nothyng regardyng the miserable people liyng in every strete, offendyng every clene person passyng by the way, with theyre fylthy and nasty savours. Wherefore may it please your marcifull goodness, (enclyned to pytie and compassion,) for the releffe of Crysts very images, created to his own similitude, to order by your high authoritie, as supreme hed of this Chyrche of England, or otherwise by your sage discrecion, that your Mayer of your Cytie of London, and his brethern the aldermen for the time beyng, shall and may from henssforthe have the order, disposicion, rule, and governaunce, bothe of all the lands, tenements, and revenewes apperteynyng and belongyng to the said Hospitalls, or any of theym; and of the ministers which be, or shalbe withyn any of them. And then your Grace shall facilie perceyve, that where now a small nombre of Chanons, Preests, and Monkes be founde, for theyr own profitt onely, and not for the common utilitie of the Realme; a great nombre of pore, nedy, sykke, and indigent persones shalbe refresshed, maynteyned, and comforted, and also healed and cured of theyr infirmyties, frankly and freely, by Physicions, Surgeons, and Potycaries, which shall have stipende and salarie onely for that purpose: so that all impotent persons not hable to labour, shalbe releved; and all sturdy beggars not wylling to labour shalbe punyshed. For the whiche doyng, your Grace shall not alonely merit highly towarde God, but shew your selffe to be more charitable to the pore than your noble progenitor King Edgar, foundour of so many Monasteryes: or Kyng Henry the Thyrde, renewer of Westminster: or King Edward the Thyrde, foundor of the new Abbey: or Kyng Henry the Fyfte foundor of Syon and Shene; but also shall have the name of conservatour, protectour, and defendour of the pore people, with their contynuall prayer for your helthe, welthe, and prosperitie long to endure.

Your humble and most obedyent servant,

RYCHARD GRESHAM."[n]

This petition for the city hospitals was in part granted; and the grant was subsequently confirmed by Edward VI. That the petitioner had attracted the favourable notice of the monarch, and was approved by his ministers, may be reasonably inferred from the letter itself; in which the writer, in the fulness of his heart, appeals at once and with confidence to the highest authority in the land. He was familiar with Lord Crumwell, (who in early life, "beyng at Antwerpe, was reteined," says Foxe, "of the Englishe Marchauntes to be

[n] Cott. MS. Cleop. E. iv. f. 222.

their Clerke or Secretary, or in some such like condition placed perteinyng to their affaires,")[o] and Audeley, the Chancellor: but he preferred addressing his "most redowted, puysant, and noble prynce," his "most dradd, beloved, and naturall sovraigne Lord," the irascible and impetuous Henry himself. That monarch, stained as he was in his latter days with crime, showed himself in the beginning of his reign keenly alive to the claims of men of merit, and to such was ever easy of access. One would wish to remember him only as the king who loved 'to be merry' with Sir Thomas More at Chelsea; "whither," says Roper, "on a time unlooked for he came to dinner with him; and after dinner, in a faire garden of his, walked with him by the space of an hower; holdinge his arme about his necke."

But the letter of Sir Richard Gresham which is best known, and has been most often quoted, is that in which he declared his anxiety to erect a Burse or Exchange in Lombard-street, for the convenience of merchants. On this head we shall have more to say hereafter; but that Gresham's letter may be understood, it is necessary to observe that at this period it was the custom of mer-

[o] Acts and Monuments, ed. 1576, p. 1149. Some valuable notices of Crumwell are given by Sir H. Ellis, in the second Series of his Letters, &c. vol. ii. p. 116.

chants, for the transaction of business, to assemble twice every day in Lombard-street; where they were necessarily exposed to the inclemency of the weather, and other inconveniences which had long been severely felt. Such however is the tendency of mankind to adhere to ancient usage and resist innovation, that when, in the year 1534 or 5, the king proposed to the citizens that they should remove their place of meeting from Lombard-street to Leadenhall,—a building admirably adapted for their accommodation, to judge from Stowe's description,—the proposal was declined; being negatived at a meeting of the common-council by a show of hands.[p]

The project, so often unsuccessfully mooted, Sir Richard seems to have had much at heart. He had visited Antwerp, where a Burse had newly been erected, and in 1537 had submitted to Crumwell (then lord privy-seal) a design for a similar edifice, which he was bent on seeing constructed at home. Before retiring from his mayoralty in 1538, he made another effort in furtherance of his favourite project, by calling the circumstance to his lordship's remembrance in the following words:—" The last yere, I shewyd your goode lordeshipe a platte, that was drawen howte for to make a goodely Bursse in Lombert strette,

[p] Stowe's Survey, ed. 1720, book ii. p. 152.

for marchaunts to repayer unto. I doo supposse yt wyll coste ii M *li.* [£2000] and more, wyche shalbe very beautyfull to the citti, and allsoo for the honor of our soverayngne lord the kinge. But," he adds, "ther ys serten howssis in the sayd strette belongyn to Sir George Monnocks; and excepte wee maye purchesse them, the sayd Bursse cannot be made. Wherefor, yt may please your goode lordshipe to move the kyngs highnes to have hys most gracious lettyrs directyd to the sayd Sir George, wyllinge and allsoo commaundynge hym to cawse the sayd howssys to be solld to the mayer and commonaltye of the city of London, for such prices as he dyd purches them for; and that he fawte not but to accomplyshe hys gracious commandement. The lettyr," he observes, "must be sharpley made, for he ys of noe jentyll nature;[q] and that he shale giffve further credens to the mayor, I wyll delyver the lettyr, and handyll him the beste I can; and yf I maye obtayngne to have the sayde howssys, I dought not but to gather oon M pounds [£1000] towerde the bulldynge, or I departe howte of myne office. Ther shale lacke

[q] Not *gentle* perhaps, but certainly benevolent. According to Stowe, he re-edified the decayed parish church of Walthamstow; built a bridge there, founded a hospital and a free-school, and endowed alms-houses for thirteen poor persons. He was lord mayor in 1514.

noe goode wylle in me. And thus our Lorde preserve your goode Lordeshipe in prosperous helthe, longe to contynewe. At London the xxv daye of Juylly, [1538.]

All yours, att your Lordeshipes
Comandement,
RYC. GRESHAM."[r]

What reception this application met with, does not appear; but with the additional obstacle of the houses, and the 'unjentyll nature' of their owner, it can be no matter of surprise that it was unsuccessful, and that the citizens remained undisturbed in their old place of resort. With Sir Richard Gresham, however, rests the honour of having originally projected the 'goodely bursse,' which his son was happily possessed of the means as well as the inclination, thirty years later, to construct. He had also the wisdom to imitate his father in his other acts of benevolence and charity, which is far higher praise.

In consequence of the representations of Sir Richard Gresham in the letter above mentioned,

[r] Cott. MS. Otho. E. x. f. 45. Ward (who has been followed by every subsequent writer) was incorrect in assigning to this letter the date of 1531; as will appear from a careful consideration of its contents. He has also erred in stating it to have been addressed to Audeley, while privy-seal,—an office which Audeley never held. I am indebted to the acuteness of Mr. Robert Lemon for the detection of Ward's error.

permission was granted to merchants to exercise the privilege of exchanging, without restraint; an advantage of which they had been deprived by royal proclamation,[s] and which they could no more be without, says the writer, "than the shippes in the sea can be wythoute wattyr." A long letter on this subject is extant, written at the time by the Lord Chancellor Audeley to Crumwell.[t]

It has been observed in a preceding page, that Sir Richard Gresham was an accredited financial agent of the state, and was frequently employed in its service. He is repeatedly mentioned in this capacity in the State correspondence of Henry the Eighth's reign: Sir Edward Carne, for instance, (the English ambassador in Flanders,) in 1539, thanks Crumwell for having sent him "a bill from Mr. Gresham for 50*l.*, to be received of his factor at Barowgh:"[u] Wriothesley, a few weeks after, begs the same nobleman "to thank Maister Gresham;" adding, "I have for

[s] Grafton's Chronicle, sub anno 1530.

[t] It follows Sir Richard Gresham's letter in Cott. MS. Otho. E. x.; being the document which Ward has so sadly mangled in his Appendix, No. I.

[u] Sometimes written Burborough, the modern Bourbourg; situated a little distance south of Gravelines. The letter is dated from Brussels, 8th January, 1538-9.—Flanders Correspondence, State-Paper Office.

meself and my fellowes recyved at his hande sithens I arryved here, besides the money for the plate, 710*l.*,"[v] and Sir Thomas Wiatt, writing probably about the same time to Henry VIII., says, "Here is here, abowte the provision, Mr. Parker, Mr. Blunt, and Mr. Gresham, your majesty's servants."[w] So that, supposing the personage here referred to, to have been in each instance Sir Richard Gresham, (which was probably the case,[x]) we may presume that he was actively engaged from about the year of his mayoralty until 1540, when the king required his services at home, on business of a different nature.

The surest road to Henry's favour was a willing acknowledgment of his ecclesiastical supremacy; and in this, like many of his elders and betters, Sir Richard Gresham was not deficient. Nor does he appear to have been one who, at an earlier period, opposed himself to the mandates of the imperious monarch. In 1532, it was unfortunately his duty, as sheriff, to receive into his custody and commit to Newgate, James Bainham, Esq., a Protestant gentleman of the Temple, who suffered martyrdom in Smithfield on the

[v] From Brussels, 3rd March, 1538-9.—Ibid.

[w] Harl. MS. No. 282, f. 119. Parker and Blount belonged to families afterwards ennobled.

[x] See the Postscript to Cott. MS. Galba. B. x. f. 96.

30th of April; and now, in 1540, (having been already appointed one of the commissioners for taking the value of the benefices of London, before the suppression of the abbeys,) he was, together with his brother Sir John, in the commission under Bishop Bonner for persecution upon the six articles. The character of that commission is too well known to require comment. Foxe calls it "the whip with sixe strings." We will only mention, that at this period the king bestowed upon him some broad church lands in Yorkshire; from which circumstance the reader must draw the most charitable inference he is able.

It was with reference to the former of these commissions, (to which he was appointed in 1536,[y]) that Sir Richard, writing to Crumwell on the 25th of July, 1538, says, "I have received your lordshippe's lettyr by Doctor Peeter, whereby I doe perceyve that the Kyng's pleasser ys, that the monastery of Wallssyngham shale be dissolved. Wherunto I am, and shalbe conformable in alle things to hys highness pleasure; and by the commissyners I have whrytten in such weysse to the Prior, as I dowght not he shale make noe staye in the same."[z] Nor did he; for

[y] Strype's Eccl. Mem. ed. 1822, vol. i. p. 276.

[z] Cott. MS. Otho. E. x. f. 45.

Dugdale relates that Richard Vowell, the prior, surrendered the priory of Walsingham, with all its possessions, to the king, on the 4th of August following.[a] A few weeks after, when the hospital of St. Thomas of Acre shared the fate of Walsingham Priory, Gresham was instrumental in securing it to his company, who erected the Mercers' chapel in Cheapside on its site.[b]

The remainder of the postscript to Sir Richard's letter to Crumwell, last quoted, is too interesting to be omitted:—"Yt maye please your good Lordshipe to move the king's highness to be soo goode and gracious lorde unto me, that I may beg of his grace serten launds in Northeff [olk,] late of the bysschopys launds; callyd Thorpe, Blowesse, Hevyngham, Byghton, and Battysford. The vallewe of them ys CL *li.* [150*l.*] by yere, aftyr the ratte of xx yeres purchase. The some ys iij M *li.* [3000*l.*] whereof it maye please hys grace to be deffaulkyd i M *li.* [1000*l.*] wyche I was commaunded by the Lorde Cardynale to delyver to the Duke of Buckynghame at hys goynge over to Guynes, as by ii obligations remaynynge in the custody of mastyr Whrysseley, (wherein stande bowndyn the sayd ducke with other for payment to the kyngis usse,) yt maye appere.

[a] Monasticon, fol. 1817–29, vol. vi. P. i. p. 71.

[b] Weever's Ant. Fun. Monuments, ed. 1631, p. 400.

And the reste, wyche is ii M *li.* [2000*l.*] I shale content and paye unto hys grace in redy mony. And thus our Lorde preserve hys noble grace in prosperous helthe longe to contynew. Amen."

"To the ryght hoñable and hys
synguller goode Lorde, my Lorde Prevy Seale."

It will have been perceived, from some of the preceding passages, that the writer of this letter was one in whom Henry's ministers had confidence: and this further appears from an entry in the Privy-council book, under the year 1540, when several persons were apprehended as "setters forth of a naughty booke made by Philipp Melanchton against the King's Acts of Christian Religion." The entry states that "Henry Dubbe, stationer of London, beyng sent for as suspect, was dismissed; and declared by the report of Sir Richard Gresham, knt., and John Godsalve, one of the clerks of the signet, to be (as far as they could perceyve by thexamination of hym) inocent in that mater."[c]

From about the year 1541 until the time of his death, we hear no more of Sir Richard Gresham, except that he received five successive royal grants of church lands,[d] the latest of which Henry

[c] Proceedings and Ordinances of the Privy-council of England, edited by Sir H. Nicolas, 8vo. 1837, vol. vii. p. 101.

[d] See Appendix, No. III. for the particulars of these grants.

bestowed in the last year of his reign,—sufficient proof of the regard he entertained for the old knight. Without much fear of erring in our conjecture, though the annals of the county are silent on the subject, we may follow Gresham at this period, when his actively spent life was verging to its close, into the retirement of Intwood Hall, in Norfolk. That Intwood belonged to his son, who often resided there, has been frequently stated; but it does not appear to be known that, from the few traces of the old Hall which yet remain, the prior residence of the father is established beyond doubt. In the garden at Intwood are the ruins of an old porch, on either side of which, beneath the label which surmounts the arch, is an escutcheon carved in stone,—one bearing the initials R. G., encircling a grasshopper; and the other representing the arms granted to Sir Richard during his mayoralty. Over the door of the kitchen we find, similarly carved on two shields, a cypher[e] and the letters

[e] This is generally called a *merchant's mark;* but, I think, incorrectly. The same representation (with the addition of letters) is to be found on the seals of many private gentlemen of the time: see, for example, the seal of Sir Thomas Kytson the elder, in Gage's History of Hengrave, in the plate facing page 170. Cyphers, carved on either side of the door-way, seem to have been once a prevailing fashion in Norfolk: they are of perpetual recurrence at the present day in Norwich, and other parts of the county.

R. G. fancifully connected. So that Intwood Hall, as it appears in plate IV., must have been erected by the father of Sir Thomas Gresham, sometime between the years 1538 and 1549, when he died; and thither, during that interval, he no doubt often retired. It seems probable, however, that even during these latter years of his life, he was more or less employed in the service of the crown; since, a few weeks after his death, arrangements were made for transferring to Sir John Williams a sum of money "growing out of the sale of certain demi-launce harnes, stele saddells, &c., apperteigning to the King's Matie;"[f] which, at the time of his decease, Sir Richard held.

Unfavourable as some of the preceding passages unquestionably are, and insufficient as the combined evidence may appear to enable us to form a correct estimate of the character of this individual, we should perhaps err were we not to assign to him a place in the foremost rank of the worthies of London. In giving his son the benefit of a college education, contrary to the practice of the commercial order of that, or indeed of a subsequent period, he showed himself possessed of enlarged views and of an enlightened understanding; and may be pronounced to have been in advance of the age in which he lived. He was of a disposi-

[f] MS. Council-book of Edw. VI., April 1st, 1549.

tion singularly energetic and enterprising: and let it be recorded to his honour, that however fortunate as a merchant and favoured as a courtier, he was yet not so engrossed by the cares incidental to a mercantile career, as to be insensible to the beauty of loftier speculations; nor so spoiled by having basked in the sunshine of court favour, as to become selfishly callous to the wants of his less fortunate fellow-creatures. On the contrary, it is remarkable that though we know of but few of his letters, they every one afford evidence of a most humane disposition. The city of London had, perhaps, never before known a greater benefactor; and it is but charitable to ascribe the harsher features of Sir Richard's character to the intolerant spirit of the times in which he lived. His connexion with Bainham's martyrdom in particular must be leniently viewed; since it does not appear, from Foxe's narrative, that Gresham exercised any severities towards his unfortunate prisoner, and only discharged the duties of his office in taking him into his charge. The share which the great Sir Thomas More is stated to have had in that transaction,[g] so strangely at variance with the wonted mildness and modest bearing of that illustrious man, should incline us to look with clemency on the errors of spirits of

[g] Acts and Monuments, ed. 1576, p. 1000, et seq.

an inferior order, committed during a period of popular excitement unparalleled in the later annals of our history.

Sir Richard Gresham died at Bethnal-green, where he generally resided, on the 21st of February, 1548-9,[h] and was buried in the church of St. Laurence-Jewry; the coat of arms which had been granted to him during his mayoralty, being placed over his tomb. It was taken down, however, according to Stowe, by Sir Thomas Gresham, who substituted for it the old family coat.[i] He had been twice married; first (in 1517, probably,) to Audrey, daughter of William Lynne, Esq. of Southwick, in Northamptonshire; secondly to a widow named Isabella Taverson,[j] who

h From the original Inquisition found on the death of Sir Richard Gresham, obligingly communicated by J. Salusbury Muskett, Esq. of Intwood Hall: (enrolled among the *Inquis. post mortem*, an. 4, Edw. VI. nu. 77. Rolls Chap.) The inscription on his monument (Stowe, ed. 1720, book iii. p. 45,) incorrectly states his death to have occurred on the 20th of February, which happens to be the date of his will, (Prerogative-Office, Populwell. quire 31.) Sir Richard's monument was not erected till after 1559; and the inscription also misstates the names of his children,—another proof that such evidence cannot be safely relied on.

i Stowe's Survey, ed. 1720, b. v. p. 176.

j Her maiden name was Worpfall. She made her will April 23rd, 1565, and it was proved on the 28th of the following month; her death must therefore have occurred during the interval.—Prerogative-Office, Morrison. quire xvj.

survived him. By his first marriage he had four children,—two daughters, Christiana, who married the wealthy Sir John Thynne, of Longleat[k] in Wiltshire, from whom the Marquis of Bath is descended; and Elizabeth, who died unmarried in 1552, and bequeathed the bulk of her property to her sister Lady Thynne, "who," she observes, "hath been very good unto me these four years." Sir Richard Gresham had also two sons, the younger of whom is the peculiar subject of the ensuing pages. He states his nett annual income,[l] at the time of his death, to have amounted to 850*l.* 2*s.* 6*d.*, of which Lady Gresham inherited 282*l.* 7*s.* per annum; Sir John, 188*l.* 13*s.* 6*d.*; and Thomas, afterwards Sir Thomas Gresham, 94*l.* 10*s.* 8*d.*[m]

These earlier members of the Gresham family seemed to demand a brief memorial of their fame and fortunes, as having laid the foundation of their descendant's celebrity; but they must not be suffered any longer to withhold us from contemplating the character and actions of Sir Thomas himself, who seems to have inherited all the better

[k] At Hawnes, in Bedfordshire, the seat of Lord Carteret, is preserved a view of Longleat, as it appeared anciently.

[l] In the Inquisition just quoted.

[m] His will was proved 20th of May, 1549. He left rings to all his friends, not forgetting Protector Somerset and his lady, to each of whom he left a ring of the value of five pounds.

qualities of his ancestors, while in personal merit he certainly far surpassed them all.

He was the second son of Sir Richard Gresham, by his first wife Audrey, daughter of William Lynne, Esq., and seems to have been named after his uncle, the rector of South Repps. He was probably born in London in the year 1519.[n] Of his youth we know nothing, except that he had the misfortune to be deprived of a mother's care at the tender age of three years; and that he was subsequently sent to Cambridge, and admitted a pensioner of Gonville Hall. When the usage of that period and his father's station in society are taken into consideration, it will not perhaps be unreasonable to presume that, as a young man, Sir Thomas Gresham discovered abilities or inclinations above the common order, that he should

[n] Fuller, indeed, says that he was born at Holt, in Norfolk, (Worthies, vol. i. p. 138,) but probably did not give himself any trouble to ascertain the fact: and as Holt was the residence of an elder brother, and Sir Richard Gresham lived and was buried in London, there is no reason to refer the birth of his son elsewhere. Dr. Ward states London to have been his birth-place, but conceals his authority, (if he had any,) as well as his grounds for assigning Gresham's birth to the year 1519. I have followed the learned Professor in this date, which is very probably correct; inasmuch as Sir Thomas could not have been born in 1520, and yet have been twenty-six in 1544, (as stated on a portrait shortly to be described); nor can he reasonably be supposed to have been born in 1518, since his elder brother was *triginta et amplius* in 1550, as appears from the Inquisition already cited.

have been admitted to the enjoyment of so high a privilege as an education at Cambridge. This must, however, remain a mere matter of conjecture, since even the date of his entrance cannot be ascertained; no register of so early a period being in existence at Gonville and Caius College.[o] Here he imbibed that attachment to the Protestant faith which is conspicuous in all his subsequent correspondence, and for which his Hall was then distinguished ;[p] and to his residence at Cambridge must of course be ascribed that taste for literature, and that love of learned men, which distinguished him throughout life ; and which none of the subsequent cares of business, calculated as they are to engross the whole energies of the mind, were ever able to extinguish in him. Dr. Caius, in his Annals of the College which bears his name, and of which he was co-founder, notices Gresham in the following terms :—"Unà nobiscum," says he, "per juventutem hujus collegii, pensionarius erat Thomas Gresham, nobilis ille et ditissimus mercator, qui forum mercatorum Londini (quod bursam seu regale excambium vocant) extruxit." These words occur in a beautiful folio

[o] There is no register of the College antecedent to the year 1560.

[p] Strype's Life of Parker, ed. 1821, vol. i. p. 12.

MS. on vellum, preserved in an iron chest in the treasury of Caius College.[q]

It was, perhaps, not so much inclination as expediency which made him a merchant. But the advantages to be derived from foreign commerce were then so considerable, that with the splendid examples of his father and uncle before him, it can be no matter of surprise that he was induced to forsake a quieter walk of life, for one of honour and emolument. His father evidently destined him for commercial pursuits, by binding him in his youth apprentice to his uncle Sir John Gresham; in consequence of which he was, in 1543, admitted a member of the Mercers' Company, being then in the twenty-fifth year of his age. Ten years afterwards, writing to the Duke of Northumberland from Antwerp concerning

[q] It is entitled, "Annalium Collegii de Goneville et Caius, a Collegio cōdicto [condito?] libri duo, per Joannem Caium unum fundatorū et custodem ejusdē, año Dnī, 1563." Ward gives the passage incorrectly; he reads "doctissimus" instead of "ditissimus," and "mercatorium" instead of "mercatorum." A copy of the MS. on paper, preserved in the same College, and entitled "Annales Collegii nostri de Goneville et Caius," &c., is probably the authority to which Ward had access, and led him into the flattering error of attributing great learning to Sir Thomas Gresham. Both MSS. were kindly consulted for me by the Rev. John Lodge, of Cambridge, whose courtesy and readiness to facilitate literary inquiries, all who have had occasion to visit the public library of the University must have experienced.

commercial matters, he says, "To the wyche syence I myselfe was bound prentisse viii yeres, to come by the experyence and knowledge that I have. Nevertheless I need not to have bynne prentisse, for that I was free by my Father's coppye: albeit, my Father Sir Richard Gresham being a wyse man, knew, although I was free by his coppye, it was to no purpos, except I were bound prentisse to the same; whereby to come by the experience and knowledge of all kinds of merchandise."[r]

This may be as proper a place as any other to mention, that my reading has led me to quite a different conclusion respecting the estimation in which merchants were formerly held, to that entertained by the elegant author of *Illustrations of British History*. Mr. Lodge considers that the nobility of other days kept themselves at a distance from even the first members of the commercial order:[s] but I believe the contrary will be established by the following pages. What is strange, the nobles appear among the most enterprising speculators, and were themselves traders on the grandest scale. In Queen Mary's reign, for instance, when the Muscovy merchants were incorporated, (that is to say, the first English

[r] The letter is dated April 16th, 1553.—Fland. Corr. St. P. Off.

[s] Illustrations, &c., vol. iii. p. 151, Note.

company which traded to Russia,) the most powerful of the nobility stand foremost in the list of members.[t] The Earls of Leicester and Shrewsbury sent out joint-adventures to Muscovia in 1574; on which occasion the first-named peer writes to his friend, "I assure you yf I had had 10,000*l.* in my purse, I wold have adventured yt every peny myself."[u]

The earliest contemporary notice of Sir Thomas Gresham, occurs at this period of his history. He is mentioned in one of the despatches of Seymour and Wotton to King Henry VIII., written from Brussels in the month of June, 1543; and appears already in the character of a merchant of some importance, although but twenty-four years of age. "The Regente hathe granted a lycense for the gonne-powder and salpeter bought for your Highnes; the whyche we have delyveryd to *yonge Thomas Gresham*, solycitor of the same."[v] Allusion is here made to Henry's preparations for war with France, which led to the taking of Boulogne in the ensuing year. He is again mentioned in March, 1545, by Secretary

[t] Strype's Stowe, ed. 1720. b. v. p. 260.

[u] Lodge's Illustrations, &c., vol. ii. p. 125.

[v] Fland. Corr. St. P. Off. The Regent was Margaret Queen of Hungary, who governed the Low Countries for her brother, Charles V.

Paget, who writes to Petre from Brussels concerning an arrest of merchandise which had taken place by order of Charles V. This unjustifiable step was occasioned by Henry's having seized certain Flemish ships which were carrying assistance to the French; and the writer is speculating on the consequences likely to result to the merchant-adventurers. "Some in dede shall wynne by it; as William Lok, Sir Richarde Gressam *and his sonne*, and William Gressam, with such other for the most parte that occupie sylkes, who owe more than they have here. But Mr. Warren, Mr. Hill, Chestre, and dyverse others a greate nombre, ar like to have a greate swoope by it; having muche here, and owing nothing or little."[w]

Between the writing of these two letters, his marriage occurred. His wife, Anne,[x] was the daughter of William Ferneley, Esq., of West-Creting, in Suffolk; and widow of William Read, a gentleman of good family, whose ancestors were settled at Beccles in the same county. Read

[w] March 3, 1544-5.—German Corr. St. P. Off. Both these passages were kindly shown me by Mr. Robert Lemon.

[x] Her younger sister, Jane, was married to Sir Nicholas Bacon, the Lord Keeper. Their father, William Ferneley, Esq., who built the house at Creting, had been a citizen of London.—Bp. Tanner's MSS. No. 226, fol. 52.

styles himself in his will "citizen and mercer of London," and appears to have been on terms of intimacy with the Gresham family; for he appointed Sir Richard overseer of his will, and left him a legacy of 10*l.* and a black gown.[y] He died in the beginning of 1544; and that his widow was married to Thomas Gresham in the course of the same year, appears from a curious full-length portrait of the latter, preserved at Weston-Hall in Suffolk, inscribed with his wife's initials and his own name, accompanied by a date. The painting alluded to is in Holbein's best manner, and represents a well-proportioned young man, rather above the middle height, clad entirely in black. He wears the same small cap and solemn-coloured cloak which appear in his later portraits; but the present one is particularly interesting, because it exhibits him at so early a period of his life. Holbein has given him an intellectual brow, and a mouth full of expression. His features are regular, and eminently handsome; and his general aspect singularly mild and engaging. The beard and moustaches are short. On either hand he wears a ring,—in that day a mark of distinction; and in his right hand he holds a pair of gloves: at his feet, on the pavement, the artist has thought

[y] Prerogative-Office.—Pynnyng. quire iii.

proper to introduce a skull. On the right of this portrait, which is about the size of life, is written

. 1544 .
THOMAS
GRESHAM.
Z 6
T G

and on the left,

A G
LOVE · SERVE ·
AND OBEI ·
T G

while on each side of the black frame is inscribed, in letters of gold, the motto DOMINVS · MIHI · ADIVTOR, followed by the letters T. G. The Thruston family, to whom this portrait belongs, formerly resided at Hoxne Abbey, in Suffolk; and there the picture had probably hung, ever since the priory of Benedictine monks at Hoxne was granted to Sir Richard Gresham.[z]

The owner of this interesting picture [a] possesses another relic connected with Gresham's hasty marriage,—his supposed wedding-ring, which is preserved in an ancient miniature jeweller's chest. It opens horizontally, thus forming two rings, which are nevertheless linked together, and respectively inscribed on the inner side with a Scripture posy. QVOD · DEVS · CONIVNSIT is en-

[z] 38 Henry VIII.—Tanner, Not. Monastica.

[a] John Thruston, Esquire, (not Thurston, as Ward writes it,) of Weston-Hall, Suffolk; to whom whose courtesy I am indebted for an opportunity of inspecting the objects here described.

graved on one half; and HOMO · NON · SEPERAT, on the other. The ring is beautifully enamelled, and contains two stones; corresponding with which, in a cavity inside the ring, are, or rather were within the last twenty years, two minute gold figures of loves or genii; one of which has disappeared. To this relic the reader has been already introduced in the initial letter of the present chapter.

It appears from Read's will, that he left two sons, William, afterwards knighted, born in 1539, and Richard; both of whom lived to years of maturity. His clear annual income, derived from his own and his wife's estates in Suffolk, amounted to 138*l.* 15*s.* 4*d.*, of which 67*l.* per annum descended to his eldest son. Such was the income of a gentleman considered wealthy in the reign of Henry VIII., and such the expectations of his heir.

How many children Gresham had by his wife has not been recorded: we hear but of one, Richard, who must have been born before 1548, since in that year his name occurs in his grandfather's will: but an incidental mention of "my powre wiffe and children" in 1553–4,[b] shows that he had

[b] In a letter dated Jan. 18th, from Antwerp.—Fland. Corr. St. P. Off.

others, which he must subsequently have known the bitterness of losing.[c]

These brief memorials comprise all that is known with certainty of the early life of Sir Thomas Gresham. It appears that, although for the first few years after his marriage he made London his home, his business frequently carried him to Antwerp,—the great focus of commerce at the period of which we are speaking. But he was not destined to continue long in a private station. He was already distinguished as a merchant possessing uncommon tact and ability; and a remarkable juncture in the financial affairs of the kingdom having occurred, he was soon called upon to take an important part in their management, being then in the thirty-second year of his age.

[c] Unless the allusion be to his son Richard, and to Anne, his natural daughter.

THE BURSE AT ANTWERP.

CHAPTER II.

[1551 TO 1553.]

OFFICE OF ROYAL AGENT—GRESHAM'S APPOINTMENT, AND REMOVAL TO ANTWERP—SOME ACCOUNT OF THAT CITY—TRANSACTIONS WITH THE FUGGERS AND SCHETZ—GRESHAM'S DISSATISFACTION—HIS FINANCIAL SCHEMES—THE DUKE OF NORTHUMBERLAND HIS PATRON—HE NEGOTIATES WITH THE AMBASSADOR OF CHARLES V.—HIS PROSPERITY.

HE office of Royal Agent, or as it was sometimes called King's Merchant, or Factor, was of very early origin. It naturally arose out of the exigencies of an imperfectly organized system of finance; which, when the country was threatened with

The old Bourse at Antwerp. *First proof*

war, or some other source of heavy expenditure, recognised but two modes of replenishing the coffers of an impoverished treasury; viz. to levy subsidies by an unjustifiable stretch of arbitrary power,—or to induce wealthy merchants, under sufficient security, to advance the sums required. The former of these methods, which in remote times was doubtless had recourse to in the majority of instances, and with most success, was too convenient ever to be totally relinquished:[a] but as the commercial wealth of Europe increased, the practice of obtaining loans from the opulent merchants settled in Germany and the Low Countries became more and more prevalent; until it was finally found expedient, on the part of government, to employ an agent for the express purpose of negotiating them. This was always some one of high ability, influence, and integrity, whose province it was, in addition to the immediate duties of his office, to supply the state with whatever was required of foreign production. It was also expected of this servant of the crown, that he should keep the privy-council informed of whatever was passing abroad; and

[a] Among the State Papers of Queen Mary's reign, there exists an original instrument, dated September, 1557, authorizing commissioners to raise a compulsory loan throughout the counties of England.—Domestic Corr.

he was not unfrequently called upon to negotiate with foreign princes in the additional capacity of ambassador.

The office of "agent for the crown, with the trading interest, or as it was called King's Merchant," says an elegant modern writer, "was one of the highest importance and trust; inasmuch as it united the duty of raising money for the royal occasions by private loans, with that of protecting and cherishing the sources from which they were derived." It is to be observed, that this office was distinct in itself, and altogether independent of the occasional employment of one or more domestic financial agents.[b] It is from a misapprehension on this head, that so many erroneous statements have been circulated relative to the father of the subject of this memoir.

One of the earliest merchants who enjoyed this appointment was William de la Pole, father of Michael, Earl of Suffolk. In 1338, he lent Edward III., at Antwerp, a sum equivalent to at least 400,000*l.* of our money;[c] on which, in addition to several grants of crown lands, he was created Chief Baron of the Exchequer and a Knight Banneret. He is styled "dilectus mercator et

[b] The extracts from the Council-book of Edward VI., given in Note [u], page 18, will prove this.

[c] Viz. 11,000*l.* and 7500*l.*—Fædera, vol. v. p. 91.

valectus noster" in all public instruments; and in 1389 was succeeded in the same capacity by his son Michael, who dwelt in his father's house in Lombard-street, near Birchin-lane. The latter died at the siege of Harfleur in 1415, and was succeeded by his son, another Michael, who fell at Agincourt. It would not be an uninteresting subject of inquiry to trace the successive occupants of this office, after it went out of the De la Pole family, until the reign of Henry the Eighth; when the duties of Royal Agent had devolved to Stephen Vaughan, much of whose MS. official correspondence, extending from 1530 to 1546, may be found in the British Museum. It is a circumstance deserving of notice, however, that neither Vaughan, nor any other individual who filled this office, enjoyed it to the same extent as Sir Thomas Gresham; whose administration of the affairs of the crown was very nearly uninterfered with: whereas, notwithstanding Vaughan's nominal agentship, he is styled merely "the King's ambassador in Flanders," in 1538; and Hutton, in the same year, is repeatedly mentioned as "the king's ambassadour *and agent* in the lowe countreys." The salary, or as it was called 'the diets' of either, was twenty shillings *per diem.*[d]

[d] Arundel MS. No. 97, Plut. fol. 32, b. 41, &c.

As none of Vaughan's letters preserved among the State Papers bear a later date than 1546, (about which time he enjoyed the office of Under-treasurer of the Mint,[e]) and he did not die till 1550, it is probable that he had the good sense to retire from public affairs, and pass the last few years of a busy life in domestic privacy. We may reasonably presume this, of one who could write such a sentence as the following:—"I am purposed to go to Loveyne, and there to lye all the Lent, and applye my books; wherefore I praye you, helpe me to be quyet." The name of this interesting individual, history associates with that of Tindal the Reformer; 'whose boke inclosed in lether,' he transmitted through Crumwell[f] to Henry VIII. "It is unlikely," he said, "to gett Tyndall into England, when he dayly hereth so many things from thense whiche feareth hym." Among other important trusts, he was employed in 1538 and 9, conjointly with Wriothesley and Sir Edward Carne,[g] to negotiate respecting the intended match between Henry the Eighth and the Duchess of Milan; and when Wriothesley

[e] Ruding's Annals, 4to. vol. i. p. 66.

[f] See the long and curious letter which Crumwell addressed to Vaughan on this subject.—Cott. MS. Galba. B. x. f. 338.

[g] A letter, subscribed with their names, may be seen in the MS. referred to in the preceding Note, (fol. 127.) It is dated from Valenciennes, Oct. 25th.

and Carne were recalled in 1539, he was left ambassador resident in Flanders, and succeeded John Hutton as governor of the company of the merchant-adventurers; offices which he seems to have held conjointly with that of Royal Agent.

Many of Vaughan's letters are amusing. I cannot abstain from subjoining a specimen, in which he exposes to Lord Cobham his motives for entering a second time into the holy state of matrimony. "My Lord, I am so often and perpetually dryven from my howse, having many children and things in my howses, that I have byn compelled to take a wyfe. I have one, and one hath me. And bycause I wold avoyde the keping of ii howses, I am mynded to mary her as shortly as I can. But bycause I have no hope to go into England before Halontyde, I am mynded to sende for her to Calles, and mary her there: but if I so doo, then must I intreat your Lordship to bryng my wyfe to your lodging, and to mary her within your chappell, without any folisshe wonderyng. Whan I come, I shall not be able to tary above ii or iij dayse; but must return, and so shall she. If it please your Lordship for iij dayse to lett me be so bolde, your Lordshipe dyd me muche pleasure. I praye your Lordship to lett me know your answer to my wyve's matter of her comyng to you. And thus I praye God send yow helthe. From Andwerp, the vijth of March.

Your Lordship's humble

S. VAUGHAN."[h]

"To the right honorable lord, my Lorde Cobham, Lorde deputie of the Quene's Majestie's town of Calles."

Vaughan wrote occasionally from Antwerp, but most often from Augsburg in Germany, where he principally resided; the majority of his transactions being with Anthony Fugger and Nephews,—merchants, or, as they are sometimes called, bankers, of that city. The name of their ancient house occurs so perpetually in the financial history

[h] Harl. MS. No. 283, l. 218. Another short extract from a letter to Lord Cobham may not be unacceptable. "My schole M^{r} in London, Mr. Cob, goith from me. I dare no longer kepe hym. This I thought to signifie unto your Lordeship, bycause of your sonne, that after my schole M^{r} wer gon, he shuld not be provyded. . . . . Men suspect me for kepyng hym: but, as God helpe me, I never had an honester man in my company, nor I think ther be no honester man. What his opynyons be, I know not: I leve those to be iudged by other. It ys a great displeasure to me to lack so sad [serious] a man as he ys, in my howse to teach my children; specially seying I am dryven so often from home."—Ibid. l. 240. In another place Vaughan says,—"In the same lettre I enclosyd a letle clowte wth nedills, which I sent to the gentilwoman your daughter; whom I heard wysshe she myght [have] some: which are fynde good nedills."—Ibid. l. 247.

of the period, and so often in the ensuing pages, that a brief account of the family will not be inappropriately introduced in this place.

To say of the Fuggers that they were in their day the wealthiest merchants in Christendom, would be to record the circumstance least deserving of commemoration in the history of this once powerful and illustrious family.[i] They merited the far prouder title of the Medici of Germany. We gather from old writers that they formed extensive libraries, and collected at a great expense ancient MSS. of the classics, which they caused to be printed: Huldric Fugger, in particular, devoted himself to this object, and employed the celebrated Henry Stephens to collect bibliogra-

[i] "Elle avait amassé des Trésors prodigieux par son commerce dans les Indes Occidentales; ensorte qu' Antoine Fugger, Chef de cette Famille, nommé d' ordinaire Fokker, et qui mourut dans sa Patrie, disposa par Testament de plus de six millions d'écus d'or. Ses richesses immenses ont donné lieu à une façon de parler qui est encore usitèe dans ces provinces, où l'on donne le nom de *riche Fokker* à un homme d'une opulence peu commune."—[Van Loon, Hist. Met. des Pays Bas, fol. 1732, vol. i. p. 436.] We find here explained the origin of a whimsical appellation, used colloquially among ourselves. In the Atrium Heroicum of Dom. Custos, fol. 1600, are twelve well-engraved portraits of the Fuggers. Some curious particulars concerning this remarkable family are collected in a Note to Dibdin's Library Companion; but the best general account is to be found in Jacob's Historical Inquiry into the Production and Consumption of the Precious Metals, vol. ii. p. 25, et seq.

phical rarities. Dying at Heidelberg in 1584, he bequeathed his magnificent library to the Palatinate; and left a fund for the maintenance of six poor scholars, as well as a provision for the poor. We have a somewhat less particular account of Anthony and Raymond Fugger, 'merchant-kings,' who resided chiefly at Augsburg, and, it would seem, in little short of regal splendour ; but those who have made mention of them, describe in high terms their collections of pictures and antiques, and bestow lavish praise on the beauty of their gardens, and the taste and magnificence displayed in their houses. Well might a family have been magnificent, of which a single member was able, in the sixteenth century, to furnish a monarch with twelve hundred thousand pounds sterling![j] The Fuggers were ennobled by Charles V., who gave them in feoff the lordships of Kirchenbergen and Weissenhorn.[k]

These merchants, though they belonged to Augsburg, had also an establishment at Antwerp,[l] where they continued to reside till the year 1590. Their spacious residence, built by

[j] T. G. to Cecil, Aug. 24, 1561.—Fland. Corr. St. P. Off.

[k] Bayle's Dict. fol. 1740, vol. ii. p. 515; and Van Loon, Hist. Met. &c., vol. i. p. 437.

[l] There is among the Cotton MSS. an original acknowledgment of "Anthonius Fuggerj et Nepotes," for 152,000 livres of Flanders. It is dated from Antwerp, 24 September, 1546.

Anthony Fugger, is still to be seen in that city, and preserves the name of *het Fugghers huys* to this day.

On the death of Stephen Vaughan, which occurred early in 1550,[m] the field was left altogether open to his successor, Sir William Dansell, whose correspondence commences where that of Vaughan terminates. Besides the office of Royal Agent, Dansell enjoyed that of receiver of the court of wards and liveries; and having been bred at Oxford,[n] was probably a man of some pretensions to learning. Respecting his merits in his official capacity, it is not easy at such a distance of time to speak with certainty; but it is clear that his administration of the king's affairs was the reverse of satisfactory to the council. In May, 1549, they wrote sharply to him; complained that he was remiss in answering their letters, and upbraided him with his unskilful mode of proceeding; adding, "the bruit is blowen over London of the taking up of bolion for his Majestie, and of

[m] His will (in which he styles himself 'Esquire,') was proved 26 Feb. 1549–50. He left three children, and had been twice married: one of his wives being probably the rich widow whom he requested a friend to select for him, as he said he knew that there were many such in the city of London. He dwelt at the sign of "the iii leggs in Chepe."—Prerogative-Office. Coode. quire v.

[n] Vide infrà, note [n], p. 66.

such price that it is great marvell: and as may be most credibly and certainly judged, ye have hindred the King's Majestie to a wonderous notable some,—as is supposed, above 40,000*l.*; so that except ye have prepared alredy very muche for his highnes, we cannot conjecture how to excuse you: but ye have done his highnes marvelous evill service."[o] Dansell defended himself in a long letter, in which he tried to prove that, in the transaction of which the council complained, (wherein he had been assisted by 'one Thomas Gresham,') he deserved no kind of blame.[p] A copy of his letter he inclosed to his friend Sir Thomas Smith; to whom on the following day he writes, "I take God to witnes, yf I had xl thousand lyves, and shuld have spent them all, I could not have done more in this matter than I did." But his protestations had no weight with the council, who only renewed their expressions of dissatisfaction and displeasure: on which Sir William, astonished apparently at the rough usage he was experiencing, remonstrated more earnestly with their lordships; quaintly declaring, "I am right sure I never offended you; and it seemyth me that you suppose me a very blunt beast, without reason and discretion."[q]

[o] May 17, 1549.—Flanders Correspondence, St. P. Off.
[p] 25th May.—Ibid. [q] 27th June.—Ibid.

Sir William Paget, writing from Germany to Sir Thomas Smith at this period, expressed his opinion that the council were too severe with Dansell. The truth seems to be, that however well intentioned, he did not possess the requisite abilities for the office he filled; and he must have been a man of unpardonably dilatory habits, to say no worse of him, or he would not have been "revoked from his office of agent, by reason of his slacknes,"[r] in April 1551. In the following December affairs had come to such a pass, that the council, instigated apparently by one John Dymock who had preferred certain charges against Dansell, ordered him "to make hys imedyate repayre home;"[s] that they might receive from himself an account of his transactions, and examine him relative to the practices of which he had been accused. But he neglected to obey the summons; with characteristic sluggishness delaying

[r] This was on the 6th of April: on the 26th we find mention of "A letter to Mr. Dansell, that the Lordes arr contented he shall remaigne in Flaunders as governor, till he shall have other commandement from hence." (MS. Council-book of Edward VI.) Like Vaughan, therefore, he appears to have resided in Flanders in the additional capacity of governor of the merchant-adventurers.

[s] 29th Dec.—Ibid. John Dymock had been committed to the Tower the day before.—Ibid. A letter from him to Lord Cobham, dated Amsterdam, 2d April, 1546, is in the Harl. MS. No. 283. p. 368.

his return until the 31st of the following March, when "he was comitted to the custody of Mr. Hobby."[t] In the mean time, their lordships being at a loss to know what course to adopt, called in several merchants to consult with them as to the most advisable mode of extricating the king from the difficulties in which he had become involved. Of the number of these was Thomas Gresham, who has himself briefly recorded his first interview with the youthful king and his ministers in these words: "I was sent for unto the counsell, and brought by them afore the King's Majestie, to knowe my oppynyone (as they had many other marchaunts) what waye wythe leaste charge his majestie might growe out of debt. And after my device was declared, the King's highness and the counsell required me to take the room in hande, wytheout my sewte or labour for the same."[u]

It may be worth remarking in this place, that

[t] Ibid.

[u] Cott. MS. Otho. E. x. fol. 43. We hear little of Dansell after this period, except that he was occasionally commissioned to buy plate and gunpowder in Flanders. Among those who presented New Year's gifts to Queen Elizabeth, his name is of frequent recurrence. (See Nichols' Progresses, &c. passim.) Notwithstanding their relative position, Gresham and he appear to have continued friends. Dansell survived Sir Thomas, and died, apparently unmarried, some time between June 1st and August 18th, 1582. He dwelt in the parish of St. Mary, Aldermanbury. By his will he bequeathed to the University of Oxford, whereof

although none of Gresham's family had ever held the office of Royal Agent before him, not only his father and uncle, but his brother and himself had been repeatedly employed previous to this event, in the service of the crown, as domestic financial agents. "Thomas Gresham, mercer, of London," is frequently noticed in this capacity in the Council-book of Edward VI., long before the disgrace of Dansell; with whose duties in Flanders, his own in no degree interfered. He must therefore, about this period, have been frequently brought under the eye of the council; and in addition to the favourable testimony afforded by the confidence which had been already reposed in him, we may reasonably infer, from his having been 'sent for' on the present occasion, that he enjoyed the reputation of being one of the most enlightened merchants of his day. The experience he must have acquired during the seven years of his life he had already passed mostly at Antwerp, must obviously have rendered him one

he "was a scholler in tymes paste," 100*l.*; which amount was to be distributed in sums of forty shillings, among "the poorest schollers of the said University, which are disposed to give themselves to lerning." (Prerogative-Office, Tirwhite. quire xxxiv.) A specimen of his autograph may be found in the Harl. MS. No. 283. art. 179. The letter, which is dated from Antwerp, 17th August, 1545, has been accidentally omitted in the general Index.

of the fittest persons that could have been selected to confer with their lordships on the difficulties which now beset them.

Never, perhaps, was the judicious counsel he offered more needed; for the king's financial affairs then began to wear an alarming appearance, having been conducted up to that period with very little dexterity, or rather with none at all. The expensive wars carried on with France[v] had obliged Henry VIII. to incur debts, which, not being always in a condition to discharge, he was compelled, as often as his bonds became due, to renew on most disadvantageous terms. The annual interest on his bonds amounted to 40,000*l.*; which (while the exchange was reduced to sixteen shillings Flemish to the pound sterling) he was compelled to pay in English money; and he was required, at every renewal, to purchase jewels or wares, and sometimes both, to a large amount, as a consideration for deferring the liquidation of the debt; which, combined with the exorbitant rate of interest, necessarily operated much to his disadvantage. Thus in Henry's reign, Vaughan, writing from Antwerp to the Secretaries Paget and Petre, says of a rich merchant named Jasper Dowche, "he offerith to serve the King's Majestie this next somer dewring the space of vi

[v] See the Appendix, No. IV.

months, with c thousand ducats every month, during the nomber of vi monthes foresade, for reasonable interest, and upon the obligacons and bond of London; so the King's Majestie woll please to take a jewell therewith, which he priseth at c thousand ducats, and swerith it is so much worth. It ys a great poynt dyament sett about with other poynt dyaments, lik a rose."[w] During the following reign, we find another curious instance of this kind of transaction, (which, having passed into precedent, it was not easy to discontinue,) in the MS. journal kept by Edward VI. [1551, April,] "25. A bargaine made with the Fulcare for about 60,000*l.* that in May and August should be paid, for the deferring of it. First, that the Foulcare should put it off for ten in the hundred. Secondly, that I should buy 12,000 marks weight, at 6 shilinges the ounce, to be delivered at Antwerpe, and so conveyed over. Thirdly, I should pay 100,000 crounes for a very faire juel of his, four rubies marvelous big, one orient and great diamount, and one great pearle."[x]

[w] January 31st, 1546-7.—St. P. Off. A day or two after, he addressed the king to the same effect; adding, "herein I forbeare to trouble your Majesty with long wryting; by cause the saide Jasper hath largely sett foorth all these his offers in wryting, which I sende unto your Hyghnes herewith."—Ibid.

[x] In the same Journal, under 9th May, 1550, we find 2500 Cinquetales [Quintals] of Powder bought, in consideration of a debt of 30,000*l.* being "put over an year."

This iniquitous imposition on the part of the money-lenders was of old standing; and, sanctioned by the usage of preceding reigns, it had at last grown into a custom. But the ministers of King Edward, who had to conduct the finance of a country impoverished by his father's extravagance, and who were ever at a loss for supplies to meet the annual expenditure,[y] resolved in future to resist every attempt to repeat it: a resolution of which Gresham, in accepting the office of Royal Agent, was ignorant, and which at first brought him into considerable difficulties.

It was either in December 1551, or in the following January, that Mr. Gresham was called upon to serve the king; and that he might the better attend to the important duties which now devolved on him, he removed with his wife and family to Antwerp; and established himself in the house of Jasper Schetz, a merchant, with whom he had long been connected by the ties of friendship, and under whose roof he had been accustomed on previous occasions to reside.

It will be remembered that at the period of which we are speaking, the Low Countries were in the zenith of their prosperity. Second to no European state in a commercial point of view,

y See Murdin's State Papers, passim. The ordinary 'device' for reaching the sum required, was a sale of crown-lands, church-plate, and bell metal.

they yielded to none in wealth and magnificence. Towns and villages, abundantly scattered over the face of the country; hamlets, worth more than the cities of a poorer realm; a soil densely inhabited, and cultivated to the utmost possible extent; an intelligent and industrious race of people, excelling in every elegant and useful art;—such, in its better day, was the spectacle presented by a country, which even in its decline awakens the interest and commands the admiration of the traveller: exhibiting in the productions of its schools of painting, and pre-eminently in the remains of its ecclesiastical splendour, glorious proofs of the taste and magnificence of its former inhabitants.

Flanders began to obtain commercial eminence at a very remote period. It was celebrated for its woollen manufactures in the twelfth century; and in the fourteenth had become the resort of traffickers from all parts of the world. Ghent and Bruges, in particular, acquired distinction about this period; but Bruges, though a smaller town, far surpassed its rival in importance. Here, in 1385, according to an ancient writer, merchants from seventeen kingdoms had their settled domiciles; besides strangers, who repaired hither from countries then almost unknown. In consequence of occurrences which it is unnecessary to particularize, the immense trade of Bruges was transferred to Antwerp in 1487; and from that moment, the latter city rapidly advanced in importance, until it became the centre of civilization and the most conspicuous commercial capital in Europe. About the year 1550, it was no uncommon sight to see two or three thousand vessels at one time in the Scheld, laden with merchandise from every quarter of the globe.[z] Our merchant-adventurers are said to have established a factory there as early as the year 1296;[o] but it was not till the 11th of October, 1558, that the Hôtel van Lyere, or residence of the Burgomaster of that name, was finally ceded for their accommodation, on condition that, if unforeseen circumstances should induce the English to withdraw from Antwerp, this property should revert to the town on their departure. A representation of this beautiful specimen of Burgundian Gothic architecture is given in the annexed plate, from a drawing preserved among the archives of Antwerp, bearing the date of 1474, which was probably the year of its erection. At an early period, this mansion obtained the designation of the English House; by which name it is frequently mentioned in contemporary history. Albert Durer, in the

[z] Huet. Memoirs of the Dutch Commerce.

[o] It is evident from the Fædera, (vol. iii. p. 482,) that the English stapled their wools at Antwerp before the year 1314.

Plate III.

Thof van Lyere, or English House.

FRONT OF THE HOUSE OCCUPIED BY THE ENGLISH MERCHANTS AT ANTWERP.

From a drawing made in 1474, preserved among the Archives of that City.

narrative of his journey through the Low Countries, notices this structure with peculiar commendation: and here it was that Charles V., when he made his triumphal entry into Antwerp in 1520, was entertained by the Burgomaster Van Lyere. Some readers will contemplate the annexed outline of the English-House with more interest when it is mentioned that our ambassadors, journeying to or from foreign courts, were usually domiciled within its walls on their arrival at Antwerp. It was hither that the English merchants, resident in that city, habitually retired in times of disturbance and danger; and here they were confined by order of the Duke of Alva, in the memorable outbreak of 1568, hereafter to be particularly noticed.[a]

Over the factory at Antwerp successively presided Sir John Hackett, who died in 1534;[b] John Hutton, who died in 1538; our old friend Stephen Vaughan, who died in 1550; and Sir William Dansell, who was superseded by John Fitzwil-

[a] This edifice is now converted into a military hospital. It stands in 'Rue des Princes,' formerly called the 'Rue Neuve.' For the original of the annexed drawing, I am indebted to M. Verachter, keeper of the Archives at Antwerp.

[b] "I have been at Douay, where good Mr. Hackett departed," says Thomas Leygh, writing to Vaughan on the 6th of November, 1534. "His corpse was sent to Calais the Wednesday before my coming, which was on Saturday night last."—Cott. Galba. B. x. f. 48.

liams. All of these were distinguished men,—well bred and well educated, and capable of exercising the functions of an ambassador when occasion required. Of the first, Stephen Vaughan, addressing Crumwell from Antwerp in 1530, speaks in the following terms: "Maister Hackett, which laye in these partes for the kyng's higness, and sollycitoure to my Lady Margaret (deceased) for the kyng's affayres, I thinke is now gone into England; or havinge lycense, intendeth to go. Who I most hartily praye you to have recommendyd to the kyng's higness; asserteyning you that his grace shall not be provyded of a man that more substancially shall handle his matters in these partes this xl yeres, ne one that shall do more in these partes than he, and excedingly well enterteyned and beloved with all the great men of these partes; which he hath purchased with his wisdom, his gentyll humanyty, and great cost and charges: and peradventure to his highness little knowen. I have been always excedingly well enterteyned with him: which nothing moveth me so much to his prayse, as his worthy prayses, vertues, and comendations."[c] Hutton is well known as a financial and diplomatic agent. Of Stephen Vaughan and Sir William Dansell, enough has been said to render further notice of

[c] Cott. MS. Galba. B. x. f. 43.

them in this place superfluous. John Fitzwilliams was an ancestor of the noble family who bear his name, and had been Sir Richard Gresham's servant in 1539.[d] His voluminous correspondence is preserved in the State-Paper Office, and would be important to any one desirous of minutely investigating the contemporary history of Flanders.

Antwerp, though not the capital of the Low Countries, in consequence of its maritime position, threw Brussels and every other Flemish town into the shade. Its population was estimated at nearly 100,000 souls. An old historian, who dilates with excusable fondness on the numerous attractions of this city, represents it as unparalleled for its internal splendour, and for the worth of its inhabitants,—a race of merchants, who attracted hither traders of all other nations: English, French, Germans, Danes, Osterlings, Italians, Spaniards, and Portuguese; of which, however, the Spaniards were by far the most numerous and considerable. These strangers resided permanently at Antwerp, conforming to its laws and usages, but in all other respects preserving the manners of the different countries to which they respectively belonged; so that this city, under the prudent rule of Charles V.,—notwithstanding the latent sparks of national jealousy between the Flemings and

[d] Ibid. f. 96.

Spaniards, never completely extinguished, and which the events of subsequent years fanned into a mighty flame,—exhibited, for a period, the uncommon spectacle of a multitude of nations living together like one large family; where each used his own customs, and spoke his own language. The inhabitants themselves were eminently hospitable and ingenious: it was not uncommon, says Guicciardini, to meet with a lady who could converse in five, six, or even seven different languages; "Chose," he adds, "vrayement commode et admirable." To complete the picture, he declares that on every side, and at all hours, were to be seen signs of festivity and merriment; there was a constant succession of gay assemblies, nuptials, and dances; while music, singing, and cheerful sounds prevailed in every street."[e]

Some curious particulars are recorded concerning the nature and extent of its commerce with the different countries of Europe; but what is said of its trade with England will be most interesting to the English reader. The exports from Antwerp consisted of jewels and precious stones, bullion, quicksilver, wrought silks, cloth of gold and silver, gold and silver thread, camblets, gro-

[e] Guicciardini, Description de Tout le Pais Bas, &c. 1568, p. 152–3.

grams, spices, drugs, sugar, cotton, cummin, galls, linen, serges,[f] tapestry, madder, hops in great quantities, glass, salt-fish, small wares, (or as they were then called, merceries,) made of metal and other materials, to a considerable amount; arms, ammunition, and household furniture. From England, Antwerp imported immense quantities of fine and coarse woollen goods, as canvas, frieze, &c., the finest wool, excellent saffron in small quantities, a great quantity of lead and tin, sheep and rabbit-skins, together with other kinds of peltry and leather; beer, cheese, and other provisions in great quantities; also Malmsey wines, which the English at that time obtained from Candia. Cloth was, however, by far the most important article of traffic between the two countries. The annual importation into Antwerp, about the year 1568, including every description of cloth, was estimated at more than 200,000 pieces, amounting in value to upwards of four millions escus d'or;[g] or about twelve hundred thousand pounds sterling:—a sum which was yearly expended in Antwerp, and invested in low country manufactures adapted for the consumption of the English market.

[f] Guicciardini adds "moncaiars" and "demi-ostades," of which I do not know the meaning; unless ostades were *worsteds*.

[g] Guicciardini, ubi suprà, p. 163, and p. 167.

Let it not be imagined that Sir Thomas Gresham took up his abode at Antwerp under a vulgar roof. The family of Schetz was one of the most distinguished in that city; and Jasper was the most distinguished member of his family. He was the eldest of three brethren, and in a peculiar degree inherited from his father, Erasmus Schetz, a taste for letters.[h] However unfavourable to such pursuits his office of King's Factor may seem,—for Gresham's friend was principal factor to the Emperor Charles V.,[i]—we are informed that he achieved for himself the reputation of a poet, and was a distinguished connoisseur of coins.[j] It would be tedious to enumerate all the lordships he held, and the honours to which he attained; of which the post of Treasurer-general of the Low Countries was not the least considerable. We are informed that,[k] towards the close of his life, he took a prominent part in public affairs; and died at Mons en Hainaut, on the 9th Nov. 1580, at the age of 67;[l] leaving three

[h] Ibid. p. 150. [i] Ibid. p. 155.

[j] Van Loon, Hist. Met. des Pays Bas, 1732. i. p. 60.

[k] Vander Vynckt, Histoire des Troubles des Pays Bas, 8vo. 1822, i. 388.

[l] His portrait may be seen in Van Loon, (vol. i. p. 60,) on a medal, struck in 1569. Round the head is the legend "Gaspar [us] Schetz, D [ominus] de Grobb [endock], æt. lvi." The reverse represents an hour-glass, with the motto "L'heure

sons, the two eldest of whom proved brave soldiers, while the youngest rose to eminence in the Church.[m]

Mention has been made of the brothers of Jasper Schetz, who were associated with him in the career of commerce, and shared his eminence and distinguished fortunes. So remarkable was the unanimity in which these three amiable men lived, that it was commemorated by a medal struck in 1556; having on one side, the armorial bearings of the family, (a crow with wings displayed,) encircled by the names of the three brothers, "Gaspar, Melchior, Balthasar Schets;" and representing on the other, two crows,—an emblem of concord, with the motto "Concordiâ res parvæ crescunt."[n] Such was the family in which Gresham became domesticated, and such the characters which he selected for his friendship. I have the less scrupled to introduce them to the reader, because they appear to have been the family with which he was most intimate. When he speaks of Jasper Schetz, he calls him "my very friend."

Our merchant did not, however, live at Antwerp by any means uninterruptedly; for, by his own

viendra;" encircled by the words "Tempora fata dabunt." Date, 1569.

[m] Van Loon, ubi suprà.

[n] Ibid. i. p. 61.

account, during the two first years he served King Edward, he posted from Antwerp to the court, on receiving very short notices, no less than forty times. We cannot of course trace him through all his journeys; but of several, we have distinct intelligence. The first we hear of, occurred in January 1551-2;[o] at which time he was sent to Antwerp with a commission to negotiate concerning the payment of certain moneys owing to the Fuggers. In this, his earliest transaction, we find associated with him Sir Philip Hoby; who, writing to Cecil from Dover on the 15th of February, 1551-2, inquires whether a certain sum shall be taken up at Antwerp "to the King's Majestie's use; for suche interest and in suche manner as was lately commened of, at Gresham's being at the courte."[p]

Next, in order of date, comes a letter which the council sent to Thomas Gresham at Antwerp, from Westminster, on the 24th of February, 1551-2. Their lordships notice with approbation that he had secured a loan from Lazarus Tucker of 10,000*l.* for six months, on interest at the rate of 14 per

[o] A long letter from Gresham to the Duke of Northumberland and the Earl of Pembroke, dated from Antwerp, May 10, 1552, is preserved among the Cott. MSS., Galba. B. xii. f. 189; and is the earliest letter from him I have been able to discover. It will be found to contain more political than financial intelligence.

[p] Fland. Corr. St. P. Off. Hoby was Master of the Ordnance.

cent. per annum. They inform him that the debt due on the last day of April, was 14,000 *li.* Flemish; and furnish him with the following instructions how he was to proceed: "Marry, for your first proceedings, this we would should be done. Since the bullion cannot be had of William Damsell, and so the licence which should have beene had of Schetz not to any purpose,—it shall be well done to take the x M *li.* [10,000*l.*] upon the interest of VII *li.* in the hundred for vi months; and with parte thereof, make up that which shall be lacking of the dett which must be paid the last of this month: which lack, we think resteth about iiij M *li.* [4000*l.*] and so shall vi M *li.* [6000*l.*] remaine; out of the which the Schetz may have one thousand pounds, which the King giveth them, and so shall remain v M *li.* [5,000*l.*]. Except that Mr. Hoby shall have neede to have some piece for his necessaries, the which may be lent to him. And then that v M pounds [5,000*l.*] may remaine well toward the paiment of xiv M pounds [14,000*l.*] which shall be due the last of Aprill.

"Having made this paiment, due the last of this month, and taken order for the safe custodie of the rest of the x M pounds [10,000*l.*] which is now borrowed, we would that ye made your speedie repaire home; to th' intent we might more certainly conferr with you, not onlie for the paiement of the said xiiij M pounds [14,000*l.*] now the last of Aprill, and for the putting over of the sum of xlv M pounds [45,000*l.*] payable the xv of May,—but also for your further proceedings in the bargaine of the bell-mettall. For the which, seeing the Schetz have desired a month's day to give answer, we doubt not but if you will make speede to returne, ye may be both here, and perchance (as cause shall require) go into France also; and returne thither by the month's ende, to receive the Schetz answer. And thus differing answer of the rest untill your returne, we wish you good successe in the service of the King's Majestie. From Westminster, the xxiiij[th] of Februarie, a[o] 1551[2]. If you may convenientlie, we would ye made Mr. Hoby privie to this our letter.

Your loving friends,

NORTHUMBERLAND. J. BEDFORD. E. CLINTON.
T. DARCYE. W. CECILL."[q]

The Fuggers received in March, "in full payment of one of the King's Majestie's bondes," upwards of 63,500*l.*; and on the 30th of April, the sum of 14,000*l.* more.[r] As these two pay-

[q] Copy. Additional MSS. No. 5498, fol. 36. b.
[r] Cott. MS. Galba. B. xii. fol. 185.

ments, which were thought very considerable, had occurred within the same year, the council wrote to the Fuggers in the beginning of May, stating, that for the present the king only meant to pay them 5000*l.* of the debt of 45,000*l.* still outstanding; and that they must have patience, and "put over the rest according to the old interest, 14 per cent."[s] The affair seems eventually to have been otherwise adjusted; and is only worth recording, as illustrative of the financial history of the period.

It appears from the written statement of Gresham's transactions, which he presented to Edward VI. on his return from Antwerp in the beginning of August 1552, that between the 1st of March and the 27th of July, his payments had amounted to 106,301*l.* 4*s.* 4*d.* His own travelling expenses for "rydynge in and owght eyght tymes" during that period, together with those of the posts who had conveyed his letters to and from the council, had amounted to 102*l.* 10*s.* 0*d.*; and he had concluded his mission by giving his friends a feast, which forms the last item in the account. "Paid," he says, "for a supper and a banckett that I made to the Fugger, and to the Schetz, and other that I have hade to do withall for your Majesty, sens your Hightnes haythe comytted

MS. Journal of King Edward VI.

this great charge unto me, the 28 de July, anno 1552, 26*l.*"[t]

That so large a sum should have been expended on a single entertainment, proves either that it was conducted on a scale of extraordinary splendour, or that the necessaries of life were very expensive at Antwerp. Probably it shows both. 26*l.* in 1552 was equivalent to about 250*l.* at the present day; and the persons feasted do not appear to have been more than twenty in number. One is inclined, indeed, to presume that this ancient merchant was famous for the magnificence of his banquets, from a circumstance I will here relate. In "An Inventorie of all the goods of the righte honorable the Countesse of Leicester and the righte worrshipful Sr Christopher Blounte, knighte, in Essex House," made in the year 1596, on the occasion of Blount's attainder, a curious enumeration of thirty-three paintings occurs, to each of which a valuation is attached. "ii pictures of my Lorde of Leicester" were valued at 13*s.* 4*d.*; the portraits of "the Lorde

[t] The autograph document here quoted, with all its superfluity of figures and intricacy of Roman numerals, is to be found in Cott. MS. Galba. B. xii. f. 185, 184, and 188. It was originally written on two or more sheets of paper pasted together; but these have become disconnected, and the volume itself having sustained considerable injury by fire, the document is in many parts illegible. See Appendix, No. V.

of Denbighe," the "Prince of Orrenge his sonne," "Julius Cæsar," "Penelopey," "Sir William Goodere," "Mr. Cavandishe," and "the Queene of Hungarie," were valued at 5*s*. each; while "Fryer Bacon" was considered worth only 3*s*.: but "i *picture of Sir Tho. Gresham his banquett*" was estimated at 5*l*.[v]—a sum which suggests the obvious inference, that the painting alluded to was an extraordinary performance; perhaps a very large piece. This, together with seven other pictures, was brought to Essex House (formerly the Earl of Leicester's town residence) from his lordship's mansion at Benington; and probably had come into his possession during the period of his campaign in Flanders, after the death of Sir Thomas Gresham.

Such an entertainment seems to have been a customary act of hospitality on similar occasions; for when Gresham was preparing to quit Antwerp in subsequent years, he generally announced to Sir William Cecil his intention of feasting the queen's creditors. "As tomorrowe I doo make a bancket to all the Queen's Majestie's crea-dytters; whom I doo inteande to make as good

[v] From the obliging communication of my friend Dawson Turner, Esq., in whose valuable and very curious library the original MS. from which this extract is taken, is preserved. For some account of it, see the Appendix, No. VI.

chere as I can," he says on one occasion: and on another, "Sir, this weke I do inteande to banket the Queene's Majestie's creditors, bothe younge and olde; as knoweth the Lorde."

Hitherto matters had gone on smoothly enough; but when, at the latter end of August, further sums, amounting to 56,000*l.*, became due to the Fuggers and Schetz, Gresham was sent over to Antwerp with instructions to persuade those merchants to postpone the term of payment for six months. To this they consented on certain conditions, which Gresham repaired home to lay before the council in person. But their lordships would agree to nothing short of the prolongation of the king's debts on the original terms. Very reluctantly, therefore, he retraced his steps, authorized only to conciliate, and solicit the forbearance of the creditors.

A part of the Instructions with which he was furnished, it may not be improper to transcribe. His memorial states, "That whereas the said Thomas had commission of late to put over certain debts due by the King's Majesty the 15th and 20th of August, that is to say 44,000*l.* Flemish to the Fulkers, and 12,000*l.* to the Schetz; wherein, although he travailed, he could not hitherto accomplish the purpose of his commission: therefore his Majesty's pleasure is, that the said

Thomas shall return over the seas thither again, and see what more good he can therein do, for the performance of his former commission; and follow the same to the most advantage of his Majesty. And if he cannot so do, then shall he repair to the Fulkers, or their agents in Antwerp, and delivering to them such letters as be there prepared, shall declare unto them how desirous the King's Majesty would be to have now, at their day, made ready payment of the money due; but that in this troublesome time of the world, it behoveth his Majesty so to consider his estate, that for divers great and weighty considerations, his Majesty otherwise is moved to employ the same money which was prepared for their payment. And therefore his Majesty doubted not but the said Fulkers will be content to think this consideration reasonable, and not forget the benefits and good bargains they had had of the King's Majesty, with good and true payments at all times made; and assure themselves, that were it not for weighty causes, his Majesty would not at this time defer any such payment. Wherein his Majesty the rather hopeth of their contentation, for that Antonio Fulker himself, being herein conferred with by his Majesty's Ambassador with the Emperor, seemed ready to gratify his Majesty, not only in this matter, but also a greater."—"These humble and gentle words," observes Strype,[u] "was the King fain to use to his creditors, to incline them to defer his payments, and keep up his credit with them."

Gresham's dissatisfaction at this mode of proceeding, sets his character in a favourable light. He arrived at Antwerp on the 20th of August, 1552, and not immediately finding the parties of whom he came in search, he could not refrain from expressing his displeasure in a long expostulatory letter to the Duke of Northumberland, the leading member of the council. This letter is dated the day after his arrival; and though an unpromising specimen of his correspondence, is sufficiently important to be laid before the reader in all its essential parts.

"It maye please your Grace to be advertised, that as the 20th of this pressent, I came unto this towne of Andwerpe in safetye; whereas I fownd neyther Jasper Schetz, nor the Fugger's factor, (being at Brussells, and lookyd for tomorrow at the forthest, being the 21st daye). With whome I shall treat according to soche commissione as the King's Majesty haythe given me; wisshing at this tyme that yt maye please God to send me soche good succes, as that the King's Majesty's honner and creditt, maye be nothinge touched. For that

[u] Ecclesiastical Memorials, &c. 1822, vol. ii. p. i.

yt shall be no small grief unto me, that in my tyme, being his Majesty's agent, anny merchant strangers shulld be forssid to forbear their monny agaynst their willes: wyche matter from hensforthe must be otherwayse foreseen, or else in the end the disonnestye of this matter shall hereafter be wholly layde upon my necke, yff any thinge shuld chance of your Grace, or my Lord of Pendbrocke, otherwise than well; for that we be all mortall. Wyche matter I doo not dowght, yf God send you life, you will foresee in tyme: wherein I will advertise you my poor and sympell advyce at large.

"But ere that I doo proceed anny further in this matter, I shall most humbly requyre your Grace to pardone me of this my writing; for that this matter touchyth the King's Majesties honnor and credit, wyche I am bownd by my othe to maynteyne and keep: as also the very love and obedience I doo owe unto you, puttethe me cleane out of feare to wryte unto you this my full mynd at large."

What follows, explains the difficulty Gresham had experienced:

"Fyrst, it maye please your Grace to understand that at my comyng home, I browght with me two bargaynes for to discharge the King's Majesty's dett, due the 20th of August, amownting to the sum of lvi M *li.* [56,000*l.*]; as allso an overplus to remayne in the King's hands for the space of a yere: and that was, I offered lii M [52,000*l.*] in reddy monny, after the rate of xii *li.* upon the hundred for a whole yere. And therewith, the King's Majesty shuld have takynne Manuel Ryssis jewel, wyche I offered once to you for viii M *li.* [8,000*l.*]; with another dyamownd of the vallew of one thowsond poundes. Wyche jewel I showed to the counsell at Alltham,[x] being there my Lorde of Willshire, my Lorde Darssay, my Lorde Warden, Sir John Gates, and Mr. Secretarye Syssell; and they made their reckonyng the jewels to be worthe nothinge, were they never so perfette or orient.

"Secondly, I offeryd them a bargayne from the Fugger for the prolongacione of xxv M *li.* [25,000*l.*] and to have taken v M *li.* [5,000*l.*] in fustians: wyche also dyd not lyke them; saying that there was no other remeddy, but that the Fugger and the Schetz must forbere with the King's Majesty at this tyme; and that they would have them prolongyd for another yere, withowght takyng of anny merchandize or jewels. Wyche matter dyd not a littil abash me, considering how things heretofore hath been usyd. For, as your Grace dowth

[x] Waltham, where the council had sat on the 7th, 8th, and 10th of August, 1552.—Council-book of Edward VI. MS.

right well knowe, when the King's Majesty's Father dyd fyrst begynne here to take up monny upon interest, Mr. Stephen Vaghan being his agent, a took the fee penny in merchandize: eyther in jewels, copper, gundepowder, or fustians. And soe the matter hayth passid ever since in taking of wares, when the King's Majesty made anny prolongacyone, until the charge thereof was commyttyd unto me. Wherein I travelyd to the uttermost of my power, and by the means of my friends I fownd the means to serve the King with xx M *li.* [20,000*l.*] withowght takyng of anny jewels or merchandize, as your Grace best knoweth. And to be playne with your Grace in this matter, I was fayne to give forth my owne [word] that this monny shuld be paid at the just daye, or else the King's Majesty could never have hadd yt."

The writer proceeds to expose the great disadvantages likely to ensue from the course he had been ordered to adopt with the king's creditors; adding, "To be playne with your Grace in this matter according to my bowndyd dewtye, veryly if there be not some other ways takynne for the payment of his Majesty's detts, but to force men from tyme to tyme to prolong yt, I say to you, the end thereof shall neyther be honnorable nor profitable to his Highness.

"In consideracyone whereof, if there be none other ways takynne forthewith, this ys to most humbly beseche your Grace, that I maye be dischargyd of this offyce of Agentshipe. For otherwise I see in the end I shall resseve shame and discredit therebye, to my utter undoing for ever: wyche ys the smallest matter of all, so that the King's Majesty's [honour] and creditt be not spotted therebye, and specially in a strange country; where as at this present his credit is better than the Emperor's, wyche I praye to the livinge God, long to contynew. For now the Emperor gevethe xvi per cento, and yet no monny to be gotten," &c.

These and similar details he follows up by observing, that as soon as he obtains an answer from the Fugger and Schetz, he will repair with it to the court; and trusting that he shall succeed in accomplishing the wishes of the king and his council, he adds: "And then I do not dowght, yf that my poor and sympel advyce may be hearde and take playse, I doo not mistrust but in two yeres to bring the King's Majesty wholly out of dett; wyche I praye God to send me life to see that day.

"And for the accomplishement of the same, my request shall be to his Majesty and you, to apoynte me out weekely xii or xiii c [1,300*l.*]

poundes to be secretly resevyd at one man's handes; so that yt maye be kept secret, and that I maye thereunto trust, and that I maye make my reconning thereof assewredly. I shall so use this matter here in this towne of Andwerpe, that every day I will be sure to take up ii or iii c *li.* [2 or 300*l.*] sterlinge by exchange. And thus doing, yt shall not be persevyd, nor yt shall not be no occasyone to make the exchange fall. For that it shall be takynne up in my name. And so by these means, in working by delyberacione and tyme, the merchaunts turn also shall be servyd. As allso this shuld bring all merchaunts owght of suspicione, who do nothing to [wards] payments of the King's detts; and will not stycke to saye that ere the payment of the King's dett be made, yt will bringe down the exchange to xiii*s.* iiii*d.*, wyche I trust never to see that daye.

"So that by this you maye perseve, yf that I doo take up every daye but ii c *li.* [200*l.*] sterling, it will amownt in one yere to lxxii M *li.* [72,000*l.*]: and the King's Majesty oweth here at this present i c viii M *li.* [108,000*l.*] with the interest monny that was prolongyd afore this tyme. So that by these means, in two yeres, thinges will be compassed accordingly to my purpose set forth; as allso by this means you shall neyther troubell merchaunt-adventurer, nor stapeler, nor merchaunt-stranger," &c.[y]

The remainder of his letter is devoted to a project that the king should make a staple of lead, taking into his own hands all the lead in the realm, and prohibiting the exportation of any for five years, from which Gresham anticipated very beneficial results: since the price of that commodity, he said, would rise at Antwerp, where the king "might fede them" as they had need, from time to time. By these combined means, he would keep his treasure within his realm, and extricate himself from the debts in which his father and the late Duke of Somerset had involved him: and thus, says Gresham, "Your Grace shall doo his Majesty soche servyse as never Duke dyd in Ingland, to the renowne of your howse for ever." The letter concludes with the latest intelligence of the Emperor's movements, and such general foreign news as the writer judged would be most

[y] August 21st, 1552.—Cott. MS. Galba. B. xii. f. 209, 12, 10, and 11, (sic.) This letter has been very incorrectly printed by Strype, in his Ecclesiastical Memorials. ed. 1822, vol. ii. pt. 2, p. 484. He had the advantage, however, of inspecting it in its perfect state, when it terminated as follows:—"Not mistrusting, ere the year goeth about, to save the King's Majesty of 20,000*l.* in the payment of his debt, if I may be credited; wherein I shall not let to forsake my own trade of living, for the better serving of his Majesty."

acceptable to his exalted correspondent: for in that age, when newspapers were as yet unknown, it was to such sources that the statesman looked for intelligence, whether foreign or domestic; and Northumberland had an agent or a spy in almost every capital city of Europe.[z]

The scheme suggested by Gresham in this letter, met with the approbation of the council; for we find that, on the 22nd of September, Sir Edmund Peckham, treasurer of the mints, had orders "to pay Thomas Gresham 1052*l.* 8*s.* 4*d.*" But in less than eight weeks, whether because the weekly disburse was found inconvenient, or for whatever reason, we learn from the Council-book of the period that "he (meaning Gresham) is given to understand that the payment of 1200*l.* that he was wont to receyve weekely of Mr. Peckham, is stayed: because that manner of exchange is not proffitable for the King's Majestie. And that yet, nevertheless, he may make ex-

[z] An idea of the extent to which this mode of communication was carried, may be formed from a document in the State-Paper Office, entitled, "The names of sundrie forren places, from whence Mr. Secretary Walsingham was wont to receive his advertisements." Besides domestic intelligence, derived from every part of the kingdom, thirteen towns in France are enumerated, seven in the Low Countries, five in Italy, as many in Spain, in Germany nine, in the United Provinces three, and three in Turkey.

change of that same that he hath already receyved."[a]

The preceding, however, was only one of many schemes suggested by this enterprising merchant for raising the rate of the exchange at Antwerp in favour of England. To this object, indeed, he directed all his endeavours, and was constantly devising expedients to check whatever he perceived had a contrary tendency. The long and frequent letters he addressed to the Duke of Northumberland and the Privy-council on this subject, abounding in the minutest explanatory details, prove how little the nature of such operations was then understood,—how thoroughly Gresham appreciated their importance,—and, lastly, which is perhaps not the least curious circumstance, how attentively he was listened to by one, whom historians represent as engrossed by plans of private ambition; and whose habits and exalted rank one might well suppose would have rendered a voluminous correspondence on such a topic the reverse of agreeable.

At the risk of being found tedious, it seems advisable to dwell a little longer on a subject, which at this time occupied all Gresham's attention. The nature and tendency of his operations will appear from the following passage in his letter to

[a] 13th Nov. 1552.—Council-book of Edward VI. MS.

the Duke of Northumberland, dated the 16th of April, 1553. "The exchange keepyth here at xix*s.* viii*d.* and so I have no dowght but that it wille contynew; and rather lycke to ryse than to fall, whiche is one of the chieffyst poyntes in the comenwell that your Grace and the king's Majesty's counsell hath to looke unto. For as the exchange rysethe, so all the commodites in Ingland fallyth; and as the exchange fallyth, so all our commodites in Ingland risyth. As also, if the exchange risyth, it wille be the right occasion that all our golde and silvar shall remayne within our realme; and also it is the meane that all other realms shulld bringe in gold and silver, as heretofore they have done."[b] He proceeds to explain some of the principal causes of the decline of the exchange, and to suggest as a remedy the absolute necessity in future, of making none but those who had served a regular apprenticeship of eight years, free of the company of the merchant-adventurers; for he showed that to the inexperience of many members of the company, the evil against which he was contending was principally attributable.[c] But the most notable

[b] Flanders Correspondence, St. P. Off.

[c] In the same letter, and others written about this period, Gresham makes such remarks on the prominent features of the commerce of his day, as prove that he was neither an inactive

of all his expedients for raising the exchange and bringing the crown out of debt, (an expedient to which he twice had recourse in King Edward's reign,) was to detain the fleet of the merchants when it was on the point of sailing for Antwerp, and compel the proprietors of the merchandise to engage, on their arrival, to furnish the state with certain sums of money, to be repaid at an appointed time in London, at a fixed rate of exchange,—of course the highest which they could be brought to accede to.[d] Of this we shall have occasion to speak more at length in a subsequent page; enough has been said to explain the following passage in Gresham's letter to the council, dated from Antwerp, 28th April, 1553, which is too characteristic to be omitted. "It may like your Lordships to understand, that as the 27th of this present, being at Brussells, I received your honnor's letter of the 24th of this pressent, whereby I perseve that you are through with the staplers for 25,000*l.*, and with the merchant-adventurers for 36,164*l.* 16*s.* 8*d.*:

nor an inattentive observer of that which was passing around him. In the Appendix, No. VII., will be found some extracts from his official correspondence at this period,—not very attractive, perhaps, to the general reader, but interesting to any one who feels curious to read the confidential letter of a first-rate merchant of the sixteenth century addressed to the prime minister, and to obtain an insight into the nature of his operations.

[d] See the Appendix, No. VIII.

trusting that you have brought them to have for every pound sterling 23*s.* 4*d.*; for withowght doubt the exchange will ryse, if you have so done, and now never like to fall again. Wherewith I have so plagued the strangers, that from hens forth they will beware how to meddyll with the exchange for London; and as for our own merchants, I have put them in such a fere that they dare not meddill, in giving them to understande that I would advertize your honnors if they should be the occasion thereof,—which matter I can soon spy out, having the brokers of exchange, as I have, att my commandement; for there ys never a bourse, but I have a note what money is taken up by exchange, as well by the stranger as Englishman. So that there ys no doubt but that the exchange will keep pound for pound, and better; for that all our flete ys here arrived in safety, praise be to God."[e]

How correct Gresham was in the results he anticipated from these and similar measures, appeared in the sequel by the success which attended them. He found means in a short space to raise the exchange from sixteen shillings Flemish for the pound sterling, to twenty-two shillings, at which rate he discharged all the king's debts; and by this means money was rendered plentiful

[e] Flanders Correspondence, St. P. Off.

and trade prosperous, while the credit of the crown became established on a firmer basis abroad than it had ever been before. All this he foresaw; but the merchants, at the time, complained loudly of his proceedings, and it required no slight dexterity to appease them. "My uncle, Sir John Gresham," said he, writing to the duke about this time, "hathe not a littel stormyd with me for the setting of the price of the exchange; and saythe that yt lies in me now to doo the merchaunts of this realme pleasseur, to the increas of my poore name amonges the merchaunts for ever." Presently he adds, "I have thought good to advertize you yt is no marvell my uncle Sir John Gresham doth storm at the matter; for that a hathe bought iiii or v thousand pounds in woolls; —assewring your Grace he and I was at great words, lyke to fall out; but ere we departtyd, we drank eche to other."[f]

The reader must have already anticipated the remark, that Dudley, Duke of Northumberland, was Gresham's early friend and patron. In 1549, that nobleman, being then Earl of Warwick, had been sent into Norfolk to quell the insurrection which broke out there during that year; and he had lodged, on the night of the 23d of August, at

[f] "Scryblyd in hast in London, the 17th day of May, aº 1553." St. P. Off.

Intwood-Hall,[g] a house about three miles distant from the town of Norwich, and which had been built by Gresham's father, as mentioned in the former chapter, and left by him to his eldest son; but where Thomas Gresham may very well have resided, according to the statement of the county historian, which derives corroboration from the fact that in subsequent years it was frequently his residence, and became his property. The earl's visit to Intwood was perhaps the occasion of his first acquaintance with its owner; and it may have partly led, two years later, to Gresham's appointment to the office of Royal Agent, "which," as he says himself, addressing the duke,[h] "was by *your* preferment." That Northumberland entertained a mean opinion of Dansell's abilities, and regarded Gresham, from the beginning, with a favourable eye, is clear from the correspondence of the period: nor is it less certain that his favour alone was sufficient to make the fortune of a subject. It is universally acknowledged that "he bore all the sway at court;" and with the title of a duke, exercised the authority of a king.

Intwood-Hall was for a long time Gresham's

[g] Blomefield's Norfolk, ed. 1806, vol. iii. p. 246.

[h] See Gresham's letter "to the Duckes grace of Northumberland, and to my Lorde of Pendbrocke."—Cott. MS. Galba. B. xii. fol. 189. It bears date 10th May, 1552.

only country-seat, and hither he seems to have been for many years in the habit of occasionally retiring with his family. The annexed outline has been copied, by favour of the present proprietor,[1] from an ancient oil-painting of the Hall in his possession, and represents it as it appeared about the time of which we are speaking : very undeserving, certainly, of the epithet of "my *poore* howse at Intwood," as, in that amusing spirit of self-depreciation in which our ancestors occasionally indulged, it was frequently called by its master. The architecture seems Flemish; or rather, the house was built in a style which forcibly recalls the buildings represented in Flemish pictures,—a circumstance which the habitual residence of its founder at Antwerp would sufficiently explain, no less than the immense number of Flemish artisans which from an early period settled in Norfolk. The very painting from which plate III. is copied, was most probably the work of a Flemish artist. The figures seem almost to establish this. Dutch in their costume and build, each holds a stick, as the boors of Teniers generally do; and the group is accompanied by a cur of low degree, with a crisp curling tail.

Few traces of the old Hall at present exist, the

[1] J. Salusbury Muskett, Esq., whose civilities I gladly avail myself of this opportunity gratefully to acknowledge.

site being occupied by a house of quite modern construction. The garden, however, preserves much of its former character; retaining its ancient raised terrace-walks and turreted walls. Here, too, the ivy-covered ruins of the red brick porch, which may be seen in the drawing, have been suffered to remain: where, in the spandrils over the door-way, as already mentioned, carved on two escutcheons, are found the arms of Sir Richard Gresham, (who doubtless built Intwood-Hall,) and his initials encircling the family crest, a grasshopper. The same initials and a cypher also occur over the servants' entrance, as well as over the door of one of the sleeping apartments. It is only on either side of the garden door, on two shields within the spandrils, that the plain shield used by Sir Thomas Gresham is discoverable, together with those of the Mercers' Company: so that, as might be expected, there remain at Intwood more traces of the father than of the son. The surrounding scenery is picturesque and park-like; and hard by the Hall is the village church, which is reached by a walk through the garden. But I fear this will be regarded as a digression.

As a proof of the high estimation in which Northumberland held the master of Intwood, it may be worth recording, that in the year 1552, being at Windsor, he selected him as a proper person to sound the ambassador of Charles V., (under whose dominion it will be remembered that the Netherlands at that time were); and to endeavour, as it were casually, to discover from him in the course of conversation, what disposition was entertained by the government he represented towards England. This, Gresham was easily able to accomplish; the nature of his own occupations, and the disturbed state of the Netherlands, so prejudicial to his own personal interests, furnishing him with a sufficient excuse for fixing on so interesting a topic. In consequence of what passed between them, the ambassador wrote to the court of the regent; and on Gresham's return to Antwerp, the subject was resumed. "The Regient," says he, writing to the duke, "hath made great inquirye of me, of my frynd Jasper Schetz, what manner a man I am, and whether I was a man of honestye and credytt to be trustyd: whome dyd informe the Regient, that I have bynne these eight yeres in his howse, knowing me to be a right onnest man, reporting to her Grace much more of me than I am of worthyness. Where upon the Schetz was commandyd to commen with me in the matter; whome askyd me upon what occasion I movyd this matter to the Emperor's Imbassador."[k] Gresham so explained the matter to his friend, that the regent,[l] in token of amity, communicated to him through her treasurer, Monsieur Longyne,[m] several important letters and papers which had been intercepted on their way from Mary, queen of Scotland, to the French king. This is related in the sequel of the letter just quoted, which was soon followed by the arrival of Gresham himself; who related to the council at length what had passed between him and the emperor's minister. Longyne, he said, had even gone so far as to open to him a proposal for a closer alliance between their respective countries, which was to have been cemented by the contemplated union

[k] Antwerp, Nov. 16. 1552.—Haynes' State-Papers, 1740, p.132.

[l] Mary Queen of Hungary, who in 1531 had succeeded her aunt Margaret, as Regent of the Low Countries for Charles V.

[m] Mr. Treasurer Longyne, arriving at Antwerp on the 12th of April, 1553, fell sick next day, says Gresham, "of a hot burning agew, and as this day [13th] has lost his remembrance and his speech, so that our Lord have mercy upon him; for the fyssisians say plainly, a shall never escape ytt. I will insure your Grace, the King's Majestie and his realme has lost a secreat and assurid friend." On the 19th we learn that "Treasurer Longyne ys departyd this world, being sicke in this towne of Andwerpe but iiii days." (Flanders Correspondence, St. P. Off.) Guicciardini (p. 45) says, that "Orlando Longin, Chevallier et Seigneur de Cappelle, was President of the Chamber of Commerce at Brussells."

of Edward VI. with the daughter of the king of the Romans. The negotiation seems to have led only to many mutual protestations of good-will; but it serves to show what opinion was entertained of Mr. Gresham at this time, though but few months had elapsed since he had been called upon to serve the state.[n]

Thus actively engaged, and almost in constant residence with his wife and family at Antwerp, Gresham entrusted the conduct of his affairs in Lombard-street, to his London factor, by name John Elliot. This person obtains frequent notice in King Edward and Queen Mary's Council-books, as the representative of their majesties' agent, when the duties of his office detained him at Antwerp; but of Elliot's history, I can discover nothing.[o] He was succeeded, after a few years, by Richard Candeler, who belonged to a respectable Norfolk family, and whose seal is represented in the wood-engraving which precedes my preface. When business carried Gresham to the court or the council, his concerns in the Low Countries were left to the able management of a far more

[n] See Haynes' Collection of State-Papers, fol. 1740, p. 132 to 142; where all the letters and documents here alluded to are printed. King Edward, in his Journal, has given a brief but admirable review of the whole transaction.

[o] Not even his will; which was certainly not proved at the Prerogative-Office at any time between 1553 and 1594.

remarkable individual than either of these,—a Welshman, named Richard Clough; who resided permanently at Antwerp, and concerning whom we shall have much to say hereafter. At first, mindful perhaps of the fate of his predecessor, Gresham effectually protected himself against similar treatment, as far as it could arise from any misconstruction on the part of the council, by rarely entrusting his affairs with them to an intermediate agent. He seldom even corresponded with their lordships, but communicated personally with them as often as he had occasion, travelling as his own post; which accounts for the fewness of his letters extant, written at this period. The route he was accustomed to pursue is probably indicated by a contemporary writer, who estimates the distance from Antwerp in Brabant to Bruges, at 15 Brabant miles; from Bruges to Nieuport, 7; thence to Dunkirk, 4; and to Calais, 6:[p]—a journey which occupied three days when diligently performed, and for which a post-rider was paid 4*l.* or 5*l.* This was, in fact, the route followed by 'the post' himself, who left Antwerp weekly, and appears to have distributed the contents of his *malle*, or trunk, in London on the fourth day: but Gresham seems quite as often to

[p] R. Rowlands. "The Post for divers Partes of the World," &c. 1576, p. 51.

have crossed the channel from Dunkirk. After awhile, we hear of the servants he was accustomed to employ on this service, which was always accompanied with much personal fatigue, and not unfrequently with much personal danger. We have repeated mention of Francis de Tomazo, who, in December 1553, had been in Gresham's employ four years and a half; when, being sent with despatches to the council, his master obtained for him at their lordships' hands the lucrative office of Queen's Post at Calais,[q] as a reward for his faithful services. So much, indeed, of peril and occasional hardship was incurred by such messengers, especially when they had bullion to transport, that we find Gresham on the same occasion requesting the council to give another of his servants 'comfortable words,' by way of encouragement.[r] The person he alluded to was John Spritwell, for whom, when he carried his letters to the council in 1555, Gresham solicited the reversion of the Postage at Calais; observing that he was "a very fitt man for the room, for that a can speak all kynds of languages, and [is] a Callisian borne; whome is a very painful man, and a man to be trusted in matters of charge, having had the tryall of him these v

[q] To the Council, Ant. 24 December, 1553.—Fland. Corr. St. P. Off.

[r] To the same, Ant. 28 Dec. 1553.—Ibid.

yeres." He had also the reputation of being as good a post-rider as any in Christendom.[s] Spritwell was already the Queen's Post at Dover; and in 1561, in consequence of De Tomazo's death, his master obtained for him the promotion he desired. "Francis De Tomazo," says he, "the Queen's Majesty's Post, ys departed; of whose soul Christ have mercy."[t]

Another of Gresham's posts, or servants whom he was in the constant habit of employing for the purpose of safe and speedy communication with the council, was William Bendlowes; Thomas Dowen, or Denne, was another; and James Brocktrop a third: Thomas Dutton and Robert Hogan seem also to have been in his employ at this period. Of his several factors established in Spain, he mentions Edward Hogan at Seville, and John Gerbridge at Toledo. There are letters of his servants, Henry Garbrand written from Dunkirk; several from John Weddington, with 'advertisements out of Holland and those partes;' and an immense number of Richard Payne's, dated from Middleburgh: in addition to which, Gresham had paid agents who sent him regular intelligence from most of the principal kingdoms of Europe.—It may be Dutch painting to descend to such par-

[s] To the Council, Ant. 27 Oct. 1555.—Ibid.

[t] To Cecil, Ant. 2 Sept. 1561.—Ibid.

ticulars; but some of these poor fellows perhaps merited the brief chronicle they have here found; and besides the pleasure of rescuing even a humble name from oblivion, what has been said seems in some measure illustrative of the principal subject of my narrative.

It was Edward Hogan, I presume, who sent Gresham the memorable 'payre of long Spanish silke stockings,' which he presented to Edward VI.; and which Stowe has commemorated in his Chronicle, as 'a great present.' The gift derived its value from the rarity of the object; "for you shall understand that King Henry VIII. did weare onely cloath hose, or hose cut out of ell broade taffaty; or that by great chance there came a paire of Spanish silke stockings from Spaine."[u] So that, although silk stockings had been brought into England a few years prior to the reign of Edward VI., Gresham's gift constitutes the earliest distinct mention of the introduction of that article of dress into this country.

We have nothing to add to the preceding notices of Mr. Gresham at this period of his life, except that he had the satisfaction of repeatedly receiving from the council expressions of their approbation of his management of the affairs of the crown. The young king himself was

[u] Stowe's Chronicle. ed. 1631, p. 867.

so sensible of the services this intelligent merchant had rendered him, that three weeks before his death he bestowed upon him lands worth one hundred pounds a-year; accompanying the gift with the encouraging words,—"You shall know that you have served a king." The saying was princely, and could hardly have been suggested by his preceptors; as some writers, (I know not why,) are fond of insinuating was the case with every rational thing Edward the Sixth said, and every noble action which he performed. The person addressed has himself recorded this anecdote, in a memorial which will presently be inserted at length; and of which a specimen is given in the fifth plate, exactly as it proceeded from the pen of the writer.

In relating this circumstance, Gresham probably alluded to Walsingham, and some other manors in Norfolk, granted to him by an instrument bearing date six days before King Edward's death. But although that young prince has left on record his opinion,—"I think this country can bear no merchant to have more land than 100*l*.," it is certain that the preceding was by no means the only instance of bounty Gresham received at his royal master's hands. Westacre-Priory in Norfolk, which was of much greater value, was also bestowed upon him in the last year of Edward the

Sixth's reign.[v] It is now a heap of picturesque ruins: but Sir Thomas made it his residence occasionally; and when he died, the effects were estimated at a sum[w] which proves its internal arrangements to have been as princely, as its external appearance was imposing.

[v] Tanner's Not. Mon. The revenue, according to Dugdale, was 260*l.* 13*s.* 7*d.*: according to Speed, 308*l.* 19*s.* 11*d.* In the estimate of Gresham's property at the time of his death, Westacre is valued at 150*l.* *per annum.* Tanner states that a house of Grey Friars at Caermarthen was granted to him, 5 Edward the Sixth.

[w] 1650*l.*

ENGLISH, FLEMISH, AND VENETIAN MERCHANTS OF THE 16th CENTURY.

CHAPTER III.

[1553 TO 1558.]

CONSEQUENCES OF MARY'S ACCESSION—GRESHAM'S MEMORIAL TO THE COUNCIL—SIR JOHN LEGH—TRANSACTIONS AT ANTWERP—GRESHAM IS SENT INTO SPAIN—EXTRACTS FROM HIS LETTERS—ABDICATION OF CHARLES V.—COMMERCIAL NOTICES—GRESHAM AMONG HIS FRIENDS AT ANTWERP.

AFFAIRS were in this prosperous position with the subject of our narrative, when the death of perhaps the most promising prince who ever occupied a throne, brought forward a royal successor, who, however much she may have been maligned and misrepresented by historians, was certainly the least popular sovereign who ever swayed the destinies of England. On the accession of Mary, Gresham found himself suddenly supplanted in his office of Royal Agent,—a circumstance easily accounted for, when it is remembered that his patron was the very nobleman who now showed himself most hostile to the queen's succession. He was, besides, personally obnoxious on the score of his religious opinions; and found a bitter enemy in Gardiner, the Roman Catholic bishop of Winchester, whom the queen restored to the see of which her predecessor had deprived him. "When the King, your brother, died," said Gresham, writing to Queen Elizabeth in 1558, "for rewarde of my servise the Bishoppe of Winchester sought to undoe me; and whatt soever I sayd in these matters," (alluding to some great measures of finance,) "I should not be creditted."

The injustice of which he complained, and the grounds on which he founded his claims to different usage, will best appear from the following memorial; drawn up by himself, apparently some time in August 1553: on the 22d of which month, Northumberland, to whom it contains an allusion, paid the price of his unlawful ambition on the scaffold. This document, though it will occasion some repetitions, is here given at length; as a valuable historical record, throwing light on the financial condition of England at the period to which it refers, and deriving peculiar interest as having proceeded from the pen of Gresham himself, whose history it illustrates in his own words. He is addressing the lords of the council:—

"Fyrst, before I was called to sarve the King's Majestie, one Sir William Danssell, knight, was his agent. At that tyme his Majestye was indebted in the sum of two hundred three score thowssonde powndes Flemyshe: for the discharge whereof, and for other causes to me unknowen, the said augent was written unto to come home, which he reffused to doo. And thereupon I was sent for unto the counsell, and brought by them afore the King's Majestie, to knowe my oppynyone, (as they had many other marchaunts,) what way, wythe leaste charge, his Majestie might growe out of debt. And after my device was declared, the King's highness and the counsell required me to take the room [place] in hande, wythout my sewte or labour for the same.

"Secondarly; before I was called to sarve, there was no other ways divised to bring the King out of det, but to transporte the treasure out of the realme; or else by way of exchange, to the great abasing of the exchange; for a pownde of our current money there, was browght [down] in vallew [to] but xvi*s*. Flemyshe; and for lacke of payment there at the dayes appointed, for to pressarve his Majestie's credit withal, [it was customary] to prolong time allsoe upon interest: wyche interest, besydes the losse of the Exchange, amownteth unto xl M *li.* [40,000*l.*] by yere. And in every soche prolonggation, his Majestie was inforced to take great parte in jewels, or wares, to his extreme losse and domayge; of which xl M *li.* [40,000*l.*] losse for interest, yerely, I have by my travall clerely discharged the said King every peny. Wythe out wyche prevenssion, the Queene's Majestie had been indebted at this her enttrye into the imperyall crown, in the sum of fore hundred thousand pownds; besides the saving of the treassore within the realme; without tacking of juells or wares, to the King's losse or disprofit.

" Thyrdely; where[as] at the tyme of my entrey into th'offis, I founde the Exchange at sixteen shillings the pownde, I fownde the means nevertheless (without any charge to the King, or hinderance of anny other,) to discharge the Kinges whole dettes, as they grew dew, at xx*s.* and xxij*s.* the pound; whereby the King's Majestie, and now the Quene, haythe savid one hundred thowsand markes clere.

" Forthely; by reasson that I raissed the exchange from xvi*s.* unto xxij*s.* (whereunto it yet remaynethe,) all forreyne commodities be fallen, and sollde aftyr the same vallew; to the enriching of the subjects of the realme in their commodities, in small process of tyme, above iii or iiij C M *li.* [3 or 400,000*l.*]

"Fyftely; by reason of raising of the Exchange from xvi*s.* unto xxii*s.* the pownd, (Flemyshe monney,) like as in tymes past the golde and silvar was abundantly transported oute of the realme by the abasing; even so, contrary wise, nowe it is most plentifully brought in ageynne, by the rayssing. For there ys come alredy, of late, above i C M *li.* [100,000*l.*] into the realme; and more and more will daylly doo.

"Sixtely; it is assuredly known, that when I toke this sarvis in hande, the Kinge's Majestie's credit on the other syde was small; and yet, afore his deathe, he was in such credit both with strangers and his own marchaunts, that he myght have had for what some of monny he had desyred. Whereby his enymyes began to fear him; for the commodities of his realme, and [his] power amongst Prynsis, was not known before. Wyche credit the quennes highness haythe opteyned, if she were in necessity for money at this present daye.

"Seventely; to th'entent to worcke this matter secretly, for the raising of the exchange I did only use all my own creditt with my substance and frends',—to the intent to prevent the marchaunts, bothe strangers and Englishe, who allwayes lay in wayte to prevent my devisses: as [also] when th' exchaunge felle, to raise it agayne, I bare some one tyme losse of my own monies, (as the Kinge's Majestie and his counsell well know,) ii or iii c *li.* [2 or 300*l.*]. And this was divers tymes done; besides the credit of fivetye thoussownd pownd, wyche I tooke by exchaunge in my own name, withowght using the King's name; as in my accownnt and letters remaynyng, wyche I sent to his majestie, evidently aperythe.

"And Eightly; for the accomplishement of the premises, I not onely lefte the realme, with my wiffe and famylye, my occupying and whole trade of lyving, by the space of two yeres; but also postyd in that tyme xl tymes, upon the Kinge's sendding, at the least, from Andwerpe to the Courte; besides the practising to bringe these matters to effect,—the infynyt occasion of writting also to the king and his counsaylle,—withe the keeping of reckonings and accomptes, (onely bye my own hand-writting, for mistrust in so dangeros a busines of preventers, whereof were store too manny); untill I had clerely discharged all the foresaid debt, and delyveryd all the bondes clere, to the great benefit of the realme, and profit of the Queene. For in case this debt had bene let alone, and differyd upon interest iiii yeres or v, her Majestie should have fownd it amount to xv hundred thousand powndes at the least. Wyche (God be prayssyd!) is ended, and therefore careless at this daye.

"For consideracyone of my great lossys, and charges, and travayles taken by me in the causes aforsaid, yt pleased the kinge's majestie to gyve unto me one hundrethe powndes to me and my heyres for ever, thre weckes before his deathe; and promysid me then [with] his owne mowthe, that he wold hereaftyr se me rewardyd better; saing, *I shulld knowe that I sarvid a kinge.* And so I dyd fynd him; for whose sowle to God I dayly praye.

"Finally; if upon the consideracion of the former articles of my service made, (wyche is all trewe,) ye shall thinke them mete to be shewed to the queene, and [it shall be] her Grace's pleaseur to accept them,—(allso as I may have access to her hightnes the rather therebye,)—I doutt not to do her grace as good proffitable service, bothe for her and her realme, as the former service of her brother dothe amounte unto. Nevertheles, hitherto I do perceive that those whiche served before me, wyche browght the King in debt, and tooke wares and juellis upp to the

Kingis great losse, are esteemed, and preffered for their evill servis; and contrary wise myself discountenaunced, and out of favour. Wyche grevythe me not a little, for my dilligens and good sarvice taken to bringe the king and queenes hightness out of dett clere. Wyche understanding of my service, that her magesty may take in good parte, is as moche as I required.

"As I was inselinge of the letter enclossid herin, I received a letter out of Flanders; whereby I understand, that as well my plate, howshold stuffe, and aparell of my selfe and wyfe, (wyche I have sent and preparid into Andwerpe to serve me in tyme of my servys there,) by casualty of weather comyng from Andwerpe, ys all loste. And now, God helpe poor Gresham! Allso the Lord of Northumberland dowthe owe me iiii c *li.* [400*l.*] for a juell and wares, that my factor solld hym in my absens; trusting that the Queene's Majestie wilbe good unto me therein."[a]

That Gresham had been unfairly treated cannot be doubted; but dismayed perhaps by the ruin of his late patron, and the evil plight of his friends at the court, he apprehended greater misfortunes than actually fell to his share. With respect to that part of his memorial in which he enumerates

[a] Cott. MS. Otho. E. x. f. 43. A fac-simile of the most interesting passage in this memorial will be found in plate v.

among his other grievances a courtier's want of punctuality in his payments, (and *that* courtier his late patron,) we forbear, at such a distance of time, from commenting upon it with severity, because the evidence we possess is of too imperfect a nature to warrant us in so doing; but the argument certainly seems extraordinary. Let it suffice to have expressed surprise at this passage in a remonstrance which, in every other point of view, is just and forcible, and which doubtless procured for its author the redress he desired and deserved; for I cannot but presume that it is to this letter, or to one which accompanied it, that allusion is made in the minutes of the Privy-council, when they met at Richmond on the 27th of August: "Received from Thomas Gresham a letter to the Queene's highness of the 16th of August, with bands under the broad seal of England, and the seal of the City of London," &c. The consequence was, that when the council assembled on the 4th of September, Gresham, being at Antwerp, was desired "to make his indelaid repaire to the Court:"[b] but their lordships' letter, according to a minute in the margin of the Council-book, was 'staied agayn,' and not sent till the 9th. This message may be deemed equivo-

[b] MS. in the Council-Office. See Haynes, pp. 176, 179, & 181.

cal; and, taken singly, it has undoubtedly an ominous sound: but viewed in connexion with circumstances to be immediately noticed, it is susceptible only of a favourable interpretation. His enemies had perhaps already begun to perceive that their machinations would not only be unavailing against him, but that they were even likely to recoil on themselves. We should, in truth, have come to the conclusion that he had been the object of neglect, rather than of actual injury; seeing that he was so speedily, and, as will be shown, so completely restored to the personal favour of Mary: but the following passage, in a letter addressed by him to Sir William Cecil eight years afterwards, proves that this was not the case; and that he would have been sacrificed on her accession to the throne, had it not been for the timely interposition of a certain Sir John Legh. "My frynde Sir John a Leye ys not yett come from the water of Spawe, whom hath written that he will be here this next week; whom I doo not doubt but that your honnor shall fynde a man of his word and promes, for his coming home: praying you to be a good master and assurid frynd unto him, at this my humble sewte, in all his sewtes. For verily, sir, *it was the man that preserved me when Queen Mary came to the crown;* for the which

I do account myself bound to hym during my life."[c]

This mysterious announcement naturally leads us to inquire who "Sir John a Leye" was; and in truth, he is a somewhat mysterious personage: for, although he is to be clearly identified, only just enough is discoverable concerning him to make one anxious to discover more. That he should have been the man who preserved Gresham when Queen Mary came to the crown,—a moment when the life of many a distinguished Protestant was in jeopardy, and the whole state was convulsed to its very centre,—is enough to prove that, whoever he may have been, he was a Roman Catholic gentleman who possessed the ear of the queen, and in a remarkable degree enjoyed her confidence. That such was indeed the case, is almost all that is known concerning him; except that he had been in his youth in the household of Wolsey, and that he was all his life a great traveller,—a circumstance which is commemorated in his epitaph. He had visited the Holy Sepulchre before 1538; in which year he was thrown into the Tower, on suspicion of belonging to Pole, or being privy to his dealings.[d]

[c] Antwerp, 6th Sept. 1561.—Fland. Corr. St. P. Off.

[d] This I gather from Cott. MS. Cleop. E. vi. f. 380,—a letter which Sir John Legh unquestionably wrote.

It is related in the life of Cardinal Commendone, that when that ecclesiastic came over to England in August 1553, (a few weeks after Edward the Sixth's death,) on a special message to Queen Mary from Pope Julius III., he was at first unable to obtain access to her majesty. Every avenue to the palace had been closed, and strict measures taken to prevent her from communicating with strangers. In this difficulty, he says he accidentally met with 'John Ly,' whom he had known intimately, and to whom he had even rendered considerable services at Rome, whither Sir John had fled for conscience sake in the preceding reign. On discovering that his friend was in the councils and confidence of the queen, and having obtained from his lips an insight into state matters of the most private nature, Commendone did not hesitate to entrust him with his secret; and communicated in turn the real object of his mission: requesting Sir John to present him to Mary, which with some difficulty his friend accomplished.[e] This of course occurred within a few days of the period to which Gresham makes reference in his mention of Sir John Legh. The same person obtains notice in the despatches of

[e] La Vie du Card. Jean Fr. Commendone, &c. 4to. 1671, p. 50–1. This event is noticed by our best historians, but completely slurred over by them all.

Noailles, the French ambassador at Mary's court, by the name of the 'Sieur Jehan a-Ly;' and Noailles relates a circumstance which proves Legh to have been, what indeed he is there called,—'favori de la dicte dame.' "The communications of a-Ly," continues this writer, "must necessarily be of greater value than any which others can furnish, from his opportunities of access to Mary, with whom he is familiar." In another place Noailles says, "The said a-Ly is called Howard, [s'appelle de Havart,] being a near kinsman of the Duke of Norfolk, and brother to the young Queen, who lost her head in the reign of Henry VIII."[f] This is a mistake; but that Sir John Legh was highly connected, and related to the Duke of Norfolk, is certain. His cousin Joyce, whose sister he appears to have married, was the mother of Queen Catharine Howard.[g] As already observed, he had been all his life a great traveller; and on the present occasion we find him mentioned as being on the continent, on his way home from that once-fashionable resort—the Spa.

To Sir John Legh then, according to his own account, Gresham was indebted for preservation

[f] Negociations de Noailles, 12mo. 1763, vol. ii. pp. 245, 247.

[g] As appears from an examination of the wills of the family in the Prerogative-Office. A few genealogical particulars derived from this source will be found in the Appendix, No. IX.

when Queen Mary came to the crown. It is only surprising that, concerning so interesting a character, books should be completely silent. The previous history of a man who had ready access to Queen Mary in the remarkable August of 1553, merits investigation ; and we feel naturally prepossessed in favour of one, who availed himself of his high privilege to befriend the absent and the friendless, whatever their religious opinions might be. If I may be allowed to hazard a conjecture on a subject concerning which it is impossible, without some direct evidence, to speak with certainty, I would suggest that as in the course of his travels Legh must frequently have had occasion to sojourn at Antwerp, it was there that he probably became acquainted with Gresham. The death of King Edward doubtless brought Legh, in common with many other exiles of the same religious persuasion, into England ; and he became privy to all that passed in the council-chamber of the new queen. Touched with sympathy for a young man whose fortunes were suddenly blighted,—perhaps whose very existence he perceived to be in jeopardy, (for Gresham's phraseology admits of the gravest interpretation,) —he interfered in his behalf, and procured his safety. He was sufficiently Gresham's senior to have felt even a paternal interest in his welfare ;

while his own large fortune and high connexions altogether preclude the idea that his actions were influenced by any interested motives.

The evidence of what passed during the first few weeks of Queen Mary's reign, is not sufficiently circumstantial to enable us to trace the early movements of her Privy-council with the minuteness and accuracy we could have wished. It is certain, however, that financial matters were among the foremost which occupied their attention: and it seems that, rather than avail themselves of the services of the late king's financial agent, who was notorious for his strong Protestant bias, they took upon themselves to procure supplies by writing directly to the Fuggers at Antwerp, and commissioning certain persons (men whom Gresham had superseded in the former reign) to negotiate the required loans. This we learn from Gresham himself. The only additional evidence we possess on the subject, relates to the endeavours of one Christopher Dauntsey, who seems to have been patronised by Sir William Petre, one of Mary's secretaries; but Dansell also found some employment, and I presume it was to him that Gresham alluded when he wrote,—"I do perceive that those whiche served before me, wyche browght the Kinge in debt, are esteemed and preffered for their evill servis."

There are only two of Dauntsey's[h] letters remaining among the State-Papers of this period: one addressed to the council, and the other to Secretary Petre. Both are dated the 10th of November; and state that, on his arrival a week before, he had presented the letters with which he was furnished to the Fuggers: whose answer was, that because Dauntsey had not kept his appointment with them, they had parted with 100,000 ducats to the emperor, Charles V. They had given his factor notice of their intention a month previous; to which, receiving no answer, they concluded that Queen Mary had no need of money, "and are now unfurnished, tyll their letters with bills of exchange do come out of Spayne, which they look for dayly." Meantime, they promised him forty or fifty thousand pounds in the course of a week or two; and Dauntsey took up of Lazarus Tucker (a leviathan of those days) 50,000 ducats, or 100,000 gilderns for a year; to be repaid on the 1st of November, 1554, with the expectation of obtaining shortly 100,000 gilderns

h His arms seem to show that he was of foreign origin; but the name he bore is identified with the brightest annals of the metropolis. Alderman William Dauntsey, a mercer, in 1542, founded and liberally endowed a free-school and some almshouses at West Lavington, in Wiltshire. He left 40*l.* in his will to Christopher; whom he mentions as "my kynnesman, beinge prentisse."—Prerogative-Office, Spert. quire xxii.

more. But let the newly-appointed agent say a few words for himself:—

"Sir," he says, addressing Petre, "it maye please your Mastershipe that this knowlage was gevyn owt here before my comyng; which is a hinderans to the Queene's Majestie in the enterprise [?], as also a pretendyd [intended] defacing of my service to the Queene's most excellent Majestie, my mistress. And yet, havyng my full affyance in your Mastershipe's accustomed goodness of your good report unto the Queene's Highness, and my honorable Lords all, [I trust] that it shall be for this tyme taken in good part: doubting nothing but [I] shall advanse unto the Queene's Majestie a more sum in a short space. Thus my trust is in your good Mastershipe; whose accustom is to set forthe all thyngs to the best, and prefer all men by your goodnes."

This he follows up by humbly offering a few suggestions, concerning which it is not easy to form an opinion; indeed they are set forth in such lame phraseology, that it is difficult to understand what Dauntsey meant. One thing is clear, however: that he expected to "advantage the Queene's Majestie a good piece of mony; having tyme enough for it. This is my poore advize: I submit all to your honors.

"For bullion or sylver, your honnorable pleasures known, I could furnishe the Queene's Majestie for a good porcyon and tyme reasonabell.

"Thus I rest your Mastership's to commaunde: whereof, to do your Mastership servis to my smalle power, according to my dewty, ye shall be assewred.

Yours,

CHRISTOFUR DAWNTESEY."[i]

"In Andwarpe, the xth of November, 1553.

"Sir, his name is Lazarus Tucker."

The council must have become already sensible of the evils which awaited them with so inefficient an agent in Flanders as Dauntsey. He had kept them for a week in the dark as to what supplies they had to depend on, and wrote at last to say that he had met with a disappointment. In this emergency they seem to have turned to Gresham for assistance; since I find a paper, dated the 13th of November, entitled, "A memoriall gyven by Thomas Gresham to the Queene's Majestie," which sets forth the terms on which he was willing to resume his office; ending with these words: "Finally, the said Thomas Gresham requireth, that forasmuch as he hath, as well in the time of our late sovereign Lorde Kinge Edward, as in the tyme of the Queene's Majestie now being, received dyvers and great sums of monny, and made pay-

i Fland. Corr. St. P. Off.

ment of the same againe, wherefore he hath not yet accompted; that it may please the Queene's Majestie to appoint such persons as shall be her pleasure, to take his account; whereto he is redy."

His Instructions bear the same date as these "Articles," as they are called; and correspond with them in tenour precisely. In fact he dictated his own Instructions, which are nevertheless by no means favourable to himself; and they differ in form from all his subsequent ones, not even naming him as the Queen's Agent. They are given at length in the Appendix;[j] which makes it only necessary in this place to mention that his orders were to take up at Antwerp the sum of 50,000*l.* for the space of a year, on interest after the rate of 11 or 12 per cent.; on the security of the queen's bond, and that of the city of London, under the great seal, as had been customary in King Edward's time. All sums which he took up at interest, or by exchange, he was instructed to convey to London with the utmost possible secrecy, in such coins of gold and silver as he thought most meet; loading them at Antwerp, on any ship bound either for London or Ipswich. Not more than 1000*l.* was to be adventured on one bottom; but he was authorized to send the value of 3000*l.* over land, from Ant-

[j] No. X.

werp to Calais, and so to London, by any of his servants or other trusty person going into England: the risk, in either case, being sustained by the crown. He was allowed for his diet, twenty shillings a-day; and was to be remunerated for all expenses for messengers, letters, and the carriage of treasure.

The case was evidently urgent, for he left England immediately; reaching Antwerp at 8 o'clock on the evening of the 17th of November. I hope the reader will not object to peruse the letter he addressed to the Privy-council the day after his arrival. His generous behaviour towards Dauntsey, and the temperate spirit in which he notices his transactions, raises Gresham considerably in our estimation.

"Yt maye please your honnors to be advertized, that as the xvii^th^ of this present I arryved in this town of Andwerpe, at viii of the clocke at nyght; and as the xviii^th^ I spake with Lazarus Tucker as touching the ii c thousand carolins that he offered (by his letter wrytten to me) to lett upon interest for a xii monthes daye, after xiii upon the hundred. His answer was, that forasmuch as that I stayed so longe in making of him answer, a hath concludyd with Christopher Danssey after the same rate; and his bonds be maid to paye the fyrst of November, a° 1554. And by his bargayne, as he sayeth, he must paye the money by the last of November : so that by this reconning, the Queene hathe but a xi monthes for xii monthes; wyche money shall stand her Majestie in, (if it take place) above xiiij *per cento.* Wyche matter is here so much spoken of, that I dare not attempt anny man for taking up of money upon interest, till further your plesseurs be known. And as your honnors do right well knowe, the Queene's Majcstic's commission is not to exceed xii *per cento:* wherefore, bothe for the Queene's honnor and credit, I will staye till further her Majestie's pleasure and yours be known. For I will informe you, this matter hath beene very openly handelyd, and marvelusly undiscretely. Considering how the said Lazarus did make to mc first this offer, the Queene's Majestie and your honnors maye proceed therein as you shall thinke good; but this is to asserteyne your Lordeships, if this bargayne take place, the Queene's Majestie and your honnors maye not looke to have no monny under xiii or xiiii *per cento:* wyche, with pollitycke handeling, might as well [have] beene had for a xi or xii upon the hundred, and the merchaunts right glad thereof. This, for my discharge, I have thought good to advertise[k] you with expedycione: most humbly

[k] *To advise,* in the sense in which merchants at present use

requyring your honnors as to accept this my rude writing in good parte.

"So that my poore advyce is, better it is for me to stay for a month, (considering how this matter is spred abroad,) than presently to proceed. And for the better accomplishement of the premises, if it shall so stande with the Queene's Majestie's pleasure and yours, I desire to have a commission under her broad seale for the taking up of money upon interest, so that I doo not exceed xii *per cento;* so there be no sum mentioned in the commission. For that upon this rumor, if Mr. Danssey's bargayne doth not take place, they will desire to see my commission. Whereby the Queene's Majestie shall save, in the sum of L M *li.*, one thousand poundes.

"Assuring your honnors that afore Mr. Danssey's comyng, monny was here delivered at x upon the hundred; wyche is no small grief unto me. [But] if your honnors may forbear a month or two, I doo not doubt but to bringe all thinges [to pass] according to your hartes desire; and to accomplish all my devices accordingly.

the term, is manifestly only a corruption of the word in the text, frequently written "adv^r^tise:" but whereas our forefathers employed the legitimate noun *advertisements* for the intelligence conveyed, we have so far lost sight of the origin of the commercial verb *to advise*, that the term for commercial intelligence is invariably *advices*.

"Also, as this day, I spake with Mathew Urtebo [?] the Fuggers' factor, who showed me a letter whereunto was dyvers of my Lordes hands (as you best know); by the wyche I doo perceve that Mr. Danssey offered[1] from hym a hundred thousand crowns to the Queene's Majestie, upon interest: wyche he utterly denyeth, and [says] that a never spake with Mr. Danssey in any suche matter. To the wyche your honnors' letter he will make answere accordingly.—Further it maye please you to understand, that as this day at xi of the clocke, I delivered Mr. Danssey the Queene's Majestie's letter: who departed suddenly upon the sight thereof; who shall declare your honnors of this proceeding more at large. Requiring your Lordeships for to bear with him (the rather) for that a hath not [before] hadd the handeling in such waytty affaires; wherein, for my parte, I judge a hath done his best."[m]

Then follows the freshest intelligence at Antwerp, and some observations respecting the emperor's movements, which it would lead us away from our subject to consider. An extract from Gresham's next letter, written a week after, will be more to our purpose. The queen, he says,

[1] Here Gresham had begun to write "your honnors;" but he checked himself, and drew his pen through the words.

[m] 18 Nov. 1553.—Fland. Corr. St. P. Off.

had better "have given Dauntsey 10,000*l*., than ever to have proceeded in this matter, both for her honnor and credit's sake." After which, he continues as follows:

"This daye [November 26th] Lazzerus Tucker came unto me upon the Bourse, and asked 'whether I had any answere whether his bargayne shuld take place or not;' requiring me 'that I wold thinke no unkyndness that a hadd not concludyd this bargaine with me, according to his offer made to me by his letter:' and [saying] that 'a stayed xx days for answere.' My answere was, 'I cold tacke it but in good parte; and that there was no fault in me, for that I knewe not the Queene's Majestie's pleasure afore my present coming awaye.'" Gresham told the money-lender that he could only marvell, both that Dauntsey should have offered, and that Tucker should have required such interest, considering what excellent security was given by the government.

"His answer was, that 'a had concludyd a bargaine, and that a looked to have his bargen kept: for that a knew that the Counsell had wrytten to the Fuggers for monny.' . . . . . . Further a dyd declare unto me, that at the fyrst a concludyd with Mr. Danssey but for i C M [100,000] floryns; and that aftyrwards, the said Danssey came unto him, and requyred, and prayed him to furnishe hym with i c m more: which a showed me that a had it not of his own, but was fayn to take it uppe upon his own credit, to doo the Queene service. Which (here writing) was small proffit to the Queene, but to *his own* proffit. For that he tooke it uppe aftyr x *per cento*, and woll make the Queene paye xiii: and forbearing the month, it is xiiij and better, upon the hundred. So that by this his proceeding, he hath been the very occasione of the raising of the interest; wherein the Queene's highness and your honnors may proceed as to you shall seem best, for this is most trewe that I doo write you. Most humblye requiring you as to accept this my writing in good parte, and [to believe] that I doo not write you hereof in the disprayse of anny man, nor in my own prayse; for that as yett, as I have done no good, so have I done no hurte nor domage in the premises. But according as I have written you, if this bargain doo take place of Tucker's, you maye not looke to have any monny upon interest under xiij upon the hundred; by the reason this matter is so spread abroad, and advices given throughout all Cristendome." [n]

By this time, the council must have perceived their mistake, if they had not perceived it before.

[n] 26 Nov. 1553.—Fland. Corr. St. P. Off. Dauntsey's contract is dated Nov. 16th.

We learn from Gresham's letter of the 6th of December, that they sent him out the customary bonds for 113,000 florins: but this 'nothing contented' Dauntsey, who proved that his contract was for nearly twice that sum. Gresham sent for their lordships' inspection, a copy of the contract, properly authenticated: "certifying your Lordeshipes this to be the very trew coppye, whereunto Danssey hath subscribyd his name, at the commandement of the Queene, my mistress. Wherein it may please your honnors to have a further consideracyon; for that this matter toucheth the Queene's honnor and creditt, as also Danssey's creditt and name, to his undoing for ever if it shuld not take place. Wherein it maye please the Queene's Majestie and your honnors to be good unto hym; for this Lazzerus Tucker is a very extreme man, and very open mouthed. As also, according as I have wrytten you, a hathe dyvers partners in the bargayne; and considering the letter that your Lordeshipes have writtin him, wherein you do [ac]knowlege Danssey to be her Highness' servant, he doth now ground himself not a littill upon that worde. In consyderacyone whereof, and considering how fair Danssey hath passed in the matter, and that it shall touch the Queene's creditt, as well as [that] the young man shall be undone thereby,—it is most meetest [for] this bargayne to take place: wherein, eftsoons I most humbly requyre you to be good Lordes unto hym. And for my parte, I do not doubt ere that two monthes dothe go about, to recover the domage thereof; as allso to optain monny, better cheape, upon interest: wyche, without doubt, I must have a tyme to bringe it about. . . . As you knowe, I left the Queene in suche credit, as they [the merchants] sought to me at home, at my doors, to take their monny: trusting to see that day agayne, for all this misfortune, if it maye please you to creditt me, and tarry the tyme." [o]

I have purposely detained the reader with these lengthy, and, I fear, somewhat tedious particulars, partly, because no abridgment seemed capable of conveying as good an idea of Gresham's manner as some extracts from his actual correspondence; and partly, because the inferences to be drawn from the whole transaction, as therein developed, appeared by no means destitute of historical interest.

His object was to export bullion from Antwerp, which was forbidden by law; and the undertaking was consequently full of danger. He was ordered to adventure only one thousand pounds sterling on one vessel; yet so strict was the

[o] 6 Dec. 1553.—Fland. Corr. St. P. Off. On the 27th of March, 1562, Gresham writes, "Lazzerus Tucker is departyd!"

scrutiny on the part of the Custom-house officers at Antwerp, that when, notwithstanding the impediment of Dauntsey's proceedings, he had succeeded in collecting a quantity of treasure, he was obliged to resort to such expedients for the transportation of it, as nothing but the most dire necessity of the state can excuse. Foreseeing that "for such money as the Queene should take up, the greatest payment would be made in Spanish silver rials, which would be very massy to convey," he proposed to the Privy-council that he should buy pepper; loading four bags on every ship which left Antwerp, and secreting in every bag two hundred pounds in money. Also, as the baggage of an ambassador is permitted to pass at the Custom-house without examination, Gresham proposed that Sir John Mason, the English ambassador at Brussels, who would depart for England on the arrival of the Bishop of Norwich, should carry over with him twenty or thirty thousand pounds.[p] These suggestions were approved by the council. In the margin of his letter, against each passage, one of the members has written, "agreed," or "to be done." They were not acted upon, however; for in his next letter Gresham writes,—"Whereas I have wrytten unto your Lordeships to have com-

[p] 6 Dec. 1553.—Fland. Corr. St. P. Off.

missione to buy pepper for the better conveying of my charge, now my mind is altered; and [I] requyre to have commissione to buy i M [1,000] demi-lances harness, wyche will be better for the purpos, to the great strengthe of our realme: and is better than treasure, which maye not pass without the Emperor's passport. Advertising your honnors I have beene at Brusselles, and have conferred with the Right honnorable Sir John Mason, who will doo his best to get me one in his own name, or in some other nobelman's name; but as for the passport for bullion, he will not medill, without a hath commissione: wyche is the chefest poynte I need in all my devyces, being a thinge most expedyent to be put in proufe with expedissione.

"Also I doo now requyre (for that the Queene's stuffe shall be packed in harness, in great dry fatts,) I request to have comyssion that I maye put in every dry fatt iij M *li.* [3000*l.*]; and to layd upon every waggon iij dry fatts, for the avoyding of the great charge of waggon-hyre and charges of men, if [I] shuld send no more than iij M *li.* in a waggon at a tyme. Whiche matter it may please you to have in consideracyon, as to you shall [seem] best. But to 'courage your honnors, after this sorte I conveyed the like for the vallew of one hundred thousand markes in one yere, in my own name, and was never touched."[q]

From his correspondence about this period, preserved in the State-Paper Office, though it unfortunately relates entirely to business, several hints are to be derived illustrative of the nature of the trust reposed in Gresham, and the conditions on which he held the office of Queen's Agent. We are chiefly struck by the frequency of his letters. On the present occasion, for instance, though some are evidently missing, we have despatches dated the 18th and 26th of November; the 6th, 8th, 20th, 24th, 28th, and 31st of December; the 1st, 13th, 18th, 21st, and 31st of January; the 6th, 15th, and 21st of February; and the 1st of March: and, what is singular, the writer commonly addressed on the same day the council collectively; some individual member, as the secretary, whom he knew to be well disposed towards himself; and lastly, the queen. Occupations sufficiently pressing to require such constant correspondence, render it not surprising that Gresham should have declared to the council,—"I shall not let to give up all my whole occupying, and trayde of lyving, for to serve her Majesty; as I did no less in the King's Majesty's lyfe-tyme:"[r]

[q] 6th Dec. 1553.—Fland. Corr.St. P. Off.
[r] 20th Dec. 1553.—Ibid.

and that he should have deemed it necessary to solicit permission to return to England for a short season, when he had completed his business,—assuring the council, in December, that "there would be nothing done at Antwerp during the hollidays, nor x days after."[s] Permission was immediately sent him, but he was not able to avail himself of it for several weeks. In the middle of January he stated that he hoped, before the end of the following month, to be prepared to quit Antwerp: "whereby I may come to the finishing of my account, and that I may have my *quietus est* of her Majestie; whatsoever may chance of me, that my powre wife and children maye knowe their substance from her."[t]

Just before leaving Antwerp, he gave the council notice of his intentions in the following words: "Pretending, by the leve of God, to departe this towne the iij[rd] daye of Marche: and the occasyone I doo send you this treassor before my coming, is onely [because] I will come clere through the serche of Gravelyne, without anny charge; for that I cannot escape but that the Cappitayne and serchers will banckett me; and all their chere is in drynцke, wyche I can very ill away withall: but it must needs be done, for the better compassing

[s] 20th Dec. 1553.—Fland. Corr. St. P. Off.

[t] 18th Jan. 1553-4.—Ibid.

of my business hereafter. Advertising your honnors that I did send the Capitayne of Gravelyn xii ells of fyne black velvett; and every customer, and sercher, viij ells of blacke cloth, for their New Yere's gifte. And in the doing thereof, I made the right honnorable Sir John Mason privye: for that [at] all tymes of nyght, the gates of the town were open to my servants, as they came with the treasure."[u]

The vice here glanced at, which many an old painting has taught us to associate with our ideas of ancient Flemish manners, is again noticed in subsequent parts of Gresham's correspondence: as in the following passage, for instance, which at a subsequent period he addressed to Sir William Cecil. "The Count of Elverston, ambassador to the Emperor, departed this day to Brussels; who desired me to do his most humble commendation to the Queen. He speaks as much honnor of her highness for her Majesties gestes and Royall entertainment, as a nobellman can do. The said county speaks much honnor of the Lord Robert Dudley; who desyred me lyke wyse to do his commendations to him, and to Sir Thomas Parry, and you; so that my lady your wife were not forgotten. Sir, *what great cups of wyne went out upon these recommendacions, I will not molest*

[u] 1st March, 1553-4.—Flanders Corr. St. P. Off.

you wythall; for that it ys not commendable in England, as it is here," &c.[v]

Count Egmont, a name which will never be forgotten in Flemish story, and concerning whom we shall have more to say hereafter, was in the mean time sent into England on an embassage from Charles V. to Queen Mary. He came partly to advise with her majesty concerning the treatment of the rebels, against whom the emperor recommended severe measures; and partly to negotiate respecting the approaching alliance between the crowns of England and Spain. One passage in the Instructions with which he was furnished is to our purpose, and must be quoted. "Considering," says the emperor, "how unable the Queen is to equip her ships of war,—which yourself and others who have visited England state arises principally from the want of gunpowder, military stores, ropes, and other necessary tackle; seeing that the want of powder has been remedied by our licence to Gresham for the exportation of the same,—you may inform her Majesty that we will give the said Gresham further licence to transport into England whatever other necessaries the country may require."[w]

[v] Ant. May 29, 1560.—Fland. Corr. St. P. Off.

[w] Translation. Feb. 18, 1553.—From a transcript in the State-Paper Office of some MSS. at Brussels.

This was written in the middle of February, 1553-4; and in the beginning of March, Gresham returned to England. On the 15th, the queen appointed commissioners to examine his accounts, [to satisfy] all his claims for debts, as well as to indemnify him for all costs and charges incurred in the performance of the duties of his office, by himself, his servants, factors, or deputies; and he was allowed "for his diett xx*s*." per diem, during all the time he had been agent to herself or her brother.[x]

Compared with the salaries of ambassadors at the same period, this allowance seems small; and in truth, like every other public servant, Gresham repeatedly complained that his salary did not defray his necessary expenses. On the other hand, there were large emoluments arising out of his office, to which I presume the ambassadorial dignity was a stranger. In order to form an opinion as to how far twenty shillings a-day was a liberal allowance, the reader may like to be informed what was the 'diet' of other officers of the state when sent abroad. Lord William Howard received 6*l.* per diem, on proceeding as commissioner into the Low Countries in 1558. Sir Thomas Chamberlayne went on his embassy into Spain in 1560, with 3*l.* per diem; and in 1561

[x] Rymer's Fædera, vol. xv. p. 371.

with a diet of five marks, or 3*l.* 6*s.* 8*d.* Cecil was allowed 4*l.* when he was sent into Scotland in 1560; and the diet of Sir William Pickering, travelling towards Germany in 1557, was four marks, or 2*l.* 13*s.* 4*d.* But then it must be remembered, that the contingent expenses of all these persons far exceeded any to which Mr. Gresham was exposed.

He had scarcely returned to England, ere his services in Flanders were again required. At a meeting of the Privy-council at St. James's on the 27th of March, Sir Richard Southwell, master of the ordnance, informed their lordships that there remained in the Tower but "fourteen last[y] of powder; which portion being by their Lordships considered to be far too little for all events, and therefore thought meete to be supplied with all convenient speede, they did resolve that whereas the said Mr. Southwell had heretofore warrant directed unto him, whereby he was authorized to give order unto Thomas Gresham to provide xl M [40,000 lbs.] weight of saltpeter in Roche; he should now, for a further supply, give order in like manner to the said Thomas Gresham to make provision out of Flanders of xx last of well-chosen serpentine powder, over and besides the saltpeter aforesaid. And forasmuch also as the said office

[y] A last of gunpowder is 24 barrels, or 2400 lbs.

of the ordinance is among other things presently unfurnished of Harquebushes, it was further resolved by their Lordships that the said Mr. Southwell should in like manner take order with the said Thomas Gresham to provide v c Harquebushes from out of Flanders, over and besides other v c for the which he hath warrant addressed out unto him already. And in case he cannot conveniently make provision for the xx last of serpentine powder aforesaid, that then he provide the quantity of lx M weight of saltpeter more than the xl M weight before remembered; so as in the whole there may be the full portion of one thousand weight provided."[z]

The country does not appear to have been very urgently in need of these supplies, since ten weeks were suffered to elapse ere Gresham returned to Antwerp. In the beginning of May he took his departure; being made the bearer of despatches to the emperor from Simon Renard,—Charles the Fifth's ambassador at the English court. Renard's letter is written in cypher, and contains the following allusion to the subject of these pages:—

"Gresham, the Queen's Agent, bearer of the present letter, is about to take his departure from hence, and wait on your Majesty in order to obtain

[z] Council-book of Queen Mary, MS.—From a faithful transcript shown me by P. F. Tytler, Esq.

a passport for exporting out of the Low Countries the gunpowder, saltpeter, harquebuses, and harness enumerated in the enclosed memorial, for the Queen's service. She begged me to write for his obtaining this licence; which I could not refuse to do, for reasons well known to your Majesty."[a]

On the 12th of May, Gresham arrived at Antwerp; intent on the speedy performance of the business which was the object of his journey: but some delay was occasioned by the feast of Whitsuntide, which fell about that period; and he wrote to Secretary Petre,—"I shall most humbly requyre you to informe the Queene's Highness [of the same,] and my Lordes of her most honnorable Counsell, that it may appere unto them there is no losse of tyme on my behalfe."[b]

After ten days of active occupation he prepared to quit Flanders, in order to set out on a journey into Spain, which was his ulterior and chief object on leaving England. He had taken up of different merchants at Antwerp, in bills of exchange, 320,000 ducats; which were made payable at the fair of Villalon, and other places in the same kingdom. This sum he was instructed to carry out

[a] Translation. London, May 6, 1553.—From a transcript in the St. P. Off. of Renard's MSS., preserved at Brussels. For this passage also I am indebted to the individual mentioned in the preceding note.

[b] Ant. 13th May, 1554.—Fland. Corr. St. P. Off.

of Spain in bullion; taking up a further amount, to produce the total sum of 500,000 ducats. Hence his present expedition, concerning which he wrote to the Privy-council from Antwerp on the 26th of May, (1554,) as follows:—

"It maye please your most honnorable Lordeships to be advertised, that as the xxij[nd] of this instant, I departid out of this town of Andwerpe, to come homewards: and toke my journey by the waye of Brussels, to knowe whether the Emperor and the Regent wolde command me any service to be done in Spain. And for answer of this matter, with the advyze of the Queene's Majestie's Ambassador, I repayred to the Bishop of Arras; declaring unto him the cause of my coming, and why and wherefore I went into Spayne. Who used me very gently; demanding 'whether I had suffycyent pasporte for the sake thereof, out of the partes of Spayne.' My answer was, 'I knew not to the contrary; for that the Queene's Majestie and your Lordeships had takyn order wyth the Emperor's Ambassidor for the same.' To that a made me answer, that 'in very deed the Ambassador had written unto the Emperor thereof; wherein his Majestie was not yet resolved: and now, considering the great alliance that is now between us, they wold proceed with as *bonne foye* wyth us as we dyd with them.'"

How important a character the ecclesiastic was with whom Gresham had this conversation, every one at all acquainted with Flemish history well knows; no less than the conspicuous part he subsequently played in influencing the destinies of Flanders. His name will frequently recur in these pages. At present I have only to observe, that by his advice, Gresham applied to the queen, (sister to Charles V. and regent of the Low Countries,) for the passport which was declared indispensable to the success of his journey.

"Wyche matter being by me movyd to the Queene, her highness answered that she wold so doo: demanding of me for what sum I wold have the passporte made? Giving her grace to understand that the Queene's Majestie had moved the Emperor's Ambassador for the sum of v c m [500,000] dockats; that I hadd takyn uppe thereon in Andwerpe for the sum of iij c xx m [320,000] dockats, and that the Queene's highness dyd pretend to take up the rest in Spayne. Upon that answer, her Majestie commandyd me to put *that* I wold have, in writing; and then she wold move the Emperor in the matter. Wherein I tooke the advyze of the Queene's Ambassador, and made my demand in writing. And uppon the delivery thereof, she willed me to stay for iiij or v days; for that Mons[r] de Erasso (the Emperor's secreatory for the Spannyshe tongue) was at Andwerpe, who hathe the ordering of all suche matters: and [I then] made my returne hither. Uppon whom I doo give my attendance, and shall follow him to Brussells, till that I have optayned the Emperor's pasporte. For without his Majestie's licence, there will be no gold nor silver sufferid to be caryed out of Spayne: wyche was the cheffyst point shuld have beene fyrst sorryd [sorrowed, cared] for, as I dyd no less advertise your honnors in the begynnyng of this matter." [c]

Having obtained the emperor's passport, Gresham returned to England; and in the month of June 1554, set sail for Spain. The sheet of instructions, or as it was called the 'Memorial,' with which he was furnished on this occasion, is dated the 12th of June, and will be found in the Appendix.[d] He was directed to "make his repayre with as convenient spede as he may towards Spaine, embarking himself at our ports ether of Darmouth or Plimouth, where we have caused a vessell to be put in redynes for his transportacon, —from whence he shall procede on his voyage as sone as wynde and wether shall gyve hym leave."

[c] T. G. to the Council, 26 May, 1554.—Fland. Corr. St. P. Off.

[d] No. XI. The original is preserved in the State-Paper Office, Spanish Corr.

King Philip was at that time expected out of Spain; and Lord Howard of Effingham,[e] the high admiral, had been sent with a fleet to convey him in safety to the shores of England. This circumstance is alluded to in the provision made at the time for the payment of the navy; "for the better supplement whereof, our pleasure is you shall call unto you such factour or factours as Thomas Gresham, our agent in Flanders, hath at this present there in Spaine; and of such money as our said agent hath agreed for to be delivered and received to our use there, cause so much to be paid over to our well-beloved cousin, Benjamin Gunson, treasurer of our Admiralty."[f] It was presumed that Gresham would reach Spain before his majesty's departure, and he was furnished with instructions accordingly; these were however of no avail, since on the 19th of July, Philip landed at Southampton, and was married to Queen Mary six days after.[g]

Of several letters written by Gresham on his arrival in Spain, unfortunately only one remains; and the only other notice of his sojourn in that country is a letter from the council, written in a

[e] For a memorandum relative to this nobleman, see the Appendix, No. XII.

[f] The Queen to Lord Privy-Seal, May 9, 1554.—Domestic Corr. St. P. Off.

[g] Cecil's Diary, Lands. MS. No. 118, p. 91.

tone which they had never before used towards him. It is dated from Richmond, August the 15th, 1554, in reply to his of the 10th of July; and expresses dissatisfaction at the fewness of his letters, and the tardiness of his proceedings; respecting which, by the way, their lordships were very ill qualified to form an opinion. "We perceive," say they, "you mean to send the said treasure to Cales [Cadiz] by your servant, to be shipped there, and yourself intend, that done, to make your repair homewards by land; which thing semeth very strange unto us: and surely we cannot but much marvell that you would comit the doing and order of a matter of such great charge and importance to your servant, or any other but yourself. . . . . . As touching the passport for the 120,000 ducats that remain above the 200,000 ducats that you have already a passport for,—ye shall do well to sue for the same at the Prince of Portingale's hands."[h]

On the 21st of November, Gresham addressed the council from Valladolid, but his letter is unfortunately lost. Leaving Medina del Campo on the 23rd, he arrived on the 26th of November at Seville, whence his next despatch was written. He expressly mentions that he 'departed in post from Meddyna de Camppo;' and well he may,

[h] Spanish Corr. St. P. Off.

for the distance surmounted in those three days was nearly three hundred miles; and certainly cannot have been less, if, as seems probable, he took the road through Toledo. The letter alluded to, which is dated the 30th of November, details the difficulties he had daily experienced, and the obstacles which were thrown in his way by the Spaniards; who yielded unwilling credence to the letters he brought from his own government and from the emperor, and viewed his operations with no slight degree of jealousy,—a sentiment for which there was obviously sufficient occasion. Previous to his arrival, Hogan had received 100,000 ducats; and the sudden removal of so vast an amount of treasure was productive of consequences more disastrous to the people of Seville than Gresham anticipated. "For my part," said he, "I am not abell with my pen to set forthe unto you the great scarsity that is now through all Spayne;" and one of the oldest banks in Seville having suspended payment in consequence of his operations, he adds with much concern, "I fere I shall be the occasione they shuld play all banke-rowte [bankrupt.]" He proposed, therefore, that returning himself to England, he should leave his factor, Edward Hogan, to receive the remainder of the sum at leisure; in the payment of which he says there would have been no difficulty or delay, if the ships which were daily expected from the West Indies had arrived.[i] In the mean time, having obtained his despatch on the 30th, (the day he wrote,) Gresham says that at five o'clock in the evening he started with two of his servants to see this treasure shipped at 'Port Riall' (Puerto Real, over against Cadiz,) "in such good merchants' ships as might be found there." It was packed in fifty cases, marked each containing 22,000 Spanish silver rials, or 2,000 ducats. At this point we lose sight of Gresham in Spain, and hear no more of him till the spring of the following year, when he had returned to Antwerp.

The letters just cited were addressed to the Privy-council; but Boxoll, Queen Mary's principal secretary, was the person with whom Gresham chiefly corresponded. That statesman was evidently well disposed towards him,[k] and occasion-

[i] Spanish Corr. St. P. Off.—From "A note of suche summes of monny as came unto the hands of Thomas Gresham, and passed from hym in the tyme of Queene Mary," preserved among the Lansdowne MSS. (No. 113, art. 19,) and given in the Appendix, (No. XIII.) it appears that the total amount of money received in Spain was 97,878*l.* 15*s.*

[k] See the rough draft of his letter to Gresham, 10th June, 1558, (Fland. Corr. St. P. Off.) where he says, that "he is ready to do him any pleasure in this time of his absence."

ally sent him a confidential letter of kind advice. Thus, when Philip was engaged in his military operations in Flanders, Boxoll recommended his friend to be mindful and ingratiate himself with the king: "knowing that you looke for some advertysement from hense at my handes, I have thought good to advyse that you shall do well, in all your greate affaires, from tyme to tyme to repaire unto the King's highness; taking orders at his hands, (yf he will give you any,) or at the least making him privie to that you are willed to do. Whereby ye shall the better accomplishe your charge in this service, beinge there amongst his highness subjects; and fynde the more helpe and favour in doing the same. And thus fare you hartily well. From the Court, at Grenewiche, the vith of Apryll, 1558."[1]

This was good counsel; for, as many of our historians have truly remarked, Queen Mary lavished much unrequited tenderness on her husband; and seems to have been in love with him to the last. The accomplished Sir William Pickering, ambassador at the court at Brussels, and Mr. Gresham in his official capacity at Antwerp, never addressed her majesty, in consequence, without informing her of the state of the king's health; and, as far as they were able, of his move-

[1] Copy.—Fland. Corr. St. P. Off.

ments. Pickering, for instance, writes to the queen from Brussels, as follows: "Methought it not amis (because I was not cauled for all the while) to procure the knowyng of his Majesty's pleasure concernyng myne owne abode here, or my repaire homewards. And so, submittyng myself (as was most mete) by my most humble and willyng offer unto whatsoever thing it lyked his Majesty to dispose of me, I requested Don Antonio [de Toledo] to move his Majesty in that behalf. That he did; and uppon Tewsday last, towards the evenyng, he brought me into the park at Brussels, where I found the King's Majesty breaking upp of a buck that he himself had stricken a lytell afore. As his Majesty hadde eynded his pastyme, it pleased him to declare his gratefull taking of my simple service in good worthe; and in such sorte, that I must needes acknowledge, whatsoever it hath been or shalbe, it may be by no meanes answerable unto the least part of his Majesty's incomparable benignitie and bountifull goodnes towards me."[m] But our business is with Gresham, who it will be seen wrote with the same detail and minuteness as his friend.— "I have been at Brussels," he says on one occasion, "by the order of Mr. Pickering, with the sum of 1,500*l.* for the despatch of Capitayne

[m] Brussels, July 24, 1558.—Fland. Corr. St. P. Off.

Walton; whereas I sawe the King's Majesty in right good health, (thanckes be given to God,) upon St. George's daye, in his robes, and the Ducke of Savoie with hym; which feast was verrie honnorablie and solemly kept by his Majesty, with all his nobills and gentillmen about him."[n] In another letter he writes, "I have been at Brussels; whereas I spake with the Kinge's Majestie the xvith, xviijth, and xixth of this present, for a licence of three hundred thousand crownes to pass into his realme and your's: he being in as right good helth as your highness' harte can desier, (prayse be given to God!) And his Majestie hath grantid you the whole licence of the said iij C M crownes, to pass at one tyme, with one hundred thousand at once; in giving me a great charge I shuld conveye this monny with as much secresy, and as small brewte [noise] as I coulde devise; by reason of the great scarssity that is here at this present. Which, God willing, shall be done, when your Grace's pleassure therein is known."[o] Next month, previous to returning home, Gresham addressed the queen as follows:

"According to my most bounden dewtie, I shall (afore my departure) gyve my attendance

[n] T. G. to Queen Mary, Ant. April 26, 1558.—Fland. Corr. St. P. Off.

[o] The same to the same, Ant. May 23, 1558.—Ibid.

upon the King's Majestie for to knowe his pleasure, yf a wolle commande me anny servize to your highness; and therewith repaier to your Grace with dilligence. Who (thankes be to God!) is in right good helth at Brussels, and now in a great forwardness with his armye of horsemen and footmen: being stronge, at this instant, with 10,000 horsemen, and 30,000 footemen at the least; and within these xii daies, a shall have 16,000 men more at his cittie of Namewre. The Dewke of Savoye, his Majesty's Capitayne-generall, doth departe from Brussells at this daye, for the conducte of them into the filde: beseechinge our Lorde to sende his Majestie helth, and victorie over his enemyes."[p] With some such passage, more or less picturesque, (and a more entertaining instance will be given in its proper place,) Gresham always prefaced more important intelligence;—for he was accustomed to send to the queen herself a report of his progress in liquidating the debts of the crown; and to detail the sums taken up, as well as the names of the Low Country merchants with whom he negotiated, as unceremoniously as if he had been addressing his factor, Master John Elliot, of Lombard-street. So primitive a practice seems to belong to a

[p] T. G. to Queen Mary, Ant. June 20, 1558.—Fland. Corr. St. P. Off.

remoter age, and to carry us back to the annals of a much earlier reign.

It cannot fail, however, to seem yet stranger, that Gresham should have received from Queen Mary in return, letters of a similar tenour to those which he addressed to her. One might have supposed that his communications to a lady of such elevated rank were merely a matter of form; that they were laid before her perhaps, but never read. Such certainly was not the case. There remains among the State-Papers the copy of a letter sent to Gresham by the Privy-council on the 21st of January, 1553–4, on which it is distinctly stated, "This was written from the Queen hirself." For the reader's satisfaction, I will quote the most interesting passages it contains: though Mary's genius for business would be better seen in the passages omitted. It will be perceived that his exalted correspondent speaks in the person of her ministers: "Wheras by your lettres it appereth, that some of those with whom you have concludyd bargaines there, fynde some faulte with the Queene's Majestie's bondes, for that the same be not sealed with hir own seale; you shall understand, that albeit the said bonds were sealed with none other seale than was at that time usually occupied throughout all England, (for that this newe seale was not then made);

yet hir highness is contented, that in case they that fynde such fault have any occasion to send into England for any other business of theirs, and do return their said olde bonde, they shall have [it] newe-made forth agayen, under hir Majestie's own seale, to their satisfaction.[q]

" And whereas you seem to be in some doubt whether you may sende home golde or silver, you shall receive herewith a note of an assay taken here, both of golde and also of silver : both which when you shall have well considered, we pray you to send some suche coynes as you can get, either golde or silver, and [such as] may be most profitable for the Queene's Majestie.

" We sende unto you herewith also, one other scedule, conteyning certayn coynes of diverse countries; praying you to sett upon every coyne how they be currant there ; and at what price you thinke best they should be currant here, for the Queene's grace's most advantage: and so to return the same unto us with your opinion accordingly.[r] . . . . . .

" And whereas you write that you have pre-

[q] On the 3rd of June, 1556, " Dirrick, the graver of the mint," was " appointed to make and new-grave the great seal."—Privy-council Book of Queen Mary, MS. Dirrick was a Dutchman.

[r] This schedule, with Gresham's remarks upon it, will be found in the Appendix, No. XIV. It may gratify the curiosity of some readers.

pared a furnesse to melte down suche Spanyshe ryalls as you shall receyve there, requiring our advices therein ; we have thought good to signifie unto you, that the Queene's highness' pleasure is, that in case you may without breache of the lawes of that country melte down the said coyne, and that the same may be commodious to her Majestie, you shall then do therein as you have devised. But otherwise, not to meddle withall : for her highness woold be lothe, having entred so strayte an amitie as she hathe don with th' Emperour, to be seen to breake any lawe of his in so weightie a case ; or to do therein otherwise than she woold be done unto."[s]

Besides the care of providing money in Flanders to meet the necessities of the state, we learn from Gresham's correspondence that many other duties devolved upon him. It was expected of the Queen's Agent, that he would keep the council constantly informed of all that was passing in his neighbourhood, or rumoured beyond seas ; a task, the faithful, frequent, and expeditious performance of which was rendered particularly acceptable by the imperfect system of communication in those days, and which Gresham's position enabled him to perform in a most satisfactory manner. It was, moreover, his province to supply

[s] 21 Jan. 1553-4.—Fland. Corr. St. P. Off.

the country with whatever articles of foreign manufacture were required, as arms, plate, or jewellery. Thus, in King Edward's Journal, (11th Feb. 1552–3,) Sir John Gresham is said to have "delivered of armour, 1100 pair of corselets, and horse-men's harnesses very fair;" and on the expectation of a visit from certain French noblemen, we find that "provision was made in Flanders for silver and gold plate, and chains to be given to these strangers."[t] Accordingly, throughout Mary's reign, we find Gresham repeatedly commissioned to purchase arms and ammunition, which the hostilities so hotly maintained by King Philip had rendered necessary for the security of the realm. In March, and again in June, 1558, he and Alexander Bonvisi (a merchant of Lucca) were employed conjointly;[v] and Gresham's progress in his commission, as might be expected, forms the subject of all his letters written about those periods, to the exclusion of what would be to us more acceptable matter. In May, he stated that he had shipped on board four ships, (in order to divide the risk,) military stores to the value of 2600*l.*: they consisted of the materials of which

[t] King Edward's Journal, MS. June 4, 1551.

[v] See the note of "Provisions made, and to be made, in Flanders," 31 March, 1558. (Appendix, No. XV.) Also the commission dated 11 June, 1558, in Rymer's Fædera, vol. xv. p. 486.

gunpowder is manufactured, together with many hundred morions, sleeves of mail, dags, &c., and his agents were at the same time actively engaged in Germany in procuring additional supplies.[w]

Other services of minor importance were occasionally required at the hands of the queen's factor. When an ambassador, or other servant of the state was sent into Flanders, he was generally instructed to look to Gresham for the discharge of his salary. Sir William Pickering, who in the beginning of 1558 was sent to King Philip at Brussels,[x] and thence directed to proceed into Germany, brought with him a warrant to Mr. Gresham for the payment of 200*l.*, and his diet of four marks, or 2*l.* 13*s.* 4*d.* per diem;[y] being commissioned to join "the musters," or, as they are

[w] See Gresham's letters to Boxoll, Ant. 26 April, and 7 May' 1558.—Fland. Corr. St. P. Off. They are noticed in the Appendix, No. XV.

[x] See Queen Mary's letter to Gresham, 10 March, 1557-8.—Ibid.

[y] "From the 8th of this present March, during his abode in our said service." The same to the same, March 1557-8.—Ibid. Gonçalo Perez, in the name of King Philip, ordered Gresham (June 10, 1558,) to pay Sir William Pickering 40,000 florins.—Dom. Corr. St. P. Off. In No. 5755 of the Add. MSS. in the British Museum, at f. 17, is a bill under the hand and seal of Sir William Pickering to Thomas Gresham, Esq. for the receipt of 40,000 florins of the Rhine, at twenty-five stivers Brabants the piece; that is, 8333*l.* 6*s.* 8*d.* Flemish; for the payment of 3000 Alemands for one month's wages and diet. 9 June, 1558.

elsewhere called, "the bands of Almaignes,"—a troop of 3000 men, whom it was proposed to enrol in the English army. Gresham was instructed, shortly after, to pay one Herman Pepper for the armour and weapons with which he had contracted to supply these soldiers:[z] and a banner being required by the same troop, he was instructed to provide it, and to be careful that it should be of the queen's colours, "white and green, with red crosses."[a]

However interesting and important Gresham's foreign intelligence may have been considered by the Privy-council at the time, the spirit of it has altogether evaporated through age. Our sympathies are far more alive to the domestic rumours, in which, like the rest of the English merchants settled at Antwerp, he was naturally so deeply interested; and concerning the authenticity of which he so frequently wrote to inquire. The intelligence of Wyatt's rebellion, in 1553–4, filled the merchants with dismay. "Here is newes come," says Gresham, "that the commons be uppe in Kent, and that Sir Thomas Wyatt shuld be

[z] Queen Mary to Gresham, 8 June, 1558.—Fland. Corr. St. P. Off.

[a] The same to the same, 18 May, 1558.—Ibid. He was ordered (3 May) to pay Will. Watson, a merchant who was employed to buy masts and other tackle, by order of the officers of the Admiralty, &c. &c.

their Captayne, with dyvers other gentilmen. As allso I do perceve by this bringer, my servant John Spritwell, [that he] was steyed by the waye, with threttening wordes ; as he shall declare unto your Lordeshipes." [b] In less than a week it was currently rumoured and believed at Antwerp, " that the commons of Cornewall, Cheshire, Norfocke, Suffocke, and Kent were uppe ;" [c] and that Sir Thomas Wyatt was " on Blackheath-field with 20,000 foot-men," ready to " sett uppon the Citty of London." Such was the effect produced upon the queen's credit by this intelligence, that Gresham says, " glad was that man that might be quit of five shillings." It was " no small comfort to her Majestie's poore subjccts," when Spritwell, his servant, " brought newes of the honnorable victory that the Queene had over the rebelles :" on receiving which joyful tidings, the English merchants caused wine to be drunk, and bonfires to be lighted in the streets ; a great peal of guns to be fired, and one hundred crowns to be distributed

[b] T. G. to the Council, Ant. 31 Jan. 1553-4.—Ibid.

[c] " The ii daye of this present, I received your honnor's letter of the xxviii of Janyver ; wyche was no small comfort unto me and to all the Queene's Highness frendes, to hear in what stay our countrey was in, save onely Kent : wyche I have not letted to publishe. For the rumours were here," &c. The same to the same, Ant. 6 Feb. 1553-4.—Ibid.

among the poor of the town.[d] Sir Thomas Cheyney, (treasurer of the household, lord-warden of the Cinque Ports, and lieutenant of the county of Kent,) writing to the council on the subject of this insurrection, has the following curious passage:—"Yt is a great dele more than straunge to see the beastlynes of the people, to see how earnestly they be bent in this theyr most develishe entreprise; and will by no meanes be persuaded to the contrary but that it is for the comen welthe of all the realme. They say and protest before God they meane to her grace no hurt: but for all that, I pray God kepe her out of their daungier."[e]

The extraordinary supposition that the queen was about to become a mother, when she was in truth afflicted with dropsy, did not fail, before it reached Antwerp, to assume the serious form of an actual occurrence: nor could less have been expected, after the great pains which had been taken at home to fill the public mind with expectations of an heir to the crown. Gresham writes thus to the lords of the council on the 4th of May, 1555:—"It maye please your most honnorable Lordeships to be advertised that as the ii[nd] of this present, here came newes along the seas by men

[d] T. G. to the Council, Ant. 15 Feb. 1553-4.—Fland. Corr. St. P. Off. Spritwell brought the news the day before.

[e] 'From Sherlond,' 1 Feb. 1553-4.—Dom. Corr. St. P. Off.

of this country, that the Queene's Majesty was brought a-bed of a yonge Prynce, the last of April; whiche newes contynewed here till the iiii[th] day. And as the thyrde day, the Regent, being in this town of Andwerpe, about 7 of the clocke at night, dyd cause the great bell to ringe, to give all men to understand that the news was trewe. Signifying unto your honnors, that as the ii[nd] day, upon the aryvall of the fyrst newes, the Quene's highness' mere merchants, according to their most boundyd dewtye, caussyd all our Inglishe ships to shoote off with such joy and triumph as by man's art and pollisey could be devysed, in the presence of the Regent, with all her nobills and gentillwomen. Whereupon the Regent presently sent our Inglishe maroners one hundred crowns to dryncke. Trusting in God the news to be trewe; for as yet, I, nor none of our nacion hath no certayne wryting thereof."[f]

Notwithstanding a certain degree of concern which this passage in Queen Mary's history excites, there is something irresistibly ludicrous in the accounts transmitted to us of the extent to which the delusion alluded to was indulged. "All the court," says Grafton, "was full of midwives, nurses, and rockers; and this talk continued almost half a year, and was affirmed true by

[f] T. G. to the Council, Ant. 4 May, 1555.—Fland. Corr. St.P.Off.

some of her physicians, and other persons about her; which seemed both grave and credible. Insomuch that divers were punished for saying the contrary."[g] On the 3rd of May, the Bishop of Norwich received "the sodeine good newes of the Quene's Highnes moost joyfull deliverance of a nooble Prince: whereupon, to laude God, *Te Deum* was solemply sung in the Cathedrall Churche, and other places of the cytye [of Norwich], wyth woonderfull joye and muche gladness of all people throughowte all the whole cytye and the countrye thereabowtes."[h] "The parson of Saint Anne within Aldersgate," says Foxe, "after procession, and *Te Deum* sung, took upon him to describe the proportion of the child; how faire, how beautiful, and how great a prince it was, as the like had not been seen."

But by far the most extraordinary circumstance connected with this delusion has never yet been noticed in print. There is in the State-Paper Office an original letter to Cardinal Pole, *signed by Philip and Mary, announcing the birth of a prince* as an event which had already occurred. "Whereas it hath pleased Almighty God of his infinite goodnes to adde vnto the great nomber of other his benefites bestowed vpon vs, the gladding

[g] Chronicle, ed. 1569, p. 1350.

[h] Ellis's Letters, first Series, vol. ii p. 190–1.

of vs with *the happy deliverie of a prince.*" The date is left blank, but the letter is endorsed "29th May, 1555."[i]

Passages such as the foregoing, however, are comparatively of rare occurrence in Gresham's correspondence at this period. Whatever favourable disposition towards him Secretary Boxoll may have entertained, there seems to have been wanting that cordiality between them,—the fruit of intimacy and similarity of sentiment,—which alone can impart interest to a correspondence; and however honourably treated by the council, and favourably noticed by the queen, Gresham generally confined himself in addressing both, to the strictest details of business. Nor did he yet consider himself so firmly established in the good opinion of their lordships, as to render superfluous frequent explanations of his proceedings; and details, which now seem minute and tedious in the extreme.[k] Of some of them he was distrustful: especially of that ill-favoured[l] old Roman-Catholic nobleman, Paulet Marquis of Winchester, the lord-treasurer; who, jealous of Gresham's weight

[i] Domestic Corr.—See Rapin, vol. ii. p. 43.

[k] *e. g.* To the Council, 5 Oct. 1555; to the Queen, 24 Feb. and 15 March, 1555-6; and to Boxoll, 29 May, 1558, &c. &c.—Ibid.

[l] I will defend this epithet by referring the reader to the portrait of Winchester, in Naunton's Fragmenta Regalia, ed. 1797.

and influence in all matters of finance, showed himself his enemy on more than one occasion, and sought to undo him.[m] A note of the queen's debts in Flanders,[n] and an account of sums of money taken up from time to time to discharge them,[o] form in consequence the general topic of his letters ; diversified only by an occasional note of payments made, or a memorandum of what bullion,[p] arms, or ammunition[q] he had shipped from Antwerp under King Philip's licence, and sent home by order of the council.—The statesman who had made any figure during the reign of King Edward, if, like Sir William Cecil, he hoped to shine in the court of Elizabeth, had in truth a difficult game to play in the days of Queen Mary.

[m] See especially Gresham's letters to Sir Thomas Parry, from Antwerp, 22nd and 29th of June, 1560.—Flanders Correspondence, St. P. Off.

[n] The documents of this class appertaining to Mary's reign in the State-Paper Office, are six in number. They are undated.

[o] See his letters to the Council of 11 Nov. 1555, and 24 Feb. 1555-6; to Boxoll, 1 May, and to the Queen, 12 April, 1 and 23 May, 1558. There are besides three undated documents of this class.—Ibid.

[p] See his letters to the Council of 8 Dec. 1553, 1 Jan. 6 and 21 Feb. 1553-4.—Ibid.

[q] See his letter to the Council of 6 Feb. 1553-4, where he mentions "gunpowder shipped under this mark (the broad arrow) in the margent;" to Boxoll, of 15 May and 6 June, 1558; and to the Queen, of the same date.—Ibid.

Such was the nature of Gresham's occupations at Antwerp; and such, more or less, were his employments from the period of his return from Spain in the beginning of 1555, until the 16th of June; on which day it is recorded in the Acts of Queen Mary's Privy-council that he presented to their lordships nine "obligations or bonds, as well of hir Highness as of the Cittie of London, which heretofore passed for the sure payment of certayne summes of money due to sundry merchants strangers. . . . . All which bonds were cancelled, and sent to the Lord Treasurer to be laid up in the Queene's treasury; and to deliver the Citty's to the Lord Maior, by the said Thomas Gresham."[r] In September, having paid another brief visit to his wife and family in England during the interval, Gresham returned to the scene of his occupations on the 4th of October,[s] in time to witness one of the most remarkable scenes recorded in history,—namely, the abdication of supreme power by the Emperor Charles the Fifth, in favour of his son Philip. This event occurred at Brussels on Friday the 25th of October, 1555, attended by a ceremony of which Sir John Mason, a statesman of high intelligence, who was at that

[r] Council-book of Queen Mary, MS.

[s] T. G. to the Council, Ant. 5 Oct. 1555.—Fland. Corr. St. P. Off.

time our ambassador resident at the court of Brussels, transmitted to his government a minute description.[t] The States of the Low-Countries being assembled in the great hall of the court, which was richly decorated for the occasion, the emperor entered about four o'clock in the afternoon, accompanied by King Philip, the Queen of Hungary, (his sister,) and a train of nobles; together with the knights of the order of the Toison d'or, wearing the collars of their order. The emperor took his seat in the highest part of the hall, placing Philip on his right, the queen on his left, and next to her the Duke of Savoy. The nobles and others being seated, the occasion of that extraordinary meeting was briefly declared by one of the Privy-council; after which the emperor rose and addressed the assembly. He reminded them of the long period of forty years, during which he had been their lord and governor; and declared "what travailes he had in this space susteyned, having made xl notable voyages,

[t] The document alluded to, endorsed by Sir John Mason, is in the State-Paper Office. It corresponds very nearly with the relation of the proceedings of that memorable day given by Robertson, or rather by La Strada, from whom it will be found that Robertson derived his information: but it has the charm of being the narrative of an eye-witness, and corroborates the date of the emperor's abdication, respecting which the biographer of Charles V. expresses some doubt.

which he rehearsed particularly; having passed viii tymes the Levant seas, thrice the Spannish seas, having been iiii tymes in France, twice in England, twice in Affrike, and sondry tymes in sondry other places." But he felt that he was no longer adequate to discharge the duties imposed upon him by Almighty God,—his infirm health and debilitated frame admonishing him to resign to a younger and abler hand the sceptre he was no longer able effectually to wield: he therefore made cession of all his estates to his son Philip, whom he earnestly exhorted to maintain the Catholic faith, and to whom he required his subjects to transfer the oath of allegiance by which they had hitherto been bound to himself. The step he was taking, he assured them, was without any view to the prolongation of his own life; for he entertained no hopes of recovery, and left his people with real sorrow. No one had ever had "a lovinger sort of subjects;" and if he had ever unwittingly omitted the performance of any of his duties towards them, or in the course of his life erred in the administration of government, he now asked their forgiveness. "And here he brake into a weeping, whereunto, besides the dolefulness of the matter, I think he was moche provoked by seing the whole company to doo the lyke before; [there] beyng in myne opynion not one man in the whole assemblie, stranger or other, that dewring the tyme of a good piece of his oracion poured not oute abondantly teares; some more, some less. And yet he prayed them to beare with his imperfection, proceeding of his syckly age, and of the mentioning of so tender a matter as is the departing from such a sort of dere, and most loving subjects."

Philip made a dutiful speech in reply, and concluded by offering "to kiss his father's hands; but being not suffred so to doo, they embraced each other in soche sorte as might well appere a loving meeting between the affections of the father and the son." Mary, the Queen-dowager of Hungary, who for five-and-twenty years had ably presided over the interests of all present, as regent of the Low Countries, having briefly addressed the assembly on the subject of her government, now announced her intention of following her brother, Charles V., into his retirement. A complimentary speech was made her in return; after which, "the Emperor arose, and every man retired to his lodging."

The various but uniformly flattering conjectures which different writers have advanced as to the real motive which induced Charles V. to take this extraordinary step, affords a curious illustration of the biographer's proneness to entertain exalted conceptions of his hero. When the emperor's deplorable health,[v] and the concomitant impairment of his mental faculties are considered, there seems good reason for suspecting that he was the victim of premature old age, and verged on dotage while he was yet in his prime. So melancholy a spectacle may be more easily rendered pathetic than ennobled. An event of so much importance to the Low Countries, however, seemed deserving of particular notice in this place; not only because Sir John Mason has supplied us with some graphic touches which are omitted by the biographer of Charles the Fifth in his elegant narrative of the same occurrence; but because it is from the emperor's abdication that those intestine broils may be considered to date, which subsequently convulsed the Low Countries, and eventually led to the decay of their commerce, and the expulsion of the English from those parts. They have obtained in history the expressive name of "Troubles,"—a word which conveys a just idea of their character. At present it will be enough to state concerning the Low-Country troubles, that although they originated in the deep-seated jealousy which had existed from the very outset between the Spaniards and

[v] See Sir Richard Morysine's curious account of Charles the Fifth's illness, in Lodge's Illustrations, vol. i. pp. 165–8–9.

the Flemish people,—feelings which it required all the address, and even the personal influence of Charles V. to counteract and render inactive,—they owed their most aggravated features to the arbitrary line of policy pursued towards them by King Philip. Haughty in his manners, and secret in his councils, his disposition soon estranged from him the affections of the people he had to govern. He did not scruple to offend their civil prejudices, by living altogether surrounded by persons of his own nation; and in the matter of religion, exasperated them by enactments which were at once violent and arbitrary. As yet, however, he was occupied by the hostilities with France in which he had been engaged since the year 1551; and it was principally to attend to these, that he had left England and Queen Mary, and taken up his residence in the country conceded to him by his father. The governorship of the same having in the mean time become vacant by the departure of the Queen of Hungary, the Duke of Savoy, Philip's favourite and most successful general, was deputed to govern in her place.[w]

[w] In the State-Paper Office (Flanders Correspondence) is preserved a MS., bearing the date of 1555, which might be of service to the historian of this period of history. It extends to sixty-four pages, and is entitled, "Forme de Police, et Regime pour le Pays-Bas."

Whether in consequence of the intrigues of the lord-treasurer, or from whatever other cause, Gresham's occupation of the office of royal agent was frequently interrupted during Mary's reign. This may be gathered from the mere inspection of his correspondence, in which there are some wide gaps: but the circumstance is confirmed by himself; for though Mary reigned for five years and some months, he states in one of his letters that he served her but two years,[x]—a statement which may be thus explained. Queen Mary began to reign in July 1553, and in the month of November, we find that Gresham was employed in Flanders; from which time his correspondence proceeds regularly, till about Midsummer 1554, when he went into Spain. There he remained, as we know, for some of the winter months; but he had either not yet returned in the following February, or he had found two rivals, in the persons of John Gresham (probably his cousin) and Nicholas Holbourn, who were at that time employed in Flanders.[y] From May 1555 to March 1556, his correspondence is only interrupted by the visits to England which he made in the interval: one in June, for the purpose of presenting at the

[x] From his letter, which will be found in the Appendix, addressed to the Earl of Leicester; dated London, 10 Nov. 1568.

[y] The Queen's letter to them, dated Feb. 1554-5, is in the State-Paper Office.

council-table the cancelled bonds and obligations of the queen and the city of London; another in September; and a third in December: at which time, six months having expired since his last attendance, it is recorded in the acts of the Privy-council, that at a meeting held at St. James's on the 8th instant, he waited on their lordships with six cancelled bonds, as before. He continued to give his periodical attendance at the council-table ever after;[z] and as the bonds of which he was the bearer had been generally renewed for the term of six months, he usually re-appeared at intervals of about half a year: but from March 1556, his correspondence is not resumed until the month of March 1558, in the November of which

[z] On the 22nd Nov. 1555, it is recorded in the minutes of the Privy-council, that five bonds signed by the queen, and the counterpart made out and sealed by the lord mayor and citizens, "were delivered to John Ellyot, factor unto the said Thomas Gresham, to be by him conveyed over to the said Mr. Gresham." Elliot had already attended for this purpose on the 2nd, and 14th of November; and on the 8th of May, and 2nd of March following, his name recurs. On the 19th June, 1556, "Thomas Gresham, Esq., the Queene's Majestie's agent in Flanders, brought to the Lords of the Council [at the Star-Chamber] these xii severall bonds following;" of which the particulars are enumerated. On the 23rd November, 1556, Elliot presented certain cancelled bonds; and on the 24th December, Gresham in person brought nine others. He attended with six more on the 31st of May, 1557.—From the original MS. in the Council-Office; whither I have to thank Mr. R. Lemon for conducting me.

year Queen Mary died; so that his letters during this reign extend, with more or less regularity, over a period of about twenty-six months. Both Sir John Mason and Sir Walter Mildmay appear to have encroached upon his province; having been severally engaged, at different periods, in the duties which properly appertained to him as royal agent. But it was to injuries of a more serious character that he alluded, when he spoke in after years of "how he had been handelyd in Queen Mary's time:" either the machinations of the lord-treasurer, or the events of the first few tempestuous weeks of Mary's reign, was probably what he meant.

With reference to Gresham's visit to England last particularized, namely, that in December 1555, the following letter deserves perusal. It has been already mentioned that he was accustomed to correspond with the queen from Antwerp, minutely informing her of his progress in every financial operation. Of this class of his letters there exists no specimen more beautiful than one which he wrote on the 19th of August, 1555, "To the Queenes most excellent Ma[tie];" enclosing "A breffe abstracte touchinge the state of your Majesty's holle dettes in Flanders; wythe the days of payment when the said dettes shall growe dew, as here aftyr too your hightnes maye more playnly apere." [a] But the following letter, written "from Laytton" on the 23rd of December, besides other points of interest which it contains, incidentally reveals to us the intercourse which continued to subsist between Gresham and his royal mistress during his sojourn in England, when his occasions brought him hither.

"It may please your most excellent Majestie to be advertised, that at my last access I had to your highness, your Grace's pleasure was that I should confer with my Lorde the Bishop of Ely, the Lorde Paget, and Sir William Peter, as touching your debts and charge beyond the seas. And [it] being dark nyght when that I departed from your Majestie, I thought it not convenyent to molest my Lords that nyght,—thinking the next day to have accomplished your Majesty's commission; which I could not do: for that I was visited with a hott burning agew. Nevertheless, according to my most bowndyd dewty, I sent unto my said Lordes and Sir William Peter, the next day, my factor John Elliot; to singnify unto them your highness' pleasure: wherein I perceived they were most redy to accomplishe the same, so farre forthe as that they had your Majestie's commyssione so to doo. And for that

[a] Fland. Corr. St. P. Off. The "sum totall owing in Antwerp," was at that time 148,526*l.* 5*s.* 8*d.*

my Lorde the Bishop made answer a shuld be absent for iiij or v dayes, and my Lorde Paget also, by the reason of my continual syckness I stayed till the coming of my said Lordes; or untill suche tyme I had beene able to have come to have conferred with their honnors. Which, as yet, I have not done; but alwayes have geven my Lorde of Ely, and my Lorde Paget, and Sir William Peter to understand what money I had received of your Majestie's warrant of X M *li.* [10,000*l.*]: advertising your highness that I have received at this instant, iiij M *li.* [4,000*l.*] whereof I have delyvered by exchange the sum of ij M *li.* [2000*l.*] at xxi*s.* vi*d.*; wyche will redound muche to your Majestie's honnor and credit, as allso your proffyt. Which ys the chiefest thinge (one of them) that your Highness ought to consider.

"Since the which tyme, it maye please your Majestie to understand, that as the xxist of this present, my Lorde Treasurer sent me worde by my factor, John Elliot, that a had taken upon hym to confer wyth me to paye all your Majestie's debts: and that a was come to London to geve order for the payment of the sum of V M *li.* [5,000*l.*] towards the payment of the X M iiij C liij *li.* vi*s.* viij*d.* [10,453*l.* 6*s.* 8*d.*] Flemish, that your Majestie oweth to Alexander Bonvyze the xxvth of Janyver next. And for that your Highness hath appoynted me to confer with other of my Lordes, according to my most bowndyd dewty, and [the] trust that it hath pleased your Grace to have reposed in me, I have thought it most expedient for my discharge to advertise you of the premises. Most humbly beseeching your Majestie that I maye knowe your further pleasure therein: wherein I shall most reverently follow your Majestie's order, wheresoever it shall stand with your Grace's pleasure to appoynte me; so that it shall stand with your Majestie's honner and credit, and for the proffit of your Majestie and the realme.

"And thus, for feare of molesting your Majestie with my longe writing, I shall praye to God to geve me grace and fortewn that my servyce maye be always acceptable to your highness. As knoweth our Lorde, who preserve your nobell Majestie in helthe, and longe lyfe, and longe to rayne over us, with increase of muche honnor. From Laytton, the xxiij[rd] of December, in the year of our Lord God xvclv, [1555.]

By your Majestie's most humble and
faythefull obedient subject,
THOMAS GRESHAM, mercer."[b]

"To the Queene's most Excellent Majestie."

[b] Fland. Corr. St. P. Off.

The interruptions of his official duties, however unwelcome they may have been in other respects, afforded Gresham leisure for the pursuits of commerce; which, until the year 1552, he had prosecuted with equal assiduity and success. A few remarks on this subject may not be unacceptable in this stage of our story, and will not certainly be out of place.

The words Mercer and Merchant-adventurer are familiar to many persons, who perhaps do not attach a very definite idea to either term. By the former appellation, in remote times, was meant any dealer in small wares; but as the commerce of this country became more extended, the operations of the mercers assumed a more important character; and the words *mercer* and *merchant* became nearly synonymous. In the year 1364, the mercers had become extensive dealers in woollen cloths, of which the manufacture was introduced into this country from Flanders by Edward III. about thirty years before; and in 1393 they became incorporated.[c] Under the title

[c] Their existence as a company may be traced as far back as the year 1172, though they were not incorporated till 1393. They take precedence of all the other city companies, and number among their members, says Hall, "several kings, princes, nobility, and ninety-eight lord mayors." Sir Richard Whittington, whose romantic tale is familiarly known to every one, was a member of this company; as was Sir Geoffrey Bullen, maternal

of Merchants of the Staple,—by far the most ancient of our trading societies,—they had long been famous; and in the reign of Edward the Third had attained high distinction and eminence. That monarch has been justly styled the father of English commerce; for the encouragement which his predecessors had held out to the Flemish merchants was fluctuating, and it is from his reign that a progressive improvement is to be dated. It was he who, in 1374, made Geoffrey Chaucer, the poet, comptroller of the customs; on the express condition that he should write with his own hand the registers or entries belonging to his said office; and never act by a deputy or substitute.[d]

To legislate for commerce, henceforth became the leading object of parliament; and wool, as the staple produce of the country,—the principal article of export, and chief source of revenue,—was the subject of almost every statute. It must not be lost sight of, however, that Edward the Third patronised commerce that he might be enabled to carry on his expensive wars with France.

grandfather to Queen Elizabeth; and, what is a yet greater boast, Queen Elizabeth herself; who honoured the mercers by becoming a free sister of this company. It is a remarkable fact, that there is scarcely a single mercer in the Mercers' Company at the present day.—Herbert's Hist., &c., and Stowe by Strype, passim.

[d] Fædera, vol. vii. p. 38.

So urgent were his necessities at one time, that he was fain to borrow gold and silver plate of the religious houses; and in 1339 he pawned his own and his queen's crown for 50,000 gold florins of Florence, or 8338*l.*,—equivalent to upwards of 160,000*l.* of our money.[e] Woollen cloths continued to be the mercers' most important article of traffic, until the time of Elizabeth; in the latter part of whose reign silks were used in such abundance, that the mercers became mostly silk-merchants. They consisted, says Strype, "much of such as sold rich silks brought from Italy, who lived chiefly in Cheapside, and St. Lawrence Jewry, and the Old Jewry."

From the society known by the name of Merchants of the Staple, arose in 1358 another, called the Company of the Merchant-Adventurers. They did not obtain this appellation till the reign of Henry the Seventh; but they were incorporated by Edward the First as early as 1296, when they established a factory at Antwerp, and employed themselves in the manufacture of woollen cloths. Edward the Third, seeing the flourishing condition of their trade, encouraged them to come over with their looms into this country, which they accordingly did; and the experiment succeeded so well, that he soon prohibited the exportation of

[e] Fædera, vol. v. p. 101; and see Anderson, vol. i. p. 311.

English wool: finally, having induced cloth-makers and cloth-workers to come over in sufficient numbers, he prohibited the importation of all foreign cloth into the realm.

The prosperity of the merchant-adventurers was permanent, and Sir Thomas Gresham, with many other mercers, was enrolled among them. Certain privileges and immunities, originally granted to this company by charter, had been confirmed to them by every successive monarch since their incorporation; and few as they were in number, they virtually monopolized the commerce of the country. They constituted a fellowship, which was under the control of a governor elected out of their own body; and they appointed deputy-governors for all their residences at home and abroad. Mr. Hussey was their governor in Queen Mary's time. Thoughout the ensuing pages, incidental notices of their mode of proceeding will often recur, which I will not here anticipate. In the beginning of Elizabeth's reign they were in the habit of sending their cloths twice a year, at Christmas and Whitsuntide, into the Low Countries; about 100,000 pieces of cloth being shipped annually, which amounted in value to at least 7 or 800,000*l.*: and the merchants were accustomed to equip on these occasions a fleet of fifty or sixty ships, manned with the best seamen in the realm. I find that, once, Gresham alone sent "4,500 western kerseys of the best sort, which sold with great profit to the Italians at Antwerp."[f] From this incidental notice, we may judge of the nature and extent of his private operations.

It has been already mentioned that our merchant passed the Christmas of 1555 in England; at which period we obtain sight of him among the number of those who presented New Year's gifts to Queen Mary. "A bolte of fine Holland, in a case of black leather," is mentioned as having been presented by Mr. Thomas Gresham; who received in return "oone guilt jug," weighing sixteen ounces and a half,—a larger present than was bestowed on most men of his quality. His friend, Sir John *A-lee*, offered at the same time "a prymer, covered with purple vellet, and garnished with Damoskyn work."[g] This was in January, 1555-6; about which time we have a proof that the services Gresham had rendered the queen were deemed satisfactory; for she bestowed upon him the priory of Austin Canons at Massingham Magna in Norfolk, together with several minor benefices.[h] It was to a promise of one of

f Cott. MS. Galba. B. xi. fol. 264.

g Nichols' Illustrations, &c. 1797. Sir John received a gilt jug, weighing 15 oz.

h He received, besides, the manor and rectory of Langham and

these grants that he must have alluded, when, addressing the queen on the 27th of October, 1555, he "most humbly besought her highness to licence him to put her in remembrance of the 131*l.* land, that it had pleased her, of her royal goodness, to give him, towards the augmenting and stay of his living, for the service he had done her Majesty, and for the good service he did intend to do her; which," he adds, "shall be no small comfort to me and all my friends."[i] In another place he says, that the lands which Mary granted him amounted, altogether, to the yearly value of about two hundred pounds.

From more than one passage in his correspondence, we are led to believe that the queen felt a personal interest in him; and her friendly disposition about this time is evidenced by the substantial marks of favour he received at her hands. To this period, however,—namely, the spring of 1556, where a hiatus of two years occurs in Gresham's correspondence,—we must probably refer the hostile act of the Marquis of Winchester, al-

advowson of the vicarage; the manors of Walsingham and Narford, besides those of Merston and Combes, and the advowson of their respective rectories.—Tanner's Not. Mon., and Blomefield's Norfolk, vol. vi. p. 232, and vol. ix. p. 8. In the Appendix, No. XVI., will be found a letter from Sir Thomas Gresham to Archbishop Parker, requesting him to institute the bearer to the living of Massingham.

[i] Fland. Corr. St. P. Off.

luded to by the subject of our narrative in the following reign. That nobleman, he says, sought to ruin him by "informing the sovereign with half a tale, ... once in King Edward's time, and once in Queen Mary's time. And when his Lordship came to see the state of myne account, a found the prince rather in my debt than otherwise."[k] He occupied himself in Flanders, however, with the pursuits of which some account has been just given; while King Philip, engrossed by his schemes of military ambition, was lavishly squandering the thousands which Gresham had been so careful in former years to provide. To what accident he owed his restoration to office in the last year of Mary's reign, we are not informed; but his Instructions are extant, bearing date the 12th of March, when he was directed to prepare himself for another journey into the Low Countries.

The reader may not be displeased, for once, to peruse a part of the original instrument with which, when he took such journeys, Gresham was provided. On the present occasion he was ordered "to take with him full information of the bargayne offered to Germayn Scioll by Chemany, for 100,000*l.* for one yere." To ascertain "before his going, the quantities of powder, saltpetre, and

[k] To Parry, 22 June, 1560.—Fland. Corr. St. P. Off.

other provisions to be made there, for armours and munitions of warre: and to make provisione on that side, to our use, of such parcels as we or our counsail shall appoint. . . . . . And he, being thus informed, to pass by post to Andwerp, and with all speede to speake with the said Chemany to understand whether the said bargayne will be performed or not. And if the same will take place, then to send word hither in post thereof: sending withal full instructions for the bonds and assurances to be made here."

He was next to wait on the king; to deliver sundry letters, to communicate the effect of his Instructions, and to sue for a passport for the exportation of military stores and treasure.

"The premises beyng declared to his Majestie and his pleasure known, for the answer thereof the said Gresham shall with all diligence repaire to Antwerp agayne; travailing according to his accustomed good diligence and wisdom, both for the speedy receipt to our use of the said 100,000*l.* bargained for by the said Scyolle, and for the borrowing of one hundred thousand poundes more, for one yeare, at such favourable interest as he may; foreseeing that he exceed not to charge us with more than fourtene at the uttermost, for the interest of everie hundred, besides brokerage. Wherein, the better service he shall do us, the better shall he give us cause to have good consideration of him."

Scioll had married Cicely, the daughter of Sir John Gresham, and was therefore the husband of Thomas Gresham's cousin. If his "bargain did not take effect," the queen's agent was ordered to take up 200,000*l.*; and to grant, for the security of the merchants, the usual bonds under the great seal. "The said Gresham to have allowance and retayne in his owne handes for his diets, of such money as shall come into his hands, twenty shillings by the day; the same to begin the first of this present March." He was also "to have allowance of four clerks, everie of them at sixteen-pence by the daye." He was authorized to reimburse himself "for the prices of any provisions; or for the charges at all tymes of posting of himself and servaunts; and for the charges of sending of any messengers either to our deerest Lord and Husband, or to us; our Council, or otherwise for our service." Allowance was also to be made him "for the hire of such houses as he shall think necessarie for the sure keeping of our treasure, powder, and other munitions; and for the charges of carriage and sending the same, by lande, fresh water, or seas." His instructions finally set forth, that his oath was the only proof which would be required by the commissioners to be hereafter appointed to audit his accounts; and he was guaranteed against any loss which he might otherwise sustain, in case "the money now permitted to go in Flanders as valued money, by just authority there should be called down."[l]

Gresham continued in Flanders until the month of June 1558; during all which time he was incessantly engaged in buying ammunition and collecting military stores.[m] He had not been gone many days, when Boxoll wrote him the friendly letter from which an extract was given at page 157. It begins as follows:

"After my hartie commendacions. Whereas at your departure from hence you received lettres from my Lordes of the Counsell unto the King's Majestie, they doubt whether you have delyvered the same or no: for that in your first lettres you did advertize nothinge thereof. Wherefore I praie you, as soone as you can, let me understande what you have done therein; that I may resolve the Queene's highness in

[l] Copy. 12th March, 1557-8.—Fland. Corr. St. P. Off. An abstract of this document is to be found in the Cott. MS. Galba. B. xii. fol. 256.

[m] According to Rymer, he was commissioned on the 11th June, 1558, conjointly with Alexander Bonvisi, a merchant of Lucca, to procure "3,500 Hackequebutts; 1,000 Pistoletts; 500 Pondera de Macches; 100,000 Pondera Petre Salse; 3,000 Corseletts; 2,000 Mourreyens; 3,000 Iron Cappes; 8,000 Lanceas vocatos, *Launces and Pykes*."—Fædera, vol. xv. p. 486.

the same, if she shall aske me the question." He then recommends him to give his frequent attendance on King Philip, and to make his Majestie privy to "all that he is willed to do." [n]

To this good counsel Gresham immediately attended. He had no sooner received Boxoll's letter, than he wrote as follows to Queen Mary:

"It may please your most excellent Majestie to be advertised, that as the xii[th] of this present, I received your highness' letter, (in Brussels,) of the iiii[th] . . . . . . As also I received a lettre from my Lords of your most honorable council, and another from the Countie de Feria unto the King's Majesty; which lettres I delivered with myne owne hands on this day, at x of the clock in the forenoon, at his comyng from the Grey Fryers of Boytendalle, three English myles from Brussells, whereas he hathe kept this holie tyme of Ester; whom, (thanks be to God,) is in right good health, as your Majestie's owne harte can desyre. And according unto your Majestie's instructions, I certyfyed his highness of this x M *li.* [10,000*l.*] that I have taken up, and of all other my proceedings, which he lyked very well; and said he stayed only for the comyng of the Capten of the Almaignes; and upon his comyng, he would gyve me order for the payment of such

[n] Copy. 6th April, 1558.—Fland. Corr. St. P. Off.

money as they should need. To the which I made answer, I was ready to accomplishe the same, with any other devyce it shuld please his Majestie to commaunde me. Then he commaunded me that I shuld advertize you with diligence of certain intelligens that he had from Deep [Dieppe] in France, which he gave me in writing: and here inclosed I sende you the same writing, with as much diligence as I can." [o]

Before conducting our merchant back to England, I will give extracts from two other letters, written during his present journey: the first "To the right honnorable Mr. Boxoll, Secretary to the Queene's Majestie;" and the second, to the queen herself. "Other I have not to molest you withal," he writes, (solicitous to see his own personal accounts with the state liquidated,) "but that it maye please you to be so good unto me as to be my meane to the Queene's Majestie, for the obteyning of her Highness' pardone upon my accompt. Whereof I have written to her Majestie, and my Lordes; trusting that her highness wolle deal with me as the King's Majestie, her late Father, delt with my aunsistors. And the rather, for that my poore name and credit was of late at a great staye, bothe here and in England, for the servize heretofore done to her

[o] Ant. 12th April, 1558.—Fland. Corr. St. P. Off.

Majestie."[p] To the queen he writes in the same strain: "This is most humblie to beseeche you, to licence me to be a suitor unto you for your Grace's pardon upon my account: which I wolde not seem to molest your Majestie withall at my departure out of England, seeing how much it stood your highness upon; whereby your grace shuld conceve any disobedience in me. Which is a thinge that my master and unckell Sir John Gresham had allwaies of the Kinge's Majestie, your late Father, undir his broad seall of England, in this case of servinge. Trusting that your Majestie wolle deall with me, as your Father delte with my ancestors."[q]

In June, Gresham "thought it expedient to forbear for a season to take up any more sums by way of interest; and made suit to come over for one month;" to both of which proposals the council acceded; and he was desired by their lordships "to advertise the Admirall of the tyme he should be in full arrediness to take shipping, that order might be taken for his waftage over with the treasure."[r]

In October 1558, after three months spent in England, Gresham was again despatched to Ant-

[p] Ant. 1st May, 1558.—Fland. Corr. St. P. Off.

[q] Ant. 26th April, 1558.—Ibid.

[r] The Queen to Thomas Gresham, June 1558.—Ibid.

werp, for the purpose of obtaining a fresh loan. He was ordered "to repaire with convenient speede to our deerest Lorde and husbande the Kyng; and after delyverie of such lettres as he shall receive from hence for that purpose, to sue to his Highness in our name for his good favour and licence to [be allowed to] provide and carry thence into England, such sums of money as followeth."[s] The sum specified in his commission was 100,000*l.*, which he was ordered to take up for the space of a year. He wrote to the queen, to his friend Secretary Boxoll, and to the council, from Dunkirk on the 17th of October; giving Mary an account of his interview with her husband, which unfortunately has not been preserved. He informed Boxoll in a confidential way, that on the 15th, he had presented the Queen's 'token' to King Philip: but to the lords of the council he communicated graver matters, which the reader may not object to peruse.

"It maye please your Lordeships to be advertised, that as the xv[th] of this present I delyvered unto the King's Majestie your Lordships letter, lying incamped upon the French King's ground beside the castle and towne of Owssye, whiche doth apperteyne to the Countie of Egmonde; being ix Inglish myles from his Highness' towne

[s] Copy. 1st Oct. 1558.—Fland. Corr. St. P. Off.

of Heading. And according to the Queene's Majestie's instructions, I declared unto his Majestie that my comyng over was for the taking up of iij c thousand crownes upon interest. And after he had perused your Lordship's letter, incontynent his Majestie sent me worde by the Countie de Feria, that I shuld tarrie no longer for his answer; for that he wold write to his Chancellor Scheff for my dispatch in all things I shuld demande of him for the Queene's Majestie's behoof.

"The occurrents be, that the Kinge's Majestie's commissioners, and the Frenche Kinge's, be att an Abby called Sercant; where the Queene's Majestie's comissioners be likewise treating of a peace, which I praie God send. For that the Kinge's Majestie doth pretend, verrie shortlie after, to be in Ingland: who is in right good health, (thankes be given to God!)

"Also it maye please you to understande, I made my repair backe agayne to Downkirk, to write to the Queene's Majestie and to you this my letter; where I founde Sir William Pickering verrie sore sicke of this new burning agewe: who hath had four sore fittes, being very low browght, and in danger of his life if they continew in this extremyty, as they have done. Having delivered him your Lordships' letter; of whom I have re-

received by the verteu thereof, the sum of three thousand six hundred pistolettes, at vi *s.* vi *d.* Flemish, the pece. Which monny, as this daye, I do carrie backe agayne to Andwarpe, till further your Lordships' pleasures be known: whereas I shall do my best to proceed in my charge, according to the trust the Queene's Majestie and you have reposed in me. As knoweth our Lord, who preserve your Lordships in helth and long life, with increase of honnor. From Downkirk, the xvii[th] daye of October, 1558.

At your Lordships comandement,

THOMAS GRESHAM, mercer."[t]

"To my Lordes of the Queene's
Majestie's Prevey Counsayl."

On the 23rd, he wrote from Antwerp; addressing on the same day, as was his custom, the secretary, the Privy-council, and Queen Mary herself. In his letters to the council he writes,—"Whereas heretofore I have moved your Lordeships for a present to be made to Jasper Schetz, of a chayne of gold of v or vi hundred crownes [value,] as also to Lazarus Tucker, Linshalls, and others, of iii hundred crownes,—it may please your Lordships to have them in remembrance; for that it will serve

[t] Fland. Corr. St. P. Off. I have omitted a postscript relative to Pickering's money transactions.

the Queene's Majestie's turne, dyvers and sundry wayes, more than I will molest your Lordeships withall." A few lines from his letter to Queen Mary—the last she received from him,—likewise deserve insertion: "By my letter of the xviith of this present, written from Downkirke, I certyfied your highness that I had delyvered your ringe unto the Kinge's Majestie. . . . . . The currants [occurrences] be here, that as the xviii[th] of this present, the Kinge's Majestie did remove his camp from Hawssye, lying upon the French kinge's grownde, into his owne grownde: being in right good healthe, (thankes be given to God!) And here is no other communycacion but of peace, which I pray God sende: as knoweth our Lorde, who preserve your nobell Majestie in helthe and long life, and long to raygn over us with increase of honnor. From Andwerpe, the xxiii[rd] of October, a° 1558.

By your Majestie's most humble
and faythefull obedient subject,
THOMAS GRESHAM, mercer."[v]

"To the Quenne's most excellent
Majestie."

With these three letters, his correspondence during the reign of Queen Mary ceases. She

[v] Flanders Correspondence, St. P. Off.

died a few weeks after they were written,—probably while he was at Antwerp; and a fresh page was opened in the life of Gresham, as well as in that of every other courtier and statesman of the period.

From the peculiar nature of our inquiry, we have been led to consider this portion of history, which the student is accustomed to regard as a period of blood and terror, chiefly in its financial character. The subject of my narrative was absent from England during nearly all this reign; and it is only in letters of a more private description than any of his which are known to exist, that we should find allusions to cruelties, which as an Englishman he must have viewed with indignation, and as a Protestant with abhorrence. It is probable, also, that the Marian persecution affected him only in so much as it brought him into contact with a vast number of intelligent persons, who were driven by the distracted state of affairs at home, to seek for security on the continent; and of whom so many found an asylum at Antwerp. One of these was John Foxe,[w] the martyrologist, who consoled himself while abroad with compiling his laborious *Acts and Monuments:* the biographer of this venerable divine states that Sir

[w] Life of Foxe, prefixed to his Acts and Monuments, ed. 1684.

Thomas Gresham "held him in great account," and frequently made him his alms-giver.

In June 1555, he had a visit from Sir William Cecil, who mentions in his common-place book that he left Calais, in company with Cardinal Pole, on the 3rd of June, on his way to Antwerp, whence he had returned by the 26th of the same month.[x] But besides Foxe and Cecil, great names are not wanting at this period, with whom he may have employed those intervals of leisure, which, fortunately, even the most pressing duties afford. That Gresham delighted to cultivate the friendship, and in the most delicate manner to encourage the labours of literary men, the author of a little work to be hereafter mentioned, expressly assures us from his own experience was the case. There is reason for believing that the celebrated geographer Ortelius was one of the eminent characters whose friendship he enjoyed: and if Richard Verstégan and Richard Rowlands were indeed one and the same person,[y] the author of the *Restitution of Decayed Intelligence* is also to be considered as one of his friends.—Nor must we in this place omit to notice the poet Church-

[x] Lansd. MS. No. cxviii. fol. 89, 91, 78, and 79.

[y] I believe that Sir T. Herbert, who began his Travels in 1626, is the first who mentions the identity of Rowlands and Verstégan.—Travels, &c. ed. 1677, p. 396.

yard, who found a patron as well as an admirer in Sir Thomas Gresham. He mentions the latter in more than one of his poems; and it was he who, many years after, composed the play and pageant for the entertainment of the queen, when she visited Gresham at Osterley. This interesting character was at once a poet and a soldier, and passed many years of his eventful and ill-fated life in Flanders;[z] where, doubtless, his intimacy with Sir Thomas Gresham began. I will presently cite a passage in Low-Country history, which associates the name of the poet with that of our merchant.

Had a more careful life been written of the celebrated Dr. John Caius, co-founder of Gonville and Caius College, Cambridge, we should doubtless have been able to add his name to the list of those who occasionally dignified Gresham's retirement at Antwerp with their society. In 1556, that eminent man published at Louvain a little medical work, which he inscribed to Sir John Mason, the English ambassador at Brussels; and it is not to be supposed that when in the neighbourhood, he omitted to visit his prosperous fellow-countryman at Antwerp. They were both of an age,—had come from the same county,—and studied together at the same college. By a singular

[z] See the Appendix, No. XVII.

coincidence, which Dr. Caius himself records,[a] the one was afterwards engaged in the erection of the college which bears his name, while Sir Thomas Gresham was watching the progress of his Exchange. They were kindred spirits, and must certainly have been friends.[b]

There is also the strongest presumptive evidence that a friendship subsisted between the celebrated painter Sir Antonio More, and the subject of this memoir. They were coetaneans; and their intimacy is clearly referable to a period antecedent even to the appointment of the latter to the office of Royal Agent in 1552,—an office which may reasonably be supposed to have collected around him all who needed a patron or a friend. Gresham sat at least three times to More for his portrait: first, in the year 1550,—which is the date on a painting that used to hang in the common parlour at Houghton, formerly the seat of the Walpole family. Horace Walpole characterizes this as "a very good portrait of Sir Thomas Gresham." It is a half-length, and represents him nearly full face, with his doublet unbuttoned, and both his hands resting on a table,—perhaps a counter. He wears on his head, as

[a] In the MS. quoted in page 46.

[b] For some notices of Doctor Caius, see the Appendix, No. XVIII.

usual, a black cap, and in his right hand holds his gloves; of which latter article of dress, by the way, it may not be improper to observe, that when introduced into ancient portraits, it is intended to denote something significant of the person represented. In proof of the high estimation in which embroidered gloves were anciently held, Stowe relates that when Edward de Vere, Earl of Oxford, many years afterwards brought Queen Elizabeth a pair from Italy, she was painted with them in her hands.[c] I know this portrait of Gresham only from the engraving in the "Houghton Gallery;" the picture itself having been transported to the Hermitage at St. Petersburg, when the collection was purchased by the Emperor of Russia. The engraving is not calculated to convey an exalted notion of the beauty of the original painting, but nevertheless possesses considerable interest.[d]

A second portrait of Gresham by Sir Antonio

[c] Lord Northwick possessed a magnificent portrait of the Earl of Surrey (?) by Titian, who has represented the earl with both his gloves on.

[d] J. B. Michel was the engraver: the print was published in 1779, but the proof bears date a year earlier. The picture is stated to be 2 feet 1 inch by 2 feet 9¾ inches. Mr. Dawson Turner informs me, that in the private estimate given by Farringdon to Lord Orford, on the sale of his gallery, the portrait of Gresham was valued at 40*l.*; but that the value finally affixed to it was only half that sum.

More, is to be seen at Titsey-Park, the residence of William Leveson Gower, Esq. This picture was the property of the Countess Dowager of Northampton as late as 1792; when an engraving of it appeared. The circumstance of its having originally belonged to the Compton family, is not perhaps fancifully accounted for by the residence of the three first Earls of Northampton at Crosby-place,—in the same parish as Sir Thomas Gresham, and immediately opposite his house. This portrait subsequently passed into the hands of G. Watson Taylor, Esq., and was sold at the Erlestoke sale in 1832, for 42*l.* It represents a man of mature age, sitting in a chair, clad as usual in a solemn-coloured suit, with a small cap on his head, and a pair of gloves in his right hand. The engraving by Thew from this picture, does the original great injustice; it was published in 1792, but has since been re-issued, and the date on the plate altered to 1823.

From a third portrait of Sir Thomas Gresham by More, the engraving which forms the frontispiece of the present volume was made by permission of its liberal possessor, Joseph Neeld, Esq., M.P. A minute examination of the original serves to show that the person represented was a favourite subject with the artist, for he has devoted uncommon labour to the work. The face is full of detail, and delicate lights which are no longer clearly distinguishable; but enough remains to impart a high degree of interest and value to the piece. The same sober costume is observable in this, as in all the other portraits of Gresham. In his girdle he wears a dagger, and from it depends an ancient purse or pouch, on which his right hand rests. In his left hand he holds a small object resembling an orange, but which a learned antiquary informs me is *a pómander.*[e] This sometimes consisted of a dried Seville orange, stuffed with cloves and other spices; and being esteemed a fashionable preservative against infection, it is frequently represented in ancient portraits, either suspended to the girdle or held in the hand. There is extant a curious portrait of Bourchier Lord Berners, wherein that nobleman is painted holding a pomander. In the eighteenth century, the signification of this object had become so far forgotten, that instead of pomanders, *bonâ fide* oranges were introduced into portraits,—a practice which Goldsmith has so happily satirized in his *Vicar of Wakefield.*[f]

[e] I am indebted for the information to Sir Francis Palgrave. Some further remarks on this picture will be found in the Appendix, No. XIX.—Concerning *pómanders*, see Nares's Glossary.

[f] "My wife and daughters happening to return a visit at neighbour Flamborough's, found that family had lately got their pictures drawn by a limner, who travelled the country, and took

At Antwerp, then, and frequently in the society of such men as we have mentioned, did Gresham live during the greater part of Queen Mary's reign. Of course his daily companions were men of a different stamp,—merchants of many nations who made Antwerp their home. In order to illustrate the costume of the period, a merchant of our own country, of Flanders, and of Venice, is represented at the commencement of the present chapter; copied from Vecellio's *Habiti Antichi e Moderni*, a book well known for the beauty and spirit of its wood-engravings, which have had the good fortune to be ascribed to Titian. The descriptive part of that work is not without interest. Of our own countrymen the author says, "These merchants do not affect a showy style of dress, but wear useful cloths of various colours: their cloaks are of fine black cloth. They are excellent sailors, and pirates." Considerably different from the English costume was that of the Low-Country merchant; who, to protect himself against cold, worc a fur coat which fell as low as the knee. Beneath, he wore a close vest of rough cloth, secured with buttons, and reaching half-way own his thigh. His head was protected by a cloth cap lined with fur; and his legs covered with

likenesses for fifteen shillings a-head . . . . . . There were seven of them, *and they were drawn with seven oranges*," &c.

hose of chamois leather. In Vecellio's opinion, his breeches, which were stuffed out with cotton, were more useful than ornamental.

We were speculating on the society which Gresham must have enjoyed at Antwerp; and in addition to the names which have been already enumerated, among the Flemings themselves the Schetz and some members of the Fugger family must be particularly mentioned; for these merchants exhibited the rare combination of great wealth, with a passionate love of letters and the fine arts,—unlike Lazarus Tucker, and some other enormous capitalists whose names recur so perpetually in the financial correspondence of this period; who, one fancies, must have resembled in their persons those old men with whom Rembrandt so loved to darken his canvas:—men with grizzled beards and black significant eyes; who hold in one hand a staff, and in the other a money-bag.

"Thus farre," (to use the words of a worthy chronicler[g] on a similar occasion,) "thus farre the troublesome reigne of Queen Marie, the first of that name, (God grant she may be the last of hir religion,) eldest daughter to King Henrie the Eighth."

[g] Holinshed.

MAINAN ABBEY: CLOUGH'S HOUSE IN CAERNARVONSHIRE.

CHAPTER IV.

[1558 TO 1562.]

QUEEN ELIZABETH AT HATFIELD—CHARACTER OF CECIL—CLOUGH'S DESCRIPTION OF CHARLES THE FIFTH'S FUNERAL — FLEMISH AFFAIRS—LOMBARD-STREET—GRESHAM IS KNIGHTED AND SENT TO THE COURT AT BRUSSELS—SPECIMENS OF HIS CORRESPONDENCE—HIS PROCEEDINGS IN FLANDERS—COUNT MANSFELD—SIR JOHN GRESHAM—THE LAND-JEWEL—LETTERS OF GRESHAM AND CLOUGH—THE CUSTOM-HOUSE IN 1561—THOMAS CECIL.

QUEEN Elizabeth's accession was a joyful event to all England. Her youth, and the trials to which she had been exposed, had interested the hearts of the people in her favour; while her well-known attachment to Protestantism, unimpaired by the evidence she gave of a conciliatory disposition towards all classes of her subjects, were forcibly contrasted by the persecution which had marked her sister's reign. The people were not a little rejoiced to find themselves released from the authority of a king who had taken no pains to render himself popular, and who belonged to a nation which they had ever regarded with jealousy and dislike. This was, in short, the epoch from which all who had suffered from the bigotry or caprice of the late queen and her ministers dated the revival of their hopes and honours : for Mary's attachment to Popery had made her overlook the merit of all who entertained Protestant opinions.

Of the number of these was Sir William Cecil, who at the beginning of her reign had been dismissed from the secretaryship, and who had been able to weather the storm which had shipwrecked so many, only by withdrawing from the immediate notice of the court, and taking a comparatively insignificant part in public affairs. But with his characteristic sagacity, foreseeing that the evil could be of but temporary duration, he had taken care in the meanwhile to secure himself in the good opinion of the Princess Elizabeth; and the time had at last arrived when he was to reap the reward of his prudence.

Mary died in London, on Thursday, the 17th of November, 1558; at which time her sister Elizabeth was residing at Hatfield in a state of retirement so equivocal, that it seems scarcely to have merited the name of liberty. Hither, several nobles and leading statesmen immediately repaired, to convey the welcome tidings of a vacant throne, to tender their allegiance, and, on Sunday the 20th, to hold a council, at which Sir William Cecil was appointed principal secretary of state. Indeed it is evident from the papers of this interesting period, that Queen Elizabeth, with remarkable sagacity, entrusted to Cecil the regulation of every thing connected with public affairs, from the very first moment she attained the honours of sovereignty. There are several loose sheets of memoranda in his hand-writing extant, dated November the 18th,[a] (being only the day after Queen Mary's death,) on which he has noted down the heads of matters requiring immediate attention;—memoranda of a character at once so important, comprehensive, and multifarious, that it is impossible to peruse them without surprise and admiration.

The removal from office of Bourne and Boxoll,—Queen Mary's two secretaries, who were also strong papists,—and the immediate promotion of Sir William Cecil, were indispensable acts; and among the few exceptions to the practice wisely

[a] Domestic Correspondence, St. P. Off.

observed by Elizabeth, of displacing as few of the ministers of the late queen as possible. Boxoll's behaviour on the occasion sets his character in a favourable light, and commands our applause: for instead of interposing obstacles to his successor in office, it is clear, from a few of his letters to Cecil dated about this period, that he cherished no sentiment but that of anxiety to afford him all the assistance in his power. He subscribes them in the language of affection—"Your lovinge friend, Jo. Boxoll."[b] One, in particular, dated only two days after Queen Mary's death, calls for notice from the interesting circumstances it reveals. It seems probable from its contents, that

[b] So little is known concerning the history of Secretary Boxoll, that the two following extracts from Queen Mary's Council-book will not be unacceptable. Under the 23rd of September, 1556, we find, "This daye was Mr. Boxall, warden of Winchester College, sworne and admitted *one of the King and Queene's Majesties' Counsell at large;* and as one of the Maisters of Requests, and a counsailor of that corte."—On the 21st of December, the following entry was made: "This daye, Mr. Doctor Boxoll, Archediacon of Ely, was sworne and admytted *one of the Kinge and Queene's Majesties' privie Counsell.*" (MS. in the Council-Office, f. 418, and f. 478.) These minutes, besides their biographical value, lead to the important inference, that to be of the 'Council at large,' and to be of the 'Privy-Council,' were different things; and consequently, that a man might be Queen Mary's counsellor without belonging to the Privy-council. The former phrase seems equivalent in its signification to the term 'Privy-council' at present; and 'the Privy-council,' as used formerly, was what we now call 'the Cabinet.'

Thomas Gresham, when that event occurred, was out of England; and we learn from the same letter, the melancholy and remarkable use to which the great seals, attached to the bonds which he must have been expecting at Antwerp, were applied. His financial occupations in Flanders were of the highest importance, or they would not form the main subject of the very first communication which the late secretary addressed to his successor in office. Boxoll's letter accompanied a number of documents essential to the conduct of public affairs: "the commission made to my Lords now beyond the sea, with their instructions, and all such letters as have been whrytten by the late Queen," &c. "which," he says, "I have put in order, in such sorte as a man coming home in a sharpe fytte of a quarten meight do. You shall receyve also herewith, Gresshames doings towching borrowing of money to the use of this Realme, and the said Quenes highnes late deceased. The letters are in ii packets;—th' one of the last yere, —th' other of this presente. The two Bandes whereof I spake vnto you of, cannot be founde: they were left in the bedde-chambre of the late Quenes highnes, to be signed with her hande; and *at the ceringe of the corse* (*as Clarencieux saieth*) *converted to that use.* They import nothing. . . . . . . You shall fynde," he adds, "in Gresshames lettres wrytten this last October to the Queenes highnes, my Lords of the Counsell, and me, the Marchants names, and the somes of money that are to be conteyned in theis bandes nowe to be maid presently." This letter was written from St. James's, on the 19th of November, 1558, and was delivered to Cecil the same night.[c]

Gresham may have been out of England on the day Queen Mary died; but he cannot have been far off, and certainly lost no time in repairing to Hatfield after that event. As already stated, Cecil was with the new queen on Friday the 18th, which was the day after her predecessor's decease: a single day elapses, and we learn, on the best possible authority, that on Sunday, when the first council was held, Gresham presented himself before Queen Elizabeth, and formed one of the group of statesmen who might be seen assembled at Hatfield on that interesting and memorable occasion. Some years afterwards, in a retrospective mood, he fortunately relates this portion of his history; and supplies us with a characteristic saying of Queen Elizabeth at their

[c] Domestic Correspondence, St. P. Off.—Another of Boxoll's letters in the same glorious repository, is dated "from my howse in Canon Row." Cecil also lived in Canon-row, Westminster, though he was now at Hatfield. How interesting does that narrow little street become in consequence!

interview, which is worth preserving. These recollections were suggested, in 1560, by an attempt which the Marquis of Winchester made to injure him with Queen Elizabeth during his absence; and again in 1563, by a threatened reduction of his stipend: of both which acts of injustice he complained most bitterly to his friend Cecil. "It maye please you," he says, "to be a meane unto the Queene's Majestie for me; and to put her in remembrance of my servisse done this fyve yeres, that she maie have some remorsse upon me,—according to her Majestie's promis that she maid me, before you, at her highness' house at Hatefylde, the xx[th] of November, an° 1558, when her highness came to the crowen: and that was, (upon the dyscoursing how I was handelyd in Quene Maryes tyme for my good servisse,) her highness promised me, by the fayth of a Quene, that 'she wold not onely *kepe one ear shut to hear me;* but also, yf I dyd her none other servize than I hadd done to King Edward her latte brother, and Quene Marye her latte syster, she wold geve me as much land as ever both they did: wyche two promeses, I will insewre your honor, maid me a young man agayen, and caussyd me to entter apon this great charge agayen with hart and courage. And thereupon, her Majestie gave me her hand to kysse it; and I exsepttid this great charge."[d] When Queen Elizabeth promised Gresham that whatever evil reports might at any time reach her concerning him in his absence, she would always keep one ear shut to hear him on his return, she was no doubt thinking of a passage in her own early life; when, under sentence of imprisonment, she had "knelt with humbleness of hart, bicause not suffered to bow the knees of her body," to her sister Mary; imploring her to remember her last promise, that she should never "be condemned without answer and due profe;" adding, "I have harde in my time of many cast away for want of comminge to the presence of ther prince."[e]

Considering that up to this hour the youthful sovereign had passed a life of privacy, which can have afforded her but few opportunities of appre-

[d] On this single occasion, I have taken the liberty of blending into one the contents of two distinct letters;—that of June 29th, 1560, and October 3rd, 1563. (Dom. Corr. St. P. Off.) Queen Elizabeth arrived in London on the 23rd November, 1558.

[e] The original of this extraordinary letter (which has been often reprinted) is preserved among the State-Papers. It is entirely in the hand-writing of the Princess Elizabeth, and must have been written on Saturday, March 14th, 1553–4, the day before she was committed to the Tower. Lord Coke has endorsed it, "Queen Elizabeth, my dear sovereign's letter to Queen Mary, *in vinculis*." (Dom. Corr.) See Ellis's Letters, 2nd Ser. vol. ii. p. 253.

ciating the nature or the extent of the services which Gresham had rendered the state, it seems but reasonable to infer, that although he thus derived his commission as queen's merchant immediately from the queen herself, he was indebted to his friend Cecil for the favourable mention which must have induced that royal lady to accompany his appointment with such distinguishing marks of confidence and favour. Cecil in truth is so mixed up with every public transaction during Elizabeth's reign, that it is as difficult as it would be undesirable to disconnect him from her annals. It was one of the maxims of that eminent statesman, that information, of whatsoever nature, should be sought at the hands of those who, from their particular profession, were best able to supply it:[f] a precept which he illustrated by his own practice, when, looking around him at this critical moment for such as might assist him in guiding the goodly vessel of which he had undertaken the management through the billows, evidently aware of the experience and ability of Gresham, who was about his own age, and had commenced his career at the same time as himself and under the same auspices,[g] he showed himself careful that

[f] Peck's Desiderata Curiosa, vol. ii. p. 35.

[g] For the early life of Sir William Cecil, over which there hangs a veil of mystery never yet withdrawn by his biographers,

the crown should not want so valuable a servant, nor himself so useful a counsellor. Their lives are indeed so intimately connected, that it seems scarcely a digression in this place to sketch the character of "Master Secretary."

To write his history as it deserves to be written, would be to write the history of England during the latter half of the sixteenth century; for no statesman was ever so completely identified with the duties of his office as Sir William Cecil. But this, though it would exhibit a true picture of his daily cares, would by no means convey an adequate idea of the extent of his daily occupations. Besides all business in council, never less than twenty or thirty letters containing domestic intelligence, and an immense number of foreign despatches, (supplying the place of newspapers,) which were sent him from every part of the continent by his numberless spies, and paid or voluntary correspondents,—there never passed a day, during term-time, in which he did not re-

I must refer the reader to a forthcoming work of my kind friend P. Fraser Tytler, Esq. It is enough for my purpose in this place to observe, that Cecil was born 13th September, 1521, (see his Memorandum-book, Lansd. MS. No. cxviii.) and that on the 6th September, 1551, he was appointed Secretary of State by the Duke of Northumberland; who, in the same year, as we have seen, sanctioned, if he did not procure the appointment of Gresham to the office of Royal Agent.

ceive from sixty to a hundred petitions. These he commonly read the same night; and he cannot have allowed himself much time for sleep, or Gresham would not have presumed to send him such a message as the following: "I have commandyd my factor, [Richard] Candellor, to give his attendance apon you every morning, to know your pleasure, whether you will have anything [said] unto me . . . . . Sir, as I have commandyd him to be with you *by* vi *of the clocke in the morning, every morning*, so I shall most humbly desyre you that he may know your present answer; for that I have no man ells to do my business, and to kepe Lombard Streat."[h] His labours were so incessant, and his devotion to affairs so great, that in cases of necessity he cared for neither food nor rest, until he had brought his business to an end. "This industry," says one of his household, "caused his friends to pity him, and his very servants to admire him: and I myself, as an eye-witness, can testify that I never saw him half an hour idle, in four-and-twenty years together."

It is utterly impossible to survey his papers without surprise and admiration. Their multiplicity astonishes,—their variety altogether perplexes one. Nothing seems to have been considered too momentous for him, or too minute. His opinion

[h] Ant. April 18th, 1560.—Fland. Corr. St. P. Off.

was solicited, at one and the same time, respecting the execution of a queen, and the punishment of a schoolboy; the terms of a treaty, and a 'regulation for the lining of slop-hose;' an insurrection in the north, and a brawl in the streets of London. Queen Elizabeth did nothing without first consulting him, and was accustomed to refer even her private suits to his consideration.

We are naturally anxious to become better acquainted with such a man, and to know how it happened that he was able to accomplish so much. We desire to follow him into the privacy of his chamber; to learn how he employed his time *there;* and to be informed whether he found leisure for the sweetnesses of social intercourse, and the endearments of domestic life. A member of his household, who passed twenty-four years under his roof, and must therefore be presumed to have known him well, has supplied us with minute information on most of these points; and left on record so remarkable a character of Sir William Cecil, that we can only feel surprised to hear him generally spoken of as a sagacious statesman, and nothing more.

"After performance of business," says this writer, "(as few men about him were idle,) there were prayers every day said in his chapel at eleven of the clocke, when his Lordship and all his servants were present; for he seldom or never went to dinner without prayers. And so likewise at six of the clocke, before supper: which course was observed by his steward in his Lordship's absence." In truth, this illustrious man exhibited in his daily habits a rare combination of deep piety with great worldly wisdom. For the space of thirty years he was seldom seen angry; never excessively elated by prosperity, or depressed by adverse circumstances. "If the news which his daily letters brought him were good, he would temperately speak of it; if bad, he kept it to himself: but he was never moved with passion in either case. Neither overjoyfull of the best news, nor much daunted at the worst. And it was worthily noted of him, that though his body were weak, his courage never failed; as in tymes of greatest danger he ever spake most cheerfully, and executed things most readily, when others seemed full of doubt or dread. And when some did often talk fearfully of the greatness of our enemies, and of their power and possibility to harm us, he would ever answer—'They shall do no more than God will suffer them.'

"What business soever was in his head, it was never perceived at his table, where he would be so merry, as one wold imagine that he had nothing else to do: and ever, in his ordinary talk, he uttered so many notable things, as one might learn more in an hour's hearing of him, than in a month's reading; so that many came rather to hear his speeches, than to eat his meat. His kindness was most expressed to his children, to whom there was never man more loving or tender-hearted: and (which is ever a note of good-nature) if he could get his table set round with his young little children, he was then in his kingdom; and it was an exceeding pleasure to hear what sport he would make with them, and how aptly and merrily he wold talk with them.

"His temperate mind ever tempered all his actions. If he might ride privatlie in his garden upon his little muile; or lye a day or two at his little lodge at Theobalds, retyred from busynes or too much company, he thought it his greatest greatness and onlie happiness. As to his books, they were so pleasing to him, as when he gott liberty from the Queen to go unto his country-house to take the ayre, if he found but a book worth the opening, he would rather lose his riding than his reading: and yet, riding in his garden and walks upon his little muile was his greatest desport."[i] It is only necessary to visit the

[i] The reader will call to mind, as illustrative of Cecil's love of his garden, the letter already given in the Appendix, (No. XIX,) where he mentions his orange-tree, and expresses a wish to have

delightful picture-gallery of the Bodleian library, to see Burghley pursuing this favourite recreation. No one who has once seen the curious painting to which I allude, can ever forget it.[k]

"It was notable," continues this writer, "to see his continual agitation both of body and mind. He was ever more weary of a little idleness, than of great labour. If there were cause of business, he was occupied till that was done, which commonly was not long; and if he had no business,

some other rare plants sent him from abroad. It appears from the "Epistle Dedicatorie" of Gerard's celebrated "Herball," (fol. 1597,)—a work inscribed to Cecil after he had attained the degree of Baron,—that its author had served his lordship for twenty years. "What my successe hath beene," says he, "and what my furniture is, I leave to the report of them that have seene your Lordship's gardens, and the little plot of my speciall care and husbandrie."

[k] I shall offer no apology for presenting the reader with the two following beautiful specimens of old English correspondence. They seem as illustrative of Cecil's private character, as of Sir Philip Hoby's; and for once show us,—what similar documents so seldom show,—the man instead of the statesman:—

"After my hartie commendacons,—I have taried purposely here in the towne this iiii or v daies longer than I wold have done, bycause I desiered to speke with you; but you come so by sterts, as to-night you are here, and tomorrowe you are gone. I pray you, take your nagge, and come to Byssham; bycause I wold fayne talke with you: but above all other things, I praie you faile not to be there this Christemas, and to bring my Lady with you, to make mery there with a company of our frends,—with whome if you faile, they have promysed to burne you in your house; and I praie you exhort our frend Mr. Mildmay and his wyffe likewise

(which was very seldom,) he was reading or collecting. If he rid abroad, he heard suitors: when he came in, he despatched them. When he went to bed and slept not, he was either meditating or reading."—"At night," says Fuller, "when he put off his gown, he used to say 'Lye there, Lord Treasurer!' and bidding adieu to all state affairs, dispose himself to his quiet rest:" but it would seem as if the 'lord-treasurer' was not so easily to be put off; for Cecil was heard to say, that "he penetrated further into the depths of causes, and

to be there, that the company may be complete. Wherefore, tyll I see you there, I byd you farewell. From the blacke friers, this Twesday morning, departing the towne.

Your owne, as ye knowe,

PHILYP HOBY."

"To the right worshipfull and my very frend, Sir William Cecill, knight."

[Endorsed by Cecil, "22 Nov. 1557;" but Tuesday was the 23rd.]

"After my hartie comendacons,—I have perceived by my brother that you will not be here at Byssham this Christemas, but as gest [guest-] wise; and that my Lady will not then be here with you; all whiche I knowe doth come of my Lady, bycause she cannot leave litell Tannikyn, her doughter. You knowe how longe it is sithens I did enjoie you, and if you now deprive me and this good assemblee of your company at that tyme, I must thinke it so great a synne as cannot be either forgotten now, or forgyven herafter; and in your so doing, you shall be th' occasion why I shall not have here him whome I so moche desire, and to whome I am so moche bound,—namely, Mr. Mildmay and my Lady his wyfe. And yet, for no suche straunge thing, or great chere that here is to be had; but bycause Mr. Mason and my

found out more resolutions of dubious points in his bed, than when he was up. Indeed he left himself scarce time for sleep, or meals, or leisure to go to bed."

It is a curious feature in the character of Sir William Cecil, that notwithstanding the momentous concerns to which he daily and almost hourly devoted his attention, he would suddenly condescend to the most minute and trivial matters. He made an inventory of his wardrobe; kept an account of his daily expenditure; and one day at

Lady have promysed to be with me, who will make us all mery.

"I praie ye, desire my Lady to come, and to bringe Tannikin with her; and I hope so to provide for her and her nourse, so all the house shalbe merie, and she, notwithstanding, at her owne ease and quiete. I looke for no *nay* herunto; but, remembring how long it is sithens we last mette, so long it must be ere we depart after our next meeting, to make amends for that that is past,—and especially at this tyme of the yere. And tyll then, I byd you both farewell. From Byssham, this last of November, 1557. Your owne, as ye knowe,

PHILYP HOBY."

"To the right Worshipfull, and my very frend, Sir William Cicill, Knight. At Wimbleton, or London, or ellswhere." [Dom. Corr. St. P. Off.]

Bisham is a pleasant village in Berkshire, about two miles from Henley-on-Thames. The very ancient manor-house (in which Anne of Cleves had resided) was bestowed, in 1552, on Sir Philip Hoby, who reposes in Bisham church, beneath the same monument as his brother; whose widow (Lady Cecil's sister) wrote their Latin epitaph. 'Mr. Mildmay,' was Sir Walter, the well-known statesman. He was godfather to Cecil's daughter, Anne,

Wimbleton, weighed his wife, children, and servants; carefully recording the result of the experiment in his pocket-book. In the same curious volume there occurs a memorandum, to the effect that on the 7th of August, 1553, he "weighed in his jacket, at Mr. Bacon's house in Thames Street," 131 lb.[1] I think it unfair, however, to charge one who showed himself capable of truly great things, with littleness on this account. The facts alluded to, are rather to be regarded as indications of an extraordinary versatility of intellect, which could as readily descend to a trifle, as

afterwards Countess of Oxford, (the 'litell Tannikyn' of this letter); as appears by the following memorandum in her father's MS. Diary, under the year 1556, [Aug. or Sept. ?] "die Sabati, nocte, int^{r} horā undecimā et duodecimā, in domo mea Wesmonast. in cubiculo prox. Thamesī, edidit in partū uxor mea Mildre- int^{r} hor. 3^{a} et 4ª post meridiē da filiā que postea die lune baptizata nomē suscep. Anna, imponētibus illud Waltō Mildmay, milite, Aña Comit. Pēbrok, Aña Dña Petre." (Lansd. MS. No. 118, f. 91.) The little lady was therefore born in Canon-row; and at this time, we may presume, was about fourteen or fifteen months old.—I trust the foregoing hint concerning Sir John Mason's social disposition, will not be thrown away. Such glimpses of character come so seldom!

On the last leaf of the MS. just quoted, Cecil has made a memorandum that he had received of his wife on the 20th of December, on his "going to Mr. Hobbyes, 10*l.* in gold." So 'litell Tannikyn' and her mother, notwithstanding Sir Philip's affectionate invitation, were left behind. See Appendix, No. XX.

1 Lansd. MS. No. 118, fol. 94–6. The weighing at Wimbleton took place in 1550, when the secretary weighed 136 lbs., and Lady Cecil 122 lbs.—Ibid. fol. 41.

occupy itself with a matter of 'pith and moment.' It has also been objected to his great love of pedigrees and heraldic lore, that it betrayed a want of capacity for something higher ; but this is ridiculous censure. Independent of the ample apology which is to be made for such pursuits, the following extract from a letter of the secretary to his son's tutor, will show in what light Cecil regarded the study of genealogies. (The youth was pursuing his education at Paris). "My desyre is to have hym know the estates and familyes of the nobilite of that realme; in which nature, you know I have here bene dilligent. I wold have hym acquaynted with some herald, *to understand the principall familyes and there allyancies.*" [m] So that the secretary made his works on foreign heraldry, no less than his county visitation-books, subservient to the duties of his office. From the latter volumes, it is well known that he derived that intimate knowledge of the private interests of families, their connexions and condition, which he was frequently enabled to turn to such good account.

The chief point in which Sir William Cecil betrayed a want of greatness, was in his endeavour to make it appear that he was of better descent than he had any real claim to. He was also more

[m] Jan. 12, 1561-2.—Dom. Corr. St. P. Off.

careful of his expenditure, perhaps, than became his high rank and station; but it must be remembered that he began life humbly, and was never a rich man. Nor can I read with satisfaction his deliberate advice to his son Robert,—so full of cold worldly wisdom.[n] Something, I am aware, is to be said in defence even of this; but an apology for Sir William Cecil would be out of place in these pages.

Let me, before resuming my story, borrow a few redeeming passages from the pen of the amiable chronicler already quoted. "To conclude,—he was of the sweetest, kindest, and most tractable nature that ever I found. I have often heard him say, 'I thank God, I never went to bed out of charity with any man.' He was gentle and courteous in speech, sweete in countenance, and ever pleasingly sociable with such as he conversed withal. His piety and great devotion (the foundation of all his actions) was such, that he never failed to serve his God before he served his contrie; for he most precisely and duly observed his exercise of praier, morninge and eveninge: all the time he was secretarie, never failing to be at the Chappell in the Quene's house every

[n] It has been often printed; in Peck's Desiderata, for instance, in Macdiarmid's British Statesmen, and elsewhere. It will be presently seen that Cecil furnished both his sons with a paper of instructions.

morninge, so long as he could go. But afterwards, being by his infirmitie not able to go abroad, he used every morninge and eveninge to have a cushion laid by his bed's syde, where he praied daily on his knees, without fail, what hast or busynes so ever he had."[o] So much for the habits and general deportment of Sir William Cecil, chiefly as they are developed in the pages of one who must have been a very competent judge of both; and who can have had no interest in falsifying the truth, by advancing assertions which any one at the time could so easily have disproved. His public character is matter of history. It would have been more attractive, had his temper been more enthusiastic; and his conduct would perhaps awaken profounder sympathy, did we recognise more frequent indications of that generosity of nature, which constitutes an essential element in all characters of the highest order. But his constitution was less ardent than reflective; and if he was excluded from the privi-

[o] "When he could kneele no more, he had then his booke in his bed; and afterwards, when he could not so well hold his booke, he had one to read to him: so as, one waie or other, he failed not his prayers," &c.—The preceding notices are derived from a curious memoir of Lord Burghley, published by Peck in his Desiderata Curiosa. I have taken the liberty of transposing the contents of that work, selecting the lines and passages which best suited my purpose, from p. 15 to p. 38, (4to. ed.)

leges of genius, let it at least be recorded to his praise, that he was guilty of none of what are called its infirmities.

No sooner was Gresham reinstated in office, than his services were put in requisition. In the beginning of December, 1558, he was despatched to Antwerp, to assure the merchants of that town of the validity of all outstanding obligations; to buy ammunition, and to take up some additional sums; for the repayment of which the city cheerfully gave their bonds. His commission assigned to him, as usual, an allowance of 20*s.* per diem, "and for the time he hath been in the Realme, since his last coming over, 13*s.* 4*d.* by the day: the declaration of the dayes he hath been here, to be taken by his own oathe." On the 23rd, he received a communication from the council, ordering him to take up a further sum; all which he accomplished: and he had returned to England before the close of the year, since we find his servant Clough writing to him from Antwerp on the last day of the month, with a relation of his proceedings since his master's departure.

It was, doubtless, before he took this journey into Flanders,—nay, it can be proved to have been on the occasion of her majesty's accession to the throne,—that Gresham addressed to Queen Elizabeth the very interesting letter on the subject of finance, which will be found in the Appendix. I abstain from giving it a more honourable place, on account of its length; and because it really contains little or nothing that, under one shape or another, we have not already had from the same pen. It is nevertheless a curious and valuable document, and exhibits the merchant at his old occupation, advising the highest personage in the land on a subject which immediately affected the well-being of the state; and which, even by the best informed, was at that time but imperfectly understood. There is something almost patriarchal in the tone and manner of the whole address, wherein Gresham exposes the origin and progress of an evil, which he had made several vigorous efforts to remedy; but in combating which, he had had to contend with private enmities, as well as with the vacillations of court favour. A new page, however, was now turned in his history. The royal lady who had just ascended the throne of her ancestors, had assured him with her own lips of her good opinion and favourable disposition. Once more, therefore, did he briefly expose his views, and sketch what he conceived to be her best line of financial policy; closing his address with these words:—

"An it please your Majestie to restore this your reallme into such estate as heretofore it hath bene, — First, your hyghnes hath none other wayes, butt, when time and opertunyty serveth, to bringe your base mony into fine, of xi ounces fine. And so, gowlde, after the rate.

"Secondly, nott to restore the Still-yarde to their usorped privelidge.

"Thirdly, to grant as few licences as you can.

"Fowerthly, to come in as small debt as you can beyond seas.

"Fiftly, to keep your credit; and specially with your owne marchants; for it is they [who] must stand by you, at all eventes in your necessity."[p]

Of Gresham, we have hitherto spoken chiefly in his capacity of Royal Agent,—procuring military stores for the protection of the country, and negotiating occasional loans to meet the necessities of the government. But this employment, as it did not engross all his time, so it did not engage all his attention. He had been bred a mercer, and had exercised that craft up to the period when he was first employed in the service of the state. For the first year or two, indeed, after his appointment, he found the duties which devolved

[p] See the Appendix, No. XXI. This letter, which has never yet been printed, was found among the Lord Burghley's papers, and came into the possession of James West, Esq., who allowed Ward to transcribe it in MS. into his private copy of the Lives of the Gresham Professors; whence it is here extracted.

upon him of so pressing a nature, that he did not hesitate, as he expressed it, "to forsake his own trade of living, for the better serving of his majesty:" but the necessity for so doing was not permanent. Throughout a considerable portion of Mary's reign, as we have seen, Gresham pursued his original avocations in Flanders: and thus, under Elizabeth, after a few years we shall find him resuming his ancient practice at home; having confided the future management of his affairs in the Low Countries to Richard Clough, a Welchman, whom he left behind him at Antwerp, and in whose zeal and ability he reposed entire confidence.

This interesting individual belonged to a family which had been settled from an early period in North Wales, but which first acquired eminence in his person. His father, Richard Clough, was of sufficient consideration in Denbigh (where he followed the trade of a glover) to become allied by marriage to two families of worship;—the surname of, I believe, his first wife was Holland; and his other wife was a Whittingham of Chester. He survived to so great an age, that he obtained the epithet of *hên*, or the old; and left by these two ladies eight children, of which, if my authority is to be trusted, Richard was the fifth.[q]

[q] Harl. MS. 1971. f. 95.

In his early youth, says Fuller, he was a chorister in the cathedral of Chester, where "some were so affected with his singing, that they were loath he should lose himself in empty air, (church musick beginning then to be discountenanced,) and perswaded, yea procured, his removal to London, where he became an apprentice to, and afterwards partner with, Sir Thomas Gresham." [r] In this last particular, Fuller was quite mistaken; for Gresham, writing from Antwerp in 1553, (one year after Clough had come into his service,) speaks of him as "my factor that is here resident,—whose name is Richard Clough;" and Clough, in his last will, calls Gresham his master, and styles himself 'servant;' which in that age was not considered a term of degradation, since in the same document Clough mentions his own brother by the same name: but the confidence and friendship of Sir Thomas he certainly possessed, and while in his service, contrived by his industry and ability to amass a large fortune. He must have been accounted a man of great consideration, for as will be seen in the sequel, he married into a family of high distinction. I reserve for a subsequent page, however, what is discoverable of his personal history; there being no evidence, traditional or otherwise, of the events

[r] Worthies, &c., vol. ii. p. 594.

of his early life, except the indubitable fact that in the fervour of youthful zeal, he performed a pilgrimage to Jerusalem, where he was created a knight of the Holy Sepulchre,—"though not owning it," says Fuller, "on his return under Queen Elizabeth, who disdained her subjects should accept of such foraign honour." Pennant and other Welsh writers have, in consequence, styled him *Sir* Richard Clough, by which name he is known at this day among his descendants. However dissimilar the opinions he entertained, his strong religious impressions he probably inherited from his mother, the daughter of a Whittingham of Chester,—that family having been distinguished, as it is well known, for their adherence to a party, "whose indiscreet zeal," in the words of Isaac Walton, "might be so like charity, as thereby to cover a multitude of errors:" but who nevertheless set an early example of schism in the church, when they established themselves under John Knox, Miles Coverdale, Christopher Goodman and others, at Geneva, in the year 1555.[s]

Clough's pilgrimage to Jerusalem does not rest, as has hitherto been believed, on Fuller's

[s] Livre des Anglois, MS. 1555–1560: of which the writer possesses a transcript by Sir E. Brydges. The original of that very interesting record is preserved among the archives of the State of Geneva.

authority alone; but is mentioned by himself in a letter which will be laid before the reader immediately, though unfortunately in such general terms as not to enable one to fix the date of the event. Sandys, the traveller, gives the following account of the order of the knights of the Sepulchre, which was instituted by a king of France in the year 1099: "None were to be admitted if of a defam'd life, or not of the Catholicke religion. They are to be gentlemen of blood: and of sufficient meanes to maintaine a port agreeable to that calling, without the exercise of mechanicall sciences. . . . . . . They take the Sacrament to heare every day a Masse, if they may conveniently. If wars be commenced against the Infidels, to serve here in person; or to send other in their steads, no lesse serviceable: to oppugne the persecutors of the church; to shunne unjust warres, dishonest gaine, and private duels: lastly, to be reconcilers of dissentions, to advance the common good, to defend the widow and orphane, to refraine from swearing, perjury, blasphemy, rapine, usury, sacriledge, murder, and drunkennesse: to avoid suspected places, the company of infamous persons, to live chastly, irreprovably, and in word and deed to shew themselves worthy of such a dignity. This oath taken, the *Pater guardian* laieth his hand upon his head, as he kneeleth before the entrance of the Tombe: bidding him to be loyall, valiant, virtuous, and an undaunted Souldier of Christ and that holy Sepulcher. Then gives he him the spurs, which he puts on his heeles; and after that a sword, (the same, as they say, which was Godfrey's of Bullein,) and bids him use it in defence of the church, and himselfe, and to the confusion of Infidels. Sheathing it againe, he girts himselfe therewith: who then arising, and forth-with kneeling close to the Sepulcher, inclining his head upon the same, is created by receiving three stroakes on the shoulder, and by saying thrice, 'I ordaine thee a Knight of the holy Sepulcher of our Lord Jesus Christ, in the name of the Father, the Son, and the holy Ghost.' Then kisses he him, and puts about his neck a chaine of gold, whereat hangeth a Jerusalem Crosse: who arising, kisses the Sepulcher, and restoring the aforesaid ornaments, departeth." [t]

Sandys speaks of the order in its original and intended purity; but he describes a scene which Clough must have witnessed, and in which he was, doubtless, a performer. "They bare five crosses gules," he adds, "in forme of that which is at this day called the Jerusalem Crosse; representing

[t] Sandys' Relation of a Journey begun A. D. 1610, &c., fol. 1627, p. 159.

thereby, the five wounds that violated the body of our Saviour." This emblem occurs on the seal of Sir Richard Clough, represented in the wood engraving which immediately precedes my preface. He appears to have adopted it as a merchant's mark,—R icardi C lough S ignum being probably the words indicated by the initials which compose his cypher. The entire device suggests the idea, that in adopting it, he meant to show that his whole heart was under the influence of the Cross.[v]

Of this Worthy it is no slight thing to say, that he is to be clearly individualized, though nearly three centuries have elapsed since he quitted the

[v] See some ingenious observations on merchants' marks in the Rev. E. Duke's Prolusiones Historicæ, page 82.—Before the suggestion hazarded in the text is rejected as fanciful and improbable, it must be considered that a pious spirit is more conspicuous in the domestic observances and habits of our ancestors, than in our own. A Scripture posy was the common ornament of a chamber: it was found on a ring; or occurred as the heading of a letter. To speak of commercial matters,—there are many little religious formulæ now fallen into disuse, which once prevailed universally; and show that a more religious feeling animated our ancestors, than is fashionable with their descendants. '*Laus Deo*' was once the usual heading of every page of a merchant's journal. When goods were sent to some foreign port, the bill-of-lading, as it is technically called, invariably stated that they had been 'shipped, *by the grace of God*, in and upon the good ship,' called by such a name. A policy of insurance against sea risks, still begins with these words,—'*In the name of God*, Amen:' and up to a late date, all commercial appointments were made '*God willing*.'

scene; during which interval, few have cared to write concerning him, or to interest themselves in his history. Enough it is presumed has been stated, to reconcile the reader to the following lengthy extract from one of his letters written at this time to Gresham, who had now returned to England; if not for Clough's sake, it will be perused with interest at least for the historical value which attaches to his theme,—namely, the funeral of the Emperor Charles V.[w]

The letter is dated January 2nd, 1558–9. It begins with a few commercial details; states that Clough had already written on the 31st December, and received his master's letter of the 28th, from Dunkirk,—"wherein were letters of the Queene's Majesty to be sent to Strasbourg to one Doctor Mount, Doctor in the Lawe; and a letter of credit for 100*l.* for the said Doctor

[w] By the liberality of Mr. Thomas Thorpe, bookseller, I have had an opportunity of examining a rare and curious quarto tract in Italian, bearing the following title: *Descritione delle esseqvie svperbissime celebrate per la morte del inuitissimo Carlo Quinto Imperadore. Alla corte del serenissimo Re Filippo suo Figliolo.* M.D.LVIIII. Dated *Di Bruselle, li* 30 *di Decembre,* 1558. The account given by this nameless author corresponds very nearly with Clough's narrative; but each furnishes us with some particulars which the other has omitted. In the ensuing notes, I will supply from the Italian writer what seems deserving of preservation; and occasionally shall be enabled, from the same source, to correct some of Clough's statements.

Mount." Then he mentions how "my Lorde of Ely" had pressed him at Brussels for a loan of 200*l.*, to which he had at last acceded: "so that having done with my Lord of Ely, I came to Andwerpe, where I founde my Lord Cobbam, and have paid to him the 120*l.* and geven myne attendanse appon hys Lordesheppe for such service as I colde do; whome ys a very gentyll and sage young Lord,—wishing that wee had many such in England. . . . . Syns my coming from Brussells," he continues, "I have received and shipped Sir John Mason's cheste of books, in the ship of Antony Pettersone of Andwerpe. It ys markyd with your marke . . . . . I have allso shipped Sir John Mason's wagon,[x] with all things pertayning thereunto, in the ship of Henryke Cornelyssone of Andwerpe; wherein there is both harness for the Queene's Majestie, and part of your copper." After this, Clough proceeds as follows:—

"The next day after your departyng, I went to Brussells aboute suche matters as you gave me

[x] Before coaches were invented, *a wagon*, (or, to speak more correctly, a species of carriage so called,) was the vehicle commonly used by the highest classes. [See infrà, page 305.] In the year 1583, the day after Lady Mary Sidney entered Shrewsbury in her wagon, "that valyant knyght, Sir Harry Sidney, her husband," made his appearance in *his* wagon; "with his Troompeter blowynge, verey joyfully to behold and see."—Nichols' Progresses, vol. ii. p. 309.

commyssion to do, as afore [stated] in this my letter: where, att my beyng there, I saw the beryall of the late Emperoure Charles, whiche begane the 29th of the last month, and duryd 2 days. The order whereof was partly as here after followith.

"Fyrst, in the court [of the Palace] there was no grett seremonies of mourning, saving [that] over the court-gate hangyd about 6 yards of blacke clothe: and in the midst of the clothe, the whole bredth of the vellvet; whereon hangyd the armes of the Emperoure, paynted upon a tabel. And the lyke hangyd before the dore of the great halle within the court.

"From the courtt to the markett, or fish mart, and so from thence to the head church called Saint Golls [Gudule's,] the streets were relyd [relaid?] on bothe the sydes of the streete,—all blacke: and along those relaies, stode of the burgh of the town in black gowns; the one distant from the other about 1 fedone: and in every of their hands, a torch of wax with the Emperoure's armes uppon them, which might be in number about 3000 torches.

"The church was hangyd all with blacke clothe; and above the cloth, the brede [breadth] of a vellvett round about the churche; whereon were made fast many scutcheons of the Emperoure's armes.

"There stoode in the middell of the church a fayre herse, which was coveryd above with clothe of golde. But, by reson the candellsteks whereon the candells stoode were so thicke and blacke, the cloth of golde was lytyll persevyd; whereon myght be, by estymasyon, about 2500 candells, or 3000 att the most. But rownd about the church there stoode wonderfull many: and under the herse, the chest or coffyn for the corse, coveryd with blacke clothe.

"The berying begane about 1 of the clocke,[y] or there aboutt; and [the procession] came all out of the court in order as hereafter followyth.

"First, there came viii of the gards, all in blacke.

"After them, the schoolmaster of the towne, and all hys skollers; all in white surplessys.

"After them, the 4 orders of freres, all in copes, vestyments, and tynacells; savyng 2 of every order that went before in their owne apparell. And in every of their hands, a wax candell; which were a great many in number.

"After them, all the prysts and clerks in the towne; in copes, vestyments, and tynacells, as the freres were.

"After them, 28 or 30 Spanysh prysts, all in copes; and after them, xv abbotts, all in myters

[y] Two o'clock in the afternoon, says the Italian writer.

of golde, or syllver and gylte; set with perle and stone.

"And next after, iiii Beshopes; all in myttes [mitres] of clothe of sylver. The Beshop of Arras went alone: and after him folowyd the Beshope of Luke,[z] [Lucca,] and on either syde of hym a Beshope.

"There was carryd before the Beshope of Luke, a pese of cloth of golde, as if it had been an aulter-cloth; wyche was holden by the other two Beshopes. Whereon he put one of hys hands, and blessyd with the other.

"After them, came 200 poore men in black gownes, and hoodes on their heds, hanging over the faces; and in every of their hands a torch of wax, with the arms of the Emperoure uppon it.

"After them, the Lords and offysers of the towne of Brussells: all in black gowns, to the number of 80.

"After them, the masters and offysers of the artylery, in black gowns, to the number of 40.

"After them, the lords and offysers of the fynance; being in number 28, all in black gownes.

"After them, the Chanseler, the Judges, and offysers of the chancery; in number 60.

[z] The Italian says, the Bishop of Liege; who chaunted the mass, and performed all the religious rites connected with this ceremonial.

"After them, 24 poursuyvants of the King, in black gowns; with the badge upon their brests.

"After them, 120 of the King's household servants in gowns, beyng all Duche men; and after them, 30 Spanyards of the King's offysers.

"There followyd them, 35 of the King's pages, all in black coats, and rownd capps of cloth.

"Next after them, 40 gentylmen of the state of the Dowke of Savoye.

"After them, 50 Spanyards of the order of Saint Jago, and other orders that they have in Spayne; with white and red crossys.

"After them, 3 knyghts of the sepoulture, with the crosse of Jerowsalem uppon their brests.

"There folowyd them, 2 in black; carrying, either, 2 of the Turks drums, coveryd with the Emperoure's armes.

"After them, 12 trompetters with flags att their trompetts, with the Emperoure's armes; whereof, the grownde of the flags gold, and the egle black.

"After them, 2 nobellmen carryed two standards; 1 of Saint Androo, and the other of the fyre stalle.

"After them, a gentyllman caryed a hellmett.[a]

[a] Clough has here omitted a part of the pageant; but the 'gentyllman,' was Mons[r] de Luli, who carried the emperor's helmet with large black plumes, at the extremity of a black wand.

"Next after that, came a Shippe, about 24 foot long, or by estymasion, of the burthen of 20 tons, whiche was exsedyngly well fashyoned;[b] and costyly graven or carven, and gylted, as here after followyth.

"This shippe was carried as if [it] had been in a sea; which was so made, and paynted as if it had been a sea indeede. The shippe went in the streets by strength of men that were within it, and no man [was] seen.

"There stode in the sea before the shippe, 2 strange monsters; whom had either a brydell or coller about their necks, where unto was made fast a cord of sylk: being fast unto the shippe and unto them. So that it seemed that they had pullyd the shippe forward. Uppon the shippe, from the watter to the shrowds, were paynted all the voyages and victorys that the Emperoure had done by watter. The sea wherein the shippe went, [was] stuck full of banners of the Emperoure's armes, standyng upright; and amonxt them, many banners of the Tourks and Moores, fallen down and lying in the watter. All the shrowds, or upper part of the shippe, was costyly carven and gylte: the shrowds and masts, sails and tops, all black.

[b] This remark does credit to Clough's taste, for the Italian writer says that the ship was "simile alle antiche."

"Rownde about the sterne of the shippe was paynted all the armes of the kingdoms whereof Charles the Emperoure was kyng.

"Above, in the shippe, it [was] stuck full of banners of all the countries whereof he was go vernor.

"There was made in the midst of the shipe, after the maine mast, a stoole of estate; whereon satt no man.

"In the fore part of the shippe satt a mayde; all clothyd in browne, and in her hand an anker.[c]

"Before the stoole of estate satt an other mayde, all clothyd in white; and her face coveryd with white lampors.[d] In her right hand a red crosse, and in her left hand a chalice, with the sacrament.[e]

"In the after part of the shippe stode 1 other mayd,[f] all clothyd in red, and in her hand a hart brannyng [burning]: and at the mayne mast hangyd a stremer, with the picture of the crowsyfyxion: with many other stremers.

[c] This was Hope, "che pareva che tutta lieta volesse dar fondo, e pigliar porto."

[d] A Dutch word, equivalent to the English 'tiftany,' or 'tiffany,' which is very thin silk. *Met een hangende lamfer*, (or *lamper*): *with a tiftany hanging from the hat.*—Dutch Dictionary.

[e] This female personified Faith.

[f] This was the personification of Charity. According to the Italian, she seemed to steer the ship.

"And uppon the 2 sydes of the shippe was writyn these 2 versys, whiche you shall receive here inclosyd.[g]

"Thys was the proporsion of the shippe. But there were many more matters about that shippe, wherein I wyll not molest your mastershippe withal at this tyme; lest I shuld be too tedyus with that I have already wrytten.[h]

[g] Clough's letter contains them not; but they are supplied, by the Italian narrative, as follows. On the right,—

"Successus neque te Cæsar spes certa petiti
Destituit, donec de littore solvit Ibero,
Neptuno sternente viam, et tritonibus undis, [?]
Auspiciis veneranda tuis, transque æquora vecta
Religio tandem auriferis allabitur Indis
Luce nova irradians mersas caligine mentes."

On the left was written:

"Non auri sitis, aut famæ ambitiosa cupido,
Non scæptri persuasit honor tot adire labores;
Humani sed te generis pia cura coegit
Navibus ignotas investigare per oras
Quas ✠ sacra populos Christoque dicaras."

"Qui manca un verso," says the Italian writer; and the English reader will probably think that something more important still is wanting, in the last line especially.

[h] Some of the particulars which Clough has omitted, merit a brief notice. At the stern of the ship was a large square frame of black cloth, covered with inscriptions in letters of gold; which set forth, that under the guardianship of the last-named Virtue, the emperor, sailing over the stormy sea of life, had gained so many countries, unknown before his time, and imparted to each the light of the Catholic religion. For the numerous allegorical paintings and mottoes which were presented in addition by this curious pageant, see the Appendix, No. XXII.

"After the shippe, followyd 2 peles [pillars] of plousse houlltre [plus ultra] standyng in a sea as the shippe dyd, and drawn as the shippe was, by 2 monsters. On the topp of one of the peles was a close crowne; and uppon the other, a crown Imperyall.[i]

"After thatt, came 24 horseys, all coveryd with the armes of the countries whereof Charles the Emperoure was prynse: the trappyngs very coustyly gylllte, and stayned; being most, taffeta and satten.

"And before every horse went either an Erle or Duke, who carryed a standarde with the armes of the country that the horse following dyd represent; the horse being coveryd with the same armes, and the saddel, of the colors of the country; some white, some red, some green, and some blewe. As also, every horse had a great bunche of fethers in his hed, of the same colors. And on either syde of the horsys went a gentyllman leding of the horses, all in black: having, either, a long cord of black sylke in their hands, which was fast unto the bytt of the horse.

[i] It will be remembered, that the arms of Spain are represented on Spanish dollars between two pillars, inscribed with the words PLUS ULTRA; whence the term *pillar dollars*. On one of the pillars introduced into the pageant, according to the Italian writer, were written these words: *Herculeas* [?] *sumpsisti signa columnas*. On the other, *Monstrorum domitor temporis ipse tui*.

"Thys followyd, first, 21 horsys after the same order: but so far as I could perseve there was no horse for any Erledoms, but only Dukedoms and Kingdoms. There was the Dukedom of Brabant, Gellderlande, Bourgony, and Houstenryke; and 6 or 7 kingdoms of Spayne, as Castil, Aragone, Granada, &c. The kyngdom of Syssely, Nepolls, and Jerowsalem, with dyvers more that I dyd not well know, to the number of 21.

"After them, came 1 horse which presentyd the Emperoure's personne; being coveryd with clothe of golde with the armes of the Empire, whereof the covering or capparisons were very short.

"And after that, came 1 other horse coveryd with cloth of golde to the grownde, which stoode lyke unto the gentyllwomen's vardygalls [farthingales]; whereon was very costly imbroyderyd the Emperoure's armes: which horse represented the Emperoure.

"And after that, 1 other horse coveryd all with black to the grownd, with 1 great red crosse upon hym. These horses were led as the others were: and before these 3 horses, dyvers great standards or baners [were] carryed by nobellmen.

"After them, 5 nobellmen, which carryed the armes of the kyndoms coustyly graven and gilte, in small shields; whereof 4 of them went by two and two together. And the fyrst came, after, alone; carrying the armes of the Empire aloft, with the hellmett over it. And before these 5 men, were carryed the standard of the Empire,[k] with dyvers other standards.

"After them came dyvers heralds of armes, with their cote-armors on.

"After them came dyvers of the counsell, and 2 with great maces of sylver and gylte, or else golde.

"After them, the Emperoure's cote-armore: and after that 2 heralds of the egle.

"After them, the Duke Dalle [D'Alva,] with a black reede or staff in hys hands, typpyd with silver, as head-stewarde: and on either syde of hym, a nobellman with 2 staves, somewhat shorter than hys.[l]

"After them, the Prince of Orange carryd the sourde with the poynt downewards. And after him, the Erle of Swarsembourch [Schwartzenberg] carryd the Emperoure's collar of SS uppon a black cousshyne.

"After him, an other Lorde (whom I dyd not know) carryd the worlde and the septore: and

[k] The accounts do not correspond as to the particulars of this portion of the pageant; but we are told that the great standard of the empire was carried by Count Policastro.

[l] These were the Marquis dellas Navas, and Count Olivares, the king's stewards.

after him, Don Antony de Toledo carryd the crown Imperyall.[m]

"After him, the king of Heralds, or grefere of the Fleece, (beyng clothyd all in cloth of golde, bare heddyd,) carryd the great collar of the Fleece, with a white rod in hys hand.

"And after him came the King's Majesty [Philip,] all in blacke; clothyd in a long robe, and a hoode uppon hys hedd. On the ryght hande of hym went the Duke of Arons, a Spanyarde; and on the left hand, Duke George of Brownswick:[n] either of them held up the King's robes before. And after hym, another Duke of Spayne[o] carryed up the King's trayne.

"After the King came the Duke of Savoye, mournyng as the King dyd; havyng a hoode on hys hed; but he carryd his trayne himselfe. And after him, all the Lords of the order of the fleece, with their collers about their necks; and after them, the rest of the Lords of the Councell.[p]

[m] Perhaps it may not be deemed a waste of time and space to mention the offices assigned by the Italian writer to these great noblemen. According to him, the Marquis d' Aghilar carried the sceptre: the sword, glittering with jewels, was borne by the Duke of Villahermosa; and the globe by the Prince of Orange: while Don Antonio de Toledo carried the Imperial crown, which was covered with large pearls and the costliest gems.

[n] The Dukes of Brunswick and Artois, according to the Italian authority. [o] Ruigomez.

[p] For a further extract from the Italian narrative, see the Appendix, No. XXII.

"Thys was the order of the fyrst day, how they went to the church, where the King tarryd tyll about 5 of the clocke; and so returnyd back again, the same way, with all his offysers; not havyng neither the prysts, Bishopes, nor horses; saving only hys owne trayne. And the next day came the King's Majesty to the kyrke, with the same state that he dyd the other daye: I meane all in blacke. But there was neither the horsys, shippe, sorde, nor crowne, saving all in black; which was about 10 of the clocke: and beying in the kyrke, I dyd all that I could to have seene what was done there, but I could not. Their horses were offeryd then at the masse, and all the armes taken off them, and given to the church.

"And the service being done, there went a nobellman unto the herse, (so far as I coulde understand it was the Prince of Orange,) who standing before the herse, strucke with the hand uppon the chest, and sayd,—"He is ded." Then standing styll awhyle, he sayd—"He shall remayne ded." And then, resting awhile, he strucke again and sayd,—"He is ded, and there is another rysen up in hys place greater than ever he was." Whereuppon the king's hoode was taken off: and as I dyd lerne at others that were there, the King went home without his hoode. But I could not tarry so long to see it, because I had promised my Lord Cobham to meet hym the next day, in the morning, at Andwerpe.

"Thys was the ordre of the buryall of the Emperoure, so far as I could carry away; but and if I myght have tarryd till the next day, I wolde have had all their names that carryd the standards before the horses. It was sure a sight worth to go 100 myles to see it! Notwithstanding I have seene at Venice, (as I went towards Jerusalem,) a more number of pepel go at the buryall of one of the Synyory of Venice, (according to the order as they use them,) the lyke of thys I think hath not been sene. The Lord give his soul rest!"[q]

Clough had resided so long at Antwerp, that, as the reader must perceive, he had acquired the minuteness of a Dutch painter. Whenever he took up his pen, the spirit of one of the old chroniclers seems to have inspired him; so that, although according to his own confession he had perhaps only two or three days before sent Gresham an account of his proceedings 'at large,' it was nothing uncommon for him to cover ten or twenty sides more of foolscap paper with the description of a pageant, or some other subject involving long details, in which he delighted.

[q] Ant. 2nd Jan. 1558-9.—Flanders Corr. St. P. Off. Clough subscribes himself, "Your Mastersheppe's *Apprentis*."

Like Dogberry, he "could find it in his heart to bestow all his tediousness upon your worship." "My servant," said Gresham, in a letter written about this period to Sir William Cecil, "is very long and tedious in his writing."

Clough, however, was adequate to the discharge of all the duties which ordinarily devolved upon his patron at Antwerp; and it was only in transactions of more than usual moment that he ever required assistance. In the mean time, he corresponded with regularity and prolixity; and Gresham, who had been living in London since the preceding Christmas, was daily in communication with the secretary, aiding him with his co-operation and counsel, and occupied with the discharge of his financial duties. These form the subject of his letter to the secretary, dated the 1st of February, 1558-9; wherein he apologizes for troubling his friend with written details on subjects which he was accustomed to discuss orally. "I wolde have wayttid upon you myselfe with all these things, but it hath pleasyd God to visitte me with a Agew, which tooke me on Satturday last; having usid a littil fyssike for the reamedy thereof, trusting the worst is past." On the 11th he writes "I wolde have waytid upon you myself, but that my late sickness will not yet suffer me."[r] Were it not for

[r] London, 2nd Jan. 1558-9.—Fland. Corr. St. P. Off.

such ephemeral causes, and Cecil's habit of preserving every written paper which he received, we should have been almost without any of Gresham's correspondence during his periods of residence in England.

The following letter, which he addressed to Sir William Cecil in London on the 1st of March, 1558–9, is nearly the last of the kind with which the reader shall be troubled. It would not be right to omit a curious document from Gresham's pen, so illustrative of the financial arrangements of his day; though, for the reader's sake, I wish it could have been a little more entertaining.

"It maye like your honnor to understande, that xxx M *li.* sterling, aftyr xxiij *s.* iiij *d.*, makyth flemyshe xxxiiij M viii C xxxiij *li.* vi *s.* viii *d.* [34,833*l.* 6*s.* 8*d.*]; [a] and aftyr xxii *s.*, (as the exchange now goythe in Lombarde Streat,) xxxiij M *li.*: wych ys the halfe of the Quene's Majestie's detts that be owing in Aprill and May next. And for the payment thereof, and for keeping uppe of the Exchange, the Quene's Majestie hathe none other wayes and helpe but to use her Merchant adventurers. Wherein I doo right well knowe they will stande very stowte in the matter, by the reason of this new costome; as also for the xx M *li.* that her Hyghnes doth owe

[a] So in the original, but evidently a miscalculation.

them. Nevertheless, considering how moche yt doth import the Quene's Majestie's credit, of force she must use her Merchants; and for the compassing thereof, her highnes shall have good opportewnity both to bargayn and to bringe them to what price her Majestie and yow shall think most convenient; as the like proof was made in Kinge Edwarde, her late brother's time.

"First, yt is to be considered that our Inglishe marchaunts have at the least l or xl M cloths and kerseys lying upon their hands, reddy to be shipped; whiche they will begynne to ship, when they shall knowe to what poynte they shall trust for their custome.

"Secondly, this matter must be kept secreat, that yt maye not come to the marchaunts knowlege that you do intend to use them; and to laye sure wait when their last daye of shipping shall be, and to understand perfectly at the customers' hands, at the same day, whether all the cloths and kerseys be entryed and shipped and water-borne. And being once all water-borne, then to make a stay of all the fleete, that none shall depart till further the Quene's Majestie's pleasure be known.

"Thyrdly, that being once done, to comande the customer to bring you in a perfect book of all such cloths, kerseys, cottons, lead, tynne, and all other commodites, and the marchauntes' names;

particularly what nomber every man hath shipped, and the just and total sum of the whole shipping. And thereby you shall know the nomber, and who be the great doers.

"Forthely, apon the view of the customers' booke, you shall send for my Lord Mayre, Sir Rowlond Hill, Sir William Garrat, Sir William Chester, Mr. Alldyrman Martynne, Mr. Alldyrman Baskefylld, Lyonell Dockat, William Bowrde, Rowland Heywood, Waltyr Marller, Harry Becher [and] Thomas Ryvet: and move unto them that, 'Whereas you have shipped to the number of A, B, wyche be ready to depart to the mart, so it is that the Quene's Majestie ys indetted in Flandyrs for no small some; for the wyche, yow, my Lorde Mayre and the cytty, do stand bownd for the payment thereof. And for that yt shall apere unto you that her highness ys not unmyndful for the payment of the same, [she] hath thought good to use you, (as heretofore King Edward her brother dyd): whereby the Exchange may be kept up and raised, and to inrich this realme of fine gold, here to remain; as likewise we maye have our commodities, and forrayne, at some reasonable prices. Whereby you merchants maye flourish in the commenwell, as heretofore you have done. And for the accomplyshment of the premises, the Quene's Majestie dowthe requyre at your handes to paye in Flanders xx *s.* sterling upon every cloth that ys now shipped, after the rate of 25*s.* flemysh for the pownd sterling; and her highnes shall paye you here again at double usans. Which sum must be paid in Andwerpe; the one thyrde part the fyrst of May,—one thyrde part the 20th of May,—and the other thyrde parte the last of May.'

"Upon the utterans hereof, they will grant to nothing, till that they havé assembled the Company together. Now, having all their goods in the Quene's power, there ys no doubt but that her Majestie shall bring them to bargayne at such reasonable price as you and the rest of my Lords shall think convenient: wherein you may quallify the price of the Exchange as you shall think most meetest, whereby they may [be] the better willing to serve hereafter; considering how much the Quene's highness is indebted unto them alreddy. Giving your honnor to understand I doo not so much press upon the great price, as I do at this present to bring them to make offer to her higness to serve at some reasonable price.

"Finally, you maye not come lower than to have for every pound sterling, xxii *s.* Flemish, (for so the Exchange passith at this present). Butt I trust yt will be at 22*s.* 6*d.* ere they have fynyshed their shipping. Advertising you, yf the exchange be better in Lombard Street than 22*s.* in any wise, to make them paye aftyr that rate; or ells they do no service, but for their own lucar and gayen,—wiche in no wise I will not have them accustomyd unto at the Quene's Majestie's hands.

"To conclude, eftsoons, yf you can bringe them to 22*s.*; and, yf the Exchange be better, according as the Exchange goeth to pay there, at the days aforesaid, and here at double usance, (which ys two months;) it wolle prove a more benyfycyall bargayn to the Quene's Majestie and to this her realme than I will at this present molest you withall; for it will raise the Exchange to a onnest price. As for exsampell: the Exchange in Kinge Edwarde's time (when I beganne this practisse) was but 16*s.* Dyd I not raise it to 23*s.*, and paid his whole detts after 20*s.* and 22*s.*? wherby wool fell in price from 26s. 8*d.* to 16*s.*, and cloths from lx *li.* [60*l.*] a packe to xl and xxxvi *li.* a packe, wythe all other our commodities, and forrayners': whereby a nomber of clothiers gave over the making of cloths and kerseys. Wherein there was touched no man but the Merchant, for to serve the Prince's turn; which appeared to the face of the world that they were great losers; but to the contrary, in the end, when things were brought to perfection, they were great gainers thereby.

"Fifthly, what bargayn soever yow do conclude with the Marchants, to remember specially that they doo paye their mony in vallewyd money, (otherwyse termyd permissyone money); for that the Queene is bounde to pay yt in vallewyd mony: wyche maye not in no wyse be forgotten. For yt may chansse to coste the Queene iii or iiii *li.* apon every hundred pownds, to come by the vallewyd money,—soche scarsetty there ys thereof: wyche, in the sales of our commodytes, wolle cost the marchants nothing; for that they may sell their commodytes to pay in permyssione money for the some they shall paye for the Quene, wyche wolle not be xx*s.* permyssion money upon every cloth. Which matter, move not to the Merchants until such tyme as you have bargayned and agreed upon the Exchange; that being done, yt maye not be forgotten."[t]

I will not pause to offer any remarks on this letter: but in order that the progress of my narrative may be distinctly kept in view, think it as well to remind the reader, that since the period of Queen Elizabeth's accession in November 1558, four months had not yet elapsed; during which period, namely, in the month of December, Gresham had made a short excursion to Flanders. It

[t] London, 1 March, 1558-9.—Fland. Corr. St. P. Off.

was now March 1559, and he was required to visit Antwerp again.

His Instructions, which are dated the 5th, direct him to postpone the payment of a moiety of the queen's debt beyond seas, for a period of six months; and to obtain from King Philip, (who remained in Flanders for some time after Mary's death,) a passport which might enable him to carry into England two hundred barrels of saltpetre. Gresham's first letter from Antwerp, after his arrival, is dated the 21st of March. He there relates the impediments he had encountered in the fulfilment of the second part of his commission; to which the Duke of Savoy, Philip's favourite general, chiefly opposed himself. But on the 3rd of April he writes, that having continued till that day urging his suit at Brussels, it had been at last freely granted by the king: and he recommends that Queen Elizabeth should send "three or four of her best ships of war that are out, for the sure waifting of this munition and armour." The next instructions he received were, to put over, if he could, for three or six months the money owing to the merchants by the queen; and if he found this impracticable, to take up money in order to pay her creditors. This was on the 10th of April; soon after which, Gresham returned to London.

A few months more elapse, and we find him commissioned to retrace his steps into Flanders. His Instructions, of which the original rough draft in Cecil's hand-writing remains among the State Papers, bear date the last day of August, 1559. Gresham is there ordered to take with him from London 10,000*l.*; and with it to pay, in part, the most urgent of the Queen's creditors at Antwerp. The remainder of her debt, he was ordered to prolong for three or four months; with an understanding, that in case of need the queen would make a further payment of 30 or 40,000*l.* Furnished with these instructions, he left England, probably about the middle of September; but the first authentic evidence of his arrival at Antwerp, is his own letter of the 3rd of the following month.

Plentiful as the letters of Sir Thomas Gresham are, many more have disappeared than have been preserved to us. Such as remain, written during his present journey, relate almost exclusively to the progress he was making in collecting and transporting military stores. His last letter, which is dated the 29th of October, states that he had written on the 16th, the 22nd, and the 23rd instant; mentions the names of the creditors whose claims he had in part satisfied; and informs Cecil that the writer was only waiting for the queen's bonds, in order to be able to return home.

We will suppose Gresham restored to his family and friends in London, in the beginning of November 1559, and take leave of him for a brief space; for, having followed him up to this period of his career, it seems desirable to take a cursory view of the contemporary state of public feeling in Flanders,—a country with which, through his agency, England was in those days so intimately connected. A few remarks on this subject seem also to be naturally suggested by the emperor's death, which of itself constitutes an epoch in Low-Country history. The ceremony so minutely described in a preceding page, severed the last connecting links, as it were, between that illustrious man and a people who seemed capable of flourishing only under his sway.

It has been already observed, that the remote cause of the troubles which subsequently distracted the Low Countries, seems traceable to the national jealousy which from the beginning subsisted between the inhabitants themselves, and the Spanish settlers; who, as common subjects of the Emperor Charles V., went at an early period to reside in immense numbers at Antwerp, Brussels, and the other principal towns in Flanders. Discordant as these elements were, common interest, the strongest bond, perhaps, which connects society, kept both nations in some degree united; and the prudent and conciliating rule of the emperor enabled them to forget their mutual differences, and live together for awhile as members of one large family. The consequence of this harmonious state of things was so advantageous, that in about half a century Flanders attained the highest pitch of commercial greatness; immense wealth poured into the state on every side; and, as a necessary consequence, it was not long ere the elegant arts felt the cheering influence, experiencing here a greater degree of encouragement and support than was accorded to them elsewhere.

But notwithstanding this flattering picture, with the abdication of Charles V. the clouds which, as already stated, had occasionally darkened the horizon, began to assume a more threatening aspect, and to give indications of an approaching storm; while more active causes of excitement than national jealousy were not wanting to aggravate the feelings of either party, and accelerate the impending crisis. Philip, to whom the Flemings were but little attached, seems to have taken every step in his power to alienate yet further the affections of the people whom he had to govern; and this, at a time when the latter, by a long series of commercial successes, had acquired that impatient sense of independence which, when uncontrouled by loyal, and above all by religious principle, is sure to lead to mischief in a state. Had the king been wise, he would have conducted himself towards his Flemish subjects in a conciliatory spirit; but he set their prejudices, civil and religious, openly at defiance, and lived surrounded by Spaniards, who had his ear, and influenced all his councils. Granvelle, the ambitious and unpopular Bishop of Arras, was his especial favourite; and it is perhaps to the general ill-will which the intrigues of this proud prelate occasioned, more than to any other cause, that the subsequent Low-Country troubles are more immediately to be traced and attributed. Gresham repeatedly mentions him as being "hated of all men."

The present, moreover, was a remarkable juncture in the history of northern Europe: England, Germany, and France had for a long time been agitated by religious dissensions; and the rancour of party feeling, which still raged with unabated violence both at home and abroad, unsettled men's minds, and disseminated an unquiet spirit. Flanders, which was then what England, or rather what London is now,—the centre of wealth and civilization, necessarily felt the effects of this in an eminent degree; and the multitude of discordant elements of which that little state was composed, contributed to render it yet more susceptible of the evil influence.

Were we to adhere strictly to a chronological arrangement of our materials, it would be indispensable, before proceeding further, to recur to Gresham, whom we parted from in London about the close of the year 1559. But before so doing, we shall take leave to draw on his subsequent correspondence for a few passages illustrative of the history of the country where he passed so many years of his life; and then proceed more systematically with our narrative.

His letters occasionally supply us with notices of the state of religious feeling in Flanders: though, being unfortunately only incidental, they are also generally very brief. One may be cited, which is rather amusing. "The vyllayne fryer," he says, writing to Sir William Cecil concerning a certain preacher who had indulged himself by too freely promulgating his opinions, "the vyllayne fryer that so unreverently preached agaynst the Queen's Majesty, dare not for his life come abroad, for that the commons will dispache hym. Here be many papist knaves of our nacion, and it is thought that some of them hath sett this fryer a-worke. I shall hearken further of this matter, and as I can come to any knowledge, I shall advertize you."[u] A few days after, he says, "The fryer that so unreverently preached against the Queen's Majesty hath made a meane to Lazarus Tucker, to speak to me for to move the Company[v] that a might safely go abrode without danger of hurting; whome is sorry, as he saythe, for *that* he hath said and preached: in the which matter I will not meddill,—trusting ere that it be long, yf a doo come abroade, a shall be well bastanadoed; yf a doo escape so."[w] "The vyllayne frier" was, next week, "commanded to Brussels." A better example might perhaps have been adduced of the religious excitement then prevalent, but the personal danger incurred by the preacher, and the species of chastisement anticipated for him in the preceding passage, sufficiently indicate what must have been the temper of the times. The Queen of England was in fact very popular, not only with the English Factory at Antwerp, but also with the native inhabitants of that city. At the very juncture of which we are speaking, a

[u] Ant. April 16th, 1560.—Fland. Corr. St. P. Off.

[v] The English Factory or Company of Merchant-Adventurers, established at Antwerp.

[w] Ant. April 19th, 1560.—Fland. Corr. St. P. Off.

rupture with England seemed so probable, that the authorities of Antwerp deemed it necessary to explain to their fellow-citizens what had been their motives for the line of conduct which (under Philip's directions) they had pursued towards England; a step on which Gresham makes the following comment to the secretary: "Sir, as this ys but a cloke for the rayn, onely for to sattisfy these commens here, so I trust the Quene's Majestie wolle forsee all thinges: for the commens of this lande take this matter here the undyrfullest [wonderfullest] against the King. And they protest, that if there shulld come anny breach of war, seurly the States of this lande will never consent thereunto. . . . . . I am creadibly informyd that the Prince of Orange hathe secreatly practissyd in Brabant and Holland to come, pressently, (att the commens' hands,) by some great masse of money; and the Counte of Egmont like-wyse, in Flandyrs: but the commens will grant to none. Assuring your honnor, here ys sych a breute and sich a rewmer amonges the commens, as it ys wonderfull; and specially att this town. I wold never a belevyd they hadd borne so good will to the Quene's Majestie and the realme."[x]

While such an unsettled state of public feeling

[x] Ant. 21st April, 1560.—Fland. Corr. St. P. Off.

prevailed, the king was obviously acting a most imprudent part when he outraged the prejudices of the whole body, or took a step which was likely to give umbrage to any influential section of the community. Inconsiderable at first sight as such a ground of complaint may appear, he aggravated his unpopularity to an extraordinary extent, especially with the lower orders, by retaining in Flanders a body of 4400 foot soldiers, after the peace of Château-Cambresis was concluded; which, as his wars with France were then at an end, rendered so large a force unnecessary. Philip had dismissed all the rest of his army, but this veteran band of Spanish soldiery he still retained; to the great offence of the Flemings, who viewed with extreme jealousy so unequivocal an indication either of distrust on his part, or hostile intentions. They complained bitterly that these troops were burthensome, insolent, and rapacious; and their frequent complaints at last elicited a promise that they should be removed from the country. But their dismissal was delayed from month to month, until the grievance was made a subject of general complaint throughout the states. At last the king promised that they should be removed at the end of four months. In the mean while, he himself, on the 26th of August, 1559, took his departure for Spain,—whence he never more returned.

He left behind him a people irritated and exasperated against his countrymen to the last degree. The national jealousy which had always subsisted between the natives of Flanders and the Spanish settlers, inflamed by mutual injuries, (though the Spaniards seem generally to have been the aggressors,) had now assumed so serious an aspect as daily to threaten a collision. Every circumstance susceptible of an injurious interpretation, was immediately invested with that character: and when the term fixed for the departure of the 4400 soldiers had expired, the old complaints against them were resumed; and their dismissal demanded so loudly, that the Duchess of Parma, whom Philip had left regent of the Low Countries, procured their removal to Zealand, in order to their final departure.

Gresham's letters for a considerable period make such particular mention of this force, that its movements must obviously have been regarded as a matter of general interest, and no slight importance. He sent a spy into Zealand to observe the aspect of affairs in that province,[y] and communicated the result of his watchfulness

[y] T. G. to Sir W. C., Ant. April 18th, 1560.—Fland. Corr. St. P. Off.

periodically to the council. "I trust from tyme to tyme to sertiffye you the certainty of the quantitie of their preparacions; of how manny shippes of war, how many vittallers, how manny souldyers [they consist]: and prinsypally, to geve you to understande by what tyme they wilbe reddye. And for the better and surer intelligens, I have sent presently one into Zealland, to hym that haythe the charge thereof. As allso I have sent one Waddington, (our counttryman and a man of experyence,) into Zelland, to vissit all havens [and] portes, for the quantitie of shipes, and what preparacione of shipes of war they doo prepayre; as also vittallers, sowldyers, and ordenans; and in what tyme they will be in a reddyness: and there to remayn till that I doo geve hym forddyr order."[z] Two days after this, we learn that his emissary had returned from Zealand, stating "that all the vittals for the provission of the 4400 Spaniards were arrived out of Holland;" and that seven ships, concerning which Cecil had written, were "in a reddyness to depart." Gresham immediately sent his messenger back "for the better advertisement of all things."[a] This was in the latter end of April,

[z] T. G. to Sir W. C. Ant. April 18th, 1560.—Flanders Corr. St. P. Off.

[a] April 20, Ibid.—In this letter the ships and their appointments are enumerated.

1560; but we find that the troops in question had not arrived in Zealand by the early part of May. Gresham writes,—"The sayd sowldyers tarryeth for the payment of their wagis. They saye here that the Regent ys come hether for the dyspache of them, and for money matters; as allso to macke new governors of this towen. The tyme shall lern me forddyr, and so shall I advertize. I have not bynne wyth the Regent, nor will not, till that I have some occasion of acces: nor licke wysse to the Bishop of Aras."[b] In the course of a few weeks however, appearances became very warlike. 'Eight ships, newly vittled,' filled Gresham (whose *doer* was still keeping watch in Zealand) with apprehensions lest the Spanish soldiers should be suddenly transported into Scotland to aid the French.[c] Next month he writes to Sir Thomas Parry,—"The 4400 Spaniards be yet in their garrisons: but the saying is here now, they shall shortly depart. The eight ships in Zealand do still remain in a rediness to receive them in."[d] But Schetz assured his friend, (and he had the best means of knowing,) that the soldiers in question were destined to be sent back to Spain, and that the eight ships were to be otherwise armed:[e] the accuracy of which infor-

[b] May 7, 1560.—Fland. Corr. St. P. Off. [c] May 29.—Ibid.
[d] June 24.—Ibid. [e] June 29.—Ibid.

mation was fully confirmed by the sequel; for though rumours continued to prevail of the northern destination of the obnoxious soldiery,[f] they were ultimately ordered home by the Duchess of Parma, on her own responsibility; an act for which the King of Spain never forgave her.[g]

Granvelle, Bishop of Arras, has been already mentioned as a most unpopular character, who nevertheless enjoyed in an eminent degree the favour of King Philip. When that monarch retired into Spain, Granvelle remained behind in Flanders; and by his insolent and imperious bearing soon incurred such deep hatred, that the first noblemen of the country conspired against him, and vowed to effect his ruin. His ambition had procured for him a cardinal's hat; and intoxicated with power and pride, he had the rashness to assume towards the leading members of the state an air of haughty superciliousness. His name frequently recurs in Gresham's correspondence; and always in connexion with something indicative of his great influence, or of his unpopularity. Speaking in one of his letters of the regent, who had come to Antwerp attended by a great train of nobles and gentlemen, he says, "I do intend as tomorrow, to present myself to kisse her

[f] July 10, 1560.—Fland. Corr. St. P. Off.

[g] VanderVynckt, Hist. des Troub. des Pays Bas, vol. i. pp. 96–114.

handes, and to byd her haultesse welcome to this town: as like wyse the Bishop of Arras, *who governs the Regent and all the Councell*."[h] In 1563, Gresham writes,—"The Cardenall kepes the courte, and the prince of Orrange ys at his howse of Brydarre, and the Countie of Egmont ys at his charge in Flanders, and all nobellmen at their howsses; *and cannot brooke the Cardenall's procedings by no meanes*."[i]

His luxurious and extravagant mode of life was one of the circumstances which gave particular offence to his enemies. On a certain occasion, when a distinguished party of Flemish nobles and gentlemen were assembled at dinner at the house of our old friend Jasper Schetz, Lord of Grobbendonc, the conversation happening to turn on this subject, and especially on the bad example set by the expensive liveries worn by the servants of the unpopular ecclesiastic, Count Egmont declared that his own servants should appear in future clad in a plain livery of common grey cloth. The whim was so well relished, not only by the assembled guests, but by the other inhabitants of the town, that all the tailors in Brussels were scarcely able to produce solemn coloured suits with sufficient celerity to meet the

[h] T. G. to Sir W. C. Ant. May 3rd, 1560.—Fland. Corr. St. P. Off. [i] To the same, Oct. 3rd, 1563.—Ibid.

sudden demand. But the offensive circumstance connected with this fashion was, that on the loose sleeve then worn by servants, fool's caps were embroidered, and more frequently still, a cardinal's hat; which made it clear to the vulgar that Granvelle was satirized by the grotesque attire which had so suddenly come into fashion. To put the question still more completely out of doubt, pasquinades were circulated, and satirical verses reflecting on the Cardinal held him up to popular obloquy and derision. Some of these pasquinades Gresham seems to have sent over, for a specimen is preserved among the State-Papers of the period: and Clough, in one of his letters, thus alludes to Count Egmont's frolic,—if so ill-natured a freak deserves the name. "I wrotte you by my formalle letters of a lyverye [which it] was sayd the nobellmen wollde geve, and that their badges shuld be foolls' hedds; and nowe, as I understande by dyvers that come from Brussells, most of the nobellmens pages do wear that lyvery, made with smalle foolls' hedds on bothe the sydes of the sleve; and in the myddyst, a grete fooll's hede, with a cardynall's hat uppon yt. Thys ys declaryd here by some that have sene them; and wryttyn of abrode into all plassys, and not well lykyd by them that are wyse; for that they doutt that smalle gudness will follow."[j] These anticipations proved perfectly correct; but to show this, would be the province of the historian, rather than of the biographer. Our narrow limits forbid any thing beyond this cursory notice of an event which made more noise at the time, both in Flanders and in Spain, than seems credible. Nor must we at present delay ourselves any longer with the individual who had so large a share in fomenting the troubles which afterwards became so celebrated, and led to the memorable results to be noticed in a subsequent page.

Some time before affairs had come to this pass, indeed soon after Philip had quitted Flanders with a view to taking up his abode in future in Spain, it was resolved by Elizabeth's ministers to send an ambassador-resident to that court: and Sir Thomas Chaloner, who had hitherto represented this government in Flanders, was selected as the most proper person to fill that important post; both on account of his long experience, and his personal acquaintance with most of the individuals with whom he would have to deal. England remaining thus unrepresented at the court of the Duchess of Parma, (regent of the Netherlands,) Mr. Gresham was furnished with letters of credence, and directed to repair to her

[j] Mar. 3, 1563-4.—Fland. Corr. St. P. Off.

grace at Brussels in the temporary capacity of ambassador. It was on the occasion of this honourable and important mission, and precisely when he was preparing to enter upon the duties which it entailed, that the honour of knighthood was conferred upon him: for though in the Instructions which which he was furnished preparatory to his departure (bearing date the 20th December, 1559,)[k] he is termed 'esquire,' the knightly style is observed in an official document under his hand, which was written on the 23rd of the same month.[l] The reader will scarcely require to be reminded that this was a distinction in that age, to which a similar honour at the present day is by no means equivalent.

At this period, Sir Thomas Gresham resided in Lombard-street, which was then the handsomest street in London;[m] and, like all other bankers and merchants living in that street, he kept a shop. It stood on the site now occupied by the banking-house of Messrs. Stone, Martin, & Co., and over his door was his crest, a grasshopper, by way of sign. This was no uncommon practice even at a later period; for we are told that the sign of the house in Bread-street, where Milton's father resided, and where Milton was born, was

[k] Flanders Correspondence, St. P. Off. [l] Ibid.

[m] Hentzner's Travels, 8vo. 1797, p. 31.

the spread eagle,—an heraldic symbol, which appears in the family arms. The original sign of Gresham's shop was seen by Pennant, and I am informed continued in existence as lately as the year 1795; when, on the erection of the present building, it disappeared from the station which it had so long occupied over the door: its metallic value having probably aroused the cupidity of some of the labourers. But the term *banker*, when applied to a former age, is so likely to produce misconception, that before proceeding further, it seems advisable to explain it.

A banker in early times pursued a very different trade from that which occupies the attention of the opulent and influential class so called at the present day. It is well known that the latter derive their profits from the employment of fluctuating sums of money, deposited in their hands for convenience and safety by the public; and for the security of which, the respectability of the banker is a sufficient guarantee. But this is a refinement of comparatively recent introduction, with which our forefathers were wholly unacquainted. As late as the time of Swift, bankers gave and took a bond on receiving and lending money; and made their profit by obtaining a higher rate of interest, or usury as it was called, on the latter operation, than they allowed on the former. Ten or twelve *per cent.* was the customary rate of interest during the reign of Queen Elizabeth; at which period, we mean no disrespect to the banker when we say, that he united in his person the trades of the usurer, the pawnbroker, the money-scrivener, the goldsmith, and the dealer in bullion. A German traveller who visited England in 1593, says, that he saw in Lombard-street "all sorts of gold and silver vessels exposed to sale, as well as ancient and modern coins, in such quantities as must surprise a man the first time he sees and considers them."[n] At the period of Gresham's death, a considerable portion of his wealth consisted of gold chains. It is a curious circumstance that Lombard-street should have retained its character as well as its name for at least five centuries and a half: and it may not perhaps be out of place to mention, that within the last thirty years several gold and silver lace-men lived there; a link between the ancient and modern occupants of the street, which has now almost wholly disappeared.

The earliest money-dealers in England were the Jews, a people proverbial among us to this day for their riches; and who, if they behaved as extortioners, were certainly treated as such by our early monarchs, and became in turn the objects

[n] Hentzner's Travels.

of every description of hardship and ignominy. To them succeeded the Lombards,—by which general appellation the early Italian merchants of Genoa, Lucca, Florence, and Venice were designated.[o] They obtained a footing in this country about the middle of the thirteenth century, and established themselves in Lombard-street: making it their business to remit money to their own country by bills of exchange,[p] which was found particularly useful by the Italian clergy, who were thus enabled in an easy manner to receive the income of their transalpine benefices. In spite of the prejudices which at first obstructed their reception, they by degrees acquired a firm footing; and in process of time, became the richest merchants and the greatest money-lenders in the kingdom. In the early part of the fifteenth cen-

[o] Hence, as might be expected, a number of commercial terms have crept into our language of Italian derivation. Debtor and creditor, for instance: cash, from *cassa*, the case or chest where money was kept: usance from *usanza:* bank and bankrupt, from *banco* and *banco rotto:* journal, from *giornale:* the abbreviations for *liri*, *soldi*, and *denari;* and the often recurring *ditto*, which should be spelt with an *e* instead of an *i*.

[p] Macpherson (p. 367) gives instances of general letters of credit, as early as the year 1200. Mention is made of *literæ cambitoriæ*, or negotiable bills of exchange, in an instrument bearing the date of 1364, (Rymer, vol. vi. p. 495). In 1400, bills were drawn in sets, and worded exactly as at present. (Macpherson, p. 614: and see Beckmann's History of Inventions, vol. iii. p. 430.)

tury they advanced a large sum for the service of the state, and had the customs mortgaged to them by way of security.

We have already in some degree explained the nature of the business pursued by these early goldsmiths, or, as they are sometimes called, bankers; and pointed out wherein their operations differed from those of bankers at the present day. The transition period was about the reign of Charles the First; "until which time the whole and proper business of London goldsmiths was to buy and sell plate, and foreign coins of gold and silver; to melt and cull them; to coin some at the mint, and with the rest to supply the refiners, plate-workers, and merchants as they found the price to vary."[q] In the time of the subsequent troubles, merchants and tradesmen, who before had entrusted their cash to their servants and apprentices, found that practice no longer safe. Neither did they any longer dare, on account of the distresses of majesty itself, to use the Mint in the Tower as a place of deposit. They now began to lodge their necessary cash in the goldsmiths' hands, for the sake of greater security. This was in the year 1645, when goldsmiths first exercised both professions; and Pen-

[q] Anderson, vol. ii. p. 402; who quotes from a scarce pamphlet on this subject.

nant, writing in 1790, says that even in his day there were several eminent bankers who kept goldsmiths' shops. The first regular banker was Mr. Francis Child, goldsmith, who began business soon after the Restoration.[r]

In Lombard-street, then, at the sign of *the grasshopper*, dwelt Thomas Gresham; and I beg the reader will not lose any of the respect he may have conceived for him, on being informed that he was a banker such as I have described, as well as a mercer and merchant-adventurer; and that he kept a shop. All the trading community at the time did the same; and a banking-house is technically called *a shop* to this day. But after he was honoured with knighthood, he must have begun to look out for some other place of residence, and to think of leaving his house in Lombard-street to the care of his apprentices: for we are told that such an abode was considered unfitting the dignity of a knight. Sir Baptist Hickes, (afterwards Viscount Camden,) a great mercer in the reign of James I.,[s] was one of the first citizens who, after knighthood, kept a shop: on which account, Stowe's continuator informs us that he was remonstrated with by the aldermen, who seem to have expected that he would have altogether

[r] Pennant's London, ed. 1790, p. 361.

[s] Stowe's Survey, ed. 1720, book i. p. 287.

relinquished his trade when he obtained his title. I am not prepared to say how it may have been with Gresham; but conclude, from the letters of business which subsequently passed between him and his apprentices,—dated respectively Gresham House, and *London*,—that his connexion with Lombard-street did not cease with his knighthood. He began, however, as I have already hinted, to think of removing to some more aristocratic locality; and fixed on Bishopsgate-street, where after a year or two a mansion arose, to which he gave the name of Gresham House. I shall have occasion to recur to this edifice hereafter, and therefore dismiss the subject for the present. Sir Thomas Gresham had been appointed English ambassador at the court of the regent of the Low Countries; and we will now follow him thither in his new capacity.

He acquitted himself in the discharge of the duties of an office, which, though not altogether strange to him, was more exalted in its character than any which he had yet filled, with his accustomed ability and success: for by frequent communications with Chaloner, who did not take his final departure until the 4th of February following,[t] he became thoroughly prepared for all

[t] The event obtains particular notice in Cecil's Diary; viz. "4 Feb. 1559-60. Sir Thomas Challoner, Ambassador with the

he had to encounter in his new vocation. This accession of dignity, however, brought with it no accession of leisure, but the contrary: for the duties of an ambassador were now superadded to those of queene's merchant. On the present occasion, for example, he was commissioned to take up for the space of a year, and transport to England, the sum of 200,000*l.*: to send over the remainder of the armour and stores in his custody, (making a present of about 500 crowns to the officers of the customs, in case any serious difficulty should arise in that quarter, and interfere with the transportation of those important commodities); and he was further ordered to purchase 500 shirts of mail.[v]

After a month passed in Antwerp, he returned home in the beginning of February, 1559–60; but it was only for a few days; since, on the 25th, we find him taking his departure from London, and writing as follows to Queen Elizabeth. "It may please your most excellent Majestie to understand, that for the better profe to your highness for the conveyance of such bullion and gold as I shall provide for you, I have sent you this letter enclosed in the stone-worke; being no small comfort unto

Duchess of Parma, revoked, and Sir Thomas Gresham left agent with her." (Murdin's State-Papers.) Some of Gresham's correspondence with Chaloner is preserved in the State-Paper Office.

[v] See the 'Instructions' referred to in note [k].

me that I have obtained to the knowledge thereof, for the better conveyance of your treasure. Which thing must be kept as secretlie as your Majesty can devyze; for yf it should be known or perceived in Flanders, it were as much as my life and goods were worth."[w] From which we may presume, that he had discovered some extraordinary mode of conveying to England with secrecy the treasure he was commissioned to procure in Flanders: and the present being a farewell letter, he commended the Lady Gresham to Queen Elizabeth in these words: "I shall most humbly beseeche your Highness to be a comfort unto my poore wife in this my absence in the service of your Majestie."

On the same day he addressed Cecil from Gravesend, as follows:—

"Right honnorable Sir,

"It maye like you to undyrstand, that this morning I met upon the Thames with letters from my factor Rychard Clowghe, which I sent you by my factor Richard Candiller: wherebye you maye perceve the great scarsity of monny upon the burse, and what ado there is. As likewise, what advertisement the Regent hath out of Ingland of such munition and armour as hath beene sent

[w] London, Feb. 25, 1559-60.—Fland. Corr. St. P. Off.

home. I shall most humbly desire you to geve great charge to Mr. Blomefield for the secret receiving up of the fyne corryne powder[x] that dayly shall come from thense, and of all such other matters as I shall likewise send: and that there may be no more of my things entered in the Custome-House, wherebie any serchers or suche knaves might come to the intelligens. . . . . Sir, you shall do well that the Queene's Majestie dothe use the staplers for XV or XX M *li.* [15 or 20,000*l.*,] as you have used the Merchaunt Adventurers: wyche they doo stand in much dought that they must needes serve. For that your honnor shall understand that, two dayes past, bothe the Mayre of the Stapell, (Mr. Offley,) and my Coussyn Marshe, spake to me to be good unto them, to be a meane unto the Queene's Majestie that they shuld not serve at this instant.—You shall do well to give the attempt, and to demand XXX M *li.* although you doo take but halfe. . . . . I praye you to send me the chiffer [cypher] by your next."[y]

Gresham's next letter is from Dover, dated the 26th. It is addressed to the secretary, and contains a memorandum of all that the writer foresaw

[x] *Corn* powder is a strong kind of gunpowder, which is manufactured in *corns;* being less finely granulated than 'serpentine powder,' of which a definition is given elsewhere.

[y] Gravesend, Feb. 25.—Fland. Corr. St. P. Off.

he should require in Flanders, as bands [bonds,] &c. &c. On the 28th he writes from Dunkirk, where he had arrived at eight o'clock the same morning, after a fair passage; observing, "At this instant I received a letter from Sir N. Throckmorton, directed to Sir T. Challoner and me, which I send you here inclosed."

His first letter on arriving at Antwerp mentions the personal danger which his commission obliged him to incur:—"The great breute that runs upon me that I will rob them [the Antwerp merchants] of all their fine gold and silver: by the reasone whereof, I will insure you I am half afrayde to go abrode, but onely at the owres of the burse tyme. I am credibly informed that the merchants (Spanyards and Italians) dothe pretend to put a supplication up to the Regent against me."[z] The letter which contains this passage is long and curious, but we cannot afford to delay ourselves with further extracts. It is worth mentioning, however, that enclosed within it was a letter to Queen Elizabeth from Sir John Legh, which letter remains among the State-Papers: but nothing further is deducible from its contents, than that the writer was apprehensive of her majesty's displeasure, and that he sought to recommend himself to her favour-

[z] Sir T. G. to Cecil. Ant. March 8, 1559-60.—Fland. Corr. St. P. Off.

able notice by the communication of Flemish state intelligence.

Again we follow Gresham back to London: having the customary evidence of his presence in the great city,—a letter to Sir William Cecil, written on the eve of his departure once more for Flanders. He requests the secretary to give his servant 'the licence for the twelve tons of beer that he had obtained for him; and also to let him have the licence for my Lady Dormer, and Mr. Clarencieux for their abode there; in order that he might have the carrying over of the same.' This was the last letter Gresham wrote from London for a long period. From the beginning of April 1560, until the month of March 1561, he resided almost permanently in Flanders; and from the numerous letters he addressed to Sir William Cecil, Sir Thomas Parry, and Queen Elizabeth during that interval, the extracts which we shall next lay before the reader will be made: or if we have occasion now and then to draw on a letter written in 1559, it will only be in order that the extract thus obtained may have its full value, and be better understood.

Let us first advert to the state of public feeling in Antwerp, when Gresham returned to that city in the spring of 1560. This was a subject of which he always took such a view, and concerning which he always made such remarks as the nature of the charge with which he was entrusted might lead us to expect from his pen. After assuring Cecil how unpopular King Philip was in the Low Countries, he invariably adds some *financial* intelligence; such as the reduced state of his resources, pecuniary and military,[a] and the bad odour in which he grew with the people of Flanders. Certain commissioners, he says on one occasion, came from the court at Brussels, for the purpose of obtaining a subsidy of the inhabitants of Antwerp; but the common council of the town having secretly assembled for the purpose of deliberation, the members resolutely determined not to grant any supplies.[b] The wealth of the New World, however, more than once came most effectually and opportunely to the relief of the Spanish nation. "Here is letters come from Sevill," writes Gresham at last, "advertising that there is arrived at Calles malles [Cadiz,] 8 ships from the Indyas, ladyn with 4 millions of fine gold and silver; and that King Phillip hath for his part 1 million. As likewise they do look for 4 ships more; wishing, for my part, it were all in the Quene's Majestie's coffers, or in the Exchequer."[c]

[a] April 18, 1560.—Fland. Corr. St. P. Off.
[b] April 25.—Ibid. [c] April 30.—Ibid.

What must have conduced in no slight degree to promote the bad understanding which it is obvious existed between the Spanish monarch and his Flemish subjects, was his restless spirit, which kept them in a state of a perpetual anxiety and ferment. "On the 17th of this instant," says our merchant, writing to Sir William Cecil from Antwerp, (April 18th, 1560,) "I ressevid your letter of the xiii^th, wherbye I persseve that Kinge Phillipe's preparacione ys now apparaunt to the Quene's Majestie, for the ayde of the Frenche Kinge to subdew the Scotes; whereof our merchaunts, and other, had intelegens as sone as I hade. So that here ys soche adoo amonges our nacione, and other, for to preserve one another, as it ys undyrfull [wonderfull,] and the most parte of all the merchaunts of this towen be rydden to Barrowghe,[d] to content and paie themsellffes with our comodittes: and some be gone to see an if they can sett over the Quene's Majestie's bondes to our company for cloths and kersses; for that all men fere here that the Regent wolle macke some soddeyen arrest,—wyche newes hayth astonnyd all nacions. So that now the Quene's Majestie's credit ys at a whole steye, and all the nacion's. The procidings of King Phillippe ys nothing lickyd: I praye God torne all things to

[d] Bourbourg, as already explained.

the best."[e] The next day, what had hitherto been merely matter of apprehension, was currently reported as matter of fact: "At this instant, here ys newes come that all Dutch shipes and hoyes shulld be arrestid at London; wyche doghtless wolle causse us all to be arestid here, owght of hand."[f]

The unsettled state of affairs in Flanders, coupled with a degree of uncertainty as to what hostile steps circumstances might induce King Philip to take, was doubtless in part the cause why Gresham was commissioned, about this period, to purchase military stores to so large an amount, and forward them to London. The progress he was making in the fulfilment of this object forms, in fact, the theme of all his letters during a considerable time; for his operations, which were conducted upon an immense scale, not only gave full occupation to himself, but also to the numerous agents who were constantly employed in his service in different parts of Flanders and Germany. In every letter he enumerates how many "corselets, dags, and handguns" he had been shipping, besides saltpetre and sulphur; until at last, weary with the slow progress he was making, he begs to be allowed to adventure military stores to the value of 3,000*l.* on one bottom from Hamburg,

[e] Fland. Corr. St. P. Off. [f] Ibid.

(from which port he says that in his day *not more than ten ships sailed in the course of the year.*)[g] "And for that [which] ys all reddy at Hamborrow, I wold I were abill to persuade the Quene's Majestie and yow that it myght pleasse her highness to bere iii M *li.* venttor in a shippe, for the speaddy dispache of yt; whishing to God it were aryvyd at London in saffetye: for that the like masse ys not to be gotten together for no treassor, and spessially harness, salte petter, and sullpher. Sir, I wrote yow in my last of the great scarssite of powdyr that ys here to be hade. The Quene's Majestie should do well to macke, out of hande, *iiij or vi mylles for the macking of powdyr* for the servize of her highness' turne, if the warres contynew, or this breach of amytie shulld chaunce betwixt her Majestie and King Philipe."[h] Gresham frequently gave the secretary similar advice; showing, at this important period of our history, how inadequately England was provided alike with

[g] Amsterdam seems to have been a port of far greater importance. Weddington thus writes from "Gronnynge in Frysland," May 23, 1560: "The next esterly wyndes at Amsterdam in Holland, they look for 3 or 400 sayle of gret ships out of Est lands, appateyning to Holland; only laden with corn and other merchandize."—Flanders Correspondence, State-Paper Office.

[h] To Cecil, April 18, 1560.—Ibid. Gresham's request was granted by return of the post, as appears from the Queen's reply, preserved among the State-Papers, bearing date April 24th.

the means of aggression and of defence, and how dependent she was on foreign states for those resources, which her native energies have since abundantly supplied. In the month of May, 1560, he writes,—"It ys geven me to understonde that she [the regent] wolle not departe from this towen, (nor the counssell,) till Kinge Phillipe's resollute answer be knowen, how a will proceed agaynst the Quene's Majestie and the realm. Fynally, Sir, it ys most convenyent for the Quene's Majestie *to macke all her shipes in a redynes within the realme, and to soffer no maryners to goo, no kynde of wayse, out of the realme.* And according as I have wrytten you, I cannot see wyche waye King Phillipe can annoye her highness this yere; considering a hath nyther monny, ships, nor men; nor munission, nor armewr. Nevertheless, it ys good to dowght the worst, and to trust to no wordes: and for my part, I have given abrode that the Quene's Majestie hayth two hundred ships in a redynes, well armyd."[1]

It was not so much any direct aggression on the part of the King of Spain which the English apprehended, as the danger which might result from his aiding France with his powerful support. The cause of Mary of Guise, with the accession of such an ally, would have become formidable; and this

[1] To Cecil. May 7, 1560.—Fland. Corr. St. P. Off.

was the real reason why Gresham watched so narrowly the movements of the Spanish soldiers in Zealand; lest by one of those strokes of policy of which King Philip was so capable, a fair wind should have been availed of to transport his veterans to Leith,—a strong-hold at that time in the occupation of the French army, from which it was the object of the united forces of England and Scotland to dislodge them. Gresham says on the 18th of April, 1560,—"I am glad to hear that the Quene Dowager is entered into communication, and the Quene's Majestie's army is at Leith;"[j] and, as might be expected, the reports which subsequently prevailed at Antwerp of the progress of the siege, obtain frequent notice in the course of this correspondence. Such passages as the following cannot fail to be interesting to English ears. "Here ys a secret talk that the town of Leith had geven [yielded] by our men and the Scots' assault: whereas was lost i M [1000] men, as they say here. Sir, I most humbly beseche you, as there ys any good newes, I may hear from you wyth the fyrst; for that here ys none other talke but of Ingland and Scotland, and all men wish Scotland were once Inglish."[k] "Here ys dyvers of our nacione hayth letters of the xxxth,

[j] To Cecil, May 7, 1560.—Fland. Corr. St. P. Off.

[k] To the same, April 25, 1560.—Ibid.

from London, that the Quene's armye at Lieth haythe geven a great overthrowe to the French men, to the nombre of ii M persones; and for that I hadd letters from you of the 30th, and had no advertisement, causyth me to geve the lesse credit unto the other. Wyche newes ys here moche rejoiced at of all nacions; for that yt ys thought that Lieth shall not be abell to holde ought any longe tyme. . . . . . . Here ys none other comonycaciones but of Ingland and Scoteland; and all men wishe Lithe to be tacken, and the French men to be put owght of Scoteland. And they doo moch lament that she [Queen Elizabeth] dyd soffer this matter so longe. Therefore, Sir, I most humbly besech, as you have any good newes worthy of writing, that it maye please you I maye have them wyth the fyrst."[l] A few weeks after, we read: "Sir, here ys serteyne news spread abrode that the French King hymsellfe, in person, comyth down to New-Haven [Havre] to see his ships and his men of war shippid for Scoteland. Wyche, I trust in God, shall be met wyth all well enough; and that Leith ys dyspached one wayes or other: wyche of force must be taken, for the honnor of the Quene's Majestie, and the realme."[m] One quotation more, and I have done. "Sir, I thancke

[l] To Cecil, May 7.—Fland. Corr. St. P. Off.

[m] To the same, May 29.—Ibid.

you for your good newes of Leethe. I wold to God that matter were dispachid, eyther by fare meynes or foul meynes, for the great honnor that her Majestie and the realme should resseve thereby; wyche newes ys here longe lookyd for." [n]

A more perfect extract from one of the numerous letters addressed by Gresham to the secretary about this period, will serve as a further specimen of his correspondence, and not be out of place here.

"Right honnorable Sir:

"It maye like you to understond, that, as the xviij[th] daye, I wrote you of all things that passed here; and of the great breute and rewmers that ys here of the ayde that King Phillipe will geve to the Frenche Kinge to subdew the Scots. Wyche matter ys so takyne by all nacyons to the great dishonnor of the Kinge's Majestie, that yf any breach of war shuld chance, I beleve the Quenes Majestie shuld be more assewryd of frendes here than he. As also they say playne here, that the States of the lande will never consent to have war with Ingland. And that this ys the practise of the Spanyardes and priests, as well in Ingland as other ways: wyche mattir hath clean alteryd the credit of the

[n] To Cecil, June 16.—Fland. Corr. St. P. Off.

Quenes Majestie and of all our nacione. I have talkyd with dyvers of the Quenes Majisties credittors; and to be playne with you, every man sekes to be paid. Whereunto I have made answer, — 'Yf this had not chanssid, every man shuld have beene paid, that wolde; but now, there was none other remedy but that they must have pacience for vi monthes longger, and that I trustid by that tyme to see them paid here, or elles at Hamborow; whereas [where] I gave them to undyrstand that the Quenes Majestie wold send so manny cloths and karssez as shulde answer her highness' whole dettes, what-soevir shuld chanse. Wyche mattir likyd some verye well, and speciallye the Germans; for *that* place will be as commodyus to them, as this. . . . . . .

"Truly, Sir, here ys such a ster, as God ys the best [witness.] Wisshing, for my parte, that the Quene's Majestie were abel to make some worthy payment for the advansement of her highness' creadit; wyche will not be a littil spoken of thorowe all Cristendome. As also, all the wyse men saye here, that it ys but a tricke of Kinge Phillipe to fear the Quenes Majestie, to make her highness call her armye backe agayen out of Scoteland; and they doo not sticke to saye openly, that yf King Phillipe hathe war agaynst the Queene's Majestie, that all the nobellmen protestants in Germany will ryse agaynst hym. Sir, I cannot write you too muche howe Kinge Phillipe ys myslicked in these his procedinges agaynst our realme."[o]

Though altogether devoted in general to the discussion of the affairs entrusted to his management, Gresham's correspondence is occasionally enlivened by details of a somewhat more amusing character; which it may not be improper to notice here, before proceeding to graver matters. Passages of this complexion were elicited when a courtier, for instance, had requested Gresham to procure for him some elegant article of foreign manufacture, or other object which was more easily obtainable on the Continent than in England; and sometimes they were called forth by other circumstances. I will give some examples. "Sir," says the same writer, addressing Sir William Cecil in 1560, "it may please you to doo my most humble commendacion to my Lorde Robert Dudeley, and to declare unto him that the Queen's Majesty's Turkey horse doth begynne to mend in his foote and boddy; which doughtless ys one of the readdyst horsses that ys in all Christendom, and runs the best."[p] In about a month, he adds, (writing to Sir Thomas

[o] Ant. April 19, 1560.—Fland. Corr. St. P. Off.

[p] Ant. May 12, 1560.—Ibid.

Parry) "It may please you to show my Lord Robert, that the Queen's Majesty's Turkey horse waxes a very fayre beast; and with the Queen's Majesty's leve, I doo intend to bring [it] home myselfe."[q] In a letter addressed shortly after to the same individual, Gresham says, "I thank you for the gentill entertainment you gave to my poore wyffe, who I do right well know molests you dayly for my coming home,—suche is the fondness of women! And whereas your honour would have a great Iron chest bought for the Queen's Majesty, with a littil keye, I have sent you the keye of the fairest Chest that ys to be had in all this town, if the key be not too bigge. Iff the Queen's Majesty would have lesse, I pray you that I may know the length, and I shall cause a chest to be mayd purposely:"[r] and in the following August, addressing the same personage, Gresham says, "I sent you on the 17th overland, to Dunkirk, the young cortall[s] I gave you, with the Queen's Majesty's Turkey horse. As licke-wise I have sent you four dozen of the same black buttons you spake to me for, which costes you 48*s*. the dozen."[t]

[q] Sir T. G. to Sir Thomas Parry. Ant. June 16.—Fland. Corr. St. P. Off.

[r] Ant. July 2.—Ibid.

[s] A little horse.

[t] Ant. Aug. 18.—Ibid.

"The man that maketh the clock is out of town, this Easter hollidayes," observes Gresham, addressing Sir William Cecil: "I trust to send you it within thes x days."[v] In another letter he says, "I have written into Spayne for sylk hose both for you, and my Lady your wife; to whom it may please you, I maye be remembered:"[w] and we learn from the letter which a few days after accompanied the gift, that those for Cecil were black. "I have sent you herewith two payre of blacke silke howsen, and payre for my Lady your wiffe."[x] Silk stockings were, in fact, at this time of great rarity and value, as appears from an anecdote related of Queen Elizabeth by Stowe, the chronicler. "In 1560," he says, "her silk woman, Mistris Mountague, presented her Maiestie with a payre of blacke knit silke stockings, for a new year's gift; the which, after a few dayes wearing, pleased her

[v] Ant. April 18, 1560.—Fland. Corr. St. P. Off. Three years after, the Bishop of Worcester presented Cecil with a clock as a New-year's gift. "Suche ys the barrenness of this contrie, that yt bringith nothing forth fitt to remember youe withall; and therfor I am bold to present yow with an olde Clock in the stead of a New-years gift; which I trust ye will the rather accept, because yt was your olde master's of happy memorie, King Edward's, and afterwards your lovinge and learned brother's, Mr. Cheeke's." (Ellis' Letters, 1st Series, vol. ii. p. 195.)

[w] Ant. April 30, 1560.—Ibid.

[x] Ant. May 7, 1560.—Ibid. There is a blank in the original.

Highnesse so well, that shee sent for Mistris Mountague and asked her where she had them, and if shee could help her to any more: who answered, saying, 'I have made them very carefully, of purpose only for your Majesty; and seeing these please you so well, I will presently set more in hand.'—'Do so,' quoth the Queen, 'for indeede I like silke stockings so well, because they are pleasant, fine, and delicate, that henceforth I will weare no more cloth stockings.'"[y] Though Gresham had presented Edward VI., eight years before, with a specimen of this article of dress, as has been already mentioned, silk stockings continued for many years to preserve the reputation of exceeding value. In 1563, a Spanish ship, called the 'Little Abraham,' was plundered; and in the "Note of Goods lacking," preserved in the State-Paper Office, we find "one trusse of Granado sowing silke; and divers payre of silke hose, *the valew of which is uncertayne as yet.*"[z]

In another part of Gresham's correspondence we read,—"I trust you [Sir William Cecil] have

[y] Stowe's Chronicle, ed. 1631, p. 867. The same writer states, that the art of knitting or weaving silk-stockings by engines or steel looms, was not perfected till the year 1599, when William Lee, M.A. of St. John's College, Cambridge, taught the secret. Worsted stockings were first made in 1564: Stowe says the art came from Mantua.—Ibid. p. 869.

[z] Flanders Corr.—The document is dated May 24.

received your seven pieces of tapistry; also I have caused to be made in Germany the 100 shirts, almaign corseletts, blue and white, that your honour spake to me for:"[a] and subsequently "vi velvet chairs, and vi of Spanish lether," are bespoken for the secretary.[b] "I sent you by Spritwell your six silver candlesticks," he writes on another occasion; promising to send Cecil his "wolf-gown" very shortly.[c]

So rarely does Gresham unbend into any thing approaching to jocularity in his correspondence, that the following passage, in which he tries to be pleasant, must not be forgotten. He is speaking of the Duchess of Parma, who was passing a short

[a] Sir T. G. to Sir W. C. Ant. May 29, 1560.—Flanders Corr. St. P. Off.

[b] "From my house in London," July 27, 1561.—Ibid. It is odd that Clough, writing six days before from Antwerp, should have announced "the chaires for the Secratary, four of lether and two of velvet;" besides six stools for his master, three green and three red.

[c] Ant. Oct. 22, 1559.—Ibid. In the Domestic Correspondence there remains a memorandum of the different articles which Gresham had procured in Flanders for Cecil, who was at that time building his house at Burleigh: it is as follows: "xvi little pillers of marbill for a gallery. . . . . . xvi *li.*—ix harthes for chimneys, at 24*s.* 4*d.* . . . . . x*l.* x*s.* [?]—vi chaires of velvet, at iii *li.* the peece. . . . . . xviij *li.*—vi chaires of lether, at xxiij *s.* iiij *d.* . . . . . vii *li.*—One cloke [clocke], ... v *li.* viij *s.* i *d.*—iii great barrells of nails, at vi *li.* xiij *s.* iiij *d.* . . . . . xx *li.*—One Ton of Iron . . . . . ix *li.*—x platts for Candells . . . . . xxiij *s.* iiij *d.*—v Cases of Glasse, at iij *li.* . . . . xv *li.*"—St. P. Off.

time at Antwerp, and at whose court he now attended in his official capacity. "The Regent ys here still; and every other day rydes abowght this town in her cowche, *brave come le sol*, trymmed after the Itallione fasshone."[d] This was written in 1560, at which period coaches were so little known in England,[e] that the duchess' use of that luxurious contrivance must have seemed to the writer 'a pithy and merry conceit.' Stowe relates, that "in the yeere 1564, Guilliam Boonen, a Dutchman, became the Queen's coachman, and was the first that brought the use of coaches into England. After awhile, divers great ladies, with as great jealousie of the Queen's displeasure, made them coaches, and rid in them up and down the Counties, to the great admiration of all the beholders."[f]

The chronicler was misinformed, however, on the subject of the first introduction of coaches into England; since Sir Philip Hoby had his 'coche' in 1556, and in a letter which will be found in the Appendix, offered to send it to conduct Lady Cecil to Bisham. They were probably clumsy contrivances at this early period; for at one of

[d] Sir T. G. to Sir W. C., Ant. May 12.—Fland. Corr. St. P. Off.

[e] Some remarks on this subject will be found in the Appendix, No. XXIII.

[f] Stowe's Chronicle, ed. 1631, p. 867.—Coaches did not come into common use till the year 1605.

the first audiences which Queen Elizabeth gave La Mothe Fénélon, the French ambassador, in 1568, she entertained him with an account of the "douleur qu'elle sentoit à son cousté, pour s'y estre heurtée quelques jours auparavant, en ung coche où elle alloit ung peu trop viste." [g]

During his protracted periods of absence from England, Gresham ever and anon expresses his concern for the welfare of his wife,—so quaintly noticed in a passage already quoted. "I shall most humbly beseche your Highness," he said, addressing Queen Elizabeth in 1560, "to be a comfort unto my pore wife in this my absens in the service of your Majesty:" [h] and similar passages are comparatively of frequent recurrence in his correspondence with Secretary Cecil, and Sir Thomas Parry, to whom he alternately either recommends her ladyship, or returns thanks for the kind attentions which she had experienced at their hands. On one occasion, happening to address Cecil at five o'clock in the morning from Dunkirk, (where he had just arrived after a very rough passage,) Gresham concludes "with my most humble commendacions to my Lord Keeper,

[g] Dépêches de La Mothe Fénélon, 8vo. 1838, vol. i. p. 27:—a work of profound interest and great importance, for which our literature is indebted to C. Purton Cooper, Esq. Of what use it has proved to the writer, will presently be seen.

[h] London, Feb. 25, 1559-60.—Fland. Corr. St. P. Off.

and to my Lord Robert; so that my powre wyfe be not forgoten,—whom I will insure you was very sorrowfull to see me depart afore my accownt was fynished: therefore I shall most humbly beseech your honour, according to your promis, to be a stey and some comfort unto her, in this my absence."[i] "I shall desyre you," he says elsewhere, "to have me in remembrans for the getting owght of my pardone, and that it maye please you to dellyver yt to my powre wyffe; which wyll be no small comforte unto her."[k] And in a letter to Sir Thomas Parry, we find,—"rendering you my most humble thanks for your gentill letter; as also for the gentilness showed to my powre wyfe, who likewise would gladly have me at home."[l] It is not to be supposed from what precedes, that Sir Thomas Gresham corresponded indifferently with Secretary Cecil, or Parry, (treasurer of the queen's household); for it was only when Cecil went into Scotland, (May 30th, 1560,) to treat with the French ambassador, that Gresham, by Cecil's particular desire,[m] addressed the treasurer.

A specimen of his correspondence with this individual may not be unacceptable. The reader

[i] March 4, 1561-2.—Fland. Corr. St. P. Off.

[k] Ant. August 16, 1562.—Ibid. [l] Ant. June 22, 1560.—Ibid.

[m] See the fragment of Gresham's first letter to Parry, dated June 1 or 2.—Ibid. Cecil returned from Scotland on the 28th of July. (See his Diary, in Murdin.) There is a beautifully-written

has been already put in possession of the information necessary to render some of its obscurer passages intelligible; and a better idea is thus formed of the nature of the communication which passed between the statesman and the merchant, than can be derived from the detached passages which have been interwoven with the text.

"Right honnorable Sir,

"Aftyr my most humble comendacions, it maye like you to undyrstonde that by my letter of the xth of this pressent, I signyfyed unto you of the great overthrowe that Kinge Phillipe had at Trippolley, by the Turkes' armey; at the wyche conflycte there was lost xxx galleyes, and xxv great shippes, and all the rest of the galleyes burnte. For that now the saying is, that the Duke of Medynna Sealley [Celi] dyd forsake all his galleyes, and tocke to a forte that he new made, wyth all his men: whereas he ys vittaled for iiij months. It ys judgyd that the Turkes' powre will take it eyther by famine or otherwise. Sir, this loss ys more greater than here they will be known of, and as littil lamentid amonges his

letter among the State-Papers, dated June 7th, 1560, which Gresham addressed to Queen Elizabeth on this occasion. He had hitherto, in pursuance with her commands, corresponded with Cecil alone; but he desired that the queen should be informed that her treasurer, Sir Thomas Parry, was the minister to whom he now addressed his despatches.

subjects here,—what for his Relligione and gouvernement. And now they saye here, that king Phillipe hathe more nead at this pressent to seeke for helpe, than to helpe the Frenche kinge; because the Turke ys so strong upon hym, and the most parte of all his galleyes and shipes be takynne and lost. Therefore, Sir, the Quene's Majestie neadyth not to doubt nothing of Kinge Phillip's procedings for this yere.—Trusting in God that Leith ys either renderid or takynne by this tyme; wyche newes ys here long lookyd for.—The iiij M iiij C [4400] Spannyardes lyeth still in their garnyssones, and so will remayne, as far as I can perseve; for that the states of this lande, as yet, will consent to no payment of monny. The viij shipes that was preparid for the transportacione of them, be at Rencaynyng, in Zealand, as by Payne's letters of the xi[th] and xii[th] your honnor shall perseve; [as well as] how all thinges there passith. The shipes wherein the Quene's Majestie's velvetz and crymsyn sattyns are, be still here, bye the reason the wynde is clean agaynst them. There ys shippyd xx ꝑ casse of velvets of pille mezẽ and iij C elles of crymessyn velvets.[n] I will ship no more till this adventure be past, having in a

[n] The concealed meaning of this jargon will presently be in some degree explained. *Pille*, is pile,—a term commonly applied to velvet: the other words I am unable to explain. Equally perplexing is the technical phraseology in page 321.

redyness xx pieces of velvets more to be shipped.

"The gentillman, your son, ys in right good helthe; (as this daye Mr. Cockes came to this town); of whome you shall have muche joye and comforte, for that a ys wholly geven to all virtewsness, and to his studdye, and belovyd of all men. Most humblye desiring you to be so good Father unto hym (and the rather at my sewte) as to augment his stipend to one hundrethe crowns more by the yere; for that this countrye ys a very chargeable countrye: wherebye a maye meynteyne hymselfe somethinge like your eldest son, wyche will redound moche to your honnor. And for my parte, I shall be redy to assist him in all thinges, as I wolde doo for my own son.

"Other I have not to molest you wythall, but that it maye please you to doo my most humble commendacions to my very singewlar good Lorde, the Lorde Robert Dudley. And thus I comyt you to God, who presarve you wythe increas of honnor. From Andwerpe the xiij[th] of June, a[o] 1560.

At your honnors commandement,

THOMAS GRESHAM."[o]

"To the right honnorable Sir Thomas Parry,
knyght, Treassorer of the Quene's
Majestie's most honnorable howsholde."

[o] Fland. Corr. St. P. Off.—It was received on the 17th of June. His next letter (June 16th) conveys similar tidings. "Bye my letter of the xiijth, I singnyfyed unto yow of all thinges worthy

Sometimes, too, the letters of this ancient merchant record, however imperfectly, the *on dits* of his day. Unfortunately for English readers, he alludes far more frequently to Flemish occurrences than to those of his own country: but *these* are occasionally seen reflected in his correspondence; and, however imperfectly noticed, to us they possess a charm of which nothing can divest them. When Queen Elizabeth first came to the crown, common report was busy in providing her with a husband; and every possible and impossible alliance had been in turn suggested. Among the foremost of her suitors was King Philip; but him she at once rejected, and perhaps the Spaniard never quite forgave her for her indifference. Later in her reign, certain English noblemen were regarded as likely objects of favour; and no

of writting, and of the great ovyrthrow that King Phillipe hade at Trippoly bye the Turckes' armey. And now, they saye here that the fyrst newes I write you of ys trewe,—that the Duke of Medynna Scylly shullde be escappid wythe xij galleys, in Sissillie; and some of the said put in to Nappoles. And they saye now, that there ys manny of the King's galleys gotten into a golfe; whereas can come in but one galley at ones; so that it ys thowght the Turckes armey can doo them but littill hurte, except it be onelye by famyne. Veryly, the losse ys so great, that K. P. shall not be able to recover in iiij yeres soche a powre of galleyes and shipes together."—Ibid. *On the same day* that Gresham's former letter reached England, Lord Clinton sent the intelligence to the Earl of Sussex. Compare the preceding with Wright's Elizabeth and her Times, vol. i. p. 28.

one more than Leicester, the 'Lord Robert Dudley' of a preceding page, for whom Gresham was nursing a little favourite steed which belonged to the queen. In the gossip of Antwerp, however, none but foreign princes seem to have been considered likely matches; and as the queen's marriage was a favourite subject of discussion, Gresham often entertains Cecil with the expectations which were there and then current. The Count Mansfeld "assured Clough, (in June 1560,) that the Duke of Holst had come to England solely to treat a marriage between Elizabeth and the King of Denmark, his brother's son."—"The talk is," adds Gresham, "that the King of Finland [Sweden]'s eldest son is going to England. He hathe given the king, his father, to understand, that he will never marry except a marry the Queen's Majesty."[p] This was Eric, eldest son of Gustavus I., whose brother, John Duke of Finland, had been sent into England in the preceding year,[q] to

[p] Sir T. G. to Parry. Ant. 4 June, 1560.—Fland. Corr. St. P. Off. Respecting this date, see page 340, note [y].

[q] John, Duke of Finland, made his appearance in this country in December, 1559; as appears from the following interesting letter which Henry Knollys, who was appointed to wait upon him on his arrival, addressed to Sir William Cecil from Harwich, descriptive of his first interview with the noble stranger. The original is in the State-Paper Office, Domestic Correspondence.

"Syr, 1559.

"At 7 of the clocke yn the mornyng, thys day, y came unto

negotiate a match between him and the queen. In 1560, Gustavus died; and his son Eric, the fourteenth of that name, having succeeded to the throne of Sweden, was expected every day to make his

Harwyche: and at 9 of the clocke, after y had taryed together with Sir Thomas Smythe yn the Duke's hall more than halff an howre, y was admytted unto the Duke's presens; who, syttyng yn a chayre withowt movyng hymsellf, offered me hys hande,—as yt semed by the maner of the holdyng theroff, to kysse. But y that had bene otherwyse brought up then to kysse the hande of ony subject, other than of the parentage of my naturall prynce, after y had with reverens kyssed myn owne hande, y joyned my hande with hys, accordyng to the maner of thys owr natyve countre.

"The Quene's messag he receaved very thankfully, but her mageste's lettres he loked not on at that present; only he sayd he wolde take a tyme to delyberat, and then make me furder answer. All that y spake yn declaryng how moche the Quene's hyghnes rejoysed on hys behalff that he had escaped the perylls of the seas, and was now saffly arryved wythyn her Mageste's realme, he ynterrupted yt even as co[urtly] lovers doe; applyeng yt all together for a testymony of the Quene's good ynclynatyon towardes the lykyng of hys Embassade: wheryn he taryed so moche, that y was marveylously perplexyd, feryng lest that, upon occasyon of my wordes, he wolde take holde towardes a promyse of some ynconvenyency. Wherfor, after he had ended hys tale, y said that yt was the maner, not only of the Quene's hyghnes that now ys, but allso of all her Magesty's progenytors, at what tyme ony noble prynce, suche as he was, came hether to see other the realme or theyr personne, allways to receive them most thankfully; and to omytt no maner of curteysy, or favor, wherby they myght ether doe them honor, or shew them ony pleasure. Whereunto when he replyed nothyng, I toke my leave of hym for that tyme.

"After dyner, my lorde of Oxforde had hym forthe on hawk-

appearance at the court. "The Quene's Highnes," says a contemporary letter-writer,[r] "being every houre in a contynuall expectation of the King of Swethen's cominge, is looked for to be shortely here at Westminster; and so moche the sooner, as the works now there in hande may be finished, and brought to eny perfection; where

yng, and shewed hym great sporte, kyllyng yn hys syght both faysant and partrych; wheryn he semed to take great pleasure. Towardes nyght, as he came homwardes, y was so bolde to enqwyre of hym whether yt wolde please hym to use my servyce ony longer here; or otherwyse, yn case y sholde retorne, whether hys pleasure were y sholde say ony thyng on hys behelff unto the Quene's Magesty? He answered that he entended to wryte unto her hyghnes; and what tyme he delyvered me hys lettres, y sholde knowe furder what to say. Afterwards, yn talke of hys removyng towardes London, y was very desyerous, (by rayson of the dowtfulnes that he kept all men yn so longe tyme,) to know when he entended to take hys jorny that way. Wherunto he answered, that, by rayson hys horse[s] were moche ympayred throughe the noysomnes of the seas, they were not yet able to serve hym; but after 4 or 5 days, he thought he sholde be redy to goe. Thus moche y thought yt my duty to sygnyfye unto you by lettres, yn as moche as y am deteaned, myselff, longer then my tyme appoynted: wheryn allso y truste you wyll declare myn excuse unto the Quene's Magesty. Thus, after myn humble commendatyons, I pray God assiste you allways with hys grace, to his glory, and the honor of the Quene. From Harwyche, the 27th of Decembre. Your poor frende,

H. Knolles."

I omit the postscript, which merely announces the probability of the duke's proceeding to London by water.

[r] Frances Alen to the Earl of Shrewsbury. Sept. 3, 1560.—Lodge's Illustrations, vol. i, p. 346.

they worke bothe night and daye." So far from visiting the English court, however, in the character of a suitor, Eric never even left his capital; but solicited the queen's hand by proxy, and was a second time refused.[s]

Previous to this event, a few days in fact after the date of Gresham's letter last quoted, (June 1560,) that merchant relates to Parry a conversation which he had had with 'Mr. Arnolde Roussyngberg, the King of Sweden's counsellor,' ('a very wise gentleman,') who, after asking sundry questions, "borsted out unto me, and sayde that the King his Master's eldest son was comyng into England with 80 sayle of great ships, and 10,000 men, and with four millions of gold and silver, to come see her Majesty: and fell in great discourse of the worthiness of the young prince for his personage and wisdom, and showed me his picture. With that I thancked him, and said,—'It is good to see that the King your Master ys a prince of grett wealth, and he right well deserveth great honour and commendacion in this his proceedings.' And thus [he] departed;"[t] but the writer concludes with a recommendation of "the Emperor's son, Don Carolo," whom, he says, "all men

[s] Holinshed's Chronicle, 4to. vol. iv. p. 186.

[t] Sir T. G. to Parry, Ant. June 16, 1560.—Fland. Corr. St. P. Off.

of experience wished the Queen to marry."[u] In the preceding year, he had recommended the same individual in the following terms. "The occoraunts be here, that Don Carolo, the Emperor's thyrde sone, ys comyng into Inglond wyth a great sorte of nobellmen and genttilmen, to the nomber of iiij or v c horsys; wyche ys moche rejoissyd at here; and the aryvall of the King of Sweddon's sone [John Duke of Finland] in Inglond[v] ys nothing lickyd here, for they cannot abyde to here of hym, nor specially of his Father, for all the ryches a haythe and doth offer wyth his sone; for they saye a ys a usurppid king. Sir, I can no more write you in this, but the will of God and her Majesty be fulfyllyd! But veryly, an' pleasse your honnor, if it stande with her highness' pleassure to marye a stranger, sewrly there is nowen so meat as one of the Emperor's sons, (for that he ys nobell borne:) and, in the marrying of hym, we are sewre to have peasse wyth these towe great prynssis,—I meynne the King of Spayen,

[u] Sir T. G. to Cecil, Ant. May 29, 1560.—Fland. Corr. St. P. Off.

[v] Concerning the landing of the Duke of Finland, see Nichols' Progresses of Queen Elizabeth ,vol. i. pp. 79, 80. Shortly after this negotiation, he was committed to prison by his brother Eric XIV., and kept in chains for four years: but a similar fate awaited the unnatural monarch, for he ended his days in the same place of confinement, in 1568.

and the French King: besyde, we shall have all Germany to [our] frynde; which will be a great strength and quietness to our realme." [w]

I have thought it desirable thus to throw together some of the lighter passages in the correspondence of Sir Thomas about this period; since, without publishing his letters entire, these must either be altogether suppressed, or occur at such distant intervals as to make them seem wholly disconnected and independent of one another. But we are now to resume the thread of our narrative, and remind the reader that Turkey horses, curtals, clocks, and silk hose, though they make some figure in Gresham's correspondence, occupied but

[w] Sir T. G. to Cecil. Ant. Oct. 29, 1559.—Fland. Corr. St. P. Off. Charles, Archduke of Austria, whom Gresham here so warmly praises, appears to have been in every way deserving of his commendation. Take a description of his person and character from the pen of that ornament of nobility, Thomas Ratcliffe, Earl of Sussex; who, eight years after, proceeded to Vienna in order to negotiate an alliance between Elizabeth and the Archduke. "His Highnes is of person higher surely, a good deale, then my L. Marques; his heare of heade and bearde of a lighte aborne; his face well proportioned, amiable, and of a very good compleccōn, wth owte shewe of readness or over palenes; his countenñce and speche cherefull, very curteowse, and not wth owte some state; his body well shaped, wth owte deformitie or blemishe; his hands very good and fayer; his leggs cleane, well proporcōned, and of sufficient bignes for his stature; his fote as good as may be. So as, upon my dutie to yor Matie, I finde not one deformitie, mis-shape, or any thinge to be noted worthy mislikinge in his hole person; but, contrary wise, I finde his hole

little of his time; which was engrossed by the care of procuring military stores for England, and providing for their safe transportation: a matter, as it would appear, of paramount difficulty and danger.

Instead of offering any remarks of my own on this subject, I shall content myself with giving a few extracts from his letters, which require no comment. He writes as follows from Antwerp, in October 1559, concerning four barrels of gunpowder, marked which he had shipped for London:— "Sir, it maye pleasse yow to give a great charge to Mr. Blomfylld that thes poncheones be

shape to be good, worthy comēndacōn and likinge in all respects, and such as is rarely to be founde in such a Prince. His Highnes, besids his naturall language of Duche, speaketh very well Spanish and Italian, and, as I heare, Latin. . . . . He is reported to be wise, liberall, valeante, and of greate courage, wch in the last warres he well showed, in defending all his contreis, free from the Turk, wth his owne force onlye, and gevinge them dīvse ovrthrowes when they attempted any thinge againste his rules; and he is universally (wch I moste weye) noted to be of such vertue as he was nevr spotted or touched wth any notable vice or cryme; wch is moche in a Prince of his yeares, indued wth such qualities. He deliteth moche in huntinge, ridinge, hawkinge, exercise of feats of armes, and hearinge of musicke, whereof he hathe very good. He hath, as I heare, some understandinge in astronomy and cosmography; and takethe pleasure in clocks that sett forthe the cowrse of the planetts."—Lodge's Illustrations, &c. vol. i. p. 366.

secreatly oppenyd and wayde in the Tower: for verylly, yf it be knowen here, the parttye ys in danger of his lyfe and goodes; and by the knowledge thereof, the Prince's turne shall be disappoynted."[x] The reader will perhaps call to mind Gresham's letter of the 25th of February, 1559-60, given at page 288; from which it appears that notwithstanding this and many a subsequent caution, his doings got wind and reached the ear of the regent.

In May 1560, we meet with the following passages relative to his proceedings; from which it is sufficiently obvious what great hazards he ran in providing England with those implements of warfare which, a few years later, she turned to such good account. It is of course needless to observe, that in serving the state which he represented, he was acting in direct violation of the laws of the Low Countries, and incurring their severest penalties:[y] so that, in order to mislead a casual

[x] 29 Oct. 1559.—Fland. Corr. St. P. Off.

[y] In Queen Mary's time, he had been accustomed to apply to the king for *a passport;* or, as we should say, *a licence*, to export 'harness,' &c.; but he now entertained such serious doubts as to the probability of obtaining the renewal of that facility, that he deemed it more prudent to conceal his need of it. Philip, he said, had once given him a general and unlimited passport, "which had of late days been made frustrate." Hence his shipments from other ports, as Hamburg and Bremen. Gresham relates in one of his letters a conversation he had had with an

reader, should any of his letters have been intercepted, in his correspondence with Cecil he conventionally made use of the word *velvet* to denote *gunpowder;* and employed other terms, as *silks*, *damasks*, and *satins*, in the same enigmatical manner. He also repeatedly requested that a cypher might be sent him; but I have met with no specimen of his correspondence so disguised.

"I have secreat advertisements by one of the serchers, how the courte here hathe geven order to the customers that all soche shipes as lade for Ingland should be searchid; wych ys only to tacke me in a trip, as I am credibly informyd. I can no more wryte yow in this matter; but well fares that peny geven, that saves one hundred! I had thought to have shipped in this flote of shipes, (wyche be to the nomber of x or xii shipes,) all the Quene's Majestie's corseletts, morrions, and corries[z] that be remaynyng in this

officer of the Antwerp custom-house on this subject, wherein the latter urged him to renew his application, saying,—"I do know right well, yff a make a new seut a shall spead." The writer asks, (and in many subsequent letters repeats the inquiry,) whether he shall apply to the regent for a licence to ship 200 barrels of gunpowder "to try her good-will." The queen, he says, "only needs a passeport for gunpowder, wyche, if she will have a quantitie, must needs pass from hens."—Sir T. G. to Sir T. Parry. Ant. June 24, 1560.—Fland. Corr. St. P. Off.

[z] A *corselet* is a pikeman's armour; a *morion* is a steel cap; *corries*, I am unable to explain, unless *cuirass* is intended.

towen; but now I will steye till this brownte [brunt] be past.—In the last shipes that went from hens, I sent you x pieces of velvets, viz. v pieces of dobbill, and v pieces of pill and halfe: and for that yow write me yow undyrstond not what *velvets* should be, (and hoping that Candiller could inform you thereof, wherein I stand in dowght,) you shall undyrstand that every piece of doble geyne velvet is one thowsond [lbs.] weight of corrin powddyr; and one piece of velvet of pill and a halfe ys 1 M [lbs.] waight of serpentyne powdyr."[o]...... "Sir, yow must neades devyse some wayes wherby the thinges that be sent from hens maye be secreatly conveyed to the Tower; or ells in soch matters I shall not be able to stand her highness in small stead from hence. I have heard reported that there is a parish church in the Tower, whereunto doth resort all the Duch men of Saint Katherine's;[a] and, in my opinion, where such a number of strangers doth resort, yt cannot be chosen [but] there be some false brethren amonges them. Therefore, Sir, if it stood with the Quene's Majestie's pleasure to remove that access from thence to some other church in Saint

[o] For *corrin powder*, see page 288, note [x]. *Serpentine powder* is "a weak sort of gunpowder that is not *corned*, and will not keep long at sea."

[a] "The Duch men of St. Katharine's" occupied the site of the St. Katharine Docks. "The parish church in the Tower" is the interesting little edifice dedicated to St. Peter-in-vinculis.

Katharine's, I believe things would be more secretly usyd; wyche, in very deed, cannot be too secretly fixed and bestowed."[b] In June, he says: "according as I have written your honour, I have corrupted the chief sercher, whom is all my doer, and [who] hath right honestly desired a worthy reward: soe, by him, and through his advice, I am doing daily, as by my proceedings to you may appere. If it is discovered, there is nothing short of death with the searcher, and with him who enters it at the custom-house. So that there shall no ship depart, but I shall give the adventure of 3 or 4 pieces of velvets in a ship: likewise, I trust the three ships from Hambro', with the 9000*l.* worth of provysion, with the other from Breame [Bremen,] ladyn with Collen [Cologne] cleves,[c] be arrived with you in safety, which would be no small comfort for me to hear of. As likewise I have writtin to my servant [at Hamburg] to send away all the rest of my whole provision, by 3000 pownds in a ship, with as much expedition as may be;—being right assured, when it shall please God to send all in safety, there is no Prince in all Christendom has the like provision. And the like is not to be gotten together for no treasure."[d]

[b] May 12, 1560.—Fland. Corr. St. P. Off.

[c] Of the meaning of this word, I am ignorant; unless *cleavers* is meant.

[d] June 29, 1560.—Fland. Corr. St. P. Off. Among the State-

Notwithstanding Gresham's precautions, and his repeated injunctions that the greatest possible secrecy should be observed at the Tower, the periodical arrivals of large quantities of ammunition did not fail to attract notice; and the intelligence soon found its way to Antwerp. To use his own words, he was now "holly at his wites' ende." "For as the xiiij[th] daie [of June 1560] at vij of the clocke at nyght, the cheiffe sercher, (whome ys all my worcker, and conveyer of all my velvets,) gave me to understand that there had bynne a Inglish man wyth the costomer, and hadd informyd hym that, of late, I hade manny velvets aryvyd at London of all sortes; and that

Papers is preserved "The copy of Michell Van Dorovy's Instructions, unto Hambro, May 18, 1560."—They are in French, in which language Gresham desired his servant to correspond with him. He was ordered to load gunpowder to the value of 9,000*l.* on three ships, "under Cristofer Pruen's mark," and to hire four other ships for the same purpose. It was not, doubtless, the sea-risk which was so much apprehended in the transportation of this ammunition, as the danger of pirates. It will be seen that Gresham used commonly to insure the armour, &c. which he sent over, at 5 *per cent.* (Sept. 23rd, 1561.—Ibid.) On the present occasion, 2,000*l.* on each ship was 'adventured,' and only 1,000*l.* 'assured;' but he requested, for security, that three or four ships of war might be sent to meet and convoy home those destined for the Tower; (June 16th, 1560.—Ibid.) this, however, was deemed unnecessary.—The earliest mention I ever met with of English merchandise insured against sea-risks, occurs in a letter from Protector Somerset to the Lord Admiral in 1548.—Dom. Corr. St. P. Off.

yf he maid a general serche now, he shulld fynde a great bootye. Wyche matter, the costomer oppenyd to the sercher, (my frynde,) and comandyd hym to be wythe hym as the xvth daye, very erely in the mornyng; whereas all the costomers and he was together in conssaylle. And the matter being longe debattyd, they conclewdyd *not* to macke no serch; for if they shulde serche and fynde nothing, it wold redowen moche to there disonnestyes; and [they] sayde amonges themsellffes, that I colde not tacke it in good parte at there handes, consideryng how benefyciall I have allways bynne unto them. The sercher allegyde they had resson; and that from tyme to tyme, as the goodes was ladynne, he tocke a vew of all the shipes lading. Wyth that, said the undyr costomer,—'This Inglishman maye doo this of mallyse; for that I knowe that Mr. Gresham ys not best belovyd amonges the merchants, for the servise a doth to the prince:' and [so] at this instant [they have] concluded that nothing should be done.—Sir, if anything should be searched and found, the parties that shipped this gear for me must flye the country till their end be maid; for it runs their goods and all their lives upon. I am promes[ed] by the sercher to have the Inglish man's name.

"Therfore, Sir, on the reverens of God, I most humbly dessire your honnor that there maye be order tackynne with Mr. Blomefylde, that no man lyving maye knowe of *that* comes in, from hens forthe; for otherwisse, the Quene's Majestie shall resseve great losse, and dyvers onnest [!] men [will be] undone thereby.—Sir, I am right assurid that there comes not[hing] into the Tower, but that Sir John Yorcke and other dothe knowe of it by sartteyne of the offysers, and they doo wryte daylly to their doers here; and to be playne with your honour, I doo mystrust Mr. Yorcke's doer, whose name is Gardener."[e] The knight here spoken of, had held in succession several high appointments in the Mint, which at that time was situated within the Tower.[f] Of Blomefield, who must have been an officer of considerable authority in the ordnance department, I can give no account. Bayly, in his *History of the Tower*, makes no mention of him.

In the preceding extract, allusion is made to the jealousy with which Sir Thomas Gresham's proceedings were regarded at Antwerp, by cer-

[e] To Sir T. P. Ant. June 16, 1560.—Fland. Corr. St. P. Off.

[f] He had been Assay-master in 1544, and Under-treasurer in 1550. In 1549, being Master of the Mint, and one of the Sheriffs of London, he received the honour of knighthood at the hands of Edward VI., on the occasion of the young monarch's dining at Suffolk-House, in Southwark, (which seems to have been used at that time as a mint for striking money,) on his way to Hampton-Court. (Ruding's Annals, 4to. vol. i., pp. 66, 67, 79, and vol. iii. p. 132.)

tain of the merchants of that city: but this sentiment towards him was by no means confined to Flanders; and with no one does it seem to have prevailed in a greater degree than with Paulet, Marquis of Winchester, the old lord-treasurer. Besides any dislike which that nobleman may have entertained for Gresham on the score of religion, there was superadded, in no slight degree, the *jalousie de métier*. The old marquis being the chief financial officer in the kingdom, and having, in the discharge of his functions, amassed an immense fortune, regarded with no slight dissatisfaction the conspicuous part a private merchant was taking in directing the financial operations of the state. Winchester had successively served Henry VIII., Edward VI., Mary, and Elizabeth, (being, as he said of himself, *no oak, but an osier*,) and the esteem in which he was held at court, rendered him a dangerous enemy: so that Gresham trembled, not without reason, when he discovered about this time that his lordship was exerting his influence with the queen and her ministers, in endeavouring to effect his ruin,—an attempt which he had twice unsuccessfully made before. What seems to have principally vexed Winchester, was the secrecy with which (in accordance with Queen Elizabeth's express commands,) Gresham conducted all his operations; making no one privy to them but Sir William Cecil, or, in his absence, Sir Thomas Parry.

The treasurer took care, of course, to assign a less unworthy motive than jealousy for his inimical proceedings against the queen's merchant. He threw out suggestions that Gresham was availing himself unfairly of his advantageous position, and had defrauded the state; also, that he had remaining in his coffers, of the queen's money, 40,000*l.*: whereas Gresham declared that he had not 300*l.* remaining by him; and said that if Sir William Cecil, to whom he had transmitted his accounts, had not been in Scotland, he could have proved the fact immediately. But being forbidden even to quit Antwerp,—a circumstance which he says much disquieted him,—he wrote as follows on the subject to Parry: "Sir, I do perceive bye my servant, that my lorde Treassorer is offendyd with me because he ys not privey to all my doings; wyche I cannot doo withe-all, for that I was commanded by the Queene's Majestie to make no man privey [to them] but you and Mr. Secretarye. . . . . . This is the thyrde time that my Lord Treasurer hath servyd me this: viz. once in King Edward's time, and once in Quene Mary's time: and when his Lordship came to see the state of myne account, a found the Prynce rather in my debt than other wysse. And I assure your honour, of my faythe and powre honesty, it shall fall out so now."[g] Two days after, Gresham says,—"This is one of his Lordship's old practisses, who cares nott how things passith here, so his Lordship's torne be servyd there."[h] He protests his innocence, "whatsoever my L. Treasurer has put in her highness head to the contrary;" and in less than a week recurs to the same theme, for it seems to have given him great anxiety, and made him very unhappy:

"It ys a hevye care that so honourable a man as my Lord Treasourer ys, (and of thosse auncient yeres, and so experymentyd in prynssys affaires!) that ever a wolld inform the Soverayne with half a tale, to the discredit or undoing of anny man; and specyall of him that was absent, and not able to answhere for himselffe. According as I have writtin you, this ys the thyrd tyme that my lord Treasurer hath servid me this. All be it, caulling to remembrans the faythefull promes that it pleassid the Quene's Majestie to macke unto me at her highness howse at Hatefull [Hatfield] when her highnes came to the crowen, ... what soever her Majestie ys informyd of me in this my absens,

[g] To Sir T. P. Ant. June 22, 1560.—Fland. Corr. St. P. Off.

[h] To the same, June 24.—Ibid.

I trust in God, her Majestie, according to her promis, *will keep one ear shut to hear me*, till yt please her highnes to lyssens me to come home; which is the thinge [which] is now my wholle comfort: to the wyche I doo refer me."[i]

Parry was a good friend to Gresham. He not only counteracted the evil intentions of the lord-treasurer, by speaking to Queen Elizabeth in favour of her merchant, but he conciliated the Lord Hunsdon,[k] who, instigated probably by Winchester, had not scrupled to express his dissatisfaction openly:—

"My factor, Richard Candiller, writes me that my lorde of Hundsdone said unto hym that 'a dyd moche marvill that the Queene's Majestie's harnes came none other ways home; wherein I had moche disappoyntyd her highness: and that he thought I hade sold her harnys to the marchaunts in London, for leuccar and gayen.' Sir, I cannot but marvyll that his Lordeshipe wold make anny soche reporte upon me. For as the Queene's Majestie and you do right well knowe, I have allreddy sent home from this town of Andwerpe viij M corseletts; and then, (my pasportes being

[i] To Sir T. P. Ant. June 29, 1560.—Fland. Corr. St. P. Off.

[k] Father of Robert Cary, Earl of Monmouth, author of the "Memoirs;" in Sir W. Scott's edition of which, (1808,) a highly characteristic and very remarkable letter, addressed by him to Lord Burghley, will be found.

bannyshyd,) I was fayen to transporte all my armeur, and other munission out of Germany, to Handborow; whereas there hathe bynne for the spasse of iiij monthes, v or vj M harnys, and other provyssiones, for the some of xx M *li.*: and dayly there ys transporttyd thither from all places, as they can get carrage. Wyche masse laye there, for that the Queene's Majestie of long tyme wolde not venter above vi C *li.* in a ship: wyche, as the xth of Maye last past, I gat enlargyd to shipe in every bottome ij M *li.*, with longe sewte; for that there ys not passing xij shipes that lades from thens to London in the whole yere. And yett [further] for the more exspedycione, fering that thinges shuld be callid for, (as they be now,) I have adventoryd upon my own head, one thowssonde powndes more in a shipe; wych I have caussyd to be assewred upon the Bursse of Andwerpe. So that I trust in God it shall most playnly apere to the Queene's Majestie I have done my dewtye, and dilligens; according to the trust her highness hathe reposed in me. Being right assured, the like was never done by no subject: and (here writing unto your honnor) there ys as moche done as maye be done, by wit of man. . . . . . . Therefore, I shall most humbly desire your honnor, as to give my Lorde of Hunsdone to undyrstand how all things standyth; and all other that haythe the charge of the receipt of those provissions I have made : for, an my life lay on it, I can doo no more. Assewring you, Sir, it is no smalle greffe unto me to here of anny complante to be maid of me; considering the great care, and travaylle, and sorrow I have had, to bringe all these thinges to so good purpose : wherein I must confess I have done but my dewtye to her Majestie, an it hadd bene x tymes more."[l]

The subject of dissatisfaction with Lord Hunsdon is quite in character; and was just such as might have been expected to have had most weight with that high-spirited, warlike peer: but he was soon reconciled to our merchant; "Perceiving," writes Gresham to Parry, on the 2nd of July, "the Queene's Majestie and you ys fully satisfied in that behalf; as also, you have satisfied my Lord of Hunsdon, and that he hath always been my good Lord, and will so continew; for the wyche I thanck him: to whom yt may please you to do my most humble commendacions."[m]

The letters whence these passages are extracted, also conveyed intelligence of the writer's progress in the shipment of military stores. "The shipes wherein was ladyn the xxx peases of vellvetts, and vi c ells of crymmesyne velvets;

[l] To Sir T. P. Ant. June 22, 1560.—Fland. Corr. St. P. Off.

[m] To the same, July 2.—Ibid.

ix c lxx ells of black damask, wyth ij c lx ells of crymmesyn satyn, be departed from hens without any sercher; wyche dothe amownt to the sum of 2500*l.*: trusting in God that they have all arrived safe. Most humbly beseching your honnor that there may be all the secreasy used that may be, for the resseving thereof into the Tower: wysh-ing there were no man privey thereunto, but only Mr. Blomefylld, whome ys a very honnest, secreat gentilman, and syrcomspect in all his doinges. And dowghtless this matter cannot be too secreat kept; considering the great care and adventore it is in the transporting of it from hens."[n] Shortly after, he announces a further shipment of 'vel-vets;' and adds, "tomorrowe I doo intend to lade 15 pieces of velvets more, and 1000 ells of black damask; so that I trust you shall lack no more of that kind of silks." By this jargon, it will be remembered that a certain quantity of ammunition was signified.

The following passage in Gresham's letter of the 22nd of June, 1560, seems deserving of in-sertion: it possesses some biographical and some historical interest; and, for once, presents us with a picture. "As this daye, at viij of the clocke in the mornyng, came unto me Mr. Bewmownt, (Mr. Secreatorye Cecill's frinde,) and declarid

[n] To Sir T. P. Ant. June 22, 1560.—Fland. Corr. St. P. Off.

unto me that, as isterdaye, he came to this town with the Frenche King's ambassador. And, as he informythe me, his comyng[°] ys onely to practisse wythe some Scottishe man, to send into Scotelande wythe letters from the French King to the Erle of Arran; wherein a offers hym the whole government of Scoteland,—so far forthe he will procead no further wythe the Queene's Majestie: and [engages] that all the Frenchmen shall departe out of Scoteland, and hath offerid him his pardone. Here inclossyd, I send unto you towe letters wyche the said Mr. Bewmont dessyryd me to send yow: the one ys from hys wiffe, and the other from a frynd of his. Furthermore, the said Bewmownt informythe me that the Frenche Ambassidor haythe geven hym to undyrstond that the King, his master, hathe no great trust to King Phillipe's procedings: saying that his master hath had nothinge but wordes, and no deades of hym. Likewyse, a had with him a great discorse of me, and asked him yf he knewe me; and

[°] That is, the coming of the French king's ambassador; whose object it was to prevail upon the Earl of Arran, (a wavering man, but to whom the chief power in Scotland belonged, as nearest heir to the crown,) to forsake the English interest, and "procead no further" in making peace with Queen Elizabeth: for the Earl had deserted the French king's party, and now favoured that of the Congregation. The treaty of Leith was not concluded till fourteen days after the date of this letter. See Tytler's History of Scotland, vol. vi. page 195.

he said 'no,' but that he met me ones at the wattyr side, and that I dyd ask him, 'whether he was a Scotishe man:' and he said 'Yea:' and that I askyd hym 'what newes;' and his answhere [was] 'he knew none.' 'Well!' quod he, 'this Gresham is a parlus fellow; for it ys he that haythe furnyshed the Queene with all the money, and armour, and munition which now be transported at Handborrow, for that his passportes were banished here.' Wythe moche other talke of the Queene's Majestie's credit in thes plassis."[p]

It is, I presume, to this period of his history, namely the summer of 1560, that a financial document in Gresham's hand-writing, from which I shall give some extracts, is to be referred. It is a sketch of what he considered to be at the time the available resources of the state; and begins by stating, that "on the 15th of August next there was to be received of the Countie of Mansfield, (of whom some account will be given immediately,) 300,000 dallors; which, at five shillings each, is 75,000*l*.—40,000*l*. was to be made over by exchange, or by transportation of money. Towards the defraying of the Queen's debts, 35,000*l*. was to be paid; and lastly, 40 or 50,000*l*. was to be paid by the Merchant Adventurers upon their cloths, and 25,000*l*. by the Staplers upon their wools."

[p] To Sir T. P. Ant. June 22, 1560.—Fland. Corr. St. P. Off.

After having transcribed so long a letter at the commencement of the present chapter on the same subject, I am half afraid to recur to it. But a large class of antiquarian readers will forgive me for so doing; and requesting them to bear in mind the notable expedient developed in Gresham's letter of the 1st of March, 1558-9, given at page 257, I will extract only such portions of the present document as seem to throw light on what has gone before. "With the like practise twice done in Kinge Edward's tyme," says Gresham, "I dyd raise the Exchange from xvi *s.* to xxiij *s.* iiij *d.*: whereby, all forreyne commodities and ours, grew good cheape; and thereby, we robbed all Christendom of their fyne gold and fine silver: and by raysing of the Exchange, and so keeping of it up, the fyne gold and fine silver remaynes for ever within our realme.—Sir, if you will enter upon this matter, you may in no wyse relent, by no perswasion of the merchants. Whereby you may kepe them *in fere and in good order*: for otherwise if they get the bridell, you shall never rewle them.[q]

"I wolde [that] presentlie, the Queene's Majestie shulde give licence to our Inglish marchaunts

[q] "Assuring you," writes Gresham to Cecil, (May 14, 1560,) "that, as the merchants be one of the best members in our commonweal, so they be the very worst yf their doings be not looked unto in time; and [themselves] forced to keepe good order."

to ship; for the sooner they doo begyn, the sooner they will be laden: and for licence of long cloths, the Queene's Majestie to grant them liberally, and to let them suffer another way.

" Sir, this matter is of so great importance, as it must be kept secret. For if the merchaunts have any inkling [thereof,] they will never ship their goods; but dispatch them otherwise. . . . . .

" To conclude with this practise.—First, you shall raise the Exchange, to the 'riching of the Queene's Majestie, and the realme for ever.

" Secondly, you shall diffraie the Queene's Majestie's debt.

" Thirdlie, you shall advance the Queene's homeward credit in such sorte as you shall astonny King Philip and the French King; whereof latter [ly ?] her highness hath felt the comoditie. Which matter is of so great importance for the Queene's Majestie's honnor, and for the proffit of her realme, that *I cannot expresse unto you; but refer me to the sequalle thereof,* which shall trie all things: whiche I have atteyned unto by experience and proofe thereof. For when the exchange was at 17*s.*, I made them paie 20*s.* upon a cloth; and the next payment, for every pound, 22*s.*: and to the hindrance and domage of no man. For, whereas it shall seme to the worlde, and merchaunts, that they shall be great losers, ere xii monthes goeth about, they shall get for everie penny loste, ij *d.*; by the reason all foreign commodities (and ours) within the realme shall growe good chepe; as also all kinds of cattell and grayne."[r]

In addition to the expedient here recommended, which had been already successfully practised, Gresham was naturally anxious to discover some channel through which he might be enabled in future with less publicity to accomplish the objects of his commission: for the practical difficulties which he had to encounter as often as it became requisite to negotiate a fresh loan with the Antwerp merchants, were of the most discouraging nature. It was with eagerness, therefore, that he availed himself of an offer which was at last made to advance a considerable sum for the use of the English government. It proceeded from the Count Mansfeld,[s] a German nobleman of the highest rank and distinction; to whom, in the distribution of the government of the provinces, the dukedom of Luxemburgh had been assigned: but the estates on which he generally resided, and from one of which he derived his title, were situ-

[r] Forming part of a collection of schedules, endorsed 1560, concerning which see Appendix, No. XXVI.—Flan. Corr. St. P. Off.

[s] See Sir Thomas Gresham's "Instructions," dated Mar. 25, 1560.—Ibid. There is an engraved portrait of Mansfeld, in Stapylton's translation of Strada, De bello Belgico, fol. 1650.

ated in Saxony, and were particularly rich in mines of silver and copper.

The count employed as his negotiator in this business, one Hans Keck; whom, after considerable deliberation, Gresham despatched to the council in company with his servant Clough. "I have sent to her Highness," he says, (meaning Queen Elizabeth,) "this bringer, — my factor Richard Clowghe, whom yt may please you to credit in all things he shall declare, as though I came in personne myselfe: whom, I will inseure your honour, hath takynne great paynes in the Queen's Majesty's servize in my absens, since her Highness came to the crown; and hath right well deserved some consideration at her Majesty's hands."[t] He begged in the same letter that Clough and his fellow-traveller might not be detained in England, but sent back to him with as little delay as possible.

The documents which Hans Keck carried with him, including Count Mansfeld's letter, (on which are some remarks in Cecil's hand-writing,) are preserved among the State-Papers. The secretary, in his reply, referred the count wholly to Sir

[t] Sir T. G. to Sir W. C., Ant. April 24, 1560.—Fland. Corr. St. P. Off. In the same repository is a document, dated May 1, endorsed by the secretary,—"A Declaration unto Sir William Cecil, Knt. by R. Clough;" being the heads of the information he gave.

Thomas Gresham; whom he recommended to "send some skilful man, as Richard Clough, or such other," to the County, in order to bring the affair more speedily to issue. Clough returned to Antwerp immediately; but Keck lingered in England, to Gresham's great annoyance. At last he made his appearance, "much commending your honour, [Sir W. Cecil,] with *potentissimo*, *reverendissimo*." [v]

Gresham accordingly despatched his servant to Count Mansfeld, with a letter to that nobleman in Latin from himself, dated the 16th of May 1560.[w] We learn from his correspondence with Sir Thomas Parry, that on the 1st of June, Clough wrote from "Isnacke [Eisenach] in Saxony, sixteen Dutch miles distant from the town of Mansfeld," where he expected to arrive on the 3rd of June; and that a day or two after, "passing through the land of Nassone," Clough had written again from Syggen, where he was lodging.[x] He had probably travelled by way of Malines, Maestricht, and Cologne, and so through the south of Germany, until he entered Saxony; whence he

[v] Sir T. G. to Sir W. C., Ant. May 14.—Fland. Corr. St. P. Off. Clough got back to Antwerp on the 9th, carrying with him a letter from the queen to his master, "touching the message that Hans Keck brought from the Count Mansfield," and another from Cecil. [w] Ibid.

[x] Sir T. G. to Sir T. P., Ant. June 16, 1560.—Ibid.

proceeded direct to Mansfeld. But he was altogether so long absent, that Gresham became at last not a little anxious concerning him; and it was with considerable satisfaction that he announced his servant's safe return to Antwerp on the 2d of July,[y] in a letter which he addressed on the same day to Parry, whom he entertained with an account of what had befallen Clough during his visit. The long absence of the latter was explained by the County's having "ridden to his mines of silver and copper, sixty Dutch miles from Mansvelt; and there were no post-horses, nor they might not ryde by night."

"The Countie of Mansfylde hath geven marvellous interteynment to my factor," writes Gresham; "for, after my man came within halfe a daye's journey of hys mines, Hans Kecke, (the Countie's servant,) went afore, to inform his master of his comyng; and the next day he sent vi of his gentillmen to meet hym, viii Inglyshe myles off; and at his coming to the playce, he himself, wyth his famylly there, was at the gate to receive hym: and so hymselfe had hym into the fairest chamber in his house. And there [he] remayned

[y] The chronology of this transaction is *utterly inexplicable*, unless we suppose that Gresham's letter, dated June 4th, should have been dated *July* 4th. In short, I have assumed that he made this mistake, and believe the circumstance to be *demonstrable*.

two dayes, in shewing of his mynes of silver and copper; which is a matter of great importance. And so, the thyrde day, he took his journey to Mansfild, to his chief howse. And by the way, a shewyd him his towns and castles, whereas at dyvers places, dyvers Erles and nobellmen of his house met him; so that, ere a came to Mansfyld, he was accompanyd with i c l (150) horses: whereas a kept my man two dayes, ere that a coulde get any direct answhere, in banquetting of him. And by the way, (as other wyse,) the Counte ministered unto hym dyvers questions; and the chiefest questyon was, that he thought this money that ys tackyn uppe should have levyd sertaine soldyers; whereunto my servant made answhere, that he could say nothing therein; but that he knewe, if the Queen's Majesty should have any such nead, he was right assewrid that he should be employed afore any man. . . . . . Sir, doughtless the Count of Mansfild is a joylly gentillman, and valliant, and marvellus well loved of the nobells and captaynes of Saxony. . . . . .

"You must note that the County of Mansfild stayed my man two days at his house of Mansfild, but [only] to see his estate that he would kepe for the honour of the Queen's Majesty: where was dyvers Countes and Earles, whom was served all in silver; and in the presence of all these nobelmen, there was no remedy but my factor must fyrst waysse [wassail ?] alone, and fyrst sett at the tabell, being marvelously somtuously servyd. My factor allways calling for his resolute answhere, the thyrde day a commandyd all his horses, and my factor's, to be made ready by x of the clocke at noon; and as he was going to horseback, a gave hym these instructions, and told hym that the Queen's Majesty should paye but x upon the c for the yere's interest, and that there should be no fawte but that the afforesaid lxxv M *li.* [75,000*l.*] should be in Andwerpe by the xvth of August at the furthest. And then comes the County's Chancellor, and presentyd to my factor in his Master's name a silver standing-cup, of the vallew of xx *lib.*; and the Countess sent hym, by one of her gentill-women, a littel feather of gold and silver, of the vallew of x *lib.*; and thankyd hym for the paynes he tooke [in] this journey. And thus [he] departyd." [z]

How highly Clough prized the gift above mentioned, appears from the particular mention which he makes of it in his will. That standing-cup of

[z] Sir T. G. to Sir T. P, Ant. July 2, 1560.—Fland. Corr. St. P. Off. Gresham's account of his servant's travelling expenses during this journey, has been inserted in the Appendix, No. XXIV. with the hope that to some readers it may prove interesting.

silver, "wholle gilte," was to remain among his descendants, as "a standard," for ever; and on no account to be removed out of his mansion of Bachegraig, in Denbighshire. He brought with him besides, a letter of instructions to Sir Thomas from the County, "written in the Allemagne tongue," of which Gresham sent Parry a French translation.[a] But there were many things not contained in those instructions, which the count was unwilling to commit to writing; and these had been confided to Clough, to whom Gresham was requested to give implicit credence. All that is known of the result of his mission has been already stated: namely, that the County had engaged to furnish Queen Elizabeth with 300,000 dollars, rated at 5 shillings each, being equivalent to 75,000*l.*; which sum he promised to deliver at Antwerp by the 15th of August; and lend for the space of a year, on interest at the rate of ten per cent. per annum, on the security of the queen's bond and that of the city of London, as usual. He offered to lend 400,000 dollars more, provided the queen would give him the bond of the merchants of the Steelyard as an additional security; but to this Gresham objected, foreseeing that if the proposal were acquiesced in, a similar conces-

[a] Sir T. G. to Sir T. P., Ant. July 2, 1560.—Fland. Corr. St. P. Off.

sion would be required by the merchants of Antwerp also, in all future bargains.[b]

Notwithstanding the fair promises and flattering proposals of Mansfeld, this negotiation proved fruitless. Weeks rolled on, and no money made its appearance; until finally, the period fixed by the County himself expired, and the necessities of the state became more urgent than ever.

Gresham's discomfiture is apparent from his correspondence.[c] He had long since resolved, with the funds which Mansfeld had promised to supply, to liquidate, to the extent of 25,000*l.*, the debt of 150,000*l.* due on the 20th of August; and had therefore been comparatively at ease on the subject. How implicitly he relied on the good faith of that nobleman, and how completely he depended on this resource for accomplishing his purpose, will be seen from the following extract from a letter which he addressed to Sir Thomas Parry on the 7th of July, 1560, with reference to his above-named intentions:—"for as the payment is but littill considering the great debt, so I will insure your honnor it will not be a littill spoken of thorow all the worlde, that her Majestie, in her wars, doth make payment of her

[b] Sir T.G. to Sir T. P. Ant. July 2, 1560.—Flan. Corr. St. P. Off.

[c] He assures Parry repeatedly, that he will "have much ado to content the Queen's Majesty's creditors." (Aug. 18, 1560.)—Ib.

dettes; when neither King Philip, the French King, nor the King of Portingall, in peace tyme, payeth nothinge; whom oweth no small sums of money: wych causeth money to be here so scante, as the like was never seen nor heard of. Therefore, now, a payment of xxv M *li.* [25,000*l.*] to be equally divided among the Queen's Majesty's creditors, will doo more good to her highness' credit than the whole sum of 25,000*l.* ys worth; and by this meynes, her dets groweth the less, and the interest [is] saved. So, the 25,000*l.* deducted out of the County Mansfyld's money, there doth remayne 50,000*l.*; wych I will see transporttid by Exchange, or ells in fyne golde and fyne silver, wych shall fall out to the Queen's Majesty's fardle and proffit." [d]

With the following letter, addressed a few weeks after to the same individual, we shall dismiss this part of our subject. Its insertion serves the double purpose of presenting the reader with another specimen of Gresham's correspondence with Parry, and of exposing how the negotiation with Count Mansfeld terminated.

"Right honnorable Sir,

"Aftyr my most humble commendacions, it maye like you to understande that as the xviii[th] of this [present,] I wrote you a letter by one of

[d] Aug. 18, 1560.—Fland. Corr. St. P. Off.

my owen servaunts, by whome I sent you the cortall horse[e] I promysed your honnor; wyche I thought might have passed at Donckerke wythout pasporte, by the olde statute, being not above xii handfulls high: and, contrary to my expectacion, the Regent hathe of late given an order that none may passe; so that your cortall remaynes at Donckerk. I will try all my friends for pasporte, but I will obtayne pasporte;—wherein your honnor must have patience.

"I sent your honnor likewise iiii dozen of black bottons; as allso your xl dysshis of silver, and xii saucers be in hand, with as much expedycion as maye be. Other I have not to molest you wythall, but that I trust Sir William Cecill hath made you prevey to all my letters; whereby you shall perseve that the Countey of Mansfyllde doth not accomplishe his bargayne for the iiii C M [400,000] dollars, according to his promise. What shall come thereof, our Lorde knoweth, and I do not: but that I do perceyve by one worde that Hans Kecke cast out, the money is here allreddy; wyche is let out apon interest—(to the town of Andwerpe of long tyme, as I guess,)—wyche matter comyth the Queen's Majesty very ill to pass, for credit's sake. Nevertheless, I have so travailed that I have given full contentacion

[e] Or "horse cortall;" the MS. is not quite clear. The meaning is, a little horse.

to all the Queen's Majesty's creditors, as by my prolongacions sent to Mr. Secretary you may percieve,"[f] &c.

But the "contentacion" here alluded to, was only to be procured by having recourse to a scheme, practised as we have seen on former occasions, by which a compulsory loan was exacted from the Merchant-adventurers. On the 2nd of August, we find Gresham thus addressing Parry in London, whither he appears to have come to pass a few days:—"Other I have not to molest your honnor withall, but that it may please you to remember the Merchaunt-Adventorers, and Stapplers, and to proceed fyrst wyth the Merchaunt-Adventorers, who begynne now to enter in the Costome-house, and to layde; and by the xxv[th] of this month they shall be all laden and watter borne; (your honnor knowyth what I doo meane). And be it rememberid to your honnor, that in case if the Quenes Majesty doth mynde to refyne her base monneys within this three monthes, that then you doo demand of the marchands (at the least) for every xx *s.* sterling, xxvi *s.* viii *d.* fleymyshe; and as her Majesty ys therein mynded, to govern the price of the Exchange; for otherwyse the Quene's Majesty may be a loser therebye."[g]

[f] Ant. Aug. 26, 1560.—Fl. Corr. St. P. Off.

[g] London, Aug. 2.—Ibid.

The nature of the operation alluded to in the former part of this extract has been so fully exposed in a preceding page,[h] as to render superfluous any further commentary upon it. The specimen of official correspondence to be next given, will both illustrate the transaction, and show what was its issue. The original letter, having been addressed in the name of the queen to Sir Thomas Gresham, is of course missing; but the rough draft, in the hand-writing of Secretary Cecil, supplies us with its contents, which were as follows:—

"Trusty and welbeloved, we grete you well. And whereas order was gyven by us in our progress, that the shipps fraughted with the cloths of our merchants, this present month of August, should have been stayed, until we might have concluded some bargayne with them for the payment of 3^{xx} [three-score] thousand pounds flemysh, (that is, 30 at the 15th of November next, and other 30 at the 15th [of] March);—so it is, by negligence of such in whom the trust was reposed, they be departed, to the nombre of 34,000 cloths, and no bargayne concluded. In which matter, our treasorer of England hath by his letters from London seemed not to allow the payment of our detts by your meanes; but rather

[h] See p: 257, &c.

to have the dett of November put over to March, which we cannot yet allow. Nevertheless, we meane to have hym come to Wyndsor to us, by Saturday next; and yet, the meane season, we have thought it necessary not only to advertize you, but also to send you our lettres directed to [Mr. John] Fitzwilliam, the governor there, with whom ye shall confer how, presently, before any show-daye,[i] we maye be furnished of this loan; and then delyver our lettres to hym and the company. And whereas we require the money to be delivered [at] 25 *s.* Flemish for the xx *s.* Sterling, because we know not how the case may be reasonably compassed, we remitt it to your consideration and discretion to obtain it to pass betwixt 23 *s.* 4 *d.* and 25 *s.* And we woll you to say to the governor, that if this our reasonable request may not be granted at this tyme, we shal be occasioned to seke some other meane, that will be so hurtful percase [perchance] unto the Company, as we shall be sorry to be forced thereto; and so indede we must, and will doo. This we wryte for more speed,—doubting, if we shuld defer untill Saturday that our lettres might come too late; for that

[i] It seems to have been a practice with the merchants to fix a certain day for exhibiting their merchandize, and exposing it for sale,—called hence "a show-day." We learn from Clough's letter of March 7, 1562-3, that 5000 cloths on the two first show-days, was thought "reasonable good sales."

we be informed the show be about the 4th or 6th of September. We marvell we hitherto hear not of the receipt of the money from the Count of Manxfeldt. Gyven under our signett at Basyng. [Aug. 28, 1560.]"[j]

Basing, in Hampshire, was the seat of the Marquis of Winchester, lord-treasurer; upon whom Queen Elizabeth, now on her summer progress, was inflicting a visit. "She liked so well my Lord Treasourer's house, and his greate cheare at Basinge," says a contemporary letter-writer, addressing the Earl of Shrewsbury, "that she openly and meryly bemoned him to be so olde; 'for ells, by my trouthe,' (saythe she) 'if my L. Treasurer were a young man, I coulde fynde in my harte to have him to my husbande before any man in England.'"[k] The letter which precedes, was accompanied by the following, addressed to Fitzwilliams, governor of the Merchant-adventurers at Antwerp:[l] a rough draft, also in Cecil's hand-writing.

[j] Aug. 28, 1560.—Fland. Corr. St. P. Off.

[k] Lodge's Illustrations, 4to. vol. i. p. 346.

[l] Mr. John Fitzwilliams, whose name so frequently recurs in these pages, was the great-grandson of Robert, fourth son of Sir John Fitzwilliam, of Sprotsborough, in Yorkshire; and was therefore a man of excellent family. His wife was Elizabeth Redrigo, by whom he left Susan his daughter and heir.—From the kind communication of the Rev. Jos. Hunter.

"By the Quene,

"Trusty and well beloved, we grete you well. Whereas we have dyvers grete somes of money to be payd in the towne of Antwerp, the xvth of November and of March next,—which must of necessitie, for our honor and creditt, be then payd; agaynst which tyme we cannot transport over the sum, nether in redy mony nor by Exchange, without both our losse and yours, the merchants of oure realme, by altering and abasyng of the Exchange; we have, by advise of our councell, thought it convenient to requyre you and your company of our Merchant Adventurers, (having there now at this next mart, by means of quantity of cloths to be sold, grete somes of money to be receeved,) to paye for us to our creditors the some of 30,000*l.* flemish, at the sayd 15th of November; dew to such persons as our factor Sir Thomas Gresham, knight, shall declare unto you: and other 30 M at the said xvth of March. For the which, we shall not fayle but see [you] repayd here in our citte of London, in English money, according to the Exchange, for every 25*s.* flemish 20*s.* English, at the manner of double usance; for the which ye shall have such assurance as ye shall conveniently require. And this, we be assured ye may doo; considering as well the great sommes of money that now shall come to your hands, as also the assured lykelihood of the dayly amendment of the Exchange, the rather by your good pollicy. Herein we make an assured account of your conformity; considering how much it toucheth our honour and reputation, and how beneficiall it shall be to us and our realme to be out of debt there; which we most earnestly intend. And if you will take order that the younger Merchants, that have more occasion to use their money there, in returning home of the commodities of those parts, than the elder and richer, may be more easily assessed, (and the rather with the great sommes,) we think the burden shall be easyer, and our service the sooner accomplished. Our Factor and Agent there, can best inform you how necessary it is to have this our request granted; and that we may not, without our great dishonour and discredit have it denyed: and therefore we omitt to enlarge this matter any further unto you, requiring you therein to credit him." [m]

Tedious as this correspondence may be found, it seems desirable for many reasons that it should not be withheld; since it was precisely in similar arrangements that Gresham's co-operation was more or less constantly required. The shifts to

[m] Of this letter, which is also dated 28th August, two rough copies exist among the State-Papers.

which the statesman of that day was reduced, become curiously exposed in such letters; and some insight into the financial resources of the kingdom is obtained. The result of the present negotiation was so far satisfactory, that the Merchant-adventurers agreed to pay 30,000*l.* at Antwerp, between the 15th and last day of November; on condition of repayment in London at double usance, after the rate of 22*s.* 6*d.* Flemish. This we learn from a letter addressed to Gresham in the name of the queen, on the 15th of October: a document very characteristic of those days of high prerogative, for it goes on to state that "as the Merchants may not be able to make such sale, as they may have the said sum in full readiness by the time required, they do desire that Gresham shall assist them in that behalf; which he is accordingly required to do: that they may, if need so require, have the said somme prolonged upon Interest, *which the said Merchants will of their chardges susteyne.*" The merchants of the staple agreed, in addition, to furnish 13,000*l.*; and the remainder of the debt was to be paid out of the Exchequer.[n]

[n] From a document entitled "A minute for the discharge of the debt in Flanders, 24th Oct. 1560:" remaining among the collection of financial papers for that year, already alluded to, (note [r]. p. 337.)

The English numismatist will not fail to have noticed the mention made in a preceding extract, of the project at this time in agitation of ameliorating the coinage. Gresham, as might be expected, was in the secret long before it became generally known; indeed, it seems no unfair inference, from the letters which are next to be given, that he was the originator of the whole scheme. Among the earliest of its promoters he certainly was; for on the 7th of July, writing to Parry, he says:—"Tomorrow departs from hense Danyell Wolstat, only to confer with you if it shall be the Quenes Majesty's pleasure to refine all her highness' base money. . . . . He is an honest man, to whom I am much beholden."[o] Whereas, more than three months after, we find Francis Alen, in a letter to the Earl of Shrewsbury, noticing a rumour that the queen was about to refine her coinage, as if it were yet a profound secret. "There is like to be a calling downe of the base money I undrestande, very shortlye; and the Quene's Majestie hathe sworne that the daye and tyme shall be kepte secrete to herself; and that fewe besyds shall knowe. So as the very tyme, whensoever it chaunceth, will be so shorte and sodeyne, that men are like to have small warninge of the matter."[p]

[o] Fland. Corr. St. P. Off.

[p] Lodge's Illustrations, 4to. vol. i. p. 345.—Sept. 3, 1560.

But we are enabled from the correspondence of Sir Thomas Gresham to adduce further curious evidence on this subject,—more curious and more to the point, it is presumed, than any which has yet been made public. First in order, though not exactly first in date, is the following letter, which tells its own story sufficiently to render all preface and comment unnecessary. Not even need it be stated who was the bearer of it, or with what object he waited upon Sir Thomas Parry.

"Right honnorable Sir,

"It maye licke yow to undyrstond, that the bringger hereof ys Mr. Danyell Wollstat, (he that mackes the offer for the reffyning of all our basse monny wythein our realme); whome, according as I have writtin yow, ys a very onnest man, and substanciall anowffe for the perfformans of the same. Nevertheles, he offerrythe to put in sewrties here in the cite of Andwarpe, or ells in the cite of London, as it shall stonde wythe the Queene's Majestie's pleasseur. Other, I have not to molest your honnor wytheall; but that I shall most humbly dessire yow, (and the rather at my prefferment,) [that] he maye have your favorable inteteynement and preferment in this his sewte; and that he maye have acces unto you from tyme to tyme, for his speedye and better dispache. Assewring your honnor, yf the matter doo tacke plasse, yow shall fynde hym no unethanckefull man; for this of hymsellfe he dessyryd me to write yow. Allbeit, the enterprise ys of great importance, and the sonner it ys put in [hand,] ewre [ever?] the more honnor and proffyt it wolle be to the Quene's Majestie and the Realme: for doughtless, this will raysse the exchange to xxvj *s.* viij *d.* at the least. As knowythe the Lorde, whoe presserve yow wythe increas of honnor. From Andwerpe the viij^th^ of July, 1560.

At your honnor's commandement,

THOMAS GRESHAM."[q]

"To the Right honnorable Sir Thomas Pary, knyght, Treassorer of the Quene's Majestie's most honnorable Howsholde."

Enclosed in the preceding letter was the following, which is equally intelligible; and of which it needs only to be stated that, though undated and without superscription, it was obviously addressed, in June or July 1560, to Sir Thomas Gresham: having been penned probably at Antwerp, though the writer, as we shall see, was a native of Germany.

"Mr. Gresham,

"It maye like you to understand that we have commodity to refyne, everye mounthe, threscore thousande pounds wayght (of xii onces the

[q] Fland. Corr. St. P. Off.

lb.) of suche baysse monney as ys now corrant in Ingland, off 3 or 4 or 6 onces fyne, in xij onces. Iffe the Quene's Majestie woolde retourne suche money unto fyne money off xi onces, or there abought, we whold bynde us to make yt also; and deliver every weke, the some of the silver that we shall weekely receyve of her Majestie's deputies: and to take only, for our rewarde, for all costes and charges belonging to it, for every xij onz. fine, iij q[ter] of a onz.; and the copper that maye be savid in yt.

"And also, to provyd, ourselfes, the stoffe belonginge to the refyninge, without anny discommodity offe the Realme: whiche woolde be a great charge for us. Thearefore, before wey entre into suche enterpries, wey desier to knowe yffe her Majestie woll asseure us of all the quantity of the said money [she intends] to cause to be delivered unto us at London, to refyne. And without [such] assurance, yt ys uneacceptable to undirtacke suche chargis opon us.

"And because that some silver muste remayne in the coper in refynynge, and not be tacken out; then, in our countrey (in Germanye) we woll and must have licens to bringe suche coper out of Yngland into Germany, and there to doo withall as shall thincke us for our most proffyt. And suche silver as shall remayne in the copper, and in waste, we woll take in partye of payment of oure reward; at [such] a prise as yt ys worthe in generall: and the rest, for our reward every weeke or mounth, in redy mony. Iff here Majestie ys myndyd to intend too suche worcke, and desiers more partycularity, we are content to send one of us into Ingland for to declarre yt more at large: better by mouth, as [than] maye be doen with the penne.

"Touchinge of Bastian Solcher, wyche ys with Sir John Yorcke, hy ys the man that haythe comysion of us to move this matter to the counseyll: but [he] haythe not comodity offe the provysion, nor ys of the abillity, nor hayth any bollen to delyver,—as moche as we knowe offe hym; but he ys a man very sckylfull and practicke to suche matter. And as for our parte, your worshipe dothe knowe well anoythe [enough,] that we are men of performans, and to be trostid to suche worcke: and yffe nead should requyre, we can put suertyes for the full doynges off this enterprys.

"Heireopon, your mastershipe [may] pleasse to wryt the effect of this mattir to here Majestie, and to let us knowe here intencion as sonne as ys possible; for our frynd haythe othir thinges in handes.

DANIEL VLSTAT AND COMP[A]."[r]

[r] Fland. Corr. St. P. Off.

Such was the proposal of Wolstat, and such the despatches of which he was made the bearer. It may be interesting to a future Rogers Ruding to be informed of the names of Wolstat's partners, —the members of the 'company' who, with him, undertook and executed the gigantic task of reforming the debased coinage of England. These men were,—"Jasper Seeler, Christopher Ansell, John Lover, and Sebastian Spaydell, almaignes;" and a curious letter is extant, from Queen Elizabeth to Sir Thomas Gresham, dated the 4th of November following, wherein she certifies him "of a bargen made with these strangers for the refyning of base monies;" "and forasmuch as they stood bounde to produce sufficient suerties for the sum of 30,000*l.*, both of Englishmen and strangers, for the performance of their covenants; and had, among other Englishmen, made choice of Gresham to be their suerty for 4,000*l.*; in case he condescended to become bound for them, in such sort as by a copy of a band [bond] sent herewith, should appear unto him,—that then he was to cause the said band to be engrossed; and to seale, subscribe, and deliver the same to the hands of the governor [of the company of Merchant-adventurers.]" Gresham was further requested to solicit the Fuggers to do the like.[s]

[s] Fland. Corr. St. P. Off.

The date of Alen's letter, quoted above, was the 3rd of September. On the 27th, the value of base coins was reduced by royal Proclamation; and on the 29th, was published, in quarto, a black letter "Summary of certain reasons which have moved Queen Elizabeth to proceed in reformations of her base and coarse Monies, and to reduce them to their values, in sort as they may be turned to fine Monies."[t]

By this time, some idea must have been formed of the nature and extent of the services which were continually required of Sir Thomas Gresham. It will be perceived that he discharged the duties not only of an Agent, negotiating loans for the state; and of Queen's Merchant, in which capacity the task of furnishing the country with military and other stores continually devolved upon him; but that he corresponded with Sir William Cecil, as the ambassadors at foreign courts were accustomed.[u] When Naunton, speaking of the Earl of Salisbury, says,—"His good old Father [meaning Cecil,] was so well seen in the mathematics, as that he could tell you throughout all Spain, (every part,) every ship, with their burdens; whither bound with preparation, what

[t] Ruding's Annals, 4to. vol. ii. pp. 135–7. See also as far as page 142.

[u] Hence the preservation of so many of Clough's letters; as well as those of Payne, and others.

impediments for diversion of enterprises, councils, and resolutions,"—it is pretty evident that it was to no other than Sir Thomas Gresham that he was indebted, for a considerable portion at least, of his information. Antwerp was then, in short, what London is now,—the centre of intelligence: so that in addition to Flemish news, Gresham conveyed home the freshest intelligence respecting the Pope, derived from Rome, Naples, or Venice; respecting 'the Turk,' derived from Constantinople or Tripoli; Spanish news, from Seville or Toledo; and not least often, tidings of what was passing, or rumoured, in Sweden, Denmark, Germany, and France. In truth, the very best proof of the opinion which was entertained of his abilities by Queen Elizabeth and her ministers, is afforded by a mere inspection of the Flemish correspondence of the period during which he flourished: about the time of which we are speaking for instance, there are hundreds of his letters in existence, and but very few by any other hand,—so inconsiderable a number, indeed, as scarcely to deserve mention; and most of these relate, or are addressed, to him. This establishes beyond contradiction the interesting fact, that in conducting the policy of England towards Flanders,—a state which formerly occupied a far prouder rank among European powers than it does at the present day,

—Cecil depended altogether on the subject of these pages, and placed implicit confidence in his "advertisements."

Many and interesting are the proofs supplied by the correspondence of these two eminent men, of the watchfulness with respect to occurrences, and the system of espionage over persons which they were accustomed to maintain. In May 1560, Gresham heard that an army of 20,000 foot was encamped in Guelderland; and immediately sent a servant with fifty crowns, to remain in the camp till that sum was expended.[v] Forty or fifty crowns, he says, were richly merited by Payne of Middleburgh, and "Harry Gerbrande, dwelling at Donkirk," for their services; "from which two ports it is most convenient for the Quene to have daily advertisements,—if it were but to know who cometh and passeth from thence."[w] Richard Payne's letters to Gresham are very numerous, and sometimes they are even valuable; but the intelligence they convey, as might be expected, is mostly of local interest, and of an ephemeral character. The same remark applies to the letters of Henry Garbrand. From Toledo, Gresham had regular information sent him by his servant John

[v] Sir T. G. to Sir W. C. May 12th and 14th.—Fland. Corr. St. P. Off.

[w] The same to Sir T. Parry, June 24, 1560.—Ibid.

Gerbridge; and he was frequently the medium by which the letters of English ambassadors resident at the Spanish and other foreign courts, were forwarded to England. In April 1560, for instance, he sends his factor "a packet of letters to my Lady Montague from my Lord her husband,"—Sir Thomas Chamberlayne and Viscount Montague having proceeded at this time on an embassy into Spain.[x] "Right honourable Sir," he says, writing to Cecil the month following; "after my most humble commendacions, it may licke yow to undyrstand that as the iii[rd] of the present, at xii of the clocke at nowen, I sent you in post from hens my servant James Brocketrope, with a packet of letters: wherein was one to the Quene's Majestie, and a nother to you, which came from serteyne Princes and Dewkes out of Germany; and allso another wrytten to me from Frederick Spedt, knyght."[y] At Amsterdam, John Weddington was established, who being in the pay of Sir Thomas Gresham, furnished him periodically with "advertisements," which were as regularly transmitted to the secretary; many of them being endorsed by Cecil's own hand.[z] On one occasion

[x] Sir T. G. to Sir W. C. April 30.—Fland. Corr. St. P. Off. and see Murdin.

[y] May 7.—Ibid.

[z] *e. g.* "Advertisement from my servant Waddington out of

Weddington, writing from "Gronnynge in Frysland," gives his employer some particulars of his journey thither from Amsterdam; observing,—"the dissiples of Lutter and the Zwynglyans have great disputacions at Emden, for the right understanding of the holly Scripture. I pray God send us his holly spryte." [a]

But Gresham's most 'delicate stratagem' was corrupting King Philip's servants: for I have felt it incumbent on me not to conceal, that to compass the ends he had in view, (and as they were not selfish ends, we will not censure him quite so harshly as we should else have done,) Gresham did not scruple to obtain the co-operation, subserviency, or connivance of persons in office by a bribe, or any other means within his power. One of these was Robert Hogan, of whom Queen Elizabeth expressed to Gresham her distrust, inasmuch as he was professedly in the pay of 'her brother of Spain:' but Gresham gave very good reasons for continuing to employ Hogan, and explained to her Majesty the advantages of information derived from such a quarter.[b] In another place [c] he declares to Parry, "there is not one word spoken by the customers, and what they

Holland and those parts;" which Cecil endorses "Amsterdam, May 1, 1560."—Fland. Corr. St. P. Off. [a] May 23, 1560.—Ib.

[b] Sir T. G. to Sir T. P., June 22.—Ibid. [c] July 2.—Ib.

intend to do, but I have perfytt intelligence." Nor must I, as a faithful historian, conceal the great obligations which Gresham was under to his friend Jasper Schetz, who was "both factor and councellor to King Philip," and who gave him constant information of what was passing at that monarch's court. This individual, of whom a favourable account was given in a previous chapter, one regrets to find was not superior to pecuniary inducements. "As this daie," says Gresham, "my very friend Mr. Jasper Schetz ys come to towen, who is the King's generall factor, and one of the counsell of finance, and rewlyth the holl finance and the burse of Antwerp." The writer proceeds to tell Cecil that he had ventured on behalf of the queen, (whose religion Schetz 'favoured,') to promise him 600 crowns; in consideration of which Schetz engaged "by the xx[th] of this month, at furthest, that a commandement should be issued by the Regent that no man should take above 1 *per cent.* for the difference of current money and permission money;" which would save the queen 2,000*l.* at least. "A[d] is a man of great power and wealth, as you do right

[d] It must be superfluous to remark, that by old writers, *he* is often written *a.* "There was a quiver little fellow, and 'a would manage you his piece thus: and 'a would about, and about . . . . *rah, tah, tah,* would 'a say; *bounce,* would 'a say; and away again would 'a go, and again would 'a come:—I shall never see such a fellow." 2 Henry IV. act iii. sc. 2.

well know, and hath always been reddy to doo me all the pleasure a could for the service of our country."[e] In another letter to Cecil, Gresham requests that 500 crowns may be sent to "Sir Jasper Schetz, ... which he well deserves." The queen sent a gold chain of that value, and Schetz fulfilled his engagement: "therefore, good Sir, in respect of this worthy servize, the Quene's Majestie can [do] no less but to write hym a letter of thanks, wyth the reward at least of v c crowns more."[f] One regrets to meet with such transactions as these, but it would not be honest to suppress them; and to the philosophic reader of biography, they convey by no means an unprofitable lesson. Discreditable as they are, and (notwithstanding that they have been frequently resorted to) altogether indefensible on the ground of morality, both as regards Gresham himself and the persons whom he bribed, there is an obvious inference to be drawn from the publicity of his statements, which in some degree palliates, if it does not excuse the conduct of the parties concerned, viz. that they lived in an age when the general tone of morals, as well as of manners, was low. The reader is also requested to remember, in forming his estimate of the character of Sir Thomas Gresham, that nothing has been suppressed

[e] Ant. Oct. 3, 1559.—Fland. Corr. St. P. Off.

[f] Ant. May 12, 1560.—Ibid.

in his history, whether unfavourable or otherwise. I cannot believe that biography is an useful study, if awkward facts and discreditable doings are to be withheld, or only exposed after they have been gilded and varnished over.

The intelligence with which Schetz supplied Gresham, and the frequent services which that eminent financial officer was able to render his friend, were of a nature so little calculated to redound to his advantage, had Gresham's letters by any accident been intercepted, that after a certain period his name is invariably indicated in the correspondence of the latter by a cypher. Sometimes he transmitted the letters themselves of Schetz to the council; but it was always with a request that, "for dyvers respects, as soon as the Quene had considered them, they might be burnt." [g]

Not altogether on strangers, however, did Gresham depend for his intelligence. There is abundant evidence of the activity of his disposition and the personal exertions he constantly made to accomplish his objects. Like his illustrious friend Cecil, of whom Hoby said, "you come so by

[g] Ant. June 24 and 29.—Fland. Corr. St. P. Off. In the same repository of archives is a letter from Schetz, "à Monsieur L'ambassadeur de la Reyne d'Angleterre, le Sr Thomas Gressam, en Anvers." It is dated Brussels, June 26, 1560, and contains French intelligence: making mention of the siege of Leith, Hawkins the admiral, &c., and requesting that the letter itself might be burnt as soon as read.

sterts, as to-night you are here, and tomorrowe you are gone," he would be to-day at Antwerp, and on the slightest summons, in less than four days in London: or, as was often the case during his present protracted sojourn beyond seas, he was found writing from Brussels, and other towns in Flanders where he judged his presence desirable. On such occasions, the only mode of travelling was by post-horses; and in one of his hasty journeys he met with a fall, by which his leg was broken. His servant, John Brigantyn, writes to him from Embden,—"I am very sorye for your fall from your horse: insomuch, I was once in mynd to have seen you," &c. This was in October 1560:[h] and the injury seems to have been serious, for the queen, four months afterwards, alludes to his accident in the following terms:—"We trust after the prolongation of this February dett, your legg will be hable to cary you a shippboard, to return to us; where, both for your recovery, and for intelligence of your doings, we shall be glad to see you."[i] It appears from his subsequent correspondence, that he continued lame ever after,—a circumstance which may explain why, in his later portraits, he is represented sitting in a chair.

We thus conduct Gresham home again; for as the consecutive correspondence on which we have

h Ant. June 24 and 29.—Fland. Corr. St. P. Off.

i Feb. 13, 1560-1.—Ibid.

had occasion to draw so largely, terminates with a letter addressed to him by Queen Elizabeth on the 16th of March, 1560–1, it is fair to conclude that soon after that period he quitted Antwerp, and came to England; whither he had at last obtained permission to return, after an almost unbroken absence of eleven months, during nine of which he had vainly petitioned for that favour. The first documentary evidence of his presence in London is supplied by a "Remembrance," presented by him to Sir William Cecil in July: wherein, after enumerating several grave matters, he requests the secretary "To apoint a day when his honour and the rest of my Commissioners may meet for taking of my account; and at what place it shall be their pleasure to meet together. Finally, it may please your mastershippe to help me with iiii warrants for bukks ageynst the Mercers' feest; at such place near adjoining as your honor shall think mete." [k]

During this protracted absence from England, (namely, some time in the year 1560,) Sir Thomas lost his elder brother, Sir John Gresham.[l] He was born in 1518, and had been knighted by

[k] July 5, 1561.—Fland. Corr. St. P. Off.

[l] He obtains notice in the MS. Council-book of Edward VI., under the 20th June, 1550, as follows :—"A recognisaunce taken of S[r] John Gresham the yonger, knight, in v c marks; to appere

Protector Somerset, on the field, after the victory of Musselburgh, in 1547. Like the rest of his family, he was a mercer and merchant-adventurer, having been brought up to business under his father; and he is mentioned among the nobles and merchants who, in 1553, equipped three ships on an expedition to Muscovy; the result of which was so disastrous, that of the three ships sent out, only one reached its destination. In 1555, the merchant-adventurers to Muscovy were incorporated by Queen Mary, and the name of Sir John Gresham stands first among the assistants of the company. This was the beginning of the trade

before the Counsaill whensoever he shall be called for, between this and Mighelmas next coming."

I am indebted to the kindness of Sir Francis Palgrave for access to a curious volume of accounts, (a kind of Household-book,) mostly in the hand-writing of "Paul Gresham, of Little-Walsingham, in the county of Norfolk, gent.;" wherein there occurs the following undated entry, (probably circa 1560,) which may be worth preserving. "Syr John Gresham's reckonyng.—Rec[d] of hym ii Tonne, one quarter of an hundred, of Englyshe Irone; whereof,

Paid to Atkyns for one cwt. codde for hym, lxxiij*s*. iiij*d*.

It. more for the frayght of the seyd codde, and one hundred of lyng, from Wells to London, vi*s*.

It. more for the carriage of the fyshe frome the wharfe syde to Syr John Gresham's howse, vi*d*.

It. more for makyng the oblygacyon, and for takyng a coppy of the receyvo[r] booke, for the arrerage of the mannor of Houlte Peryers, xii*d*." [Record-Off. Chapter-house, C. i. 13.]

A few more particulars respecting this MS. will be found in

with Russia; and the prominent part taken in it by Sir John, sufficiently marks his spirit and commercial importance. He probably made no inconsiderable figure on the memorable occasion of the arrival of the first ambassador from the "Emperor of Cathaie, Muscovia, and Russeland," in 1557, whom, according to Holinshed, the merchant-adventurers of London went forth in civic splendour to meet at Tottenham. Aware of the importance of the new commerce, they were eager to make a favourable impression on the mind of their barbarian visitor: so they went on horseback, wearing coats of velvet, with rich chains of gold about their necks, and bore all his expenses. Lord Montacute, with the queen's pensioners, met him at Islington; and the lord-mayor and aldermen, in scarlet robes, received him at Smithfield; whence they rode with him to Denmark-house, then "Maister Dimmock's, in Fenchurch-street," where he was lodged.[m] I find it stated in the minutes of

the Appendix, No. XXV. As regards the preceding extract, I have only to observe that Holt-Pereers was one of the manors with which Holt school was endowed; and that "ling" is a kind of fish. "*Ling, salt fish*, and herring, for Lent to provide," says Tusser. Paul Gresham was grandson to William,—only brother of Sir Thomas Gresham's grandfather. See the family Pedigree in the Appendix, No. I.

[m] Chronicles, p. 1132.—Stowe (Chronicle *sub anno*) says they "conveyed him riding through the city to the Muscovie-house in Seething-lane."

Queen Mary's Privy-council, that on the 21st of February, 1556–7, "A lettre [was sent] to th' officers of the warderobe in the Tower, to deliver, or cause to be delivered, to Mr. Hussey, (Governor of the Marchaunts-Adventurers,) or to three of that Company which he shall send for that purpose,—a bed of estate with furniture and hangings for the chamber of the [ambassador from the] Duke of Moscovia; to be by the said marchaunts re-delivered, when the said Embassador shall be departed." A letter was also sent "to th' officers of the Jewell howse, to deliver ij pair of grete white silver pottes to the said Governor, to be used *ut suprà*."[n] The same valuable record supplies us with a few other passages of a similar tendency; proving the high consideration in which this envoy was held, by the marked attentions which were shown him.

Sir John Gresham is said to have complied with the times, in the reign of Queen Mary;[o] but there is no proof, that I am aware of, that he had ever professed the doctrines of the reformed church. He was survived twenty years by his widow, Lady Frances, daughter and heiress of Sir Henry Thwaytes, of Lownd in Yorkshire: and it would appear that he did not leave her in affluent cir-

[n] MS. in the Council-Office, f. 511.

[o] Ward's Life of Gresham, p. 5.

cumstances; for Sir Thomas Gresham bestowed upon her an annuity of 133*l*. 6*s*. 8*d*.,—in those days a very considerable income. Their only daughter and heir, Elizabeth, was married to Sir Henry Neville of Billingbere, in Berkshire; from whom the present Lord Braybrook is descended.[p] Sir Henry was grandson of the Lord Abergavenny, and had been of the privy-chamber to Henry VIII., who bestowed upon him some considerable estates in Berkshire. These are still possessed by his descendants, the grant having been confirmed by Queen Elizabeth: but it had been revoked by her royal predecessor; which seems to imply that Sir John Gresham's son-in-law was a Protestant of a less yielding disposition than many of his contemporaries. He died on the 13th of January, 1593, and was buried in the church of St. Lawrence Waltham, where a stately monument perpetuates his memory; representing himself, his two wives, and his son, kneeling. His epitaph has been frequently printed.[q]

[p] His lordship informs me that he possesses no documents relative to the Gresham family; and it would seem that the portrait mentioned in the History of Audley-End as that of Sir *John* Gresham, is only a copy from a well-known portrait of Sir Thomas. In portraits of the Nevilles, however, Lord Braybrook's gallery is extremely rich.

[q] Collins's Peerage, by Brydges; Ward's Life of Gresham, page 6, &c.

So much has been already said respecting the financial transactions in which, especially at this period of his life, Gresham was engaged, that as the only existing evidence of his occupation during this visit to London partakes of a financial character, the subject may be dismissed without comment. The correspondence of Richard Clough, which was maintained throughout the interval with unabated vigour, it will be more to our purpose to notice; and no apology it is presumed will be necessary for laying before the reader a somewhat lengthy specimen.

It is curious to observe to how great a degree, in that age, the wealth which resulted from the commercial eminence of the Flemish people had engendered a taste for pageantry and extravagant apparel. The reader was probably struck with this in the description Clough gave of Charles the Fifth's funeral; and we have seen that a leading nobleman of Flanders, to wreak his vengeance against his political adversary, had recourse to the ludicrous expedient of insulting him through the channel of costume.[r] It really seems as if this nation, which had prospered as long as its members were chiefly remarkable for plodding industry, had by this time attained a state of luxurious independence, which, while it

[r] Vide suprà, p. 276–7. Strada has an interesting account of the same occurrence: see Stapylton's trans. of his History, fol. p.178.

made a costly pageant an agreeable variety, and one which the whole body of the people were able to relish, conduced materially to render them susceptible of external impressions; and had its full share in inducing those habits, and that temper of mind, on which faction finds it most easy to work, and mould to its bad purposes.

As might be expected, the national tastes just glanced at, did not long preserve their innocent character; but were soon made subservient to party purposes, both in religion and politics. The most interesting illustration of this is supplied in the accounts transmitted to us of certain academic contests, then much in vogue; but which, like many other pastimes which delighted our ancestors, appear in description at the present day flat and unprofitable in the extreme. The performers on these occasions were companies of Rhetoricians, of which there were several in each of the principal towns in Flanders. These companies had been incorporated in ancient times, and invested with sundry privileges: it was their province to address the monarch on public occasions, in verse and prose; and each chamber, or company, adopted some emblem or device by which it was distinguished. Before presenting the reader with the following letter from Richard Clough to his master, which exhibits, with the accustomed minuteness of the writer, a curious picture of by-gone manners, in the description of a pageant of the character just alluded to, I will merely remark, in order to show its connexion with the contemporary history of Flanders, (to which we must presently recur,) that these contests, which in their origin were probably merely rhetorical exhibitions, had become the arena for political cavil; wherein, not only state questions were discussed, but the character of the minister was frequently the subject of popular censure. The reader is also requested to observe, that the same contests were made the vehicle for the promulgation of religious opinions; and had already assumed so formidable a character as to be forbidden by law, and for the space of twenty years to have been rigorously suppressed. At a convocation of the clergy, held at Haarlem in 1564, they were again prohibited, without previous examination and the sanction of the bishop of the diocese. It will be felt that such exhibitions bear the impress of a peculiar and unsettled state of public feeling.— "They were and ar," says Clough, "forbeden moche more strettly than any of the boks of Martyn Luter: as allso those plays was one of the prynsypall occasyons of the dystrouccyon of the towne of Gantt,"—alluding to the revolt of that city in 1539; on which occasion, the emperor, with his accustomed promptitude and decision, having reduced the unruly citizens to order, deprived them of the civic privileges which up to that period they had enjoyed, but of which they had shown themselves so unworthy. I cannot find it in my heart to mutilate Clough's letter, (the original of which extends over fourteen sides of folio paper,) and trust that, notwithstanding its tediousness, it will find some favour in the reader's eyes, in consideration of the historical interest which it certainly possesses.

"Ih̃us ad. 4 de August a° 1561, in Andwarpe.

"Ryghtt worshepfull Sir,

"Ytt maye plese you to understande that I sent you my last, of the 2nd dytto, by the ordinary post; wherein I wrote your mastersheppe howe things passyd att that present. Synce the weche, here hathe passyd no thinge worthye of wrytyng; savying that, as yesterday, (being the 3rd of August,) here hathe beene in thys towne of Andwarpe a wonderfull tryumfe,[s] for the wynnyng of a pryse, weche ys callyd *the Lande Juell;* beyng a skalle[t] of syllver, weche weyeth vi ownsys: for the wynnyng whereof, I dare saye

[s] Clough (and Gresham himself, a few pages further on,) seems to use this word in its Dutch acceptation, which differs slightly from ours.

[t] *Schaal* is the Dutch for a drinking-cup.

there hath bene spentt, (and shalle be, within these 10 days,) one hondrytt thowsand marks.[u] And for because I am in doutt wether your mastersheppe hath sene the order thereof in tymes past, (weche hathe not bene yousyd in xx yeres,)[v] I wyll declare you a lytyll thereof, in brefe.

"Fyrst, the Lords of the towne of Andwarpe hathe bene att greate charges in the makyng of pagents,[w] and standyng plasys to stande uppon, to geve judgement, who shalle wyn the pryse; weche was both costyly and marvelously well done.

"Further, your mastersheppe shalle understande, that in thys towne of Andwarpe ther are 3 companys or brotheroods of Reteryke; whome have every one of them a house alone; and are all 3 very exselent in that syense.

"The one company ys *the Paynters:* the other ar callyd *the Marygollde,* (whome geveth a marygollde in ther armes): the third are callyd

[u] 66,666*l.* 13*s.* 4*d.*: equivalent to about half a million sterling, at the present day.

[v] The last exhibition of the kind had occurred at Ghent, in 1539.

[w] Tooke, in his Diversions of Purley, gives the derivation of this word; but Clough's use of it seems to show that we scarcely attach a correct idea to its signification. See, for instance, what is said at page 386, respecting "*7 pagents, carryed by* 150 *men.*" In page 382, a "*pagency or standyng-place*" is spoken of.—Perhaps it may assist a person desirous of investigating this subject, to be informed that the Dutch terms for a pageant are *triomfboog,* (*boog* signifying *arch*); and *triomfwagen,* which speaks for itself.

the Olyve branche, (and do geve for ther armes a branche of olyves.)

"This Juell that is nowe to be wone, ys to be gotten by playing; and that company that can make the best answer in ther plays to the questyone that ys propoundyd, shalle wyn the juell or pryse: weche questyon ys,—'Whatt thinge doth most cause the sprette [spirit] of man to be desyrus of conyng [cunning]?'—So that thys ys the prynsypal pryse. Notwithstandyng, there are many other pryses to be wone; but they that do wyn *thys* pryse nowe, shalle carrye ytt with them to ther towne, and shalle sett ytt up in ther towne within 7 yeres; where all these townes must meet, as they have done here nowe. For every towne in thys lande hathe one company or 2 of Reteryke, so well as thys towne: for thys towne dyd wyn thys prise att Gantt, xx years past; and for because of the warres, they have nott sett ytt up tyll nowe. At weche tyme the questyon was then,—'A man beyng redy to dye, whatt was hys most hope?'—Some company saye, 'by the byrthe of Cryst,:' some saye, 'by good deeds:' some saye, 'by preyer:' some saye, 'by fastyng;' and som, 'by pardons.' And the company of the Paynters of Andwarpe saye, '*the resourreccyon of the fleshe!*'—So that ytt was conclewdyd that *thatt* was the best answere, and worthye the pryse. But ther was at thatt tyme syche plays played, that hath cost many a thowsantt man's lyves; for in those plays was the worde of God fyrst openyd in thys contrey. Weche plays were, and ar forbeden, moche more strettly than any of the boks of Martyn Luter: as allso those plays was one of the prynsypall occasyons of the dystrouccyon of the towne of Gantt.

"But to my pourpose. The Paynters of Andwarpe hath set up that pryse, and dyvers other; to say,—one to bee wone by plays, (weche ys the prynsypall:) one other, to be wone by that towne that dyd come in most costlyest, in apparrell wherewith ys least fault to be founde; to say, that all things be sutabell: an other, who hathe the best fool:[x] another, whatt company doth go solemnyst to the chourche, and dothe cause the solemnyst masse to be sunge: another, whatt

[x] In 1563, a medal was struck of "Maistre Jean Wielen Oomken;" who, from the legend,—"Prince couronné des Docteurs à quatre oreilles,"—seems to have obtained the very unenviable distinction of excelling as a fool at an exhibition of this nature, when fifty-six years of age. The Fool's object was to create the greatest degree of merriment possible, without "o'erstepping the modesty of nature." He appropriated to himself some insignificant phrase, which he contrived to render applicable to every incident. One, for instance, whose motto was, "Tout avec douceur," amused himself with a fox's brush dipped in honey; with which he saluted every one who came within his reach.

towne dothe make the most triumfe[y] in fyre: another, whatt towne dothe make the grettyst chere in banquetyng; with dyvers other.

"Thys ys the order howe the townes were apparalyd, and howe they came in.

"Fyrst, the company of the Paynters of Andwerp were all clothyd in powrpell satten and vellvett; beyng in number xl hoursys [horse-men,] all havyng shorte gownes or cassacks of that kynde of syllke, lynyd throo with wyte satten or clothe of syllver; dowbeletts and hose of wyte satten, coustyly made; wyte boots, pourpell hatts, and wyte fethers; wyth swords and speres. And all them that had vellvett, was coustly inbroderyd with syllver; whereof Mr. Mellcher Shettz[z] and Mr. Strawle[a] wer the prynsypalle, and head-men, and were so imbroderyd,—bothe ther aparell and the caparysons of ther hourseys,—that the least of them cost above 300*l.*;[b] havyng, ether, 6 footemen, all in pourpell, as *they* were.—There were more of the company, 4 herods [heralds,] 4 typ-

[y] See the remark made in note [s].

[z] Melchior Schetz, Lord of Rumpst, Willebronk, &c., was Jasper's younger brother: "homme vertueux," says Guicciardini, "et bon mathematique."

[a] Anthony Straelen, Lord of Mercshem and Ambrugghe; a wealthy burgomaster of Antwerp, whose fate is recorded in a subsequent page. Concerning him, see Guicciardini, p. 150.

[b] Equivalent, when this letter was written, to nearly as many thousands.

staves, 4 banner caryers, and 6 trompetts,—all in pourpell taffata; besydes 40 footemen in cotes of pourple taffata, with hose and doubletts of wyte satten, in all poynts suitabell to the other. And for because I have molestyd your mastersheppe thys moche with thys matter, you shalle understande the syrconstaunce[c] thereof, and howe all the companysse do come in.

"As the 3rd daye of August, beyng yesterdaye, all the lords of the town of Andwerpe, or the most part, be [were] att one of the clocke in a redyness, appon their pagency or standyng plase, wher they must geve jugement. And, att the same howre, all the townes of Brabantt, with ther companny, must be in a reddyness without the gates; where, at 1 of the clocke, the gates are openyd. And after that the companny that ar fyrst appon the markett,—to saye, the trompeters and the herawlds,—do come and declare unto the lords that they ar in a redyness at the gates, they shall come in fyrst, and passe throohout all the towne, and so before the lords. So that *thatt* beyng done, the company of the Paynters must go to the gates and feche them in by one att ownse, and presentt them to the lords; and [then go] to

[c] Clough's use of this word recalls several passages in Shakspeare, where it it employed in a similar manner; as,

"Pride, pomp, and *circumstance* of glorious war."

feche another. So that, fyrst havyng steyd themsellfes, they wente and fechyd in one of the companies of the towne of Andwerp, callyd *the Golde blome*;[d] where were 60 horssys [horse-men] all in crymysone satten and vellvett, in shourtt clokys lynyd with wyte satten; wyte satten hose and doublets; red hatts with wyte fethers; [and] wyte bootes. All ther hourses [were] trappyd accordyngly; besydes 12 trompeters and heralds, and att the least xx foote men, apparalyd accordyngly.

"After them, they fechyd in another company of Andwerpe, callyd *the Olyve branche*; wherein [were] lyke 60 hourses, all grene satten and vellvett, lynyd with wyte; with wyte hose and doublets. In all poynts so costyly as the other, bothe for foote men and trymmyng of the horses.

"After them, came in the towne of Baro [Bourbourg,] with 40 hourse men; all in tawny satten damaske, and velvet; and after them, 12 wagons[e] coveryd with tawny cloth, and in every wagon two men [were] settyng in tawny syllks, carying 2 tourches; and after, in every wagon, 2 fyre panes [pans?]. All these of Baro had red hose and doublets, and red hatts with wyte fethers, very coustly; and blak bouskyns, suitabell. So

[d] *Goudsbloem* is the Dutch for *marigold.*

[e] Vide suprà, page 242, note [x]; and especially Appendix No. XXIII. Wagon in this place has probably the meaning of *chariot.*

that the wagoners were all apparellyd in the same colours.

"After them, came in the towne of Maclyn [Mechlin,] all apparellyd in cotes of incarnasyon colore stamett,[f] made after the Enggleshe fassyon; beyng well tyed with yellow parchement. All, yello hose and doublets, red hatts and yello fethers, and wyte bouskyns. They came in with 360 horses, ryding by 2 and 2 together: the one 2 had tourches brannyng in ther hands; and the other 2, ether, a flowre in ther hands.

"There were amonxt them, 112 gentyllmen; and every one of them [had] a grett chene of golde about hys necke; and his cote gardyd with fyne golde. Every of them had one or 2 footemen, apparalyd as they wer, with yello satten doubletts, and all things accordyngly.

"They had 12 trompeters, 4 waytts,[g] 4 herawlds, [besides] dyvers and many that dyd cary armes and banners; weche was wonderfull to see. There came in amonxt them, 7 pagents, wonderful coustyly, both for the makyng and golde spent uppon them; and spesyally for the personages that dyd stande upon them, which was wonderful

[f] *Stamett* is the Dutch for *stamine*, a light sort of French stuff.

[g] I believe the earliest mention of the nocturnal minstrels so denominated, is to be met with in Nicholas' Privy-Purse Expenses of Henry VIII., under the year 1532.

to see. And after them, 16 wagons coveryd with yello and incarnasyon clothe, made of a very strange fassyon; lyke unto a canopy: and rownde aboutt the wagon hangyd xii shelds, very costyly graven and gylte, (I mene every wagon,) and the wagon within coveryd with yello clothe; wherein sett 2 men, all over apparelyd as they that were on hourse-backe,—holdynge, ether, a tourche in ther hands; and in the ende of the wagon, 2 cressetts[h] brannyng. All the wagoners, and they that dyd looke unto the cressets, were apparyllyd in all poynts as the other. The matter was so strange, that it ys too long to wryte. They were in number, att the least, 450 hourseys and men; in that lever,[i] att the least 600 persons.

"After them came in Lere [Liere] all in grene cotes, trymmyd with wyte; wyte hose and doubletts, grene hatts [and] red fethers. Four pagents, with trompeters, herawlds, and foote men accordyngly; and after them, 16 wagons coveryd with grene and wyte, with tourches and cressets in very good order: and amonxt them, xx in grene velvett; whereof Conratt Shetts[k] was the prynsi-

[h] Great torches, or beacons.

[i] *Liever* is the Dutch for *rather*.

[k] I do not remember that Conrad Schetz is any where else mentioned. He was the fourth and youngest of the distinguished brothers of whom some account has been already given at page

pall, whome dyd moche passe hys brother Mellcher in costylynes, beyng so enbroderyd with golde and syllver, that no prynsse might be any costlyer.

"After them, came in dyvers townes; some in grene, some in blak, some in orange colour, some in yello: to the number of 15 towns and companies. And with some, 100 horses; some, 200; trymmyd in all pointes as the other, with pagents and wagons; whereof Sertynggam bonsse [?] was the best of the ordinary sorte.

"But pryncipalye of all came Brussells; weche methinks was a dreme.

"Fyrst, they came in with a wonderfull meny of trompetes, heraulds, footemen, standard-berers, [and] caryers of armes; with dyvers other kynd of offysers. After them, came 7 pagents, being carryed by 150 men; and the pagents beyng so trymmyd with young chylldren in cloth of golde, silver, and satin of all colours, so embroyderyd and wrought, and to such good pourpose, that I cannot tell whatt to wryte of them. And about every pagent [rode] 4 men on horseback, with torches in their handes; apparallyd in long cotes, after the manner of polle [Poland,] of crymsone

78, and is commended by Guicciardini in his Description des Pays Bas. 1568, p. 151. Prefixed to the last-named work, by the way, are some Latin verses by Jasper Schetz.

sattin; imbroderyd and garded with golde and silver; hatts of red, trymmyd as the rest, with wyte fethers; wyte satin doublets, and wyte bouskyns; grette gyrdells of golde taffata, with their swords accordingly. After every of these 7 pagents, came 7 wagones, being all coveryd with red cloth, and gardyd with wyte, and hangyd rownd about with arms. In xxi of these wagons, were very fayre personages; some in harness [armour]; some like nuns; some lyke monks; priests; beshops; cardynells; and all kynde of relygyous men; with wonderfull devysys weche I colde nott well perseve, for that ytt was 2 of the clock att aftyr-midnight before they came in: so that I colde nott well perseve it by tourche-lyght.

"The rest of the wagons, beyng att the least in number that came after these pageants 200, (for I told 104,) were all coveryd with red, as the other; and in every wagon, 2 men syttyng, and in some 3,—in crymsone satin as the other; holding in ther hands, tourches. All these wagons were made with wyte basketts, as the marchants do youse here, and no common waggons; and in most of the wagons, 4 grett horses, all with wyte harness, draying as lemone[1] hoursys: the wagoners

[1] *Draying* horses, I suppose, are such horses as are used in *drays*. 'Lemone' I am unable to explain.

beyng apparallyd in red cloth, and gardyd with wyte.

"After the wagons, came 380 on horse-backe, all in cremysone satten, inbroderyd with golde and silver, as the other wer: after them, ther cappytayne, with 24 footemen, all in crymysone saten; wyte hose, and doublets accordingly; and after that, at the last, 25 wagons coveryd with red, full of chests and bagage.

"In fyne, I do judge to be there, 600 hoursemen, all in crymson satten, and 130 wagons: so that, with them on horseback, and they that dyd lye in the wagons, and the chillderne uppon the pagents, I judge to be 1000 persons in syllke; and in hoursys, all together, att the leste, 1000.

"Thys was the strangyst matter that ever I sawe, or I thynke that ever I shall see; for the comyng of King Fylyppe to Andwarpe, with the cost of all the nasyons together in apparell, was not to be comparyd to thys done by the towne of Brussells. And they shall wyn no more with all, but a skalle of syllver weying 6 ownsys!—I wolde to God that some of owre gentyllmen and nobellmen of England had sene thys,—(I mene them that think the world is made of ottemell [oatmeal];) and then it wold make them to thynke that ther ar other as wee ar, and so provyde for the tyme to come; for they that can do thys, can do more.

"Thus the matter endyd yesternyght, between 2 and 3 of the clocke. And thys daye, one party goyth to the churche, where will be no small ado; for as they came in order on horseback to the town, so they must go in order to the church, on foote.

"I wrote your mastersheppe by my last, that there was some news from Rome, weche at that present I cold not lerne; so that now I have lernyd whatt the matter was.—Of late, serteyne of the cardynalls in Rome had conspyred against the Pope, intending to have made a nowe [new (Pope);] and havyng callyd a consystery, where they thought to have sent hym off, and to have made a nowe, whereof the Pope had intellygens; and the cardynalls beyng in the counsell-house, the pope sent for them all and said,—'The cause that I have sent for you ys thys. I have somewhat to saye to you: butt I do command you, uppon pain of death, that what somever I do saye unto you, that you do make me no answer, nor that you do ax me no questyon, for my pleasure ys so. The cause that you have callyd this council ys, (I know ryght well) to put me off, and to make a nowe: whereof I have grett marvell. I have done, and wyll do, my best to observe sych orders as other have done before me; and yf I do amysse,—tell me, and I wyll mend. Well: for *that* ys past, I do forgeve you, for I do know who they be that were the doers hereof; but and yff I maye hear of the lyke, look for no pardone!'—So that they thatt are in fault, are in moche doubt [fear] of the Pope: whereof ytt ys thought wyll be more news very shortly.

"The Prynse of Orange ys departtyd for Docheland to be maryed to the daughter of Duke Marysse [Maurice,] with a small company. For whereas he thought to have had dyvers nobellmen of thys country with him, there ys commandment geven by the King that no man in all thys Low Countrie, bearing any offys, shall goo with him in payne of losing his offys, and [incurring] the King's displesure besyde: with expresse words, because they shall nott be infectyd with any of the herysies that ys yousyd in that countrie. Which matter it ys thought that the Duchess wyll not take in good part; which, in the end, may fall out ill: for the Prynse ys now waxing grette by this marriage, and presently his offyssers do sell most of the lands that he hath in thys country; weche ys moche spocken of nowe.

"The nells [nails] for Mr. Sakefyllde,[m] ar boughtt and shippyd in Bartolmewes Pall's [ship];

[m] Sir Richard Sackville, Under-treasurer of the Exchequer.

whome departyd from hense yesterday. All other your comyssyons by your last letter, I have observyd: whereof I wrote your mastersheppe answer by my last, att large.

"Here inclosyd, you shall receive a parcell of letters which I received from Sir Thomas Chamberlene, out of Spayne.—The Exchange passyth att 22*s.* 4*d.* usans; small store of money, and takers. Havyng nott ells to molest your mastershippe at thys presentt, as knoweth God; whome send your mastersheppe with my Lady, my Mistress, good helth and longe lyffe to the honor of God, and to your hart's desyre.

Your mastershepp's servant,

RYC. CLOGH."[n]

"To hys ryght worsheppfull Master,
Sir Thomas Gressam, knyghtt, the
Queene's Majestie's agentt, London."

Clough had scarcely despatched this letter, ere he had occasion to pen another, also to Sir Thomas Gresham. It was as follows.

"Ryght worshipfull Sir,

"Ytt maye plese you to understand that I sent you my last, this present daye att 10 of the clocke, by owre English post. Syns the which,

[n] Ant. Aug. 4, 1561.—Fland. Corr. St. P. Off.

this present hour, (being 6 of the clocke,) here arryved a post from Hambroo, with letters from Benedictus Goderman to Crystofer Prowyne;[o] wherein he wrytyth that, at that present, the Kyng of Denmarke and the Duke of Holst do arrest all the shipps that they can gett,—specially of Hambroo and Bremen. And whereas the Kyng of Denmark was in a rediness with 500 horsemen to have gone to the mariage of the Prynse of Orange, he dothe nowe nott go: so that he wryteth that he ys in doubt that there wyll rise some matter uppon it. Wherefore I have thought good to sende awaye thys letter in post, because there maye arise more matter than is looked for. From Andwerpe, thys 4th daye of August, a° 1561.

Your Mastersheppe's servant,

RYC. CLOUGHE."[p]

"To hys right worshepfull Master, Sir Thomas Gressam, knyght, the Queene's Majestie's agent in London.
haste haste haste."

It had been already intimated to Sir Thomas Gresham, (towards the latter end of July,) that his

[o] Christopher Pruen was treasurer of the town of Antwerp: concerning him, vide infrà, page 405, note [f].

[p] Fland. Corr. St. P. Off.

presence would soon be again required in Flanders; and the accustomed sheet of "Instructions" having been drawn up, he now prepared to take his departure. While he was in the act of so doing, the two foregoing despatches reached him; as the letter to be next quoted, written on the 7th of August, will show.[q]

"Right honnorable Sir,

"It maye like you to understand, that I sent you my last of the first of this present; and there inclosed, a lettre from Mr. Earle[r] by the order of Sir Richard Sackvyl: wherein I desired your honnor to be good unto me for the rate of the Exchange, for such money as was disbursed and paide here in London; and so I shall eftsoons most humblie desire you to have consideration. For, being rated at xxij*s.* vi*d.* the pound, (as the

[q] On the 1st of August, (six days before the next letter was written,) Gresham addressed a few lines to Sir William Cecil, not sufficiently interesting to entitle them to any thing beyond this brief notice; but rendered remarkable by a curious mistake of the writer. He has dated the letter "*from Andwerpe*;" whereas not a shadow of doubt can exist that it was written in London. The circumstance seems worth placing on record for many reasons, which will at once strike an intelligent reader, See also page 340, note y.

[r] William Herle, a man who occasionally found employment, (chiefly as a financial agent,) under Sir William Cecil. A multitude of his letters are preserved in the British Museum. Some account of him will be given hereafter.

auditor informeth me he hath done,) I shall lose therebie above v c *li.*[a] . . . . . .

"Pretending with the leve of God, as tomorrowe, to take my journeye towards Andwarpe: whereas I shall doe my devoir to the uttermost of my power, for the accomplishment of the premises. Most humblie desiring you to have in your remembrance the passing of myne accompt; and that it maye please you to write to Sir Walter Myldmaie to be at Enfilde, agaynst the Queene's Majestie's coming thither, (as my trust is in God and you); considering the great charge and burden that lies upon me and myne. Other I have not to molest you withall; but that your pillars of marbell be aryved in safetie. Trusting that both my Lady your wyve's chairs of velvet and Spanish lether will be here shortlie: to whom it maye please you to [do] my most hartie comendationes. And thus I commit you to God. From London, the vii[th] of August, 1561.

At your honnor's commandment,

THOMAS GRESHAM."

"Since the wryting hereof, I have received ij letters from my factor, Richard Cloughe; which I send you here inclosed, for [you] to consider at

[a] The intermediate paragraph may interest a financialist, and is therefore given in the Appendix, No. XXVI; together with abstracts of sundry schedules, and other original autograph documents relative to Gresham's transactions about this period.

your leisure: for that it is muche notid that the King of Denmark hath altered his purpose, and taketh up all the ships he can come by at Hambrow and Breamen."[t]

We cannot do better perhaps, than follow the writer into Flanders; whither he proceeded in order to receive 30,000*l.* of the merchant-adventurers, to pay a portion of the queen's debt, and to persuade her creditors to postpone for the space of a year the liquidation of the sums due in November and December. In less than a fortnight, we find him addressing the secretary, from Antwerp, as follows:

"Right honnorable Sir,

"After my most humble commendations, it maye like you to understande that I wrote you my last upon my arryvement at Donckirke; and as the xviijth I arrived in this town. . . . . . The occuraunts be, that the Kinge of Sweden hath sent comyssioners into the lande of Wyrtemburche to take up a great nomber of horsemen and footemen: some men think, to give war against the Kinge of Denmarke. Both the Kinge of Denmark and the Duke of Holst doo arrest and take up all the ships they can come bye at Hamborow and Bremen: to what purpose it is not yet here revealed. The Duke of Augustus hath sent the

[t] Fland. Corr. St. P. Off.

County of Swarssyngbourge and another County, in post to the King of Denmarke.—The Duke Augustus and nobells in Germanny dothe take in very ill parte that Kinge Phillippe wold suffer none of his nobells of this countrye to accompanye the prince of Orange to his mariage of the Duke Morris' daughter; [u] for fere that any of them shuld be corropted wyth their heresies.—The saying is, that the French King hath sent the order of Saynte Michell to the King of Denmark.

"Other I have not to molest you withall; but that I have shipped your iiij chayres of lether, and two of velvet: and the rest, of velvet, will be redy this next weeke. Most humbly beseeching you, at the Queene's Majestie's comyng to Enfyllde, to remember me for the passing of myne account, as my trust is in God and you; and that it may please you to wryte for Sir Walter Mildmaie to be there. And thus, with my most humble comendacions to my Lorde Admerall [Clinton,] and to S[r] Fransis Knowles, and to my Lady your wife, I comit you to God; whoe preserve you with increase of honnor. From Andwerpe, the xix[th] daye of August, a[o] 1561.

At your honnor's commandement,

THOMAS GRESHAM."

[u] Duke Augustus was brother of Maurice, Duke of Saxony, and succeeded him in the Electorate. He was guardian to his niece, the Lady Anne, whom the Prince of Orange married; his first wife, Anne Egmont, being dead.

"Here is no communicacyone of the King of Sweden coming into England; for that there is a practise for hym to marry the Kinge of Pole's daughter, and Imbassadors sent of both partes, as the saying is here.

"Here is nothing in this town to do, because they are styll triumphing and drynking, which of the towns shall wynne the Land Jewell; wherein hathe been spent above 100,000*l*.

"The letters out of Germanny declaryth that the Emperor shuld be very sore syck of the agew, and in great danger.—Herewith it may please you to receive one letter from Mr. Docter Mownte."[v]

These are lengthy extracts; but, without a few such specimens, no correct idea can be formed of Gresham's duties, occupations, and mode of life. For the same reason, the following disconnected passages claim insertion; written during a period when he was among the most active of Cecil's correspondents.

"Right honnorable Sir,

"It maie like you to understande that I sent

[v] Fland. Corr. St. P. Off.—Dr. Christopher Mount, or Mundt, an agent on whom Sir William Cecil was accustomed to depend for his German intelligence, resided chiefly at Frankfort or Augsburg. His letters are almost all in Latin, and occur in large numbers among the State-Papers.

you my last, of the xixth of this present. Since the wyche time there is nothing worthye of writing, but that the saying is now here that the Kinge of Sweden, the King of Polle [Poland], the Kinge of Denmarke, and the Duke of Saxony, the Landgrave and dyvers other nobells of Germanny, doth wholly joyne together agaynst the Emperor of Muscovya. As likewise the saying is, that the counsel of Trente goeth forward; whereat [it] is thought nothinge will be concludyd. Allso the Kinge of Spayen doth requyre of the states of this lande, a gift, or subsidy of money towards the payment of his debts; and they have made answer they will grante nothinge, except the Inquissition be put down; and that the land be not molestid wyth these new Byshopes, in religious matters." [w]

Take another specimen of his 'advertisements,' extracted from a letter written a week after the preceding: "Now, there is no other communicacione but that the King of Sweden for certeyn dothe come into Inglande; and that his Majestie is departed from Stockholm towards his haven of Newles, (wyche ys iiij c Inglishe myles distaunt,) and bringes with him one of his sisters, and his youngest brother, and the youngest Duke of

[w] Aug. 24, 1561.—Fland. Corr. St. P. Off.—Concerning these grounds of complaint, more will be said hereafter.

Saxony; with divers other nobellmen and gentlemen. He hathe made governor of all his country, the Duke, (his brother,) that was in Ingland."[x]

Next week, we read: "At this instant, Mr. Harvye (that was in Spayne) came unto me and said,—'For as muche as you are here wholly the Queene's Majestie's mynyster, I am come to geve you to undyrstand that I was commandyd by the Queene's Majestie's ambassador, Sir Thomas Chamberlayne, to make my repayre home; for that her Majestie's pleasure was suche. As likewise I received a letter from Sir William Cicell, by the wyche he promises me that [I] might safely come. And forasmuch as I have no other assurance from her Majestie than by the Ambassador, I have wrytten unto Mr. Secretary my full determynacion therein.'—I dyd persuade with hym all that I could, that your letter was more than suffycient; and that, if I were myself in his case, I wold upon your letter pressently make my repayre home. But as far as [I] can perseve, he will not come home except he hath some other assurance, for all my persuasion. So that herewith you shall receive his letter, and a letter that

[x] Aug. 30.—Fland. Corr. St. P. Off.—*i. e.* John, Duke of Finland, concerning whom, see p. 312, &c.

he gave me to be delivered to the Lorde Montague. He remaynes at Lovayen; and *there* is Mr. Englefyld, who intendes to make his repayre homewards very shortely; as one Prewdence, my Lady Dormer's servant, informed me."[y] In this letter occurs the passage concerning Sir John Legh, quoted at the commencement of the preceding chapter.

"The saying is here still," writes Gresham at the end of four days, "that the Kinge of Swedone for serteyne comes into Inglande, wythe a great navye, to the nomber of one hundred sayles of ships; and bringes withe hym two myllyons of Dallors, at the least. Whereof I doo right well knowe your honnor hath better advertisements by his ambassador, than I can give you from hence. . . . . . . As this daye, here is aryved my frinde Sr John Lye; who has hym most humbly commended unto you, and pretends, with the leave of God, to make his repaire home by the last of this monthe."[z]

[y] Sept. 6, 1561.—Flanders' Corr. St. P. Off.—The 'old Lady Dormer' was at this time living at Louvain, (Sir T. G. to Sir T. P., 29th June, 1560.—Ibid.); and we learn from this letter that Queen Mary's privy-counsellor, Sir Francis Englefield, who had fled over to Flanders, and had been taken into the pay of the King of Spain, had chosen the same place of retreat. At Louvain was one of the chief seminaries of the refugee Roman Catholic priests from England.

[z] Sept. 10.—Ibid.

One other specimen, written from Antwerp on the 23rd of September, 1561, claims insertion; and it shall be the last.

"Right honnorable Sir,

"After my most humble commendations, it may like you to understand that I sent you my last, of the xvi[th] of this present. Synce the wyche tyme here ys nothinge worthye of writing, but that I have receivid lettirs of the xxviij[th] of August from my doer at Handborowe; wherbye I perceive that the Kinge of Denmarke, and the Duke of Holst, and the Duke of Brunswicke, hathe released all the Queene's Majestie's armour and munission. Whereas I have attempted all the ways and practisse I can, for the dispatch thereof; but I can by no meanes compasse it. Therefore, for the better dispatche thereof afore the wyntar dothe come, there is shipped in two shippes these parcels as followeth:—

"Shipped, by the grace of God,[a] in [the ship of] Martynne Styteman,—vij c xl corselets: v c lxxij corriers: v c lv morrions;[b] wyche was the goodes that was lost at Dichemarche, and under the arrest of the King of Denmarke and the Duke of Holst, and his brother.

[a] This form of words is only now falling into disuse. Vide suprà, p. 240, note [y]. [b] Vide suprà, p. 320, note [z].

"Shipped in the Cristopher of Dyttemarche, xlij M waight of salte peter, and vij C XX long corriers.

"All wyche goodes doth amount to the some of iiij M *li.*; wyche I have caused to be assewred aftyr the rate of v *li.* upon the hundred, for the more seurtie of the seyes; wyche I beseche the Lorde to sende in safetie. Lykewise, as there can be gotten ships for London, the rest shall be shipped wythe as much expedycione as maye be.

"Here ys no other occurrants, but that the Kinge of Sweden shuld be aryved in Ingland, wythe one hundred sayles of shippes; wyche is here muche spoken of, that the Queene's Majestie wolde suffer such a nomber of shipes to come into her realme, if the Queene's Majestie and he shuld not not parte frendes. . . . . . .

"It maye please you to take order with my Lorde Treasurer, that my bills of exchange maie be paid, for the preserving of my poor name and credit; which doth not a little disquiet me: for that, as the xv^th^ of this present, there was not a penny paid. Rendering unto your honnor my most humble thankes for your goodness showed unto me in that behalf, and for the dispatch of the bondes, which I doo attend for dayly; and upon the recovery of the olde, I doo intende (with the Queene's Majestie's leve) to make my repaire home.

"Here is great communicacion how that the King of Navarre hath sent to King Phillip his ambassadors for the restoring of suche possessions as he keeps from him, of his kingdome of Navarre: and it is muche doubted some breache of warre will follow. . . . . Here hath been great talke of a great earth-quake that of late hath bynne in the realme of Naples, and hath overthrown both great towns and castels; whereat many persons have perished."[c]

The preceding letters were written during a sojourn of two months, made by Gresham at Antwerp in the autumn of 1561. From October until the end of the ensuing February, he was in London: and on New-year's day, presented Queen Elizabeth with 10*l.*, in angels, enclosed "in a purse of blak silk and silver, knytt;" for which he received in return twenty-four ounces of plate—in the shape of "oone guilt cup with a cover." Lady Gresham, whose offering was "a boxe with foure swete baggs in it," received a smaller gift in return. We are pleased to recognise our old friend "Sir John A-lee," among the personages at court on the same occasion. He gave the queen "a cofer of woode, carved, paynted, and gilt, with

[c] Sept. 23—Fland. Corr. St. P. Off.

combes, glasses, and balls :" and his reward was "oone guilt stowpe with a cover."[d]

The active mind of Gresham seems to have been as much on the watch as ever, for opportunities to benefit the state; and we cannot wonder at the esteem in which he was held, when the number and importance of his services are considered. During his long residence at Antwerp, however successful he had been in evading them, he had witnessed the superiority of the custom-house regulations in that city, over those of the same establishment in London; and he now wrote to his factor, Richard Clough, desiring him to obtain complete information as to the system pursued in Flanders; and to communicate to him the result of his inquiries in writing. This produced the following epistle, which will be perused with interest for the contrast it affords between the commercial usages of that age and the present; as well as on account of the interesting proposal with which it concludes. Nor will the reader fail to give Clough due credit for his intelligence and activity, when it is mentioned that a very few days after the receipt of his master's inquiries, he returned him the answer from which an extract is here subjoined; covering more

[d] Nichols' Progresses of Queen Elizabeth, vol. i. pp. 115 and 125.

than twenty sides of folio paper, and entering into all the details of the custom-house with the utmost minuteness.

"Ihũs ad. 31st de Dyssember, a°1561, in Andwarpe.

"Ryght worshepful Sir,

"Ytt maye plese you to understande that I sent you my last by oure Enggleshe post, wherein I wrotte you of all thyngs att large. Syns the wiche, I have received your mastershipp's of the 20th date; well understandyng the effecte thereof.

"First, whereas your plesure is that I shall make inquiry amongst your frynds here, for the order, and howe they do youse the matter in hyryng outt of their tolle or Coustom here, with the wholle systeme thereof,[e]—I have (thro' the frendeship of your gossepp, Crystofer Prowne,[f] now beyng Treasorer of the towne of Andwarpe)

[e] In the State-Paper Office is preserved a MS. extending to twenty-four sides, endorsed by Clough,—"The ordynances howe, and aft[r] what manner y[e] do yousse to hyre hout the toll and coustomes in the neder lande of brabantt and flanders." At the conclusion, are these words; "Done at Bruxelles, the ix[th] day of October, 1560."—Fland. Corr.

[f] We have met with Christopher Pruen's name before, (p. 323,) and he is mentioned by Guicciardini, p. 123. In a letter to Cecil, Gresham says, "my gossip Prewen . . . . . . declaryd unto me that ther were men of Importance had chargyd him that they knew he was a great man with me; and for the amyttey that they perseved to be betwext hym and me," &c. Ant. Aug. 29th, 1562.—Ibid.

gotten outt in Doche the pryncypall partyculars thereof; the menyng whereof is in Enggleshe, as here after foloweth."

Having entered into details which cover sixteen pages, Clough proceeds as follows:

"Sir, I am glad to heare that thys thyng is callyd for; hoping that suche order shalle be takyn therein, that it shalle be for the Quene's Majestie's profett, and the honor of the realme. For as the matter is now yoused, it is agaynst conscyence to hear the tallke that goeth, howe the Quene is disseved; which must needs be trewe, consyderyng the order that they do youse, (whiche is to no resone); [namely,] that the Quene's coustomes must stande uppon the reportt of v or vi serchers, (more or lesse,) whiche serchers are men knowne to be men that wyll be coropptyd for moneye. For, in the openyng of a fatt[g] full of syllks, some tymes I doubt it is broughtt over to the coustom house for fustyans, or suche other ware. Butt and if the Quenes Majestie will thus lett outt her coustome, I do not doubt butt she shalle feele shortely howe the matter hathe passed: or otherwise, and if hyr Majestie be not dysposed so to do, and if I myghtt

[g] A *fat* (or vat) of merchandise was a package. The word *winefat* occurs in the New Testament; and we have already met with the term *dry-fats* in Gresham's letters. Vide suprà, p. 141.

be credytyd therein, and if the Queen's Majestie wollde bestow butt ij or thre thousannde pownds once, I wollde nott doubt butt to save her fyve thousaunnde pownds every yere att the least. For, where[as] the matter is yoused att London by so many Quays crowne-serchers, wayters, and other powlyng offycers, in suche order that all the worlde dothe crye outt upon us, (as you do ryghtt well knowe,)—here is in Andwerpe but i or ii serchers. Yett I dare saye there is more coustome stollen in London in i Month, than is here in Andwerpe in one wholle yere; whiche comyth, because they here do the thyngs in order, and wee, outt of order.

"I doubt wether Mr. Secretary, or other my lords of the counsill, do knowe of some of these orders, [usages,] whiche I have hearde bothe Englishe men, and straungers moche complayne uppon: [one of] whiche is, [that] when men have their goods att home in their howsys, they must runne sometymes x days [before they are able] to gett a sercher to come [and] see the openyng of the goods. And unlesse he [the merchant] wyll geve iiii or v groats to the sercher, possybly he wyll not come in xiiij days, which is no reasone; for a stranger or Englisheman oughtt to paye butt one coustome—and nott to the quene and to the sercher bothe. Thys is a thyng dayly yousyd;

and when the questyun ys axyd unto the sercher, or waiter, 'wherefor he dothe so youse the matter,' they saye that 'they have butt xx nobles [6*l.* 13*s.* 4*d.*] wages, which they cannott live uppon.'[h] In myne opynyon, better it were that the matter were so yoused that men myghtt be servyd as they oughtt to be! For I dare saye that nott only Engglishemen, butt strangers also, are more agrevyd with thys trouble, than they are in paying of the coustome. And one thing [is certain,—that] it must needs be muche agaynst the Quene's profett. A Marchante, whattsoever he be, having a fatt or packe of sylks in hys housse the space of vi or viij days, (and consyderyng the great coustome that they do paye for it,) it ys not to be thoughtt the contrary, butt that he wyll seke all the menes he can to take out those syllks, and putt in other goods in the place. Some men will saye,—'no, because the sercher hathe putt hys seale upon it.' He that made the sercher's seale, can make the lyke; and it is to be thinkt that marchants are not the sympelyst kynd of pepell that be: for I do knowe that bothe here, (aye truly [and in] Spayne, [and] Dochelande,) men do seke out the best heddyd men that they can, to do their besynes,—specyally abroade in forren countrese. In Engglande, many wyll saye

[h] The average salary of this officer at the present day, is 300*l.*

that [these] are coustomes that hathe of long [time] bene yoused: yett, in mine oppynyon, and yf they be never so olde, and nott for the honor or profett of the realme, they maye well be broken.

"I wryte this muche unto your mastersheppe to putt you in rememberanse that when tyme shall serve, you maye breake some of these matters to Mr. Secretary; for in dede it is marvell that wee have so gude orders as wee have, consyderyng what rulers wee have in the sittey of London; suche a companny that do study for nothyng ells butt for their own profett. As for insampell: consyderyng whatt a sittey London ys, and that in so many yeres they have nott founde the menes to make a Bourse! but must wallke in the raine, when ytt raineth, more lyker pedlers then marchants; and in thys countrie, and all other, there is no kynde of pepell that have occasyon to meete, butt they have a plase meete for that pourpose.—In dede, and yf your besynes were done, and that I myghtt have the lesure to go about hytt, and that you wyll be a menes to Mr. Secretary to have hys favore therein, I wyll nott doutt butt to make so fere a bourse in London as the grett bourse is in Andwarpe, withhoutt molestyng of any man more then he shulld be well dysposyd to geve. Herein I am somwatt tedyus: desyryng you to pardone me, for beyng ownse enteryd into the matter, I collde nott stee mysellfe.[i] . . . . .

"Occurencys there is none, butt that by the letters outt of Italy, they wryte of a smalle doubt of warrs betweene the Venesyanes and Mylane: for that the Venesyannes have a towne whiche some say hathe pertaynyd to the Dukedom of Milane, whiche towne they have of late fortyfyd, and putt in a grett number of men. And, to the contrary, they wryte that the Marquis of Pyscara dothe make all the frontiers of the Dukedom of Milane strong, and hathe fournyshed them with men and munysion; butt it is thoughtt all wyll be seised; for the Venyssyans have too muche monneye in that respecte.

"They wryte allso that the Pope makyth grett labore to have a generalle counsell; and that there ys all redy att Trentt above cc Besshops. As towchyng all other your affaires, I wrote you att large yesterdaye by the Enggleshe post; havyng not ells to wrytt you att thys presentt, butt preying God to sende your worsheppe, with my Lady, grace, helthe, and long lyfe, to the honor of God, and to your hart's desyre.

Your mastershepp's Servantt,

RYC. CLOUGHE."

"As towchyng the matter for the toll, and if it

[i] A fac-simile of the original passage will be found in plate v.

were wryttyn agayne, it shullde nott be amisse; for that I am in doutt weder Mr. Secretary can well rede my hande."[j]

The result of this correspondence does not appear to have been an immediate amelioration of the system which had hitherto prevailed at the custom-house; but after a few years, a great change was wrought in this department, which was attended by an enormous increase in the revenue.[k] That a vigilant eye had for some time been kept on the merchants, is sufficiently evident; and the wealthy foreigners who had become naturalized in the city, but who were always regarded by their English neighbours in the light of rivals, had been the objects of peculiar scrutiny.

They were, it seems, in the habit of taking out a licence to export a certain quantity of merchandise, paying the same duty as English subjects; it being always understood that the said merchandise was to be their own property. Thus Bene-

[j] Ant. 31 Dec. 1561. The address as before. Lansd. MS. no. v. art. 27. The Council of Trent began to be held on the 13th of December, 1545, and terminated on the 3rd of December, 1563.

[k] In 1330, the amount received for customs is stated to have been about 8000*l.*: in 1561, the revenue derived from the same source, was 71,365*l.* 15*s.* 1*d.* It rose to upwards of 100,000*l.* in 1613; and in 1641 had increased nearly five-fold. In 1709, the customs brought in 2,319,320*l.*; and in 1789, 3,711,126*l.* The returns for the year ending January 5th, 1839, show a revenue of 31,018,843*l.*, derived from the customs and excise.

detto, or as he was more generally called, Benedick Spinola, a young merchant who belonged to one of the best families of Genoa, obtained a licence in the beginning of the present reign "for the passing 2000*l.* in custome as an Englishman, viz. 1600*l.* in clothes, and iiij c in swette wynes."[l] But scarcely had four years elapsed, ere we find the Italian called upon to sign the following confession of his fraudulent practices, in the presence of the Earl of Pembroke, Sir Walter Mildmay, and Sir William Cecil, who drew up the document with his own hand.

"27th Dec. 1561. I doo confess that I have entred in the customs' book at London, and shipped out of this realme in my owne name, and uppon my licence, the nomber of foore hundred [and] forty-foore karseys, which wer the proper goods of Ihon Justiniano of Cio, stranger. For the which I have payd to the Queene's Majestie's use but Englishmen's customs, according to my licence: and have receaved of the sayd Justinian such custom as strangers doo paye to her highness for karseys; abatyng to hym (by agreement betwixt us) viij c vppon every carsey.

"*Per me* BENEDETTO SPINOLA."[m]

[l] April 21, 1 Elizabeth.—Lansd. MS. No. xiii. art. 10.

[m] Lansd. MS. no. v. art. 48. Benedick Spinola,—a name well known in Queen Elizabeth's reign,—was the second son of Baptist Spinola, an eminent merchant of Genoa, who in 1556 refused

It will be observed that this exposure of a kindred abuse to that which particularly engaged the attention of Richard Clough, was drawn up only three days before the date of his letter to Sir Thomas Gresham.—A view of the custom-house as it appeared in Queen's Elizabeth's days, may be seen in Wilkinson's Londina, copied from a rare and ancient print. It was erected in the ninth year of Richard the Second's reign, and preserved its integrity until the general conflagration of 1666.

the dukedom of his native city.—Visit. of London, MS. in Queen's Coll. Lib. Oxford, fol. 117. The Earl of Leicester said that Benedick was the best Italian he knew in England; (Harl. MS. no. 260, art. 208,) but the subject of this eulogium found the earl very unpunctual in paying his debts, for he had occasion to trouble him with many letters on the subject.—Cott. MSS. Spinola was more magnificent in his New-year's gifts to the queen than any other man of his quality. In 1561–2 he offered "oone hoole peice of purple velvett." In 1577–8, he presented a "petticote of watchet satten, leyed al over with pasmane lace of golde and sylver, and flowers; with eight yards of pasman of golde and silver rounde abowte it, lyned with yelo taphata:" and he received in return 80 oz. of gilt plate; which was not, perhaps, quite satisfactory, for next year he only gave "a fore parte of white and tawnie satten, al over faire, embrauderid with golde and silver; and two fannes of strawe, wrought with silke of sundry colours;" on which occasion he only received "a paire of guilt potts," weighing 4 oz.—Nichols' Progresses. A copy of his will may be seen in the Prerogative-Office; it was written by the testator's friend Horatio Pallavicino, (whom he calls "mio confidentissimo . . . . . . siendo io al mio letto,") 6th July 1580; and was proved on the 29th of October following.—Arundell, quire xxxvi.

The most interesting, if not the most important point in Richard Clough's letter, is his suggestion relative to the erection of an Exchange for merchants; and although the honour of having originated that project rests, as we have seen, with Sir Richard Gresham, yet was Clough's proposal not the less original, nor a less genuine expression of individual feeling. It eventually fell to the lot of the subject of this memoir to erect the Royal Exchange; but no small credit is due to his correspondent for the earnest and hearty wishes on the subject which we have just heard him express. "Herein I am somwatt tedyus: desyryng you to pardone me, for beyng ownse enteryd in to the matter, I collde nott stee mysellfe."

From the month of October 1561, until the ensuing February, as already stated, Gresham was in London: but on the 4th of March, 1562, we find him on his way to Antwerp, addressing Sir William Cecil at five o'clock in the morning from Dunkirk, where he had arrived after a stormy passage, which he describes. To pay some of the queen's bonds, and to renew others, was as usual the object of his journey; and what seems to have occasioned him considerable anxiety, were four cases of treasure (in sovereigns)[n] which he carried with him in order to satisfy certain of the credi-

[n] Fland. Corr. St. P. Off.

tors. On the 27th of March, (having already written on the 21st, 22d, and 23rd,) he announced his intention of repairing home as soon as Clough returned from Deventer: and with the queen's leave he proposed 'to call himself to account again, it being now twelve months since he had so done.' "Trusting that now her Majestie will bless me with her Royal gift for my servize, in such sorte as King Edward her late brother, and Quene Mary her late sister did; who, as you know, gave me between them the some of 300*l.* ([in] land) a yere, to me and my heires for ever." He had rendered Queen Elizabeth more important services than both her predecessors; and, says he, "when I took in charge this business, the Quene's Majestie promised me, by the faith of a Quene, that and if I did her but the like servize I did to her late brother and sister, she would give me as moch lande as both they did." [o]

This part of our subject is brought to a close by the following extract from "A brief of the account of Sir Thomas Gresham, knight, the Quene's Majestie's agent in Flanders, for three whole yeares, and one hundred fifty and nine dayes; determyned the xxii[nd] daye of Aprell, anno quarto Dominæ Elizabethæ, [1562.]" [p]—After several weighty "charges" and "discharges," we meet

[o] Fland. Corr. St. P. Off. [p] Ibid.

with two items of which we know something:—"A yron chest 20*l.*;"—"charge of a Turkey horse 10*l.*;" and finally,

"Riding and posting charges .	£1,627	9	0
House-hire	200	0	0
Diett and necessarize . . .	1,819	3	5
	£3,646	12	5"

With regard to the second of these, it is worth mentioning, (it should indeed have been sooner mentioned,) that Sir Thomas Gresham's house at Antwerp was situated in the "Long New Street;"[q] or, as it is laid down in the plan of that city, *De Lange nieu strate*,—a situation which preserves to this day its ancient character, and was in his time the principal street in Antwerp.

During the intervals between his late journeys to and from the metropolis, he may be presumed to have been busied with the erection of the mansion in Bishopsgate-street, to which he afterwards gave his name. It is doubtless to this edifice that Clough alludes in the following passage, which occurs in a letter he addressed to his master in the beginning of 1563. "And for suche letters as I have received, so well from S[r] John Masone as other wyse, both for Spayne and Venis, I have

[q] This we learn from the address of the letters he received from his servant R. Payne, of Middleburgh. Payne generally adds, "Give the post 1 stiver."—Flanders Corr. St. P. Off.

sent them awaye: and as towching *the galary and the stones for the wyndose and walls*, they are all shippyd in the shippe of John Ryke, who departyth from hens within two or three days, at the furthermost."[r] Stowe, speaking of the houses occupied by men of worship in St. Helen's and the neighbourhood, mentions Gresham-House as "the most spacious of all other thereabout; builded of bricke and timber."[s] Like the Exchange, it consisted of a square court, surrounded by a covered walk, or piazza; and it had spacious offices adjoining, as will be seen from an inspection of plate x; the whole being surrounded by pleasant gardens, which extended from Bishopsgate-street on the one side, to Broad-street on the other.

Of Gresham-House, which is better known by the name of Gresham College, more will be said hereafter; it needs only to be observed at present, that the earliest document which mentions it by the former name, bears date the commencement of 1566.[t] Vast as the proportions of this

[r] R. C. to Sir T. G. Ant. March 7, 1562–3.—Fland. Corr. St. P. Off.

[s] Strype's Stowe, ed. 1720, book ii. p. 106.

[t] January 30, 1565–6. The document alluded to is a Latin instrument on parchment, (Gresham's power-of-attorney, apparently,) to William Fayre, gent. (Phaer, the queen's agent at the Spanish court,) for the recovery of money owed him in Spain by

mansion were, and capable of affording accommodation for so many, its inmates were in number very few. Would we picture to ourselves the group which at this time gathered round the owner's hearth, we must remember that it consisted merely of himself and his lady; Richard, his only son; and Anne, his natural daughter. Richard Payne, whom Sir Thomas employed at Middleburgh, and of whose letters a great number are preserved among the State-Papers, at the close of each generally enumerates the several members of his master's family; "hoping," like a dutiful 'bedesman,' (as he always styles himself,) that "my good Lady is well, and young master, with all other of your good lovers and friends."

At the time of which we treat, far more picturesque than at the present day, must have been the appearance of that part of Bishopsgate-street in which stood the house of Sir Thomas Gresham. Instead of crazy shops concealing an inelegant building,—such as the modern Excise-office, which occupies the site of Gresham-House,—an extensive mansion was visible, surrounded by spacious gardens. Beyond, were some ancient hostels or inns, of which the sites and signs yet remain; and im-

Diego and Martin de la Torre. The witnesses are German Cioll, mercator Anglus, Joseph Lupo, a Venetian, and Thomas Webbe, an Englishman.—Dom. Corr. St. P. Off.

mediately opposite, the eye reposed on the classic outline of Crosby-place,—then in the zenith of its glory, and occupied by one of Sir Thomas Gresham's kinsmen. That ancient dwelling had devolved by purchase to German Cioll, a Spanish merchant, who resided there with his wife Cecily, a daughter of Sir John Gresham the elder, and consequently cousin to the subject of this memoir. Cioll, who probably came over from Spain in the train of King Philip, was at this time an opulent person of some note, and in Queen Mary's days had been employed in the service of the state;[u] but from the following passage in a letter which Gresham addressed to Cecil from Osterley in 1566, he appears to have subsequently experienced some severe reverses of fortune. "I am so bolde," he writes, "as to send you a letter that my cosin Ciole hath writtin unto me, wherein I praie you, for my sake, as to helpe him to his monny, if it be possible, in this his great necessitie; whome, I will insewre you, is fallen in decay only by losse of sea, and Bankrowts."[v] This explains why, in 1566, Crosby-place passed into other hands; and why Gresham left by will to his cousin Cecily, (Cioll's widow,) of whom he

[u] Vide suprà, p. 191.

[v] March 26.—Dom. Corr. St. P. Off. See also another letter on the same subject, dated April 15, 1566.—Ibid.

was extremely fond, a considerable legacy. She continued to reside in Bishopsgate-street till the time of her death, which did not occur till the 10th January, 1609-10; when, by her special desire, she was buried in her father's vault, in the church of St. Michael, Bassishaw.[w]

To allude to Crosby-place is, surely, to recall the many historical associations which its noble Hall yet awakens; and to which Sir Thomas Gresham's having been often entertained within it, will be allowed to add another. Shakspeare has made every one familiar with that mansion as the residence of Richard III. while Duke of Gloucester; but it is not so generally known that it was also the residence of the great Sir Thomas More. All that remains of this beautiful relic of ancient splendour,—endeared to us by a thousand classic remembrances,—after the neglect of nearly two centuries, has at last attracted the attention of a few zealous spirits; and already exhibits evidence that the ruin with which it was threatened has

[w] See the abstract of her will (which was *not* proved at Doctors' Commons,) in Carlos's Historical and Antiquarian Notices of Crosby-Hall, p. 54. In the register of St. Helen's parish, we find "Cicely Cyoll, widowe, was buried in Bassyeshawe Church the 24th Jan. 1609." To which, another curious register belonging to the same parish, (containing apparently rough entries for the official volume,) adds the information, "died, Wednesday, 10 January."

been effectually averted. It is sincerely to be hoped that an attempt to preserve and restore so beautiful a relic of antiquity will meet with the support it requires, and so eminently deserves: the mere names of the several occupants of Crosby-place,—to say nothing of the mention made of it by Shakspeare,—should have been a sufficient charm to protect its venerable walls from injury.—But it is time to resume the thread of our narrative, and return to Sir Thomas Gresham; who, after a sojourn in England of nearly four months, reached Antwerp again on the 27th of July, 1562, furnished with Instructions which, if the reader has any curiosity to inspect, he must refer to the Appendix.[x]

Foreign travel began, about this period, to be fashionable with the younger members of the nobility, and private families of distinction. It may have been observed, in some of the preceding letters which Gresham addressed to Sir Thomas Parry, that the treasurer's eldest son, being on his travels, was sojourning at Antwerp in 1560, apparently under the eye of our merchant; who repeatedly requested Parry to increase the young gentleman's yearly allowance "to one hundrethe crowens more by the yere." About the same time, Thomas Cecil, the secretary's eldest son,

[x] No. XXVII.

was similarly engaged; who, having pursued his education under Thomas Windebank,[y] his tutor, for a year or two at Paris, and visited some other places of note, made his appearance at Antwerp a few days after Gresham's return to that city.

This young gentleman, (afterwards Earl of Exeter, and ancestor of the present Marquis,) was the only fruit of the secretary's first marriage with Mary, sister of Sir John Cheke; and was born in 1542. He was at this time, therefore, about twenty years of age. So little is generally known respecting this young person, that in consideration of his illustrious parentage, as well as

[y] Windebank belonged to a family not undistinguished for bravery and ability. The following particulars relative to his personal history are deducible from his correspondence: viz. that his father and mother were both dead in 1562; for he says that a certain letter which Cecil wrote him, (dated March 24,) had 'grieved him as much as his parents' death.' H. Alington, addressing Windebank from Westminster, (Feb. 5, 1561–2,) writes, "*Your predecessor,* Mr. Daye, is translated to the provostship of Eton, and is to preach before the queen this Lent." Alington also uses the words "*your father* Coxe." (This writer seals his letter with Sir William Cecil's seal, and was perhaps related to the secretary; for one *R.* Alington, addressing Cecil in Latin, styles himself '*nepos.*') In another letter, making mention of Dieppe, H. Alington adds,—" where *your brother*, Mr. Windebank, hath the leading of ii c soldiers."—Dom. Corr. St. P. Off. How Windebank was related to a namesake, who dated his will " from the Leguer at Bumble," May, 14th 1599, I know not. *That* Thomas Windebank was a soldier; and he states, as a motive for making a written distribution of his property, (which as-

on account of his connexion with the subject of this memoir (to whom he became eventually related,)[z] a few extracts are here subjoined from a correspondence hitherto unnoticed, illustrative of his character and history.

Sir William Cecil was one of those men who preserve every thing in the shape of a written document which comes into their possession,—a habit to which we are indebted, in a great measure, for our minute information respecting the occurrences of Queen Elizabeth's reign. A great part of the letters which he addressed to his son, as well as many of those which he received in re-

sumes the form of a letter to his brother Aaron,)—" I am now very often in hazard." He had another brother, Phineas; and a nephew, John, son of Aaron. His will was proved 11th Aug. 1599.—Kidd. quire lxv.—It is anticipating a statement which would be made with more propriety in the next volume, to mention here, that the tutor of Thomas Cecil was one of the four clerks of the privy signet in 1577; and that he died holding that office in 1606, having received the honour of knighthood. Wood mentions him as Sir Thomas Windebank, of Haines Hill in the county of Berks. It seems from his will that he married a widow named Reade, for he mentions Mildred, Anne, and Henry Reade as his children: he had besides a son and a daughter, Francis and Margaret. His will is dated 23rd April, 1606, and was proved 26th Jan. 1607.—Windebanck, quire 1. Sir Francis, son of Sir Thomas Windebank, was Secretary of State to Charles I., and died at Paris in Sept. 1646, leaving two sons,—Sir Thomas, of the Privy-chamber; and Col. Francis, governor of Blechingdon-House in Oxfordshire. (Wood's Athenæ.)

[z] See the Gresham pedigree, in the Appendix, No. I.

ply, besides a considerable portion of his correspondence with Windebank, have in consequence been preserved. The following is an early specimen written by the secretary to his son, in 1560:—

"I wish you blessing from God, and to deserve it through His grace. I mervell that I have so few letters from you; seing, in wryting ether of French or Lattyn, you shuld proffitt yourself. Will [desire] Wynebank to advertise me of your expencees, that I may see how your monny passeth away. In this tyme, take hede of surfetts by late suppers. If ye fynd in that contrey any thyngs mete for my garden, send me word therof. And so, God kepe you. From Hallyngbury-Morley, the 27th of August, 1560.

Your loving father,

W. CECILL."

"To my sonne Thomas Cecill,
at Pariss, or nere therto." [o]

It is to be wished that 'son Thomas,' as Cecil called his elder son, (in distinction from his favourite Robert, afterwards Earl of Salisbury,) had never given his father occasion for more serious rebuke than this letter contains. It is needless, however, to anticipate reflections which we shall be compelled presently to make on this

[o] Endorsed, "my Father to me."—Dom. Corr. St. P. Off.

subject. For the moment it suffices to state, that the young man having made a short tour, and visited in his progress Dieppe and Rouen, (of which towns Windebank sent the Secretary some account,) the travellers returned to Paris on the 24th of June, 1561. The following brief extract is from one of the tutor's letters: "Sir, I humbly beseche you, in your letters to Mr. Thomas, to remembre him that he leese not the commoditie of the morning for his proffiting in any kind of thing. I cannot perceave he hath any greate mynde to the lute; but to the cistern, he hathe. . . . . . We receaved, the ix[th] of this present, a bill of credit for 300 △ [dollars] from Mr. Gresham's man at Antwerp, to be received by us at our pleasure. I pray God we may bestowe them well.—As yesterdaie, being the ix[th], my Lord Ambassador [Sir Nicholas Throckmorton] went to the corte, to speake with the Queene of Scotland; to whom he presented Mr. Thomas."[a]

In the secretary's letter to his son, four days after, we read: "I have receaved iii severall lettres from you, but none maketh any mention at what chardg you lyve at. In any wise, be servisable, but not chargeable to Sir Nicolas Throkmorton. Begyn by tyme to translate into French: serve God daylie: take good hede to your

[a] Paris, July 10, 1561.—Dom. Corr. St. P. Off.

helth; and visitt once a weke your Instructions. Fare ye well. Wryte at ev'ry tyme somewhat to my wiffe. From London: the xiiijth of July, 1561.

Your loving Father,
W. CECILL."

"To my sonne Thomas Cecill,
in Pariss."[b]

It must be confessed, that hitherto there does not appear to have been a sufficient motive for the displeasure which Cecil expressed towards his son: at all events, it is more agreeable to indulge the supposition that the father was severe, because he considered it the most likely means of making his son approach nearer to the high standard he had proposed for his son's attainment, than to conclude that there had been, as yet, misconduct on the part of the youth, of which we are uninformed.[c] Cecil's complaints of him in general

[b] Dom. Corr. St. P. Off. The mention made in this letter of "your Instructions," recalls the well-known written precepts with which Robert Cecil was supplied by his father.

[c] Yet is there a solemnity and bitterness in the following passage, (in a letter dated the 27th Dec. 1561,) which has altogether the air of having proceeded from the heart of the writer: if it did, it forcibly illustrates the maxim, that some unsuspected care is the portion of every man,—however illustrious his rank, eminent his attainments, or exalted his station. "Children ought to be as gifts of God, comforte to their parents; but you, on the contrary, have made me carelesse of all children,—you see how your former misbehaviour hath filled me full of discon-

were, first—that he was careless in his expenditure,—a fault of the greatest magnitude in the eyes of Queen Elizabeth's future lord-treasurer; "I see, in the end," said he in one of his letters to Windebank, "my sone shall come home *lyke a spendyng sott, mete to kepe a tenniss court*:"[d] secondly, that he was idle. This is the burden of his next letter to Windebank:

"I know not what to judg, but I have had a watche worde sent me out of France that my sonne's being there shall serve hym to litle purpose; for that he spendeth hys tyme in idleness, and not in proffityng hymself in lerning. If this shal be confirmed to me agayne, I shall thynk myself much deceaved in you; and therefore, as ye meane to have creditt with me, so looke therto. If it be trew, I wold revoke my sonne; and hereof I pray you wryte to me playnely. God bless you all. From Henyngham, in Essex, the 27th of August, 1561."[e]

tentacion: and how it will be curid, I leave it to Allmighty God. I charge you, be serviseable to Allmighty God; and think of your tyme, that yesterdaie will never retourne!"—*Copy.* Dom. Corr. St. P. Off. Another letter, (also a copy,) Cecil subscribes "Your Father of an unworthy sonne."—Ibid. Let it be again repeated, that the youth to whom this was written was not yet twenty years of age; and that he lived to become good and great.

[d] Nov. 4, 1561.—Ibid.

[e] Ibid.

A fortnight later, one is sorry to read: "Suerly, I have hytherto had small comefort in hym; and if he deserve no better by well doyng, I will lern to take less care than I have doone.

"My trust is, (howsoever ye will to my sonne,) you will not, beyng thus charged, lett [leave] me deceaved; but truely and playnly advertise me of his faults. I know some of his old faults wer, to be slowthfull in keping his bedd; negligent and rash in expencees; uncarefull or careless of his apparrell; an unordynat lover of unmete playes, as dyce and cards; in study, sone weary, —in game, never. If he contynew or increase in theis, it wer better he wer at home, than abrode, to my grete chargees. It is time to end this manner of wryting, for it increaseth my greef. I have wrytten a litle herein to hym, and I wish he wold chang his rase, that I might sometime have cause to wryt comfortably. Fare ye well. From Hertford Castle, the 10th of September, 1561.

Your lovyng frend and Mr,

W. CECILL."

"I pray you Wynebank, if ye thynk that ye can pleasur me with sendyng me in the season of the yere, thyngs mete for my orchard or garden, help me; and if also ye can, procure for me an apt man for myn orchard or garden. First send me word and the chargees. You know my garden is new, and must be now applyed.

W. CECILL."[f]

The following letter from the same pen, is in a less painful strain.

"Wynebank,

"I pray you lett me know the pricees of these kynds of books following, to be well and fayre bound.

The course of the cyvill lawe, in small volumes and in greate.

The works of Tullye, in small volumes.

The courss of the cannon law, with the comments in the volume of 4[d].

I have alredy the cannon law, in the smallest volume.

I wold also understand what fayre biblees there be in Lattyn, of a great lettre: and some also in French. Which ij I wold have to lye in my chappell.

If there be any particular charts of contrees or provincees, whereof yow thynke I have none, send me word.

Of these abovesayd, I meane first to understand the chargees, before that you shall provyde any for me.

[f] Dom. Corr. St. P. Off. Vide anteà, p. 224, and Appendix, No. XIX. The allusion is, I believe, to his garden at Burleigh.

"I pray you lett Tho. Cecill put my Instructions which I gave, into French, and send me them. Lett hym also wryte to me, in French, how and in what studyes or exercises he spendeth the whole daye.

W. CECILL."[g]

"To Thomas Cecill, or
Thomas Wynebank."

Windebank's reply to this letter is preserved; and the following picture of how his youthful charge passed his time at Paris, will be perused with interest:

"Since Thomas Kendall's departing from us, this order Mr. Thomas hathe takin. In the morning, from VIII to IX of the clocke, he hathe one that readith Munster[h] unto him: that don, he hathe his houre to learne to daunse; and in these ii things is the whole of the forenoon consumid. After dynner, at one of the clocke, he goith to a lesson of the Institutes,[i] whereof he wrote his determination himself unto you,—per-

[g] Qy? Nov. 5 or 6, 1561, Dom. Corr. St. P. Off.—Endorsed 'Rec. by Hawkins.' On the 3rd of September Cecil had ended a letter thus,—"I pray you send me some registers of books there, that I maye thereof make choise to garnish my Library; for I am almost past study. Fare ye well."—Ibid.

[h] Seb. Munster. La Cosmographie Universelle, folio. Paris, 1552. "The reading of Munster's Cosmography," says Windebank, "dothe stand us in two crownes per month."

[i] The Institutes of the Law.

suaded therunto by my L. Ambassador. Toward iii of the clocke, he hathe one that teachith him to plaie on the lute; wherein, (and an houre's reading the historie of Josephus de bello Judaïco,) he bestowith the whole afternoone. After supper, he lackith no companie to talke with, for learning the tongue that waie; and besides, eyther accordith on the lute, or takith some booke in hande. This is presently the order of dividing his tyme, which I thought my duty to let you understand."[k]

Scarcely less interesting is the following outline of a tour which the tutor contemplated for young Cecil. Windebank is again addressing his patron, the secretary.

"According to your commandement, we have conferred with my lorde ambassador here, for our travaile: whose advise is, that, seing your mynde is to have us travaile, that Mr. Thomas shulde see *that* that is worthy sight, and worthe his labour and your expences; and therefore wolde have us to go as farre as Marseilles. And for the order of our waie, he wolde have us first to go to Orleance, and there to remayne v or vi daies. From thence to take the poste, as it lieth to Lyons; and by the waie, to reste in suche townes as be worthiest to be considered: in some, one daie; in some others, ij or iij daies. From Lyons, to go

[k] Paris, Nov. 12, 1561.—Dom. Corr. St. P. Off.

to Vienne; from thence to Avignon; and so to Marseilles,—all by water. Now, for our returne: he appointith it from Marseilles to Nysmes; from thence to Montpelier; and so to Tholouse, by poste. From thence, to Bordeaux by the ryver of Garonne; from thence to Poictiers, by poste or jorney, as we shall then think beste. From Poictiers to Angers; and then, to Tours, Amboyse, Bloise, Vendosme, Chartres, and so to Paris agayne. This jorney wolde be worth the travaile; but the charges will be greate to ride poste, for every poste will cost us xviij soulz a man,—that is ij *s.* iij *d.*, (reckonning the drinking penny that we must give to the guide, and to others of the sorte; and we are three, besides the guide.) So that, reckonning the charges of iiij persones for every poste, it will amounte to iij franks xij soulz: that is, about viij *s.* x *d.* of our monny, every post. And to Lyons, from hence, there are xxx posts; which will amount to cviij franks,—that may be, in crownes, xliij △, and x soulz over: and in our monny, (after vi *s.* the crowne,) xij *li.* xix *s.* iij *d.*, besides our meete and drinke, &c.

"We cannot well differ our setting forthe longer than the viijth or xth of Aprill; because of the heate that will be muche advaunced in those countreys of Prouvince and Languedoc, which I feare Mr. Thomas shall not well induer: for that I know he cannot abyde greate heate."[l]

After one other short letter from Sir William Cecil, we shall be able to speak of Sir Thomas Gresham, who has not been lost sight of, though no mention has hitherto been made of his name.

" Wyndebank, my complaynt is straung to you of my sone for his lewdness,[m] and for your so long sufferance, ... for what amendment hath he made of his wryting?—nay, what empayrement! . . . . . I see your accompt riseth great with trifles. . . . . Good Wyndebank, if there be left any spark of my recovery of a good name to my sonne, attempt all your coning. I wish you God's grace. From Westminster, the 24th of March, 1561-[2.]

Your assured good Master,

W. CECILL."

" To Thomas Wyndbank, my
loving Servant."

On a little slip of paper, which the preceding letter contained, are these words:—" That which is sharply wrytten concerning yourself, is onely to shadow mistakyng of my sone towards you; so as you may pretend greef for your owne part." [n]

[l] Paris, March 4, 1561-2.—Dom. Corr. St. P. Off.

[m] Ignorance, want of learning. So, in the New Testament, " certain *lewd* fellows," &c.

[n] Dom. Corr. St. P. Off.

The correspondence of Sir William Cecil and his son's tutor having been conducted (not without some regrets) thus far, the connexion of the entire episode with the subject which should more properly engage our attention, is shown by the following letter, which Windebank addressed to Sir Thomas Gresham from Paris. The reader will perceive that it must have reached Gresham a few days before he returned to England in April 1562; at which time he 'called himself to account,' as we have seen, and presented a statement of his pecuniary claims. The letter is as follows:—

" Mr. Gresham,

" We have received your lettre of the xx^th^ of Marche by Mr. Governor,[o] together with iii c crownes which you have sent to us by him; for the which, Mr. Cecill chiefly hath cause to thank you: and I have no lesse cause than he, for that being furnished with monny, you may think what a lightening it is to me of care that I have in this charge, whereunto my Master hath appointed me, in a strange countrey. But seeing that I am now come to speake of my selfe, surely, Sir, I cannot but with great shame confesse a

[o] Mr. John Fitzwilliams, who has been already mentioned. See pp. 73, 75, and 350.

great slackness, or rather a whole negligence in me, in that I have not of long tyme writtin unto you, as I am bounde to doo. For, next unto my Master, (and this I speake unfayndly,) I acknowledge myselfe as muche beholden unto you, as to any man in Englande: not only for your greate good will that it pleaseth you to beare to me, and for your like benefits bestowed upon me; but also for a singular affection that is within me, which constrayneth me therunto. But, Sir, I desire you not to regarde my faulte in not writing heretofore; and to think that, though I have not written, yet, with a more worthye thing than *that* is, (which is my harte,) I have bothe remembrid you, and honored you: so as if at any tyme I may doo you any service, I will be most ready thereunto during my life. Therof beseeching you to assure yourself, I cease to speke any furder.

"I send to you, herewith, a bill of my hande, acknowledging the receipte of your iij c ▵ [300 dollars]: and so I leave to trouble you furder at this tyme. From Paris, the ij[nd] of Aprill, [1562]."[p]

[p] From Windebank's rough draft, endorsed "M. to Mr. Gresham from myself, by Mr. Fitzwilliams, governor."—Dom. Corr. St. P. Off. It is rather singular that, in the same repository, the corrected draft of almost all Windebank's letters should be found, along with the originals. These duplicates of a correspondence, concerning which Cecil may have reasonably felt a little jealous, were probably delivered up to him by his particular desire when

It so happened, that on the very day Windebank traced the preceding lines to Sir Thomas Gresham, Cecil wrote a letter of heavy complaint to Windebank respecting his charge; who, though but twenty years of age, gave his friends a great deal of trouble. Next to be inserted (for they come next in order) are the father's letter and the tutor's reply; which, painful as they certainly are, lose half their bitterness when it is remembered that Thomas Cecil became an improved character as he advanced in life. In less than five years after these letters were written, he had subsided into a sober kind of personage; who, when weary of the country and the court, found sufficient vent for his naturally ardent temper in the bustle and excitement of the camp. But to return to Cecil's letter, which is as follows:—

"Wyndebank,

"I am here used to paynes and troobles: but none crepe so neare my hart as doth this of my lewd sonne. I am perplexed what to thynk: the shame that I shall receave to have so unruled a sonne, greveth me more than if I lost him by honest death. Good Wyndebank,—consult with my deare frend Sir Nicholas Throckmerton, to

the tutor and his pupil returned from their travels;—a step which has led to their preservation, instead of ensuring their destruction, as was doubtless contemplated.

whom I have referred the whole. I cold be best content that he wold committ hym secretly to some sharp prison. If that shall not seme good, yet wold I rather have hym sent awey to Strasburgh, (if it cold be possible,) or to Lovayne; for my greef will grow dooble to see hym, untill some kynd of amends may be. If none of these will serve, then bryng him home; and I shall receyve that which it pleaseth God to laye on my sholders: that is, in the middest of my busyness, for [instead of] comefort, a dayly torment. If ye shall come home with hym to cover the shame, I rather desyre to have this sommer spent, though it wer but to be absent from my sight. I am so trobled, as, well what to wryte, I know not. From Westminster, the 2nd of Aprill, 1562.

Yours assured,

W. CECILL."[q]

"To my trusty servant, Thomas
Wyndebank, at Pariss."

Shortly after which the person addressed wrote as follows:—

"Sir,

"After so many discomfortable lettres, (for so I take them to be unto you,) I wolde to

[q] Dom. Corr. St. P. Off. All these letters (except where the contrary is specified) are printed from originals.

God I could with just cause write at the last unto you that [which] might take awaie, yf not all, yet some parte, at the leste, of your griefe. But, Sir, I may not dissemble. Mr. Thomas his behaviour doth contynnew suche, notwithstanding all your severe letters,—all counsels and threatenings of my Lord Ambassador,—all shame of the worlde,—and all dangeor and inconvenience that bothe are come, and are yet to come,—that the same being known to you, it cannot diminish your grefe, but increase it. And because it is most necessary, remedy to be most speedily provided, (which lyeth not in me, nor in my Lord Ambassador to doo, yf he contynew in this country,) I cannot but let you understande that he is come to this extreamitie, that if good watch had not bene kepte, he had fled his waie from us all and you,—no man can tell whither. The meanes for monny was, that he woulde have solde all his apparell and myne. And by the meanes of a merchant, (using rather good will than otherwise,) he was upon the pointe to have had a cupple of horses, upon credit of the merchant. So farre is he transported! And when a man is in an evill mynde, [he] casteth the worste that may come to him (as he dothe): sayeng to diverse, that 'he is sure of his portion;' and that 'you cannot disinherite him.' I leve it to be thought what hope ther is of suche a one! His behaviour ys suche to me, that I can be sure of nothing in my owne custodie; which makith me very perplexed. I am sorry that you will not have him home." [r]

Before this letter reached its destination, Cecil addressed Windebank again:—

"I have wrytten a lettre to that noughty boye of myne. I have commanded hym to putt awey his servant, and to bannish his wanton lusts. I have commanded hym to shew yow my lettre. I wold gladly, if it wer possible to reform his follyes, to permitt hym there; for ij respects. One, because I know how he might pass safely into Germanny, (for I wold be lothe to have hym at Lovayne, or in any papiss towne); secondly, [because] if he shuld soddenly come thence, his departure wold disclose his lewdness, to my discomfort and shame. This you see how I wryte, lyke a fond [foolish] father. But if, without departyng thence, amendment will not insew, I care not whyther he goo. Good Wyndebank,—assaye all wayes to amend hym, without my reproche! I cold be content that he wer at Strasburgh. Fare ye well. Kepe hym from monny, and pray Mr. Throkmorton not to be weary of reforming my

[r] Paris, May 7, 1562. Dom. Corr. St. P. Off. This was the second letter which Windebank addressed to Cecil on the same day.

lewd sonne. From Westminster: the xth of May, 1562. Your loving Master,

W. CECILL."[s]

The reader may not be displeased to peruse a letter from 'son Thomas' himself; written in the French language,—concerning his proficiency in which, Cecil and Windebank expressed themselves so solicitous.[t]

"Mon tres honoré seignour et père.

"Vos lettres m'ont apportés tant de facherie, que rien plus : par lesquelles J'entend que vous estes fort corruseé contre moy,—estant adverty que J'employe tout mon temps en poursuivant les vanités d'amour. Come je suis bien marry que vous entendres chooses de moy qui sont tant à mon desavantage, (et d'avanture [peut-être] beaucoup plus qu'ilz sont,) ainsi, je ne me puis excuser en tout : mais come je suis junne, ainsi il fault que je confesse que je suis subjett à les affections qui gouvernent quelques fois ceux qui sont junnes. Pourtant, de paour [peur] de ne vous facher trop avec ma longue et facheuse lettre ; et que vous ne penses que, en usant beau-

[s] 'To my loving servant, T.W. at Pariss.'–Dom. Corr. St. P. Off.

[t] To 'have exercise of the French tongue,' and to 'see some fashons to frame him better than he is allready,' Windebank considered to be 'the ij thinges which should be the end of Thomas Cecil's remayning in any place.'

coup de parolles, je sercherois de vous déguiser le mattier, je vous supplie bien humblement de me donner vostre benediction! Si, par le passé, j'ay mis en oublie mon devoir, je vous promette de me mestre en panie, doresnevant, de me monstrer, en tout, prest de vous obéir: priant le Créatur vous avoir tousjours en sa divine garde. De Paris; le 17e de Maye, 1562.

Votre tres humble, et filz trèssobéissant,

THOMAS CECILL."[u]

"To the right honourable, & my loving Father, Sir William Cecill, knight: the Quene's Majestie principall secretary, etc."

Young Thomas Cecil and his tutor are brought into closer connexion with Gresham by the following announcement, contained in one of his letters to the secretary. He had scarcely been a week

[u] Dom. Corr. St. P. Off. Windebank, writing to Cecil on the same day, announces his intention of retiring with his young charge 'to Mr. Dammart's house,' in order to detach him from the capital. His next letter (of the 29th May) is dated "from Dammart, vii leagues from Paris." There is a note written to Windebank, while he and young Cecil were residing in this retreat, by Sir Nicholas Throckmorton; dated Paris, June 5, 1562: "From England," says that eminent statesman, "I understand that twoo of my deare frendes be dead. That is to say, Mr. Goodricke and Mr. George Medley,—twoo rare men, bothe for their giftes and honesty."—Ibid. It is a privilege to record the names of such persons.

in Antwerp, (after returning from his four months' sojourn in London,) when he received a visit from the travellers. "On the 7th," he says, "your son and Mr. Wynnyngbancke arrived in right good health; and [it] haith pleased them to accept my poor howse. Your son is much grown in heythe, and haythe bestowed his tyme very well; for that he speakyth very good Frenche, and [is as] full of sivillity and verttew as your honnor's harte can desyre. You shall doo well to let hym to go to Germanny; but I perseve by Mr. Wynnebank, they have no great store of money left, if they shuld goo into Germany: therefore your honner must needs helpe. And yf it be your pleassore, I shall give him credit to all plassis he shall goo [to], for *that* he shall lacke."[v]

Along with this letter, was sent another from Windebank, who had left Paris with his charge on the 1st of August. "We perceive," he writes, "from a letter of yours to Sir Thomas Gresham, your pleasure is that we should go to Strasburg, or Basil, till November. . . . . . To go into that country will be exceedingly chargeable, by reason of the horses, while we shall be travayling; for hyrid horses are not to be had in that country."[w]

[v] Ant. Aug. 9, 1562.—Fland. Corr. St. P. Off.

[w] "You shall doo well," says Gresham, "to send them thre good geldinges; for heare, horse-fleashe ys very deare, and hard to come bye."—Ibid.

Besides that Mr. Thomas is to be furnished of mony to spend after his own fantasy, and not at my discretion: wherein, Sir, I besich you, let us both know plainly your mynd; for Mr. Thomas is desyrous to buy many prety things . . . . . . Sir Thomas Gresham hath taken us into his house, where I am sorry to trouble him so long as till we shall hear from you, which we hope shall be within 8 days: for the mean tyme, we will see som towns of Flanders.

"As for Mr. Thomas his estate, I trust your honor will like his personage well, and his behaviour better than you have done before: and I trust that his little follye will much increase him in wisdom. I wish he wear now in England, that you might see his proffit in the tongue; lest, by his being in Germany, he shall com to forget. And so I most humbly take my leave of your honnor, and my Lady, to whom I praye to be excused for not writing. From Andwerp, the ixth of August."[x]

While young Cecil and his tutor were under Sir Thomas Gresham's roof, the secretary addressed the following letter to Windebank; who must have left Antwerp ere it reached his hands.

"Wyndebank, I thank you for the contynuance of your care over my careless sonne. I shall not

[x] Rough draft.—Fland. Corr. St. P. Off.

forgett it, by God's grace. Seing he is there, I wish hym to see Germany; for, in dede, the wound is yet too grene for me to behold hym. I have wrytten for creditt for ij c crownes, to Mr. Gresham.

"I meane to send you ij geldyngs for your jornaye. I am sorry that ye ar so chargeable to Sir Thomas Gresham. Ye may doo well to see Bruxells, Gaunt, Lovayne, &c.

"Whylest ye ar there, wryte to me of the commen talk of that contree. I pray you, teach my sonne to wryte trulyer in the orthography of the French; for I myself can fynd his faults. Lett hym wryte oftner. Send me the rest of your accompt, sence your last declaration. Sir Nicholas Throkmorton shall come home; and whatsoever he sayth, or heareth, none helpeth hym home but I.

"I pray you, kepe in remembrance that both you and my sonne serve Almighty God. 14th Augusti, 1562.

Yours assured,

W. CECILL"[y]

"To my loving servant, Thomas
Wyndebank, at Antwerp."

We learn from the postscript of Gresham's letter of the 16th, that the travellers (to whose party

[y] Dom. Corr. St. P. Off.

"Mr. Harrye Knolles," had joined himself) left Antwerp on that day for Germany: an event which is thus recorded in a letter written by young Cecil to his father:

"Mon très honoré Seignour, & Père.

"Le sixiesme de ce moys, Monsr Knoules arrivant icy à Anvers, j'entendu par luy novelles de vous que vous esties en bonne santé; & par voz lettres à Monsr Gressam, [j'ai appris] vostre volunté touchant nostre journé en Alemaigne: vouz estant d'avise que nouz ferions compagnie à Monsr Knoules. Et comme vouz nouz avez remis à la discretion de Monsr Gressam, ainsi l'ayt il donné bonne ordre à touz noz affaires. `A qui, pour le bon traittement qui [qu'il] nous a fait tout ce temps en sa maison, je vous supplie de luy remercier par voz lettres: l'ayant fait, je scay bien, pour amour de vous.—Le mesme mattin que je escrivois ceste lettre, nous soummes parties d' Anvers avec Monsr Knoules, vers Alemaigne, à cinque heures de mattin. Monsr Gressam nous a fourny de cinquante livres, que nous portons quant et nous; oultre cent escues que nous restent encores de nostre monnoye. Ainsi, prenant mon congé de vous, je vous supplie me donner vostre bénédiction: priant Dieu vous donner bonne vie, & longue, avec un prospereus successe en toutz voz affaires. Demeurant, pour faulte de moyen de recompenser le plus moindre benefit que j'ay receu de vous, vostre obligé de vous complaire toute ma vie. De Anvers, le dixcestiesme d'Aoust, 1562.

Vostre très humble & filz trèssobéissant,
THOMAS CECILL."[z]

"I have despatched your son and Mr. Wynnebank," writes Gresham in the letter above alluded to, "and given them 50*l.* in their porse; and 50*l.* more, by credit, to receive at their pleasure, till I hear further from you; and, God willinge, I shall take care and fornishe them wyth all thinges they shall lacke. Most humblye thancking yow that it maye pleasse [has pleased] yow to geve me the care of your sonne: whyche I wyll insewre [you,] I wyll looke unto as my own sonne; for, here wrytting, you have as hanssom a man to your sonne, and full of verttewe, as your own harte can desyre."[a]

On the 22nd of August, Gresham wrote as follows. The first extract is from a long letter of intelligence which he addressed to Cecil: the second, to Windebank, tells its own story. Some

[z] Dom. Corr. St. P. Off.—The address as before.

[a] Ant. Aug. 16, 1562.—Fland. Corr. St. P. Off. Of the same date are a few hasty lines, "To the worshipfull Mr. Thomas Cecill, and Thomas Wyndebanke," from their "loving and assurid frynd, Thomas Gresham," accompanying a letter of credit."—Ib.

remark may be expected on the eulogizing terms in which the writer speaks of Cecil's 'son Thomas,' compared with those in which we have hitherto found the young gentleman mentioned by his father and tutor. I can only suggest, that he may have been courtier enough to make the best of a character with which he must have been so little acquainted, and of which he can have had so few opportunities of judging, as the son of his friend and patron; and in the next place, that it is only fair to conclude that he found in him less to condemn, than from the letters of his father we have been led to expect.

"I have wryttin to the genttilman your sone, as you have willed me," says Gresham, "assewring you, whiles he was here, for all that he sawe in this towen, I sawe hym not bestow one peny in wayst; and as carefull in wrytting, and in all other things to pleasse yowe. Assewring your honnor, without flatery, yow have as hanssome a man to your sone, and as toward, and inclynyd to all vertew, as your own harte can desire: most humbly thanckinge yow that it [has] pleassed yow to gyve me the care of hym, whiles he ys in Jermany,—wherunto I wyll looke, and provid for hym, as I wold doo for my own sone. You shall not nead, now, to send hym anny geldinges."[b]

[b] Aug. 22.—Fland. Corr. St. P. Off.

The next is a letter from Gresham to Windebank.

"Aftyr my right hartie commendacions,—I doo perseve by Thomas Dowghton [Dutton][c] that you shall neade of creadit for the some of L dallors in Germanny: assewring yow, I doo take it very unkindelye at your handes, that yoursellfe wolde not speacke unto me at your being here; and cannot but marvell what yow have consevid of me, and my doinges towardes yow, that yow shullde be abasshid, or affraide to speake unto me,—considering the good will I have allwayes owed yow, and the offres I have maid yow frome tyme to tyme. And as I am one that forgets soche ingrateteudnes, so, for this tyme, I will impute it to your good nateur of shamefastnes; and, as your assewrid frinde here, I send yow a letter of creadit for the some of one hundread dallors, to reasseve of Fredericke Wolffe, the parte or the whole, whensoever you shall requyre it: to whom yow shall macke your acquyttans for so moche as yow shall resseve. And thus, withe my hartie commendacions to gentill Mr. Cecill (à la Franchoisse,) I wishe yowe bothe helthe, and saffe returne. From Andwerpe, the xxii[nd] of August, a[o] 1562.

Your loving and assewrid frinde,

THOMAS GRESHAM."

[c] One of Gresham's servants: of whom more hereafter.

"I pray yow to doo my humble commendacions to Mr. Knolles, and to Mr. Doctor Mownte. Sins the wryting hereof, I have receaved letters from Mr. Secreatory, and others to yow, wyche I send herewith."

"To my very loving frinde Mr. Thomas Winebank, geve this, in Strawesbrowghe."[d]

It is now time that we should take leave of these personages, since they have taken leave of Gresham. Their letters shall therefore be brought to a close with a few lines from Cecil to Windebank: partly, because they are written in a milder strain; and partly, because they serve to conduct the travellers well on their journey, where we shall be obliged to wish them farewell.

"Good Wyndebank. I hartely thank you for your contynuall care, had towards my sonne: I know your paynes and care ar not small. For his aboode from hence, I can be content that he wer out of Germany, and might see Italy, and pass by the Helvetians, and [so go] to Geneva. Marry, I wish you [to] have good regard to pass as unknowen as ye maye, because of the malice that I know the papists owe me; and cold be content to avenge the same in my sone. Herein, I pray you conferr with Mr. Knoolles. My meaning is, that, sence my sonne is abrood, he shuld see all thyngs requi-

[d] Dom. Corr. St. P. Off., whence the two ensuing letters are derived.

site for I: doo meane at his retorne to move hym to marry, and then to plant hym at home. I have spoken to Mr. Gresham to procure you power for monny: wherein I pray you have as good regard as ye maye, to moderat your expencees. Our newes, Mr. Knolles I thynk will report to you. I pray you lett my sonne use reverence to Mr. Knolles: and lett hym lern to weare his apparrell clenly and courtly, for of hymself he is somewhat negligent. Send me your accompt. From my hows next the Savoye, 16 November, 1562.

Your assured good Master,

W. CECILL."

Here we part with Windebank and his wayward charge. Liberal as the foregoing extracts may have appeared, the reader is assured that very many more letters have been omitted than have been laid before him; whether of the tutor, the father, or the son. This chapter, which has already grown too long, shall be brought to a close by the insertion of a curious letter to Sir William Cecil from Sir Henry Percy, afterwards Earl of Northumberland,[e] which well merits preservation. That nobleman had married Catharine, eldest daughter and one of the four co-

[e] There is a good account of him in Collins's Peerage. This gallant soldier, having distinguished himself in the North, was appointed Captain of Norham Castle in 1565. He became implicated in the cause of Mary Queen of Scots, and died or was murdered in the Tower, 21 June, 1585.

heiresses of John Neville, last Lord Latimer;[f] and it will be seen that the object of the letter-writer was an alliance which he desired to see brought about between the Secretary's 'son Thomas,' and Lady Percy's second sister, Dorothy; who eventually, as is well known, became his wife. Percy's letter will appear to be slightly out of chronological order; but it could not have been introduced in a better place than the present, where it serves the double purpose of bringing this long episode naturally to an end, and of presenting us with an interesting picture, during her girlhood, of the first Countess of Exeter.

"After my humble and hartie commendacions. Whereas I have ever bene bound by your goodnes towards me, to devise by what meanes or service I mighte requite the same; and havinge no cause sufficiently worthie for *that* I have receyved at your handes, yett have I thought good to advertise youe of this whiche I have had in my mynde sence my mariage, and before. And altho' the mater shall not seme greatelye comodious towardes youe, but that youe may advance youre house into muche greater levinge,

[f] By Lucy, daughter of Henry Earl of Worcester. The two other co-heiresses were,—Lucy, who married Sir William Cornwallis; and Elizabeth, who became the wife of Sir John Danvers. Lord Latimer died in 1577.—Collins' Peerage, by Brydges, vol. v. p. 155–6.

yet will I humbly requier youe to receyve it as procedinge from a faithefull frende.

"Youe shall understand that my Lorde Lattymore havinge foure daughters, whereof, as youe knowe, I maried one; and the seconde beinge of xv yeres, and as I supposse not muche unmete for mariage,—I have sence the tyme of my mariage kepte withe me this gentilwoman, my sister, onelie to understand hir dispossicion. And altho' I thoughte to have had some conferance withe youe in this mater at my laste beinge at the coorte, yett was I lettede; for that I wold have some tryall of the conversacion of the young woman: which I assure you is so good and vertuous, as hard it is to find such a sparke of youthe in this realme. For bothe is she very wise, sober of behavoure, womanly, and in hir doings so temperate as if she bare the age [of] double her yeres; of stature like to be goodlie; and of beautie, verry well. Hir haire browne, yet hir complexion very faire and cleare. The favour of hir face every bodie may judge it to have bothe grace and wysdome. Sir, altho' it be a dangerous matter thus much to write of a younge woman, yet do I assure you I have said nothinge more than she deservethe. Sir, for that my cousen (youre sone) is unmaried, and that God hathe indeuede youe with such gifts as is like to leave him greate possessions, yet do I thinke it not amisse if that he were planted in some stocke of honor: and if this should so fortone as my harte desiers, bothe should he be matched in a great house, as also the likelyhoode of possessions to come thereby. And consideringe the evill goverment of my Lorde [Latimer,] as also the good meanes you have to establishe and devise a saftie of that house, we, who alredie be matched with that stocke, should have juste occasion to thinke oureselves bound to youe; as also rejoice to matche with such one who mighte staye that which, withoute helpe, were in greate daunger. Perchance this shall seme unto youe that I write for my own cause. I proteste before God I do not. Marry, I muste confesse glad I wold be that the follye of my Lord should not hasard that which might come to his childerin: but the chief cause (by my faithe) is, for that I had rather to be lynked with youe than with any man in this realme. And so I hartily desier you to excepte it.

"Sir, when youe have perused this, and pawsed of the same, I pray youe lett me be advertisede. But, in any case, lett it not be knowen unto any; for that there is nobilitye which ernestely goethe about to conquor this. Howbeit, my credit is so good withe my lady, my mother-in-lawe, as also withe the younge gentlewoman, as by my advise they will be much governede. And therefore, if they should understand that I had practised in this without their consents, it should be an occasion to make my credit the worse withe them. I do perceyve my Lorde is nowe at London, where he is better to be talked withall than in the countrye: but if youe be amynded to speke in the matter, in no wayes talke with my Lorde in it before I breake it to my Ladie, and the gentlewoman: for women be willfull, if they be not first sought unto.

"Sir, if you advise of this mater, as mete it is, yet I pray youe to advertise me whether you wold have it stayed or not, any tyme: for that there is, that goethe ernestly about to obteyne the thinge. Thus leavinge to trouble you anny further, (trustinge in shorte tyme to have advertisemente from youe,) I wyshe the encrease of your honor. From the Quene's Majestie's castell of Tynemouthe, this xxv[th] of January, 1561 [-2.]

Your most faithefull, and
Assured Cousen to comaund,
H. PERCY."

"To the right honorable Sir William Cecill, Knight, Secratorye to the Queene's Majestie, and Master of the Wards and Leverys."

APPENDIX.

No. I.

Pedigree of the Gresham Family.

[Referred to in page 6, note c.]

THE following pedigree is derived chiefly from one which formerly belonged to Sir Marmaduke Gresham, Bart., of Titsey. Dr. Ward published it narratively in 1740; and it is here given, with several corrections and additions, in what appears to the writer a more intelligible shape. The introduction prefixed to the genealogy is as follows.

> "A true and exact PEDIGREE of the right worshipfull, ancient, pious, loyal, and charitable family of Gresham of Gresham in the county of Norfolk, sometimes residing at Holte, Intwood, Myleham, Walsingham Parva, and Thorpe Market in the said county; at Founteyness in the county of York; at Titsey, and Limesfield in Surry; at Osterley, and Fulham in the county of Middlesex: wherein are inserted the severall marriages and alliances to severall other worshipfull, and some honourable familys.

Which family was at once seiz'd in Norfolk of thirty-five mannors, in Suffolk of five, in Cambridgshire of one, in Kent of three, in Sussex of two, in Surry of nine, in Middlesex of two, in Somerset of two, in Derbyshire of three, in Yorkshire of nine, and of twelve granges, and severall other *villatae*, and considerable possessions in the same county, and of three mannors in the bishoprick of Durham; as appears by severall letters patent, fines, deeds enrolled, inquisitions *post mortem*, wills, and private evidences, now in the hands of some of that family. And out of which family, within the compass of an hundred and fifty years last past, there has been one baronet, nine knights batchelers, whereof one knighted in the field; one baronet's wife, and nine knights wives of the name and family of Gresham; and have issued from them in that time two viscounts, seven baronets, twenty four knights, two countesses, five baronets wives, and twenty two knights wives."

PEDIGREE OF

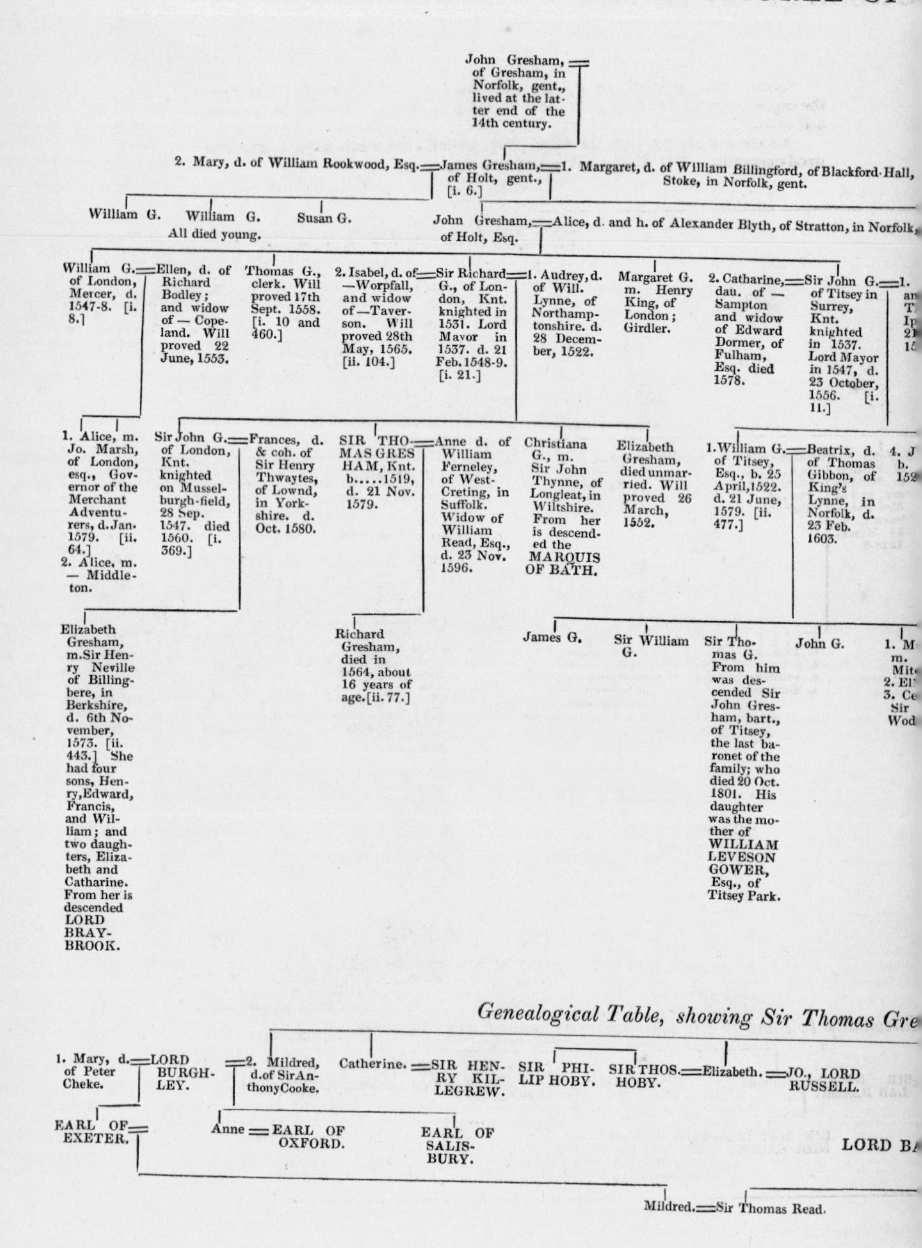

John Gresham, of Gresham, in Norfolk, gent., lived at the latter end of the 14th century.
2. Mary, d. of William Rookwood, Esq.
James Gresham, of Holt, gent., [i. 6.]
1. Margaret, d. of William Billingford, of Blackford-Hall, Stoke, in Norfolk, gent.
William G.
William G.
Susan G.
All died young.
John Gresham, of Holt, Esq.
Alice, d. and h. of Alexander Blyth, of Stratton, in Norfolk,
William G. of London, Mercer, d. 1547-8. [i. 8.]
Ellen, d. of Richard Bodley; and widow of — Copeland. Will proved 22 June, 1553.
Thomas G., clerk. Will proved 17th Sept. 1558. [i. 10 and 460.]
2. Isabel, d. of —Worpfall, and widow of —Taverson. Will proved 28th May, 1565. [ii. 104.]
Sir Richard G., of London, Knt. knighted in 1531. Lord Mayor in 1537. d. 21 Feb. 1548-9. [i. 21.]
1. Audrey, d. of Will. Lynne, of Northamptonshire. d. 28 December, 1522.
Margaret G. m. Henry King, of London; Girdler.
2. Catharine, dau. of — Sampton and widow of Edward Dormer, of Fulham, Esq. died 1578.
Sir John G. of Titsey in Surrey, Knt. knighted in 1537. Lord Mayor in 1547, d. 23 October, 1556. [i. 11.]
1. Alice, m. Jo. Marsh, of London, esq., Governor of the Merchant Adventurers, d. Jan. 1579. [ii. 64.]
2. Alice, m. — Middleton.
Sir John G. of London, Knt. knighted on Musselburgh-field, 28 Sep. 1547. died 1560. [i. 369.]
Frances, d. & coh. of Sir Henry Thwaytes, of Lownd, in Yorkshire. d. Oct. 1580.
SIR THOMAS GRESHAM, Knt. b.....1519, d. 21 Nov. 1579.
Anne d. of William Ferneley, of West-Creting, in Suffolk. Widow of William Read, Esq., d. 23 Nov. 1596.
Christiana G., m. Sir John Thynne, of Longleat, in Wiltshire. From her is descended the MARQUIS OF BATH.
Elizabeth Gresham, died unmarried. Will proved 26 March, 1552.
1. William G. of Titsey, Esq., b. 25 April, 1522. d. 21 June, 1579. [ii. 477.]
Beatrix, d. of Thomas Gibbon, of King's Lynne, in Norfolk, d. 23 Feb. 1603.
Elizabeth Gresham, m. Sir Henry Neville of Billingbere, in Berkshire, d. 6th November, 1573. [ii. 443.] She had four sons, Henry, Edward, Francis, and William; and two daughters, Elizabeth and Catharine. From her is descended LORD BRAYBROOK.
Richard Gresham, died in 1564, about 16 years of age. [ii. 77.]
James G.
Sir William G.
Sir Thomas G. From him was descended Sir John Gresham, bart., of Titsey, the last baronet of the family; who died 20 Oct. 1801. His daughter was the mother of WILLIAM LEVESON GOWER, Esq., of Titsey Park.
John G.
Genealogical Table, showing Sir Thomas Gre
1. Mary, d. of Peter Cheke.
LORD BURGHLEY.
2. Mildred, d. of Sir Anthony Cooke.
Catherine.
SIR HENRY KILLEGREW.
SIR PHILIP HOBY.
SIR THOS. HOBY.
Elizabeth.
JO., LORD RUSSELL.
EARL OF EXETER.
Anne
EARL OF OXFORD.
EARL OF SALISBURY.
LORD B
Mildred.
Sir Thomas Read.

GRESHAM FAMILY.

ARMS.—See the fourth seal in the wood-engraving which precedes the preface; the capital letter to the same; p. 19, note w, and p. 24. note i. The blazon is *argent* and *sable*.

CREST and MOTTO.—See the third, fifth, seventh, and ninth seals, in the same wood-engraving. The grasshopper is blazoned *or*.

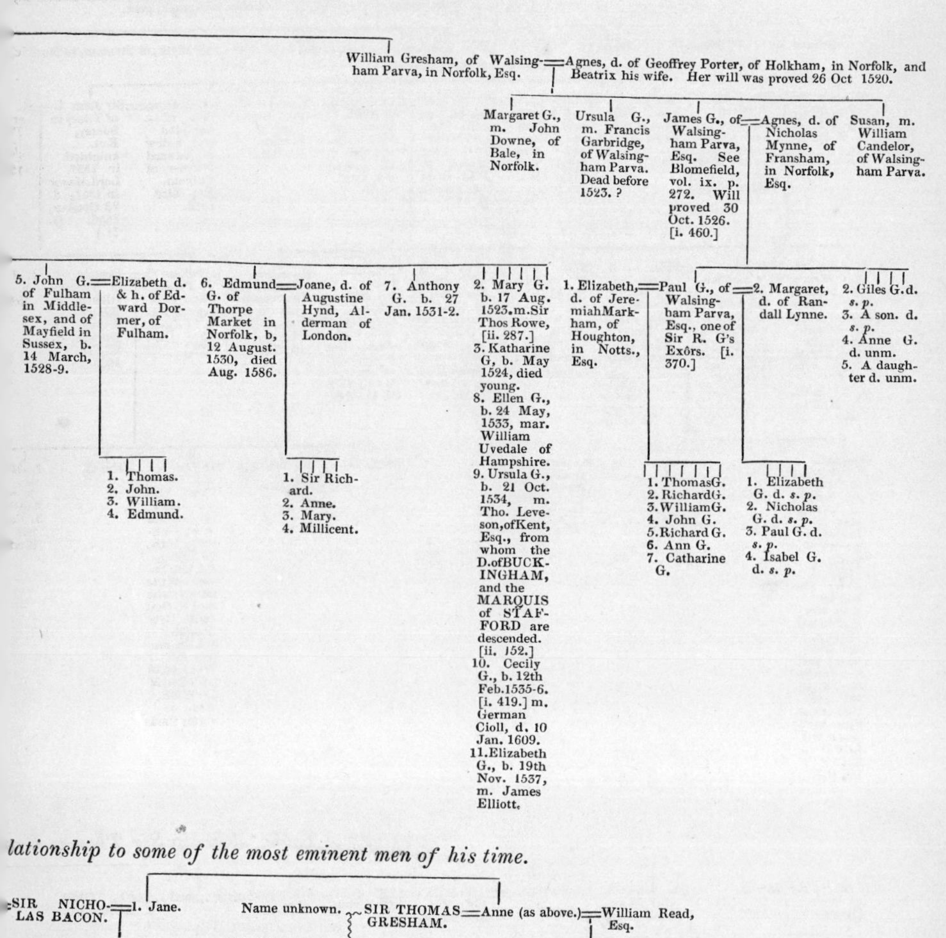

lationship to some of the most eminent men of his time.

SIR NICHOLAS BACON. = 1. Jane.

Name unknown. ~ SIR THOMAS GRESHAM. = Anne (as above.) = William Read, Esq.

SIR NATHANIEL BACON. = Anne. From her the Lord Viscount Sydney is descended.

Sir William Read, Knt. knighted in 1603. =

Far more interesting than most of the relationships indicated in the foregoing pedigree, is the following; which shall be given in the words of the intelligent antiquary and very expert genealogist by whom it was kindly communicated,—the Rev. Joseph Hunter. "John Gresham of Mayfield, cousin-german of Sir Thomas, married Elizabeth Dormer of Fulham. This is in the Baronetage; but it is not stated that she survived him, and married, 2ndly, William Plumbe, of North End, near Fulham, whose will was proved 1st March, 1593; in which he speaks of Thomas and John Gresham, sons of his wife. What gives something of interest to this connexion is, that William Plumbe was *uncle to Joshua Sylvester, the poet;* as appears by his 'Triumph of Faith.' Now, may not the Greshams have had something to do with placing Sylvester in the situation of merchant-adventurer? The poet was a frequent guest at the house of his uncle and his aunt, (by the marriage,) who had been Mrs. Gresham:

> 'I was wont (for my disport)
> Often in the summer season,
> To a village to resort
> Famous for the rathe-ripe peason.
> When, beneath a *Plumb*-tree shade,
> Many pleasant walks I made,' &c."

Another interesting relationship, pointed out by the same antiquary, but unnoticed for obvious reasons in the foregoing pedigree, is that of the Greshams to the ancient family of Clapham of Yorkshire. According to Dodsworth, (MS. cxxxv. f. 79, b.) Catharine, sister of the lady of John Gresham, one of the daughters and coheiresses of Sir Henry Thwaites, married George Clapham of Beamsley; by whom she had a son named Gresham Clapham, father of George Clapham of Beamsley, who married a Heber of Marton. The wife of Gresham Clapham was Ann Fisher, daughter and heir of William Fisher, the son of a sister (half-blood) of Bishop Ferrar, the martyr.

In Vol. II. p. 152, note, will be found a quotation from a curious list of nativities of the children of Sir John Gresham of Titsey. The result of that document having been transferred to the preceding pedigree, one other specimen of the entries may suffice. "Mary Gresham [the eldest daughter, who became the wife of Sir Thomas Rowe,] was borne the xvij daye of August, callyd octava Sancti Lawrencij, A° dñi xv^{c} xxiij: and my Lady Allen, and Mystris Kyng, and Mystrys Lock,—thes were here godmothers; and Mr. John Worsop was her godffather. Uppon the Mondaye: and God make here a good old woman." [Addit. MS. No. 6239.—*Copy*. Ex. cod. MSS. penes Edv. Rowe Mores, A.M. Soc. Antiq. Lond. soc. 1754.]

No. II.

Wills of the Gresham Family, proved at Norwich.

[Referred to in page 11, note j.]

In the will-offices at Norwich, I expected to have reaped a rich harvest of documents illustrative of the history of the Greshams; but I was altogether disappointed. The will-offices are three in number: of which the most important, known as 'the Bishop's Registry,' is situated behind the cathedral. The wills proved here date as early as 1416, and are all well indexed. Next comes what is called 'the Registry of the Archdeaconry of Norwich,' at Mr. Steward's, in Upper King-street; a very voluminous repository, and well indexed, but on a less convenient plan than the preceding. Lastly, we have 'the Registry of the Archdeaconry of Norfolk,' situated in Surrey-street, in the house of Mr. Francis. The ancient superintendents of this registry were wicked enough to index the wills according to the *Christian names* of the several testators: but fortunately this inconvenience is only partial in its extent. A search at these three repositories produced the following meagre results.

1.

4 Nov. 1420. JOHN GRESHAM, Vic. Eccl. de Hornyng̃. Leaves 12*d.* to the high-altar; two other legacies of 6*d.* each; and 40*d.* to the sub-rector of Hornyng. Leaves the rest of his property to his exõrs: viz. John Norman of Tylley; John Crosby of Hornyng; and John Dovey of Raughton, [Revington?]

[Proved, 18 Nov. 1420. Bishop's registry. *Hyrninge, quire* lxxiij.]

2.

1 Oct. 1494. JOHN PUTO, *alias* GRESHAM, Vic. Eccl. St. Andrew de Buxton, in Nowicen. dioc.

[Proved, 16 June, 1598. *Ibid. Typpes, quire* cxlviij.]

3.

23 Aug. 1520. AGNES GRESHAM, of Little Walsingham, widow. Desires to be buried by the sepulture of her husband, William. Mentions her father and mother-in-law, Jeffrey and Beatrix; and her son James, to whom she leaves her cupboard. He was to give x*s.* to his sisters Ursula and Susan. She mentions, also, her daughter Margaret Dunne;* and Agnes, her daughter-in-law.

[Proved, 26 Oct. 1520. *Ibid. Robinson, quire* xxix.]

* It will be seen from the preceding pedigree, that Margaret Gresham married John Downe (or Dunne); that Ursula married Francis Garbridge; and Susan, William Candelor,—all three Norfolk men; whose surnames, it seems deserving of notice, were also borne by three of Sir Thomas Gresham's servants.—Vide suprà, pp. 106 and 109.

4.

6 Nov. 1523. JAMES GRESHAM, of Little-Walsingham, (son of the preceding). Appoints his wife Agnes his executrix. Leaves his sisters Margery and Susan, 20*s*. each. His son and heir was Paul; to Giles, his second son, he bequeathed 20 marks if he became a priest, and 20*l*. if he continued a layman: there was also another son, and two daughters; the elder of whom, Anne, was to receive 20*l*. on her marriage. Mentions his uncle, John Gresham of Holt. "I wull," says the testator, "that my Executors do fynde a honest preste to sing for my soul, and my friends' souls in the said parish church [of Little Walsingham] by the space of one year. .... I make and ordeyne the sayd Annes* my wiff, [and] my brother Nicholas Mynne, myn executors; and my cosyng, Master Thomas Gresham,† supervisor.

[Proved 30 Oct. 1526. *Ibid. Alpe, quire* xxxv.]

5.

23 Aug. 1558. Mr. THOMAS GRESHAM, parson‡ of South Repps. Appoints Edmund Gresham, gent. his executor and doer. Witnesses, Will. Black, gent., Sir John Wilson, parish-priest. Joan Sefall, widow. Richard Sefall.

[Proved 16 Sept. 1558. *Ibid. Jerves, quire* ccxlvi.]

No. III.

Grants of Land to Sir Richard Gresham.

[Referred to in page 38, note d.]

Tanner enumerates the following.—1. The site of the abbey of Fountains or De Fontibus, in Yorkshire; 2. The site and desmesnes of the priory of Nun Kelynge, in Yorkshire; and 3. The site of the priory of Swinhey, in Yorkshire,—32 Henry VIII. 4. An Hospital of Knights of St. John of Jerusalem, at Battisford in Suffolk, worth 53*l*. 10*s*. per annum; and 5. A religious house of Knights Hospitallers at Carbroke, in Norfolk, worth 65*l*. 2*s*.11*d*. per annum, (the latter being granted jointly to Sir R. Gresham and Sir Richard Southwell,)—35 H.VIII. 6. A house of White-Friars in Newcastle, and 7. The religious house of Walknol in the same town, (being granted to Sir R. Gresham and Richard Billingford,)—37 Henry VIII. (See, however, Bourne's Hist. of Newcastle, p. 142.) 8. The priory of Benedictine Monks at Hoxon, in Suffolk, worth 18*l*. 1*s*. per annum,—38 Henry VIII.—*Notitia Monastica, passim.*

* It is often difficult, in old wills, to decide whether a lady's name was Agnes or Anne: the former word became so generally Italianized, and softened into *Annis* or *Annes*.

† The rector of South Repps, whose will follows. ‡ Vide suprà, pp. 10 and 11.

No. IV.

Military and Naval Expenses of Henry VIII. and Edward VI.

[Referred to in page 68, note v.]

Among the Domestic State-Papers an extraordinary document relative to this subject is preserved. The MS. extends over twenty-three large pages, and details the whole military and naval expenses incurred by Henry VIII. and Edward VI. during their wars with France and Scotland, the insurrection in England, the expenses of Calais, Boulogne, &c., and the charges of castles and garrisons, from Sept. 1542 to Sept. 1552. It concludes as follows: "Sm̃ totall of the charges conteyned in this booke, xxxiiij^c^iiij^xx^ xi^m^ iiij^c^ lxxj ^lib.^ xix^s.^ v^d.^ (3,491,471*l.* 19*s.* 5*d.*): whereof, in the time of o^r^ said late kinge, xxi^c^ xxxiiij^m^ vij^c^ iiij^xx^ iiij^lib.^ xij^d.^ (2,134,784*l.* 12*d.*): in the time of ye kinges Majestie that nowe ys, xiij^c^ lvj^m^ vj^c^ iiij^xx^ vij^lib.^ xviij^s.^ v^d.^" (1,356,687*l.* 18*s.* 5*d.*) and some fraction of a penny.

No. V.

Gresham's first Account; rendered to King Edward in August, 1552.

[Referred to in page 84, note t.]

In addition to the notices of this document contained in the text, much needs not to be stated. Gresham had received of Sir P. Hoby, (with whom he was at that time evidently associated in public business,) Jasper Schetz, Anthony and Conrad Relingar, divers sums, at different times, amounting in all to—106,282*l.* 5*s.* 5*d.*: of which he had paid, . . . To Anthony Fugger, 63,573*l.* 6*s.* 8*d.*: to Jasper Schetz [and his brethren,] "in recompens of soche lossis as they susteynid by the fall of the exchange, when as they maid there great provissione of corrin [corn] delyveryd in Ingland in King Henry the eyght dayes, a^o^ xv^c^xxxvi [1536,]" and for other services, 1000*l.*: further sums to the same, in payment of the king's bonds, "wyche, wth a quittance of the resset thereof, I dd then vnto yor Ma^tis^ wth mynne owne handes," 41,637*l.* 4*s.* Other payments follow, which should amount, in all, to 1090*l.* 13*s.* 8*d.*: and the schedule ends with these words: "And so remaynes to yor Ma^tis^ of the fotte of thys mynne accownt, all accownts cleryde betwxte yor Ma^tis^ and yor S^r^vant Thomas Greshm̃, the vj of August, a^o^ xv^c^lij, from the begynnyng of this worlde vntill this daye, sum . . . 249*l.* 11*s.* 8*d.*"

No. VI.

Curious old Catalogue of Pictures.

[Referred to in page 85, note v.]

The MS. quoted in the text, (constituting part of a volume of original letters and papers relative to the unfortunate Devereux, Earl of Essex,) extends over twelve folio pages, and consists principally of an enumeration of articles of furniture and linen; the whole of which are valued at 1206*l.* 15*s.* 4*d.* What proportion of this estimate the pictures formed, will be seen from the following curious extract.

"An Inventorie taken the 23rd daie of Aprill, 1596, of all the goods of the right honorable the Countesse of Leicester, and the righte worrshipful Sr Christopher Blounte, Knighte, in Essex-house, delivered by Edwarde Standishe into the charge of William Benton; and were remayninge in the howse there att the attainder of the said Sr Christopher. "In the Wardropp.

"ii pictures of my Lorde of Leicester, xiii*s.* iiij*d.*—i picture of the Lorde of Denbighe, v*s.*—ii pictures, thone of the Prince of Orrenge and the other of his wife, xx*s.*—i picture of the King of Scottes, vi*s.*—i picture of the Prince of Orrenge his sonne, v*s.*—i picture of Julius Cæsar, v*s.*—i picture of Penelopey, v*s.*—i picture of Sir William Goodere, v*s.*—i picture of Mr. Cavandishe, v*s.*—i picture of a man of Cattea, [Cathay or China,] iij*s.*—i picture of my La: Garrolde, x*s.*—i picture of my La: Sheifield, x*s.*—i picture of Fryer Bacon, iij*s.*—i picture of the Queene of Hungarie, v*s.*—i womans picture wth a whyte Tyre vppon her heade, v*s.*—i womans picture wth roses unfynished, v*s.*—vii small Flaunders pictures, vii*s.*—viii mappes, xxx*s.* Some vii *li.* vii*s.* iiij*d.*"

"An Inventorie taken the xth daie of Julie, 1596, of suche stuffe that came from Benington to Leicester-howse, from the hands of Edwarde Standishe to the charge of William Benton; and were alsoe in the howse att the attainder of the said Sir Christopher.

"i picture of Christ preaching in the Wildernesse, xiii*s.* iiij*d.* i picture of Sir Tho: Gresham, his banquett, v*li.* i picture of the Convercon of Sall, x*s.* i picture of Charitie and her Chilldren, x*s.* i picture of Suzanna, x*s.* i picture of the Duke de Savoye, v*s.* i picture of Diana and her Nymphes, viij*s.* i picture of a woman with a carelesse tyre uppon her heade, v*s.*"

The MS. from which this extract was obtained, was communicated to me, with his usual liberality, by Dawson Turner, Esq.

No. VII.

Extracts from Gresham's Official Correspondence in the reign of Edward VI.

[Referred to in page 98, note c.]

The following extract is from Gresham's letter "To the Duckes Grace of Northethomberland;" Antwerp, 16th April, 1553: being a continuation of the passage given in p. 97.

"And to be playne wth yor grace, yow shall never be abell to bringe this to passe except yow tacke away, and so be a steye of one of the greattist occasiones of the lette and steye thereof; and that ys, that yt maye pleasse the Kinges Matie and yow, wth his most honnorable conssell to macke a pressent steye, that there shall be no more maid fre of this company of the Merchant Adventores of the new hansse * from this daye forward. For veryly, the [they] have bynne and ys one of the cheffyst occasiones of the falling of the Exchange; as allso, for lacke of experience, the have browght the commodites of o^r^ realme clean owght of reputacione, as allso the marchaunts of the same, wyche in tyme past haythe here bynne most in exstymacione of all the marchaunts in the worlde; and in fewe yeres sens this acte was maid for the new hansse, the marchaunttes and o^r^ comodites haythe fallen in decaye, and licke to fall daylly more and more, except theye matter be preventtid in tyme. For as yor grace dowthe right well knowe, where there ys no order kepe, all thinges at lengthe fallythe to confewssione. So, and please yor grace, how ys yt possibell that ayther a mynsterell-player, or a shoye- [shoe] macker, or anny craftye men, or any other that haythe not bynne browght vppe in the syence, to have the ꝑssent vnd^r^-stonding of the feat of the Marchaunt Adventorer? To the wyche syence I myselfe was bound prentisse viii yeres, to come by the experyence and knowledge that I have. Neverthelesse, I need not to have bynne prentisse, for that I was free by my Father's coppye: albeit my Father Sir Richard Gresham being a wyse man, knew, although I was free by his coppye, it was to no purpos, except I were bound prentisse to the same; whereby to come by the experience and knowledge of all kynds of merchandise. So that by this ytt maye apere vnto yor grace, thes men that be maid fre by this new hansse, for lacke of experyence and knowledge, haythe bynne and ys one of the cheffyst occasions of the fall of the Exchange, as allso hayth browght o^r^ comodittes owght of reputacion, and the m̃chaunts of the same.

* The merchants of the Hanse Towns, were commonly called Merchants of the Steelyard. See page 234.

"As for a forddy[r] exsampell to yo[r] grace; yt ys not passing xx or xxx yeres agoo, sens we hadd for every xx *s.* sterling, xxxij *s.* flemyshe; and by the notable nomber that be come in by the new haynsse, for lacke of experyence and knowledge, as allso substance, haythe from tyme to tyme rowen in headlong into the feat of merchaundisse, and so enterid into creditt: and when the hadd ov[r] shotte themsellffes, and hadd bowrden themsellffes wth more then there sobstance wolld bere, bothe here and in Inglonde; then, for saving of there name and creditt, they were fayne to rowen apon the Exchange and rechange; and the m̃chants knowing the hadd nead thereof, wold not from tyme to tyme delyver there monny but at there price. So that in fewe yeres theye plenttye of thes new marchaunts com̃en in by the new hansse, what for lacke of experyense and allso substance and creditt, haythe bynne owenly the occasyone the exchange fell from xxxij *s.* to xxvi *s.* viij *d.* wyche was dowen afore anny fall of monney passid in Inglond. Wherein I doo ryght well knowe yo[r] Grace haythe forther experience in thes matters than I am abell to set forthe; nevertheleasse, according to my most bownddyd dewttye, and for the very love and obediens I doo owe to yo[r] Lordeshipe, I am so bold to wryte to yo[r] grace my powre and sympell advyze, wherein I know yow shall doo the Kings Ma[tie] hye s[r]vyze, and shall hyghly redowen to the Comenwelthe of his realme, to the renom̃e of yo[r] name and howsse for ever."

Gresham complains at some length of the injury done to the trade of the merchant-adventurer by the retailer: a brief extract may suffice.

"A dothe not only take awaye the lyving of the Marchaunt Adventorer, but in process of tyme the few nomber of xl or l retaylers in London will eat out all the m̃chaunts within o[r] realme; as allso will be a meynne [means] by the reason their bartering, to bring o[r] said commodities owght of reputacione, and make all foraign commodities in reputacyon .... In consideration whereof, the marchaunts here with one assent have maid a acte in o[r] howsse, to take effect at mydsomer next comyng (wth a peradvyzo so far forthe as the King's Ma[tie] and his most honnorable counsell be agreable to the same) that the retayller shall occupy onely his retayle, and the m̃chaunt adventorer his feat: according to be at their libertye betwixt this and then to tacke to one of them, wych they shall seem most to their proffytt," &c. &c.—Fl. Cor. St. P. Off.

What follows is an extract from Thomas Gresham's letter "To my Lordes of the Kinges Ma[tes] privey conssayll." Antwerp, 12th April, 1553.

"Yt maye pleasse yo[r] honnors to be advertisid, that by my letter of the vii[th] of this present, I singnyfyed vnto yo[r] honnors of the xsoddaynne fall of the Echange from xx *s.* iiij d. to xix *s.* Persseving now the fawte to be as moche in or owen nacyone as in strangyrs, and rather lycke to fall than to rysse, I tocke vppe by exchange of dyvers men the sũ of one thowssownd, eyght hundreth therttye seven pownds, eyght shillings sterling; wyche mackythe Flemyshe i M vij c lvj *li.* ij *s.* iij *d.* as by the accownt here inclossyd to yow maye apere. And for that I sawe or nacyone was holly uneprovydyd for the payment of the king's monny dew the last of Marche, and trustyd onely to the exchange, (wyche yff I hadd not preventtid in tyme yt wold have browght the exchange to xviij *s.* and loer, [lower,]) I declaryd to all the holle companny that the had most disobediently vssid themselffes toywards the Kings Matie, considering how franckely the Kings Matie had paid them aforehand, as well for the kepping uppe of exchange as other wisse, wherbye the shulld be no lossers; so that now ytt shall apere to the King's Matie that we marchaunts be them that dowthe kepe dowen theye exchange. And franckely I declaryd vnto them yff they tocke no nother waysse to pay me, but by tacking uppe there monny by exchange, I shulld not lett to advertisse yor honnors how theye were unprovydyd, and the particular names of them that tocke vppe anny monny by exchange. Apon this admonyshement, to bringe vppe the exchange I sett me all the brockers of exchange, some to đd me ij c *li.* some iii c, iiij c, v c, and had gaven forthe my word for iiij M *li.* And when the strangrs sawe that I began to delyver so abondantly, noo man dorst meddill wth me; as for or nacyone I was most assewred of: so that in towe borssetymes I resseyd the exchange from xix *s* to xix *s.* viij *d.* and there I trust to kepe ytt, and now rather lycke to rysse then to fall for ever. And now, here ys dyvers of or owen marchauntes has muche money to delyver, and specially staplers, and no tackers; wyche wth owght dowght wolle causse the exchange to rysse. Trusting that yr Lordeshipes hathe bargeyned wth the Marchaunt Adventurers and stapleres for to have for every pownde sterling xxiij *s.* iiij *d.*, to paye here in July and August in permissione monny; wyche and yff yor honnors had concludyd, and the thinge knowen to all men, ytt wolle bringe vppe the exchange forthewth too xxiij *s.* iiij *d.* And my powre advyze ys, yff the marchaunts dowthe requyre anny monny to be disborsyd aforehand, yow shulld in no wisse consent therevnto; for the plentye of monny amonges marchauntes dowthe causse the exchange to fall in London; and here, the plenttye of monny dowthe causse the exchange to rysse. Therefore I wold wyshe the Kings Matie to be att his liberttye in soche sorte as a was last; whereby the m̃chauntes shulld be kept hunggery from monny till opportewnyttye srvyd; whereof from tyme to tyme I shulld advertisse yow."

No. VIII.

Old Method of obtaining a Subsidy.

[Referred to in page 98, note d.]

Allusion is made to a similar, but much milder proceeding, in the following minute in Cecil's handwriting, headed "The Kynges Matie detts, wth some devise towards ye discharge of ye same."

"At Syon, ii Oct. [1552]—Vppon much communication and treaty wth theis m̃chants vndr named,—Aldermā Garret, Emanuel Lucar, Thom. Greshā, Richard Mallory, Lyonell Duckat, Thom. Eaton, Ihõ Calthropp, Rogr Martyn, Phillipp Bolde, Ihon Elliott.

"They agreed for themselves that they wold paye in Antwerpe by ye end of December of eũry cloth they had, xx*s*. to ye discharge of ye Kinges dett; requyring repaym̃t wthin iij moneth aftr ye delivery thereof," &c.—Dom. Corr. St. P. Off. King Edward VI. in his Journal mentions that on the 3rd of October, 1552, a loan of 40,000*l*. was obtained of the merchant-adventurers.

No. IX.

Genealogical Notices of Sir John Legh, and his Family.

[Referred to in page 125, note g.]

Some scanty notices of the Legh family are incidentally given in Manning and Bray's Surrey; but what is there said about them is little to our purpose, and not of much value. Moreover, the writers, being altogether unaware of the historical interest which attaches to the name of Sir John Legh, have dismissed him in a very unsatisfactory manner; merely assigning to him his place in a pedigree which is full of misstatements. In so voluminous a compilation, this might well be the case; and I only allude to the circumstance, because it constitutes a sufficient apology for the insertion here of a few genealogical particulars, which else might be considered unnecessary. They are derived almost exclusively from the wills of the family, but are offered very humbly: the requisite labour not having been bestowed upon them to secure them from the manifold sources of error, to which such inquiries are in an eminent degree exposed. It is presumed, however, that if not perfectly accurate, the following will be found a far less erroneous pedigree of Legh (as far as it goes) than is contained in the county Visitation-books. The experienced eye of a genealogist will at once perceive how much scope for misapprehension is afforded by the relationships therein expressed.

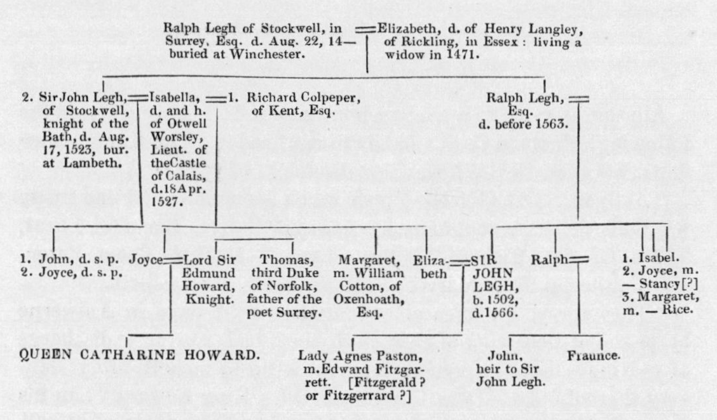

My ground for believing that Sir John Legh married as above, is the circumstance that his aunt, Lady Isabella, mentions her daughter Elizabeth as married to 'my *cousin* John Legh;' which in the phraseology of the time might well mean her nephew. This was in 1527, before Sir John was knighted. His wife's name *was* Elizabeth: and this intermarriage serves both to explain the confusion which has crept into the accounts of this family; and to produce a nearer approximation to Noailles' statement of the relationship which existed between Sir John Legh and Queen Catharine Howard.

It is not by any means my intention to give here a history of the Leghs; but only to offer, in addition to what precedes, a few circumstances relating to them which have come under my observation. They were originally of Chester: and the Harl. MS. No. 1561, (Visitation of the county of Surrey,) traces their descent to John Legh, of Ridge, in that county; assigning for their arms *gules, a cross engrailed within a bordure, argent.* Their crest was *a cockatrice, azure,* with which I find that *our* Sir John sealed his letters.

Sir John Legh the elder, made his will on the 12th of June, 1523, and it was proved on the 10th of December following. He left the manor of Stockwell, for the term of her life, to Lady Isabella Legh, who brought it in dower from her former husband. Its yearly value seems to have been 200*l.* He left, by will, to each of his nieces, Isabel, Joyce, and Margaret, (daughters of his brother Ralph,) 200 marks, as a marriage portion. To his nephew Ralph, 10*l.* a-year "to find him at Clifford's Inn;" and, after three years, 16*l.* 6*s.* 8*d.* per annum, to find him at the Temple. He left him besides 50*l.* 2*s.* 1¼*d.* a-year; 3 lbs. of wax; a capon; a pound of pepper, and two hens: the same being the yearly produce of several manors and lands which he specifies. His nephew, (the "Sir John a-Lye" of the preceding pages,) he appointed his heir, leaving him lands worth upwards of 200*l.* per annum "as appears from a writing between me and Sir John Wyndham;" with remainder to his brother,—to the testator's cousins Roger, Thomas, George, and William,—to the Lord Edmund Howard and Joyce his wife, and to their children, Henry, Charles, and George Howard, (brothers to the future queen),—"if they be good, kind, loving, and unfainedly assisting unto myn executors." These were, Sir Richard Broke, one of the justices of the King's Bench; John Rooper, the king's attorney; John Spilman, serjeant-at-law; and Roger Legh. He also left some money "to the grey friars in London, whereof I am a brother."—[Prerogative-office, Bodfelde, quire xv.]

His widow, Lady Isabella Legh, died seven days after the date of her will, which was made on the 11th of April, 1527, and proved on the 25th of the following month. Her first husband was Richard Colpeper, of Kent, Esq., who left by her, three daughters: Joyce, who married Lord Sir Edmund Howard (brother of Thomas, third Duke of Norfolk); Margaret, who married Wm. Cotton, Esq., and Elizabeth, who, as already stated, married *our* Sir John Legh. Joyce and her husband were enjoined by the testatrix to secure "the estates in Kent which descended to her from her father Richard Culpepper, or from her brother Thomas Culpepper; according to the will of Sir John Culpepper." To Lord Howard, Lady Isabella bequeathed 10*l.* that he might pray for her; and to his wife (her daughter Joyce) she left "of such stock of her's as Lady Howard had in her hands,—8 oxen, 12 kine, 1 bull, 37 wethers, 75 ewes, 48 young sheepe, 4 old hoggs, 4 yeltz, 2 small barowe hoggs, 1 bore, 15 quarters of wheat, 10 of barley, 9 loads of hay, 1 mill-horse, and 2 cart-horses." To her daughter Margaret, she left 66*s.* 8*d.*; and she enumerates an immense number of beds, bolsters, jewels, rings, dresses, crosses, beads, &c. &c, which she divided among her children: 40*l.* if I remember right, was to be expended on her funeral. To Charles, Henry, George, Margaret, and [QUEEN] Katharine Howard, (her grandchildren,) she left 20*s.* each; and to her god-daughter, Mary Howard, 40*s.* In her domestic establishment she unmbered a ghostly father, a chaplain, &c. &c.—[Ibid. Porch. quire xviii.]

In Lambeth church, in the south chapel, says Stowe, "is a fair monument of marble, engraven as followeth:—"Here lyeth Sir John Legh, Knight of the Bath, son of Ralph Legh, Esq. Lord of the Mannors of Stockwell and Levehurst, and Dame Isabel his Wife, Daughter of Otwell Worsley. Which Sir John deceased the 17 day of August, Anno Dom. MDXXIIII. And the same Isabel deceased the 18 day of April."—This epitaph has either been inaccurately copied, or it supplies us with another proof of the little value of such evidence.

We now come to SIR JOHN LEGH, of London, knight, son of Ralph, and nephew and heir to the knight of the Bath, whom we called Sir John Legh the elder. He was born in 1502, and married, as before explained, his cousin Elizabeth Colpeper,—the aunt of Queen Katharine Howard: by whom he had an only child, Lady Agnes Paston, married to Edward Fitzgarrett. One regrets to learn from his will, that he had been divorced from his wife "on certain sufficient grounds."

A most interesting letter is extant addressed by Sir John Legh to the Lords of the Council, from the Tower, where he was under confinement in 1537 or 8. It reveals several interesting particulars of his history; but it would be improper to insert so lengthy a document in this place. The original is to be found in the Cott. MS. Cleop. E. vi. fol. 380; and in Strype's Ecclesiastical Memorials, ed. 1822, vol. i. part i. p. 481-4, it may be seen printed; though so mangled as to be scarcely recognisable. Legh relates a conversation he had once at Rome with Cardinal Pole; which, in addition to the personal allusions it contains, (and the principal of these have been incorporated in the text,) is rendered interesting by his mention of St. Thomas à Becket's shrine, and the Italian storybooks he meant to read.—In turning over the voluminous Flemish correspondence at the State-Paper Office, I remember more than once meeting with letters written in the same hand-writing as the foregoing, but did not suspect their interest: never supposing that the knight, concerning whose history I felt so curious, was their author.

On the 13th of July, 1542, the poet Surrey was committed to the Fleet prison by order of the Privy-council, for having challenged Legh, who was his kinsman; but he was liberated on the 5th of August, having entered into a recognisance of 10,000 marks 'not to offer any injury to John à Leigh, Esq., or to any of his friends in future.' From this, it would appear that Surrey was in the wrong; the reader will at all events acquit him of any rivalry with Surrey [Vide Nott's Works of Surrey and Wyatt] for the affections of the fair Geraldine, who was about fourteen years of age in 1542, at which time Sir John had seen forty winters. Surrey, in fact, was very contrite, and expressly mentions "this simple body, rashly adventured in the revenge of *his own quarrel.*"—One is curious, however, to discover why Legh was committed to the Fleet in August 1547; and bound in 2000*l.* for his future good behaviour: and again consigned to durance in the following November.

Sir John Legh made his will on the 30th of April, 1563, adding a codicil on the 14th of March following: both which were proved on the 5th of February, 1565–6. The principal legacies are as follows:—To his wife, in consideration of certain property in Surrey which she had brought him in marriage, he left 33*l.* 6*s.* 8*d.* per annum, payable out of his manor of Hilton, in Dorsetshire.—To the children of his daughter Lady Agnes Paston, 300*l.* To his son-in-law, Edward Fitzgarrett, his "collar of gold with stories enamelled." He left them, besides, considerable property; but he appointed John Legh, the son of his brother Ralph, his heir: making mention of lands, manors, rents, and hereditaments in Berkshire, Bucks, and Oxfordshire, bought of Sir Francis Stone; (?) others in Surrey, Dorsetshire, Sussex, Southampton, and London, and the manor of Williton in Somersetshire. He also mentions his residence at Stanwell.—To his niece Fraunce, sister of his heir John Legh, he bequeathed 100*l.*—To Henry, Thomas, Richard, and Elinor, the children of his sister Margaret Rice, 100 marks.—To the children of his sister Joyce Stancy, 100*l.*—To Sir George Howard, 100*l.*: to his god-daughter, the daughter of Lord William Howard, 100*l.*: to Jane, daughter of Sir Thomas Arundell, 100 marks: to his cousin, Mary Martyn, 10*l.* and to her sister, Fraunce, the same sum: to M. Whetill, Esq. 100*l.*: to Edward, the younger son of Sir Thomas Paston, 100*l.*: and to his sister Katharine, 200*l.* Also legacies to the overseers of his will,—Sir Nicholas Bacon, the Lord Viscount Montague, and Roger Manwood, Esq.; and to his executors, Thomas Lovelace, Esq., Sir Thomas Cotton, Thomas Felton, Esq. of Clerkenwell, and Richard Blount his servant.—To the children of John Lovelace,—John, Henry, Arthur, and Elizabeth, 10*l.* each.—To Sir Nicholas Bacon, if he had not already disposed of it otherwise, (which he *had*,) he bequeathed his "collar of gold, with stories enamelled, or 50*l.*" To Lord Montague, his "best hobby, or any one of his horses which his lordship liketh."—Finally, Sir John Legh directed that he might be interred in the parish-church of Lambeth, in a chapel there erected by his uncle Sir John Legh, late of Stockwell, knt. deceased; or else in the parish-church of St. Margaret's, Lothburie, wherein I do presently inhabit." He directed that a tomb should be there erected to his memory, to cost 20*l.*; "and thereuppon my image and arms to be gravyn in lattyn, [latten ?] and the similitude of the cross of Jerusalem that is on my breast, cut in my flesh."—(Ibid. Crymes, quire iii.)

Accordingly, I find mention made in Stowe, of "a goodly ancient tomb in the chancel" of St. Margaret's church, Lothbury; of which we would fain have had a more particular account. Stowe or the monument is again incorrect in stating that Sir John died in 1564. (Survey, ed. 1720, book iii. p. 58.) We forgive him, however, in consideration of his having preserved the following verses, which constituted Sir John Legh's epitaph:—

"No wealth, no praise, no bright renowne, no skill,
No force, no fame, no prince's love, no toyle,
Though forraine lands by travels search you will,
No faithful service of thy country soyle,
Can life prolong one minute of an houre:
But death at length will execute his power.

For Sir John Leigh, to sundry countries knowne,
A worthy knight, well of his prince esteem'd;
By seeing much, to great experience growne:
Though safe on seas, though sure on land be seem'd;
Yet here he lyes, too soone by death opprest,
His fame yet lives, his soule in heaven hath rest."

X.

Gresham's Instructions on being sent into Flanders.

[Referred to in page 131, note j.]

"d. d. 13 Novembris, 1553.

Wher we have byn enfourmed that Lazarus Tucker and certayn other merchaunts of Andwarpe have of their own good wills offred to lende vs diverse great sumes of money,—we, remembring the great debts left unpayed at the death of our late brother, and considering that as well in respecte therof as for many other great causes, it shuld be very expedient for our suertie and the comon welth of our realme to have a good masse of money in redynes to serve in all events,—have thought good to accept the said offers. And for the better vnderstanding of the said merchaunts' meanings, and full concluding wt them, have appoyncted our said srvūnt to procede in suche fourme as followeth.

First, the said Thomas Gressham, repairing to Flaunders, shall comnaunt [covenant] and bargayn in our name and for our use wt suche merchaunts as to hym may seme most mete, for the sume of fiftie thousand pownds, or so moche vnder that sume as he may get or attayn vnto, to be lent vnto vs for one yere, to be repayed in Andwarpe at the yere's ende w[t] thinterest of xj, or at thuttermost xij in the hundreth.

And for the suertie of the repayment, we be pleased that the said Gressham shall comnaunt to delyver suche and like bands convenūts and assurance to be by vs signed and sealed w[t] our great seale, and w[t] the seale also of our citie of London, as in the tyme of o[r] late brother hath byn given in semblable cases.

And it shalbe also lawful to our servūnt to take vp from tyme to tyme during this comission, money by exchaunge vpon his own credit in Flaunders, to be delivered in London for our vse.

And all suche somes of money as the said Thomas shall take vp vpon interest or by exchaunge, shalbe by him in most secret maner sent to London, in suche coynes of golde and silver as the said thomas shall thinke most mete; to be laden in Andwarpe to London or Ipswiche in euery ship that shall depte to either of the said places, not exceeding one thousand poundes sterling in one bottom. And further it shalbe laufull also for our said servūnt from tyme to tyme to send to London over lande from Andwarpe to Calys, and so to London, by euery suche trusty pson or psons as he shall put in trust, the some of M[t] M[t] M[t] *li.* [3000*l.*] sterling, thadventure of all suche somes of money as shalbe so sent over bothe by see and lande to be born from tyme to tyme at our charge and jeopdie, [jeopardy.]

And to thintent the sayd Gresham may the bette[r] execut the charge cometted by vs pntly vnto hym, o[r] pleasure is thatt of the money to be by hym received by force of this o[r] comession he shall reteyn in [his] own hands and to his own vse, not only the dietts of xx*s.* for eūry day, the same to begyñ the day of the dat of thies pñts inclusive, and to cotynue during his abode about o[r] s[r]vice in this behalf; but also all such money as he shall pay for sending of any messangers, lettars, or treasure vnto vs. For thallowance wherof thies o[r] instructions shall be suffisient warrant to such as shall herafter have authorite to hyer his accompt for the premiss, [premises.] Fland. Corr. St. P. Off.

Copy, endorsed "13 Nov. 1553.—Tho. Greshams instructions."

No. XI.

Gresham's Instructions on being sent into Spain.

[Referred to in p. 152, note d.]

"A memoriall gyven by the Quene's hyhnes vnto hir trusty and welbeloved s^r^vaunt Thomas Gresham, esquier, hir Matie agent in Flanders, for the purposes ensuing, xii^o^ Junii, 1554.

Fyrst,—where as the sayd Thomas Gresham hath for vs, and to o^r^ use, bargayned wth dyvers ꝑsones in Andwerpe for sundrie sumes of monny, for which he hath receyved theyr bylls of exchange to be payd in Spaine,—that is to say of Anthony Fugger the sume of cxii^m^ vii^c^l ducats: to be receyved at the fayre of Villalon, lxij^m^ ducats; and the rest in the fayre of May. Of Jasper Schetz and his bretherne the sume of lxv^m^ ducats, to be receyved in the fayre of October: more of the sayd Schetz and his bretherne, the sume of xxxv^m^ ducats, to be receyved in the fayre of Villalon,—of Octavian Lomelino, the sume of xxxij^m^ ducats, to be receyved at the fayre of Villalon—xxiiij^m^ ducats; and the rest in the fayre of May: of John de Mantansse, the sume of xv^m^ ducats, to be receyved in the fayre of Villalon: of John Lopez de Gallo, the sume of xxiiij^m^ ducats, to be received in the fayre of Villalon: of Anthony Spynnole and Frederigo Imperialle the sume of xvii^m^ ducats, to be received in the fayre of May: amounting in the hole, to the totall sum of iij c thowsand vij c l ducats. The sayd Thomas Gresham, taking with hym this memorial, and themperors lrẽs of license, wth suche other things as ar prepared for hym, shall, for the receipt of the sayd money make his repayre wth as convenient spede as he may towards Spaine; embarking hymsellf at o^r^ ports either of Darmouth or Plimouth, where we have caused a vessel to be put in a redynes for his transportacion: from whence he shall procede on his voyage as sone as wynde and wether shall gyve hym leave.

And for ye better and more surer conveyance hither owt of Spaine of the sayd money, o^r^ pleasure is y^t^ the sayd Thomas Gresham shall, before his deꝑture, common wth suche marchaunts in London, ether Englyshemen or straungers, as doo trafficque in to Spaine; procuring, yf he by any meanes may, to bargayne wth them or any of them for the delyvery here vnto o^r^ vse of suche sumes of mony as they shall have occasion to employe in Spayne: whiche shall be there by hym repayed againe vnto them owt of the said mony that is to be receyved to o^r^ vse,—foreseing that we be not of this bargaine burdened wth any losse of exchange or interest.

Itm̃, at his coming in to Spayne, in caase o^r^ dearest cousin the Prince of Spaine shall not be deꝑted from thence before the money that is fyrst payable shall be receyved,—the sayd Thom̃s Gresham shall then conferre wth o^r^ right trusty and right welbeloved cousin and counsello^r^ the Earle of Bedforde, keꝑ of our privie seale, and opening vnto hym the hole circumstance of this matter, shall, by his advise and counsell, distribute amongst the best and most surest shippes of the flete that shall cume in cumpany of o^r sayd derest cousin the Prince of Spaine, so muche of the sayd mony as he shall have receyved: so as he adventure not above the sume of fyve thowsand pounds sterling in any one botome. And yf it shall fortune o^r sayd dearest cousin the prince of Spaine to be come from thence before the sayd mony can be receyved; in that caase, o^r pleas^r is, that the sayd Thomas Gresham procure to sende over by way of exchaunge, to be delyvered there, and repayed againe vnto us here or at Andwerpe vppon sight, so muche of o^r sayd mony as he can. Foreseing that we be not burdened wth any losse of exchaunge, and that the ꝑsones to whome the mony shalbe delyvered be sure and substanciall.

As for the rest of the sayd mony that cannot be sent over in suche sorte as is aforesayd, o^r pleas^r is, that for the more saffer transportacõn thereof, the sayd Thomas Gresham shall abyde the coming from thence of sume convenient flete of shippes, emongst the best and surest of whiche, he shall distribute the rest of the sayd mony so remayning; so as he adventure not above the sum of eight thowsond pownds in any one botome. Vsing for the convoyannce of o^r sayd treasure this wayes, all the best meanes and pollicie y^t he can devise.

And finally, for as muche as we have occasion to employe sume masse of treasure wth in o^r realme of Ireland, our pleas^r is that the sayd Thomas Gresham shall devise sume good and sure way, yf he can, to send vnto o^r sayd realme of Ireland the sume of tenne thowsand pounds ster. to be delyvered there into thands of the deputie of o^r sayd realme. In whiche, we wolde he employed his best industry and diligence; and bothe herein, and in the rest, to have speciall regarde, as nere as he may, to the strength of the shippes and the honnesty of the ꝑsones that shall have the conveyance of the sayd mony; vsing all the secrecie he can in the shipping and sending away thereof.

And where, heretofore, we appointed vnto the sayd Thomas Gresham towards his diets and entertainement in o^r service the sume of xx *s.* by the day, considering now that he shall by this ꝑsent service be occasioned to be at sume further expence then hitherto he hath byn,—we have thought convenient to enlarge his sayd diet, and to give him till his return out of Spayne, x *s.* by the day, from the date of thes instructions, ou^r and above his former dietts of xx *s.* the day: w^c sumes o^r pleasure is he shall receyve and pay to hymsellf owt of suche o^r treasure as shall from tyme to tyme cume to his hands.

And after he shall have dispached our busines in Spaine ꝑntly committed to his charge, we ar pleased that he doo make his returne vnto or presence, ether by see or by land, as may bee most for his suertye, and shall seme most conveniẽt vnto hym." [Copy Spanish Corr. St. P. Off.]

After the first half of this volume had been printed, the writer obtained access to Queen Mary's original Council-book. The following extracts, (which should have appeared in a former page,) seem worthy of preservation, and will not be out of place here.—7 June, 1554,—"A lettre to my L. Admyrall, [Lord William Howard,] to prepare in a redynes at Plymouthe, within xv or xx dayes at the furthest, sum convenyent barque or small pynnase to transporte from thence into Spayne, Thomas Gresham, the Quene's agent, about her Grace's affayres of greate importance." [fol. 131.]—10 June.—"A lettre to the Maior and his brethrene of Plymouth, to see in a redynes a pynnesse for the transportacon of Thomas Gresham into Spayne within three or foure daies at the furthest, yf the Lorde Admyrall have not given ordre alredy therefore." [fol. 132]. . . . . . On the 15th of August a letter was sent to Gresham, and on the 13 September.—"A lettre to Thomas Gresham, with a license signed by Th' Emperor for one C M ducates more thenne he had license for before; prayeing him to use diligence.

"A lettre to the Lorde Treasouror with a packet to Thomas Gresseham; praieing his Lordshipp to sende the same awaye fourthwith."—fol. 174. [Council-Office.]

No. XII.

Lord Howard of Effingham.

[Referred to in page 153, note e.]

The great length to which this volume has unexpectedly extended, renders it necessary to reject all superfluous matter. Concerning the Lord Howard of Effingham, therefore, it shall only be stated, that among the papers of Queen Mary's reign, [1558] there exists a curious document; describing his establishment and household of sixty persons; noticing his expenditure, the allowance he made to his wife, son, and daughter, and several other interesting matters.

No. XIII.

Finance during the Reign of Queen Mary.

[Referred to at page 156, note i.]

"A note of suche sumes of monny as came vnto the hands of Thomas Gresham, and passed from hym in the tyme of Quene Mary.

Ffyrst arrrearage left in his handes as well vppon a bargayne of fustians, as allso for the ꝑvision of certayne munition . . . . viijmt ixc xixli xiiijs xd
Redy monny receyved owt of the Quenes coffers . . . . clxxiiijmt iiijc xviijli ijs jd
Monny receyved in Spayne . . . . . . lxxxxvijmt viijc lxxviijli xvs—
Monny taken vppe vppon interest and by way of exchaunge and exchaunge . lxxxxvmt iiijc xxvli xvijs iiijd
Monny borrowed and had by the waye of lone . . . . xljmt iiijc xxviijli xijs —
Monny gotton and advaunced by the travayle of thaccomptaunte . . . . xjmt iiijc xxjli xis ixd
Sm̃ Totalis iiijc xxixmt vc xxijli xiijs —"

[Lansd. MS. No. cxiii. art. 19.]

No. XIV.

Value of certain Coins, in Mary's Reign. 21 *Jan.* 1553–4.

[Referred to in page 162, note r.]

Queen Mary's letter, alluded to as above, contained an enclosure, from which the following is an extract: "The dubble ducats of Spayne, all wtout the andrew crosse to be worthe .—The half of the same ducats of Spaine, to be after the rate .— The single Hungarian ducats, .—The Keysars [Emperor's] Royall of fyne gold, .—The frenche crowne of gold, .—The Crusado wt the longe crosse, .—The crowne of the Roose, .—The Burgonyon crowne, .— The Spanishe Ryall of silver, .—The half of the same Spanishe Ryall, .—The quartr of the same Ryall, .—The half-quartr of the same, ."

Gresham, in replying to the Council, (31st Jan. 1553–4,) says: "The dubble ducats of Spayne, all wthout the Andrew crosse, wyche ys here nowen [none] to come by, ys worthe here the pcs,—xiiij *s.*

vi *d.* . . The hallfe of the same ducat aftyr the rate,—vij *s.* iii *d.* . . The singgle Hungarian ducats ys worthe (and nowen to be gotten) ys worthe,—vj *s.* x *d.* . . The Karssers Rialls of fynne golde,—xi *s.* . . . The Crusado of the longe crosse,—vj *s.* xj *d.* . . The Frenche croween,—vi *s.* viij *d.* . . The Burgonyone crowen, vi *s.* viij *d.* . . The crowen of the rosse (and nowen to be gotten),—vi *s.* viij *d.*

"And yff yow shulld vallew this monny at thies prissis above wryttyn, wth owght dowght ytt wolle bringe dowen the exchange to xx *s.* And besydes that, yff yow shulld vallew them att anny preyce, ytt shulld causse the emperor and this countrye to thinge that yow goo a bowght to robe them of ther tressor: by the meynnes whereof, here shulld be soche strayte wayte laid att the serche and tolles, thatt no man shulld passe, but in great hassard of lossing,—to his vtter vnedoing for ever; for the emperors lawes be soche. For every pownd that ys tackynne, a forfettes x *li.*, and his boddy at the emperors plesseur, yff ytt be knowen in vij yeeres. So, by this, yow may ꝑsseve whatt danger I rowen in daylly, yff my doings shulld be perssavyd. In consideracyone whereof, my power and sympell advyze ys,—to bringe all in to the Quennes Mate owen stampe, wyche wole be a stey of all this mattr: as allso the exchange shulld be kept vppe; wherin I can adverttisse yow no more thereof then here to fore I have dowen.—Assewring yor honnors, whatt so ever price the Quenne Mate dowthe vallew them at, as she shall ꝑsently wynne by them owen waye, so, I assewre yor honnors there wolle be as moche losse by the exchange other waysse. Wherein yor honnors maye doo as to yow shall seme best in the ꝑmysses. For yff I shulld advyze you to vallew them, ytt wolle be a vneforteyn mattr; for that the exchange ryssythe and fallythe daylly, wyche ys the thinge most exspedyent in or com̃en well to to be lockyd a pon." [Fland. Corr. St. P. Off.]

No. XV.

Ammunition, &c. purchased in Flanders.

[Referred to in pages 164 and 165, notes [v] and [w].]

"Provicions made and to be made in Flaundres as foloweth, viz.

"By Alexander Bonvise:—Saltpetre, iiijxxx mt weight . . . Harquebutts complete,—iij mt ccl . . . Dagges wt there furniture,—mt. . . . Cullyn cliffes,—viii mt . . . Matches,—v mt weight.

"By Thomes Gresham:—Serpentine powder, l lasts . . . Cornepowder,—x lasts . . . Murrions,—iiij mt . . . Dagges wt there furniture,—mt . . . Skulles,—v mt . . . Sleves of mayle,—v c paier. . . . Splynts,—mt mt paier . . . Collers white,—iij c: blacke,—lxv. In all,—iij c lxv . . . Vambraces [?] white,—xxiiij paier: blacke,—x paier. In all,—xxxiiij paier . . . Taces [?] white,—xx paier, and black l paier,—lxx paier."

[Endorsed] "Vltimo m̃tii. 1558.—Note for ꝑvision of munycõn for Flaunders." [Fland. Corr. St. P. Off.]

In a letter to Parry, dated 26th April, 1558, Gresham says: "I have bargayned wth dyvers men of this towne for the some of v mt waight of sarpentyne powder, at iij *li.* iij *s.* iiij *d.* the hondred, to be delyverid all by the xth and xxth daie of the next mownthe; which is the holle rest and coppelment of the Quens Mates provissione of gowne powder. More, I have bought iiij c dages, ij c splents, ij c skolles, iij c morrians, and i c l payer of sleaves of malle; whiche I staie for shipping till forder my Lordes pleaseures be knowen: for that her is no shippes of warre for the condewt of the same."

On the 7th of May, we meet the following passage: "Here is presentlie iiij good shipes of this towne that lades for London; and the licke will not be readie this towe mownthes when they be gowne; whose names be,—Bartillmew Pallis, Thomas De Grave, Cornelis Hildernes, and Clais Cornelisson; whom I have bownde that they shall not deꝑte frome hens affore ths xvjth daie of this present. Pretending, with the leave of God, to laide in the saide iiij shippes for the Quennes Mates accownte:—xl mt waight of serpentyne powder at the least . . . x mt waight of cowrne powder at the least . . vi mt waight of salte pettir at the least . . . i mt morrions . . . ij c paier of sleaves of male . . . i c dages . . . ij c skolles . . . i c l paier of splents.—Whiche provission will amownt to the some of ij mt vj c *li.* at the least. Therefore I have writtin to my Lordes to apoynct soche convenyente waifters for the conduct of the saide shipes, as to them shall seame most meatest; for I that I will assewer you, the licke quantite of powder is not to be gotten for monye: by the reason here is no salte pettir nor colles to be gotten for monnye."

While on this subject, another short extract, serving to establish the price of certain "Armewr and Monnyssyones" in 1560, may not be unacceptable. Gresham procured for the country about that time,—"18,000 corselets, at 26*s.* 8*d.*—16,000 corriers, at 16*s.* 8*d.*—15,000 handguns, at 7*s.*—18,000 dagges, at 16*s.* 8*d.*—16,000 morrions, at 6*s.* 8*d.*—16,000 collen cleves staves, at 2*s.*—8000 pickes, at 3*s.*—260,000 of serpentine powder, at 3*l.* the cwt.—160,000 waight of corne powder, at 3*l.* 6*s.* 8*d.* the cwt.—310,000 waight of saltpeter, at 3*l*. 10*s*. the cwt.--150,000 waight of sulpher, at 20*s*.—310,000 waight of copper at 52*s*. the cwt.--60,000 waight of maches, at 30*s*. the cwt.—1790 bundles of bowstaves, at 11*l*. the cwt.—6000 pike heads, at 3*l*. the cwt.—2000 coats of mail, at 33*s*. 4*d*. each.—2000 sleeves of mail, at 10*s*. each —200 Van playnttes, at 4*s*. each . . . Sum, 108,956*l*. 13*s*. 4*d*." [Ibid.]—For an explanation of some of the preceding terms, the reader is referred to the notes in the text.

No. XVI.

Sir Thomas Gresham to Archbishop Parker.

[Referred to in page 190, note h.]

The following letter is copied from the original, in the library of Corpus Christi College, Cambridge, (MS. cxiv. Misc. i. 230, p. 627. Vide Nasmith's Catalogue, p. 160.)

"I offer most humbly commēdations unto youre grace.—Whereas I have given to the bringer hereof Great Massingham benifice in Norfolke, and understandinge that the byshope of Norrige is inhibited, who prefereth all the delays that he can, to put him of frō being induced; because he wold have yt fale in the lapse, yt he myght have the presentaciō thereof. Thus I most humbly desier youre grace yt yt may please youe at this my seute, to institute him, as well for the voydinge of charges as the losse of tyme: wherin yor Lordship shall do me a singular pleasure, and also bind this poore mā to pray for yor Lord grace's longe prosperytye. Thus I most hūbly take my leve of youe. Fro my house in Londō; the 24 of Maye, a° 1563. [?]

At yor gracis comandement,

THOMAS GRESHAM."

For the preceding transcript I am indebted to the kindness of my friend, the Rev. J. W. Blakesley, of Trinity; who informs me that the outer side of the letter, and consequently the address, has not been preserved.

Matthew Parker, second Protestant archbishop of Canterbury, was born at Norwich in 1504, and educated at Corpus Christi College, Cambridge, of which he subsequently became Master.—Who 'the bringer' of the preceding letter was, does not appear; but William Gold was presented to the living of Massingham by Sir Thomas Gresham in 1572. (Blomefield's Norfolk, vol. ix. p. 11.)—'The byshope of Norrige' must have been Bishop Parkhurst.

No. XVII.

The poet Churchyard.

[Referred to in page 204, note z.]

The profession of arms does not seem favourable to the cultivation of poetry; but among our own countrymen, the Earl of Surrey, Sir Philip Sidney, and Thomas Churchyard, afford three remarkable instances of brave soldiers who were also excellent poets. A Spaniard would enumerate Garcilaso, Camoens, Cervantes, Lope de Vega, and Calderon.

Churchyard has been his own biographer in *A Storie translated out of Frenche;* and in *A tragicall discourse of the vnhappy man's life;* which, in 1813, were reprinted in the *Bibliographical Miscellanies* published by the Rev. Dr. P. Bliss. Fiction supplies few narratives so varied with adventure as these. Churchyard's escape from prison, in which he was aided by a fair lady, one "mooneshine night, when neighbours were a sleepe," is by no means the only romantic incident to be met with in his history. He possessed in an eminent degree what the Germans call the *subjectiveness* of genius: and all his writings so abound with hints for a biographer, that it is only surprising no one should have yet been found willing to undertake the task of critically investigating his history, and weaving the materials he has himself supplied into one connected story. Mr. Wright, in a recent work, ("Elizabeth and her Times,") has rescued from obscurity three charming letters of Churchyard to Sir Christopher Hatton, (vol. ii. pp. 140, 142, 145,) and a fourth to Mrs. Penn, (p 414),—a circumstance which alone, methinks, entitles him to our gratitude.

No. XVIII.

Doctor John Caius.

[Referred to in page 205, note b.]

"John Caius, doctor in phisick, of the parishe of St. Bartholomew the less, next unto Smithfeld," died in London, July 29, 1573, and lies buried in the chapel of his college, with the laconic epitaph, FVI CAIVS. His will is rather interesting. "John Caius, Doctor in physick, of the parish of St. Bartholomew the less, next unto Smithfeld," says—"I give and bequeath unto my said colledge all my bookes, new and olde, wherein these words be written JOHANNES

Caius Collegio suo dono dedit; and I will that all the said bookes shalle be bounde in with chaines to the desks of the library there, for the common use of the students." He left money for erecting his own tomb, and for "the clearing and mending of Mr. Linacre's tombe in Paules Church in London." "To Matthew [Parker] Abp. of Canterbury, all my bookes which I have made, not yet printed; and all those that I have made that be printed and augmented; upon condition that it may please his Grace to cause them to be printed (as my trust is whollie in him that he will so do) in a faier letter and forme, altogether in one volume; and twelve of them to be given to my saied colledge, there to be kept as the other books are, and to be successivelie tyed with chaines in the library of the same colledge." To Judge Cateline he left "a ring, with a corse in a shete made upon it." To Justice Wray "a ring with a death's head," &c. The remainder of this interesting document is almost exclusively devoted to arrangements for the government and well-being of Caius College. (Prerogative-Office, Peter, quire xxxix.)

No. XIX.

On the Orange in More's Portrait of Sir Thomas Gresham.

[Referred to in page 208, note e.]

After the preceding pages were printed, I met with the following apposite passage, illustrative of Gresham's attitude. Cavendish, in his Life of Wolsey, describes the Cardinal entering a crowded chamber, "holding in his hand a very fair orange, whereof the meat or substance within was taken out, and filled up again with the part of a sponge, wherein was vinegar, and other confections against the pestilent airs; the which he most commonly smelt unto, passing among the press, or else when he was pestered with many suitors." [Singer's ed. pp. 105-6.]

M. Passavant, who saw Mr. Neeld's picture, and in his "Tour of a German Artist in England," &c. (1836, vol. i. p. 189,) pronounces it to be "of eminent beauty," explains the representation in question by stating, that Sir Thomas Gresham introduced this fruit into England as an article of commerce,—a fact which he would have found it difficult to prove; for oranges were certainly well known in England long before Gresham was born. They are mentioned in the Privy-purse expenses of Elizabeth of York, under the year 1502; and in Henry the Eighth's Privy-purse expenses, about the year 1530, frequent mention is made of a reward being given to James Hobart, (probably a gardener,) "for bringing of *oranges, dates, and other pleasurs* to the King's Grace."

Had it been stated that the orange in Gresham's hand was meant to show that he had introduced the *orange-tree* into England, there would be more difficulty in disproving the accuracy of the statement. I am aware that the introduction of orange-trees is commonly assigned to about the year 1595, on the strength of what is stated by Bishop Gibson in his additions to Camden's Britannia, (p. 166,) published in 1695; namely, that the orange-trees at Beddington in Surrey, introduced from Italy by Sir Francis Carew, were the first that were brought into England; that they were planted in the open ground, under a moveable covert during the winter months; and that they had been growing there for more than a hundred years. Bishop Gibson, however, was indebted for his information to Aubrey, [Hist. of Surrey, vol. ii. p. 160; and see vol. i. page xiv.,] who began his collections for "The Natural History and Antiquities of the County of Surrey" twenty years earlier; so that, according to this statement, the introduction of orange-trees might be referred to the year 1575; and though Sir Francis Carew at the time of his death in 1611 was a very aged man, [Manning's Surrey, vol. ii. p. 530,] there seems good reason for doubting whether some one had not been beforehand with him in bringing the orange-tree into England. A writer in the Biographia Britannica states, [art. Ralegh, p. 3475, note O,] that, according to a family tradition, "that delicate knight" (Carew) raised these trees from oranges given him by Sir Walter Ralegh, who first imported them, and whose wife was niece to Sir Francis. No part of this story, however, is entitled to credit, and Ralegh certainly can have had nothing to do with the introduction of orange-trees, as the following interesting letter, written when he was only nine years old, proves. It was addressed by Sir William Cecil to Mr. Windebank, who, as the reader will remember, was travelling on the Continent in the capacity of tutor to his son Thomas, afterwards Earl of Exeter. The original is preserved in the State-Paper Office, among the Domestic Correspondence.

"When this messengar was redy to depart, my Lady Throkmorton gave me a lettre from Tho. Cecill, wherin he maketh mention that Mr. Caroo meaneth to send home certen orenge, pomgranat, lymon, and myrt trees. *I have alredy an orrenge tree*; and if the price be not much, I pray you procure for me a lymon, a pomegranat, and a myrt tree; and help that they may be sent to London, with Mr. Caroo's trees; and, before hand, send me in wryting a perfect declaration how they ought to be used, kept, and ordred. Fare you well. From Westminster, the 25 of March, 1561.

Your assured frind and good Master,

W. Cecill."

"To my servant Thomas Windebank at Paris."

Orange-trees, therefore, were cultivated in England before the year 1561. In consequence of the request contained in the preceding letter, Windebank sent Cecil, the year following, from Paris, a lemon-tree in a tub, costing fifteen crowns; and two myrtle-trees in pots, costing a crown each. They were chosen by "my Lord Ambassador and Mr. Caroo," whose servant brought them to England along with Carew's trees. Windebank gives ample and curious directions for the culture of these plants, in a letter dated from Paris, April 8th, 1562. Ibid.

No. XX.

Another Letter from Sir Philip Hoby to Cecil.

[Referred to in page 228, note [k].]

Among the Lansdowne MSS. is another letter from Sir Philip Hoby, written to Cecil with a similar object the year before. "I have bene often tolde of your coming to Bissham," he says, "and what shulde staie youe I knowe not; but well am I assured that I have not heard one make so many promesses and performe so fewe. Peradventure my Lady staieth you, who, you will saie, cannot ride. Therto will I provide this remedy,—to sende her my coche: bicause she shall have the lesse travaile thither, and you, no excuse to make. Let me knowe by this bearer when I shall looke for you at Bissham, that my coche may come for her; for otherwise, if ye come not, there will chaunce a greatter matter than ye yet knowe of." (1 July, 1556, Lansd. MS. No. iii. art. 53.)

In that beautiful folio work, "Holbein's Portraits," there occurs an interesting head of Sir Philip Hoby. He died in 1558, and was buried in Bisham church.

No. XXI.

Sir Thomas Gresham to Queen Elizabeth, on Finance.

[Referred to in page 234, note [p].]

The source whence the following curious letter was obtained, has been already explained in the text. It is headed,—"Information of Sir Thomas Gresham, Mercer, towching the fall of the exchaunge, MDLVIII." "To the Quenes most excellant maiestye."

"Ytt may pleasse your majesty to understande, thatt the firste occasion off the fall of the exchainge did growe by the Kinges majesty, your latte ffather, in abasinge his quoyne ffrome vi ounces fine too iii ounces fine. Wheruppon the exchainge fell ffrome xxvi*s*. viii*d*. to xiii*s*. iv*d*. which was the occasion thatt all your ffine goold was convayd ought of this your realme.

"Secondly, by the reason off his wars, the Kinges majestie ffell into greatt dept in Flanders. And ffor the paymentt therof thay hade no other device butt paye itt by exchainge, and to carry over his ffine gowlde ffor the paymentt of the same.

"Thirdly, the greatt ffreadome off the Stillyarde and grantinge of licence ffor the carringe off your woll and other comodytes ought off your reallme, which is nowe on off the cheffest pointes thatt your majestie hathe to forsee in this your comon well; thatt you neavir restore the steydes called the Stillyarde againe to ther privelydge, which hath bine the cheffest poyntte off the undoinge off this your reallme, and the marchants off the same.

"Now, for redresse off thes thinges, in *an.* XV C LI [1551] the Kinges majestie, your latte brother, callide me to bee his agentt, and repossid a more trust in me, as well ffor the paymentt off his depttes beyond the seas, as ffor the ressynge off the exchainge,—beinge then att xv*s*. and xvi*s*. the pounde; and your mony corrantt, as itt is att this presentt, beinge nott in vallew x*s*. First, I practized with the Kinge and my lorde off Northomberlande to overthrowe the Stillyarde, or else ytt coulde nott bee brought to passe, ffor thatt thay woold kepp downe the exchainge by this consideration; wher as your owne mere marchantes payeth outtwardes xiv*d*. upon a cloth custome, thay paye butt ix *d*.; and like wisse, ffor all such wairs as was brought into your reallme, your owne mere marchantes payeth xii*d*. upon the pounde, the Stillyarde payd butt iii *d*. upon the pounde, which is v *s*. difference uppon the hundreth: and as they wear men thatt raine all uppon the exchainge ffor the byenge of ther comodytes, whatt did thay passe to give a lowar price then your owne marchantes, when thaye gotte v *l*. in the hundreth by your custome; which in processe off time woulde have undone your whole reallme, and your marchantes of the same.

"Secondarely, I practissed with the Kinges majestie, your brother, to come in creditt with his owne mer marchantes: and when time servid, I practised with theme att a sett shippinge, the exchainge beinge still att xvi*s*., thatt every man showld paye the Kinge xv*s*. upon a cloth in Anwarppe, to paye att doblle usans xx*s*.

in London; which the Kinges majestie payd theme riallye, which did amountte to the some off LX M*l*. Ande so, vi months after, I practissed the licke upon ther comodyties ffor the some off LXX M *l*. to paye ffor every pounde starlinge xxii*s*.: so by thes meanes, I maide plenty off mony and scarstie, and brought into the Kinges handes, which raised the exchainge to xxiii*s*. iv*d*. And by thes meanes I did nott only bringe the Kinges majestie, your brother, outt off deptt, wherby I savide hime vi or vii*s*. upon the pounde, but savid his tresore within the reallme, as ther in Mr. Secretary Sissille was most privie unto.

"Thirdly, I didd likewise cause all forraine qoynes to bee unvallewed, wherby itt might bee brought into the minte to his Majesties most fordlle; att which time the kinge your brother dyed, and for my rewarde of servize, the Bishoppe of Winchester sought to undoe me, and whatsoever I sayd in thes matters I should not be creditted: and againste all wisdome, the sayd bishoppe went and vallewid the French crowne at vi*s*. iv*d*., and the pistolott at vi*s*. ii*d*., and the silver rialle at vi*d*. *Ob*. Wheruppon, imediattlye, the exchange fell to xx*s*. vi*d*. and xxi*s*., and ther hath kept ever sithence. And so consequently aftire this ratte and manor, I brought the quenes majestie your sister out of deptt of the some of CCCCXXXV M *l*.

"Fowerthlye, by this itt maye playnely appear to your hightnes, as the exchainge is the thinge that eatts ought all princes, to the wholl destruction of ther comon well, if itt be nott substantially loked unto; so likewise the exchainge is the cheffest and richist thinge only above all other, to restore your Majestie and your reallme to fine gowld and sillvar, and is the meane thatt makes all forraine comoditties and your owne comodites with all kinde of vittalles good cheapp, and likewise kepps your fine golde and sillvar with in your reallme. As, for exsample to your hightnes, the exchainge beinge att this present att xxii*s*., all marchantes seeckes to bringe into your reallme fine gollde and silver; for if hee should deliver itt by exchainge, he disbursis xxii*s*. Flemishe to have xx *s*. sterlinge: and to bringe itt in gowlde and sillver he shall make theroff xxi*s*. iv*d*.—wherby he saves viii*d*. in the pounde: which proffitte, if the exchainge showlde kepp but after this ratte of xxii*s*. in fewe years you showld have a welthi reallme, for her the treasur showlde continew for ever; for thatt all men showlde finde more profytte by v *l*. in the hundreth to deliver itt per exchainge, then to carry itt over in mony. So consequenttly the higar the exchainge riseth, the mor shall your Majestie and your reallme and comon well florrish, which thinge is only keppt up by artte and Godes providence; for the quoyne of this your reallme doeth nott corresponde in finnes [fineness] nott x *s*. the pounde.

"Finally, and itt please your majestie to restore this your reallme into such estatt, as hertofore itt hath bine; first, your hyghtnes hath non other wayes, butt when time and opertunyty serveth, to bringe your basse mony into fine of xi ounces fine, and so gowlde after the ratte.

"Secondly, nott to restore the Stillyarde to ther usorpid privelidges.

"Thirdly, to grantt as fewe licences as you cane.

"Fowerthly, to come in as small deptt as you can beyond seays.

"Fiftly, to kepp [up] your creditt, and specially with your owne marchants, for it is thaye must stand by youe att all eventes in your necessity. And thus I shall most hombly beseech your majestie to exceptt this my [poor writing in good] partte; wherin I shall from time to time, as opertunity doeth serve, putt your hyghtnes in rememberance, acordinge to the trust your Majestie hath repposside in me; becechinge the Lorde to give me the grace and fortune thatt my servis may allwais bee exceptable to your hightnes: as knoweth our Lorde, whome preserve your noble Majestie in health, and longe to raigne over us with increasse of honor.

By your Majesties most homble
and faythefull obedientt subject,
Thomas Greshm̃, Mercer."

It must be superfluous that I should point out to any intelligent reader, that the preceding document evidently contains many errors of transcription.

No. XXII.

Further Particulars of Charles V.'s Funeral.

[Referred to at page 253, note p.]

The writer regrets to find himself under the necessity of omitting the additional particulars promised in the text: the extent which these volumes have unexpectedly reached, rendering it indispensable that *something* should be withheld.

No. XXIII.

Early English Vehicles.

[Referred to at page 305, note e.]

See also p. 242, note x; and page 383.—In Ellis's Letters, &c. 2nd Series, vol. ii. p. 253, will be found a very remarkable description of a "Wagon of tymbre work, for Ladies and Gentlewomen" of Queen Mary's Privy-chamber, (1557.)—See further on this subject, some interesting details at the end of Nicolas' Privy Purse Expenses of Elizabeth of York: see also Strutt's Dresses, &c., vol. ii. p. 90: the Northumberland Houshold Book, p. 447, *et seq.*; and above all, a paper in the Archæologia, vol. xx. p. 426, *et seq.*—The heading of a document preserved among the Domestic State-Papers of Queen Mary's reign, viz., "Ordinances devised by the Kinge and Queene's Majesties, for the order of the Postes and *Hackney men* betwene London and Dover," seems to show that the commonly received etymology of *Hackney coach* is erroneous.

No. XXIV.

Expenses of Clough's Journey to Mansfeld.

[Referred to in page 342, note z.]

The following document, (not in the autograph of Sir Thomas Gresham,) is transcribed from the original preserved in the Flanders Correspondence at the State-Paper Office. Endorsed,

"1560.—Mony layd owt by Sr Tho. Gresham for his man Clowgh's charges in his negotiation wt ye Counte Mansfeld, etc.

"Paied, the xviijth of May, ao 1560, for my factors, Richard Clowghe's charges into Germany, by comandmt of the Quene's Matie, wth a letter to the Countie of Mansefyld, as towchinge mony proffered to the Quene's Matie by his srvaunte Hans Kecke: to saie, for him and his post, and for ij horses bowght, whereof the one died; more, for the post's wages, iij *s.* iiij *d.* a daie: som̃ paied vi *li.*

"Paied, the xxijnd of Maie ao 1560, for the hire of a post wth lrẽs to Mr. Secretary; wherein I adũtized that I had dispatched awaie my factor Richard Clowghe, and Hans Kecke, to the Countie of Mansfild, for money ꝑmised by him; and of the adũtisement that there was no gondepowder to be got in Hollande . . . . iiij *li.* x *s.*

"Paied, the xvjth of June, ao 1560, for ye hire of a post to Sr Thom̃s Parry, for ye prouision of xlti last srpentyne powder, and xxx last of corn-powder; wt adũtisemt of the straight shippinge, and to convey the said powder: by reson I was like to have byn betraied by an Inglishman. As also wt adũtisemt of my sr̃vant Clowghe from Issewnock [Eisenach] in Germany, when he went to the Countie of Mansfild for resolute aunswer of the thre hundred thowsand dollars. Som̃. . . . . iiij *li.* vi*s.* viij*d.*

"Paied, the ijnd of July, ao 1560, for ye hire of a post to Sr Thom̃s Parry; wth aunswere of the Contie of Mansfild, sent him by my sr̃vañt Richard Clowghe : and that the Quene's Matie shold not faile to have at his hands, by the xxth of August, the som̃ of three hundred thowsand dollars ;—Som̃ . . . . iiij *li.* x*s.*

"Paied, ye xxiiijth of August, ao 1560, for the hire of a post wth lrẽs to the Quene's Matie and my Lordes of ye Counsell, wth lrẽs to the Quene's Matie from ye Countie Mansfild, as towchinge ye iij M dollers he had promysed to her Matie, whose aunswer upon his lrẽ written to me, wch I founde verie sclender : as also ·I wrote the same tyme for ye Quene's Mat's new bands, and the Cities of London, ... v *li.*"

No. XXV.

Paul Gresham's Household Book.

[Referred to at page 371, note 1.]

The most interesting entries I met with in the Household-book of Paul Gresham, besides that cited in the text, were the following. "It. more to Thom̃s Walgrave the five daye, to buye Thom̃s Gresham a bowe, xviii*d.*" p. 77 : [Thomas was Paul Gresham's eldest son.] "It. upon Ester-even, I rekenyd wt John Tele; and then I ought hym for iij carriages, viz. ii to Lynne, and one to Intwoodde." p. 92.—"Ao Dñi 1555. Money due to me, John Fox, from my brother Gresham, as hereafter followyth, viz. It. pd to Mr. Grene the undersherve for the staye of thextente against Mr. Thomas Gresham by yor commandment xl*s.* It. pd for the coppye of thextente againste Mr Thomas Gresham, xii*d.* It. pd for a pound of gunpowder, xii*d.*" p. 146-7.—"Pd for a Billyment and a Crepone for my cousin Katharine Gresham, vi*s.* viii*d.*" p. 147.—"Pd for a barrell of olives, 16*d.*"—"1557. It. pd to Mr Hall of Norwiche for the castynge of my cosyne Wyllm̃ water, and a purgacon with losengers, 2*s.*" p. 148.—"Shoes for Anne Gresham, 7*d.*"—"For the lying of the gravestone over my sister."—"Wyllm̃ Greshm̃ whas bornne the iiijth of Maye betwyne xj of the clocke and xij of the clocke in ao ijdo R. Edwardi sexti." p. 236. [This was Paul's second son.] Paul Gresham's signature occurs at p. 226.

I have stated in a preceding page, that the MS. from which these extracts are derived is preserved in the Record-Office, Chapter House, and was obligingly communicated by Sir Francis Palgrave. It is of the folio size, on paper, and extends to 253 pages. The entries seem to range, mostly, from 1555 to 1565.

No. XXVI.

Documents relating to Finance.

[Referred to in page 394, note [s].]

The following is the passage omitted, and alluded to in the text, (7 Aug. 1561):—"Also yt maye please you to be advertised, that my Lorde Treasurer haithe apoynted me to paie the xxvth of August in Andwarpe, the some of xliiij M vij C iiijxx iiij *li.* vi*s.* [44,784*l.* 6*s.*]: whereof the Marchants Adventrors payeth xxx M *li.* sterling. The Marchaunts Staplers vij M cc lxvi *li.* xvj*s.* more out of the Quennes reseipt ij M v c xlij *li.* xvi*s.* Some sterlinge, xxxix M viii c viii *li.* xvii*s.* iiij*d.* wyche maketh flemyshe aftir the rate of xxij*s.* vi*d.* for the pownde sterlinge,—Some, xliiij M vij c iiij xx iiij *li.* vi *s.*

As likewise, whereas the Quennes Majestie had appoynctid me, by my Instructions, fiftie thowsande powndes to be prolongid till February next, my Lorde Treasurer will have that sett ovir till August 1562, with the rest of the debt dew this August and November, whiche amounts to one hondreth thowsand powndes. And for the rest of the Quennes detts to be prolonged, to paie in June ano 1562, xiiij M iiij xx xiiij *li.* xix*s.* iiij*d.* [14,094*l.* 19*s.* 4*d.*] and in November ano 1562, xiiij M iiij xx xiiij *li.* xix*s.* iiij*d.* [idem,] and in December ano 1562, xiiij M iiij xx xiiij *li.* xix*s.* iiij*d.* [idem.]"

In the State-Paper Office, there occur (as might be expected) a vast number of documents illustrative of the finance of this country in Gresham's time: some being the accounts he periodically rendered; others, copies or abstracts with which himself or his servants supplied Cecil. I will here insert a few notices of a collection of schedules of this class, preserved among the Flemish State-Papers for 1560.

The first is 'a brief note of all such sums of money as I, Thomas Gresham, have received in Antwerp, for the behoof of the Queen's Majesty, since 1 Oct. 1558:' amounting to 310,458*l.* 14*s.*—Since the 21st December, 1558, he had paid 319,968*l.* 3*s.* 7*d.*: so that his payments had exceeded his receipts by 9,509*l.* 9*s.* 5*d.* 'To this,' says Gresham, 'must be added my expenses for charges of all kinds; as for the transportation of armour and military stores, &c. &c. and for postage and diet for eighteen months, amounting at least to 6 or 7000*l.*'—This account must therefore have been rendered in April 1560.

Three months before however, apparently, he had transmitted to Queen Elizabeth, a beautifully-written account of sums paid and received since 21 Dec. 1558. He had paid 339,996*l.* 13*s.* 4*d.*; and received 337,958*l.* 14*s.* 'And so the payments doth amount to more than the receipts, the sum of 2037*l.* 19*s.* 4*d.*'

In January 1559-60, Gresham stated that the sum total he had paid at Antwerp, was 105,195*l.* 0*s.* 8*d.*: he had received 87,005*l.* 16*s.* 8*d.*; and so rested to him, 18,189*l.* 0*s.* 4*d.* (sic.)

On the 18th March, 1559-60, the queen's debt at Antwerp amounted to 94,659*l.* 16*s.* 8*d.*

From another 'Note of the Queen's debts in Antwerp,' it appears that the sums due in October and November 1559, and February, May, and July 1560, amounted to 133,680*l.* 12*s.* 8*d.*

From another 'Note of all the Queen's Majesty's debts owing in Antwerp, 15 April, 1560,' we learn that, in May 1560, 93,659*l.* 16*s.* 8*d.* fell due: in June, 10,706*l.*: in July, 11,514*l.*: in August, 138,586*l.* 6*s.* 8*d.*; and in February, (1560-1,) 4,393*l.* 6*s.* 8*d.*: making a total of 279,565*l.* 10*s.*—Of this sum, Queen Mary owed at the time of Elizabeth's accession to the throne, 65,069*l.* 17*s.* 4*d.*—This schedule is endorsed 'Gresham's reckoning, 1 Oct. 1558, to 20 April, 1560."—There is another version of this schedule, signed *Richard Candeller.*

We learn from another document that, from 17 Nov. 1558, to 30 April, 1562, Gresham had taken up 487,502*l.* 7*s.*: he had paid 378,289*l.* 16*s.* 'And so remaineth yet owing in Flanders, 109,213*l.* 6*s.* Flemish.'

Some of these schedules are interesting from the curious catalogue of names which they contain: others are beautiful specimens of penmanship, and of ancient accounts,—being intended for the hands of royalty itself. All are of real historical value, and deserve careful consideration.

No. XXVII.

Gresham's Instructions. July, 1562.

[Referred to in page 421, note x.]

The following is a copy of the rough draft in Cecil's handwriting, (Fland. Corr. St. P. Off.) . . . . . "A chardg gyvẽ to Sr Thomas Gresham, knight, being sent to Antwerp. July 1562.

"Where we be indettid in Antwp to certen M^r^chats strãgers in several sõmes, amoũtyg in ye whole, in flẽmish, to ye some of threescore fowre thowsand, fyve hũdred twẽty three pownds, xviij*s.* ij*d.* payable in ye next mõth of August,—our pleasure is, yt ye shall pass ovr wt spede; and first, showing an apparãce that ye come to take order to paye ye same, or some good part thereof, ye shall, aftr that, procede to ye prolongation therof for vi mõths vppõ lyke interest: or if ye can possible, vppon less; and ye shall also, before ye conclude for ye prorogation, treate wt some other m̃chants to take vpp a som̃e of thousãd pownds ovr and above our present dett; which somme we wold have so answerable to vs, yt by ye x or xv of August we wold be at our choiss, whyther we wold have ye same moñy to our owne vse, or to be ẽployed in ye paymẽt of parcell of our sayd dett of August. Herin we wold ye vsed grete circũspection and spede."

END OF VOL. I.

LONDON:
PRINTED BY MAURICE, CLARK, & CO.
FENCHURCH STREET.